The Utilization of Classroom Peers as Behavior Change Agents

APPLIED CLINICAL PSYCHOLOGY

Series Editors: Alan S. Bellack and Michel Hersen

University of Pittsburgh, Pittsburgh, Pennsylvania

A Continuation Order Plan is available for this series. A continuation order will bring delivery of
each new volume immediately upon publication. Volumes are billed only upon actual shipment.
For further information please contact the publisher.

The Utilization of Classroom Peers as Behavior Change Agents

Edited by
Phillip S. Strain

Western Psychiatric Institute and Clinic
University of Pittsburgh
Pittsburgh, Pennsylvania

PLENUM PRESS · NEW YORK AND LONDON

Library of Congress Cataloging in Publication Data

Main entry under title:

The Utilization of classroom peers as behavior change agents.
(Applied clinical psychology)
Bibliography: p.
Includes index.
1. Peer-group counseling of students—Addresses, essays, lectures. 2. Peer-group tutor-
ing of students—Addresses, essays, lectures. I. Strain, Phillip S. II. Series.
LB1027.5.U85   371.4′044   81-1733
ISBN 0-306-40618-7   AACR2

© 1981 Plenum Press, New York.
A Division of Plenum Publishing Corporation
233 Spring Street, New York, N.Y. 10013

Printed in the United States of America

To all the children who have graciously and competently served as instructional agents

for their classroom peers

And to Heidi, who taught so many to love and care

Contributors

Tony Apolloni, Ph. D., California Institute of Human Services, Sonoma State University, Rohnert Park, California

Thomas P. Cooke, Ph. D., California Institute of Human Services, Sonoma State University, Rohnert Park, California

Tiffany Field, Ph. D., Departments of Pediatrics and Psychology, University of Miami Medical School, Miami, Florida

Michael Gerber, M.A., Department of Special Education, University of Virginia, Charlottesville, Virginia

Charles R. Greenwood, Ph. D., Bureau of Child Research and Departments of Special Education and Human Development, University of Kansas, Lawrence, Kansas

Michael J. Guralnick, Ph. D., The Nisonger Center, The Ohio State University, Columbus, Ohio

Hyman Hops, Ph. D., Oregon Research Institute, Eugene, Oregon

Alan E. Kazdin, Ph. D., Department of Psychiatry, Western Psychiatric Institute and Clinic, University of Pittsburgh School of Medicine, Pittsburgh, Pennsylvania

James M. Kauffman, Ph. D., Department of Special Education, University of Virginia, Charlottesville, Virginia

Mary Margaret Kerr, Ed. D., Western Psychiatric Institute and Clinic, University of Pittsburgh School of Medicine, Pittsburgh, Pennsylvania

Charles A. Peck, M. A. Department of Special Education, University of California at Santa Barbara, Santa Barbara, California

Elizabeth U. Ragland, Ed. S., Nashville-Metro Public Schools, Nashville, Tennessee

Philip S. Strain, Ph. D., Western Psychiatric Institute and Clinic, University of Pittsburgh School of Medicine, Pittsburgh, Pennsylvania

Hill M. Walker, Ph. D., Division of Special Education, College of Education, University of Oregon, Eugene, Oregon

Clifford C. Young, Ph. D., George Peabody College for Teachers, Vanderbilt University, Nashville, Tennessee

Preface

Since the early 1800's, children have been taught and encouraged to function as instructional agents for their classroom peers. However, it was not until the last decade that peer-mediated intervention was studied in a rigorous, systematic fashion. The purpose of this edited volume is to provide an up-to-date and complete account of empirical research that addresses the general efficacy of classroom peers as behavior change agents.

As a result of various social and legal developments, such as the passage of Public Law 94-142 and its accompanying demand for individualized instruction, peer-mediated interventions seem likely to proliferate. As I have noted elsewhere (Strain, this volume), close adherence to the principle of individualized programming has rendered obsolete the "adults only" model of classroom instruction. Whether the utilization of peers in the instructional process comes to be viewed by school personnel as a positive adjunct to daily classroom practices depends in large measure on our ability to carefully design, conduct, and communicate the findings of applied research. I trust that this volume will function both to accurately communicate existing findings and to stimulate further study.

My colleagues who have generously contributed their time and skill to this volume have my deepest appreciation. They have performed their various tasks in a timely, professional manner and, in my opinion, have provided considerable insight into the problems and potentials of peers as instructional agents.

University of Pittsburgh   PHILLIP S. STRAIN
Pittsburgh, Pennsylvania

Contents

Early Peer Relations

TIFFANY FIELD

HISTORICAL PERSPECTIVE ON EARLY PEER RELATIONS AND PEER RESEARCH

First, what do we mean by the term "peer"? The term connotes equivalence between individuals, equivalence of developmental level or behavioral complexity (Lewis & Rosenblum, 1975). In most research on early peer relations, the term "peer" also implies same-age, since the context in which the children are studied is usually a graded classroom, a same-age situation (Hartup, 1980b). In history (Barker & Wright, 1955) and evolution (Konner, 1975), same-age peer relations during childhood are a recent development of advanced industrial states. As Konner states,

> In the strict sense, peers are unknown in man's environment of evolutionary adaptedness and in that of his closest relatives, the Pongidae. One has to be beyond the apes to terrestrial old world monkeys to find prominent peer relations; and these are animals so distantly related to man that we may not have shared a common ancestor for 40 million years.

Konner further notes that for 99% of human tenure on earth, man was organized in small bands of hunter-gatherers. The small size and low birthrate of the bands alone precluded the existence of groups of children very close in age. Rather, a juvenile group composed of children of a variety of ages was typically found. Konner observed among the !Kung San children of the Kalahari Desert that only 5% of face-to-face contact was accounted for by peers. And in a more industralized sample, Barker and Wright (1955) reported that contacts of two-year-old children with age-mates accounted for as little as 10% of the children's daily interactions, increasing to approximately 30% among preschool children and

TIFFANY FIELD ● Departments of Pediatrics and Psychology, University of Miami Medical School, Miami, Florida 33101.

approaching 50% among school-aged children. Although considerable cultural variations in children's time with peers have been reported by Whiting (1978), it would appear that generally very little time is spent with peers in the early years.

Yet, in 1978 alone there were as many as 68 studies published in the leading developmental journals on the subject of peer relations among preschool children. This fact suggests that there may be more children attending preschool at this time, or more researchers studying early peer relations, or both. School census data suggest that more children are attending school earlier, and thereby would have contact with age-mates both earlier and with greater frequency. Some have ascribed this recent "home-away-from-home" movement of very young children to current social and political developments. These include the dissolution of the extended family, increasing numbers of single-parent families, the women's liberation movement, and equal-employment-opportunity legislation, all of which have contributed to the need for substitute caregiving. Thus, more children are attending school earlier, and the schools, at least in this country, usually feature graded or same-age classes. Peers or same-age children invariably interact, and they interact in interesting ways. Given their interesting interactions and their easy accessibility, researchers tend to study them.

Another reason for the study of early peer encounters is their relationship to a number of current social problems which also are high funding priorities. Among these social problems are autism, childhood schizophrenia, behavior disorders, learning disabilities, delinquency, hyperactivity, drug abuse, school truancy, dropouts, runaways, and teenage pregnancy. Longitudinal studies suggest that poor relations in childhood are an indicator of future problems such as these. Children who are loners are more likely to have adjustment difficulties as adults than children who are well accepted by their peers (Hartup, 1980a). Children who are rejected by their peers have higher delinquency rates as adolescents (Roff, 1961), are at risk for emotional problems including serious forms of mental illness (Cowen, Pederson, Babijian, Izzo, & Trost, 1973; Rolf, 1972), and are more likely to drop out of school (Roff, Sells, & Golden, 1972). Thus, some researchers appear to be studying early peer relations to identify early correlates of these later socialization problems. Trends in research and funding often seem to follow trends in social problems and social change.

Innumerable studies on preschool peer relations appeared in the literature of the 1930s and 1940s (Bridges, 1933; Buhler, 1933; Maudry & Nekula, 1939; Piaget, 1951). A 30-year hiatus followed with very little research on peer relations. Although some suggest (Lewis & Rosenblum, 1975) that the psychoanalytic "primacy-of-the-mother" theory and the

Piagetian developmental-sequence theory may have suppressed the study of early peer relations, there is also reason to believe that social developments contributed to this hiatus. For example, in the 1930s and 1940s the WPA and other federal programs provided early day care for children of wartime, working parents, and orphanages were widespread. Early child care in the 1950s and 1960s more commonly occurred in the home, and with this development came a series of studies on mother–infant bonding (Bowlby, 1969), attachment (Ainsworth, 1972; Gewirtz, 1972), and early parent–child interactions (Bell, 1968; Lewis & Rosenblum, 1974). Recently, with greater numbers of working mothers and earlier school placement, there has been a renewed interest in research on sibling and peer interactions. This interest is reflected by recent volumes devoted to peer interactions occurring as early as the first two years of life (Field, Goldberg, Stern, & Sostek, 1980; Lewis & Rosenblum, 1975), and by dozens of papers on preschool peer relations.

A number of the early parent–infant and parent–child interaction studies evolved into longitudinal studies. These studies suggest some continuities between early socialization with parents and later peer interactions. Bakeman (1979) notes, for example, that infants who showed disturbed interaction behaviors with their mother showed disturbances interacting with peers at preschool age. Field (1979c) also reported continuities between disturbed mother–infant interaction patterns, such as gaze aversion and minimal vocalization, and preschool language delays and behavior problems. Lieberman (1976) reported that children who had "secure" attachments to their mothers were more responsive to other children and engaged in more sustained interactions with their peers than did children who were not securely attached. Those children whose mothers provided experiences with other children in the home were also more responsive to other children in school. In a similar early-attachment study, Waters, Wippman, and Sroufe (1980) noted that four-year-old children who had been rated at 15 months as "securely" attached (vs. those who were "anxiously" attached) were sought out by other children, were socially active rather than withdrawn, were active in initiating activities or behaving like leaders, and were empathetic with their peers when distressed. Data on older children (Elkins, 1958; Winder & Rau, 1962), and on adults from the Berkeley growth study, also suggest continuities between early parent interactions and later peer interactions. Although causality cannot be inferred, these data suggest that successful early interactions with parents may facilitate later peer interactions.

Thus, the recent popularity of early-peer-interaction research may be related to the reported increase in early exposure to peers and the presumed importance of early peer relations for later socialization. In this chapter we will describe some of the data deriving from early-peer-interaction studies and speculate about some of the unique features and functions of peers as socializing influences.

Types of Studies Illustrating Peer Influence

Peer influences among animals, particularly monkeys, have been reported in field observations, in studies of peer vs. parent rearing, and in studies of the use of peers as "therapists." Studies on early peer influences among humans can be categorized as "experiments in nature," naturalistic-observation studies, manipulations of peer situations, and studies on peers as behavior-change agents.

Monkey Peer Relations

A number of naturalistic observations (Dolhinow & Bishop, 1970) and laboratory observations (Rosenblum, 1975; Sackett, 1970) of monkey relations suggest a rich variety of rough-and-tumble, nurturant, and interactive play among monkeys and their peers. Classics in the monkey literature are the studies of the Harlows (Harlow & Harlow, 1965) and their colleagues, comparing peer rearing of rhesus infant monkeys without mother contact, and mother caregiving without peer contact. Monkeys raised without mother but with peers developed strong attachments to each other and manifested proximity-seeking behaviors such as hugging and clinging. When the peer-rearing situation featured several peers, there were no observable affective disturbances in later encounters with peers. When monkeys were reared by mothers in the absence of peers, however, the monkeys showed both short-term and long-term disturbances in play behavior and affective development, showing wariness and overly aggressive behaviors. Although this study suggests more deleterious effects of peer than mother deprivation, other factors such as relative differences in numbers of monkeys and restricted cage space may have contributed to this finding. Goy and Goldfoot (1973) compared monkeys who were separated from their mother at three months and subsequently had limited peer exposure, with monkeys who had unrestricted access to both mothers and peers. More aggressive-submissive behaviors appeared in the mother-separated, limited-peer-exposure monkeys and more precocious and mature sexual development in the monkeys experiencing unrestricted access to peers and mothers. These studies, together, suggest that although peer-reared animals may develop satisfactorily, an unrestricted exposure to mothers and peers appears to be the more optimal rearing pattern.

Monkey peers have been used as "therapists" for rehabilitating socially withdrawn monkeys by the Harlows and colleagues (Novak & M. Harlow, 1975; Suomi & H. H. Harlow, 1972). Although the use of adult monkeys as "therapists" was not successful, the use of infant monkeys as "therapists" (three months younger than the withdrawn monkeys) resulted in less isolation, clinging, and self-stimulation stereotypies in the withdrawn monkeys. In addition to illustrating the socializing influence of peers, these studies provided models for research on peer relations among human infants and children.

HUMAN STUDIES

Analogs of the Animal Studies

Human analogs of the above-cited monkey studies are provided by both laboratory research and experiments in nature. The classic observation of World-War-II concentration-camp children by Freud and Dann (1951) was an appalling "experiment in nature," but one which demonstrates the power of peer rearing among human children. Six young, motherless children reared together as a group and moved from camp to camp during the war showed strong attachments to each other. As Freud and Dann noted,

> Positive feelings were centered exclusively in their own group . . . at times the children ignored the staff completely. . . . They cared greatly for each other and not at all for anybody or anything else. They had no other wish than to be together and became upset when they were separated . . . constantly asking for the other children.

Interestingly, no later emotional or behavioral disturbances were noted in these children.

Other analogs of the animal studies are provided by Hartup and his colleagues. In one study peers served as "therapists" for socially withdrawn children (Furman, Rahe, & Hartup, 1980). Preschool children were identified during naturalistic observations as noninteractive, nonsociable, or socially withdrawn, having engaged in social interaction for less than 30% of the observation periods. The socially withdrawn children were then randomly assigned to a socialization experience with another child who was either within three months of his chronological age or 15 months younger than his chronological age. The socialization experience involved 10 dyadic free-play sessions. The socialization experiences with both younger and same-age children, but particularly with younger children, appeared to enhance the interaction activity of the socially withdrawn children. Furman et al. (1980) suggested that this behavior-change process may have been related to the younger therapists providing the socially withdrawn children opportunities to be assertive and to practice leadership roles. However, since assertive or leadership behaviors were not observed this interpretation is mere speculation. In addition, this interpretation would not apply to the positive effects observed in the same-age-therapist condition. Finally, it is not clear whether these effects would generalize to the typical classroom situation featuring teachers and several children. Playing alone with another same-age or younger child in a smaller playroom may be a less distracting, frustrating situation, which in itself could explain these effects. Nonetheless, the Furman et al. (1980) data, as well as a large body of data on the use of peers as behavior-change agents and tutors (to be discussed later in this chapter and throughout this volume), do provide evidence for the power of peers. How and when peer relations and their influences evolve is not entirely clear. Although some have suggested a stage theory with parent and peer relations developing in that order and at specific ages (H. F. Harlow, 1969), there are increasing numbers of studies which suggest that peer relations happen very early, paralleling studies of parent relations, if and when there are opportunities for early peer exposure. Most of these studies have involved a naturalistic-observation methodology.

Naturalistic-Observation Studies

Naturalistic-observation studies of the 1930s, 1940s, and 1970s comprise a very large data bank on early peer relations. However, the observation contexts of these studies varied widely from institutional settings to day-care centers to home observations. In addition, peers included both strangers and friends, and very few studies traced the developing peer relations of the same children in a longitudinal design. Nonetheless, these data suggest that peer relations and peer preferences occur at a very early age. In general the relations are positive and appear to have implications for affective and cognitive development. Since this literature is very extensive, only a few examples of the peer-relation studies can be cited here.

Infant Peer Relations. Generally the literature suggests that peer relations emerge at a very early age. Peer-directed social behaviors have been observed as early as two to three months at the period corresponding to the emergence of the social smile, vocalizations, and head control. Infants attending nurseries spend considerable periods of time smiling, cooing, and craning their necks to have long looks at their peers (Field, Masi, & Ignatoff, 1979). When placed in an infant seat face to face with a peer and a mirror, the three-month-old infant directs more social behaviors to the peer than the mirror (Field, 1979a). These infants vocalized, smiled, and reached toward each other more frequently than to their mirror images. At six to eight months, when sitting and crawling emerges, infants move directly toward each other and in an exploratory fashion, poke at each other's eyes, pull each other's hair, wrest toys from each other, and then look to observe the effects of these little injustices. Finally, as if apologizing, they smile and coo at their victims (Fischer, 1973). At this stage the preferred peer, as measured by proximity and frequency of peer-directed behavior, appears to be the developmental equivalent peer, a peer who moves about and coos with matching prowess.

Studies conducted with similar-age infants in the 1930s (Bridges, 1933; Buhler, 1933; Maudry & Nekula, 1939) report fewer peer-directed behaviors and more negative than positive behaviors. However, these were institutionalized infants who were generally placed in restricted situations such as cribs and playpens with a very limited supply of toys. A comparison of playpen with "open-field" or floor play in the Fischer (1973) study demonstrated dramatic territorial behavior (regarding space and toys) of the six- to eight-month-old infants when playing in a playpen. Floor play in an unrestricted space, however, featured significantly more positive than negative peer-directed behaviors.

At 10–14 months, infants are considerably more interactive with their peers, perhaps as a function of their expanding repertoire (Field, 1979b). They are observed to follow each other on all fours, support each others' attempts to toddle, rough-and-tumble play, manipulate the same toys, and frequently respond with crying to peers' distress behaviors, as if developing empathy. Here too, however, context appears to be a critical factor, because when mothers are present, there are fewer positive and more negative (such as toy-snatching and crying) peer-directed behaviors. Varying mother presence–absence has its effects as does varying toy presence–absence (Eckerman, Whatley, & Kutz, 1975; Ramey, Finkelstein, & O'Brien, 1976; Vandell, Wilson, & Buchanan, 1979). These authors noted distinct differences between these two contexts, with peer-directed behaviors occurring more frequently in the toy-absence condition.

Environmental context, perhaps more than any other factor, may explain the discrepancies noted in the literature on infant-peer interactions. In some situations the infant directs positive or nonaggressive behaviors toward his peers (Eckerman, 1973; Field, 1979b; Spiro, 1958; Vincze, 1971), whereas in other situations more negative interactions occur (Bronson, 1974). Moreover, some report that frequent contact or familiarity with the same peers enhances interactions (Mueller & Rich, 1980), whereas others report fewer social contacts and more frequent aggressive behaviors among familiar peers in a familiar situation (Dragsten & Lee, 1973). At the same time, Lewis, Young, Brooks, and Michalson (1975) report fewer peer-directed behaviors when the peer is a stranger. In addition, although Eckerman (1973) noted little difference in mother and peer contact at 12 months, Field (1979b), Lenssen (1973), and Lewis and colleagues (1975) reported more proximity behaviors toward mothers and more distal-interaction behaviors toward peers. Since most of these studies were conducted with similar-age infants of similar socio-economic-status (SES) backgrounds, environmental-context differences across studies may explain some of the variability in findings.

Preschool Peer Relations. The preschool-age child has been studied more frequently than any other age category of children during the past two decades. Since most preschools feature same-age classrooms, most of the studies were conducted in same-age situations. Studies of the early 1970s borrowed the observation-research models used in the 1930s and 1940s. For example, observations involving coding of the Parten (1932) free-play categories (i.e., unoccupied, solitary, onlooker, parallel, associative, and cooperative play) were very popular in the 1970s (Barnes, 1971; Rubin, Maioni, & Hornung, 1976). A frequent research question, using the Parten coding scheme and the amount of positive and negative interactions, concerned the degree to which these behaviors vary as a function of age and sex.

Although most of the age differences reported derive from cross-sectional studies of same-age classrooms, confounding the question of age differences, some investigators observed mixed-age classrooms. Holmberg (1977), for example, observed 12- to 42-month-old children and reported a significant increase in prosocial initiations with age. An age comparison of three to five-year olds by Reuter and Yunik (1973) also noted an increment in peer interactions with a parallel decrease in adult interactions. A wider age-span comparison of two- to five-year-olds vs. five- to nine-year-olds by Gottman and Parkhurst (1977), on the other hand, noted a decrease in interactive play and an increase in interactions featuring information exchange and use of rules. In the absence of longitudinal studies on peer relations in the same setting, age- or developmentally related changes in peer relations must be viewed very tentatively.

Sex differences in early peer relations are reported more frequently than any other difference in the preschool literature. These appear to be confounded by context variables and by conducting the observations in same-age classes. One consistent observation is that boys interact more frequently with boys and girls with girls, and boys reinforce boys, while girls reinforce girls (Charlesworth & Hartup, 1967; Fagot & Patterson, 1969; Field, 1980a; Langlois, Gottfried, & Seay, 1973). Miscellaneous sex differences include boys being more physically and socially active (Charlesworth & Hartup, 1967) but less verbal (Field, 1980a; Langlois *et al.*, 1973), and boys preferring outdoor play (Harper & Sanders, 1975) and block-corner play (Fagot & Patterson, 1969; Field, 1980a; Shure, 1963), as opposed to girls who prefer art-area and doll-corner play. Attempts have been made to reinforce opposite-sex play (Serbin, Tonick, & Sternglanz, 1977) with some success, although removal of the reinforcers resulted in a complete reversal to unisex preferences. This study, not unlike most of the other studies reporting same-sex interaction preferences, occurred in a same-age classroom.

Data deriving from mixed-age classrooms suggest that sex differences are less frequently observed in those situations. For example, Langlois (1973) noted a greater frequency of heterosexual interactions among three- and four-year-olds than among five-year-olds. Reuter and Yunik (1973), comparing Montessori classrooms with low teacher–child ratios and university-lab schools with high teacher–child ratios, reported fewer sex differences and more frequent same-sex preferences in the Montessori school. Although the authors related their findings to teacher/child ratio, these findings might also relate to the mixed-age grouping in the Montessori school. Similarly, Bianchi and Bakeman (1978) did not find same-sex preferences in a classroom featuring minimal teacher-structured activity, whereas same-sex preferences occurred in a classroom with considerable teacher-structured activity. However, Bianchi and Bakeman failed to note that the classroom of minimal teacher structure featuring no same-sex preferences was a mixed-age class whereas that which featured same-sex preferences was a same-age class. The studies of Langlois, Reuter and Yunik, and Bianchi and Bakeman suggest that same-sex interaction may occur more frequently in same-age classes. A study by our group on mixed-age two- to five-year-olds and same-age preschool groupings (two-year-olds, three-year-olds, etc.) involving the same children, same setting, and same teachers suggests that same-sex interactions are more common in the same-age situation and opposite-sex in the mixed-age situation (Field, 1979d). But this finding interacts with age, since two-year-old boys preferred two-year-old boys and five-year-old girls preferred five-year-old girls. What appeared to emerge from these data is that children tend to interact more with their language-matched peers in either same-age or mixed-age situations. An independent assessment of language skills suggested that two-year-old girls' language skills approximate those of three-year-old boys, three-year-old girls of four-year-old boys, and so on, with only the two-year-old boys and five-year-old girls having only same-sex, language-skills-equivalent peers with whom to relate. When the children were playing in mixed-age sessions, opposite-sex interactions of two-year-old girls with three-year-old boys, three-year-old girls with four-year-old boys, and so on occurred frequently, whereas in the same-age sessions the children reverted to same-sex (also language-skill-equivalent) peer interactions, that is, three-year-old boys with three-year-old boys and girls with girls.

Thus, same-sex interaction preferences may be an artifact of our same-age groupings.

A number of preschool investigators have noted relationships between frequency of peer interactions and other behaviors such as imitation and fantasy play. Children who are high peer interactors, for example, tend to engage in more imitative play (Lubin & Field, 1980) and more fantasy play (Rubin *et al.*, 1976). Fantasy play with peers is considered an indispensable step in cognitive development through which the child becomes liberated from stimulus-boundedness, learns to understand reciprocal relations, and thereby advances toward operational and abstract levels of thought (Piaget, 1962; Vygotsky, 1967; Werner, 1948). Children who show high rates of interaction also show active imaginations in their fantasy play, and complex verbal interplay (Field, 1979d). Their complex verbal interplay is reminiscent of children's dialogues reported by Chukovsky (1963). Examples of dialogues taken from Field (1979d) follow:

> *Two boys sitting in the block area pretending to fish:*
> BOY 1: "Why are you here?"
> BOY 2: "I don't know. Why are you here?"
> BOY 1: "I don't know either."
> BOY 2: "If we don't know why we're here, maybe we should go somewhere else."

> *Two girls in the doll area:*
> GIRL 1: "I'm the mommy."
> GIRL 2: "I'm the mommy too."
> GIRL 1: "Someone has to be the daddy."
> GIRL 2: "Why? Don't mommies ever get married?"
> GIRL 1: "Let's get married!"
> GIRL 2: "No, it's my turn to be married."
> GIRL 1: "Well, if we both get married, then we can stay home with our baby."
> GIRL 2: "Here's my bed. When you see me get out of bed you spank me, but not too hard O.K.?"
> GIRL 1: "O.K."
> GIRL 2: "Ow! That's too hard! I don't like being the baby."
> GIRL 1: "But we need a baby."
> GIRL 2: "I'd rather be a tiger."

> *Girl and boy in the doll area:*
> GIRL: "You be the father because you're a boy. You're a boy, aren't you?"
> BOY: "I think so. You're a girl aren't you?"
> GIRL: "I guess so."
> BOY: "Then I must be a boy."

In this study, these highly verbal, imaginative children characteristically had a "close" friend with whom they frequently engaged in dyadic or group play. Although friendship at the preschool age is a vague construct, the children frequently verbalized concerns about friendship—in the interrogative, "You're my superfriend, right?"; the affirmative, "You're my very best friend"; or the possessive, "She's my friend, not yours," as if already according friendship a great deal of importance. The direction of effects for these fantasy-play and verbal behaviors is unknown. Children who frequently engage in fantasy play may be more verbal as a function of their fantasy play or engage in more fantasy play because they are more verbal.

Similarly, although a number of investigators have explored relationships between frequency of peer interaction and social-cognitive skills such as role-taking and classification skills, the direction of these relationships is also unknown. Piaget (1962) suggests that peer interactions facilitate a decline in egocentric thinking and thereby foster social and cognitive development. A number of studies report relationships between frequency of peer interaction and role-taking skills (Castle & Richards, 1978; M. O'Connor, 1976), classification skills (Marshall, 1961; Rubin et al., 1976; Saltz & Johnson, 1974), as well as performance on developmental assessments (Mundy, 1980), particularly verbal items of those assessments (Lubin & Field, 1980). In addition to these relationships, high rates of peer interaction are reputed to occur in children who are rated as more popular by their peers and teachers (Marshall & McCandless, 1957; Rubin et al., 1976). Others have failed to note these relationships. Jennings (1975), for example, noted that although peer popularity was related to social knowledge, it was not related to peer orientation. Similarly, Selman (1976) suggested that although children who are less popular are less likely to show high levels of social-cognitive development, children with high levels of social-cognitive development may or may not be liked by peers. Emmerich, Cocking, & Sigel (1979) suggest that "cognitive processes facilitate social adaptation, but social adaptation does not influence cognitive growth" (p. 503). Thus, although a number of relationships between rates of peer interaction and performance on social and cognitive tasks have emerged in this literature, the directions of those relationships are complex and largely unknown at this time.

HANDICAPPED AND PEER RELATIONS

A review of the sparse literature on peer interactions of handicapped children suggests a very limited range of interactions, particularly when the children have been observed in nonintegrated classrooms. For example, Spradlin and Girardeau (1966) noted a general absence of social interactions among retarded children. In both structured and unstructured activities, most of these children remained isolated from neighboring children and adults while engaging in a variety of self-stimulating and other forms of nonsocial behaviors. The presence of self-stimulation and absence of other-directed activity has been reported for groups ranging from autistic to Down's-syndrome to physically handicapped children. Typically, however, comparisons have been made between these children and chronological-age-matched children. Comparisons with developmental-age-matched controls, on the other hand, might be more appropriate and might reduce the differences between handicapped and normal children.

Hulme and Lunzer (1966), for example, observed the interactions of subnormal and normal children matched for a mean mental age of three years (although the mean chronological age of the subnormals was seven years compared to three years for the normals). Although these groups were similar on a number of interaction measures, the subnormal children were markedly inferior both in the number and level of language responses. With the exception of language skills, this study suggested that matching for developmental age diminished many of the differences between the groups. Lovell, Hoyle, and Siddal (1968) found that speech-delayed children developed fewer social-interaction behaviors than their speaking peers. Gregory (1976) also observed almost exclusively solitary play among deaf children and related their impoverished interaction to the lack of communication skills necessary to sustain interactions. Cerebral palsy has also been noted to interfere with early development of peer interactions. Poor functional mobility as well as intellectual deficits appear to be the limiting factors for this group (Hewett, 1970). Children with physical and mental handicaps may "need to be taught how to play and interact with other children" (Hewett, 1970).

A study by our group compared three classrooms of handicapped children with a classroom of normal children (Field, 1980b). The handicapped children had varying perceptual-motor handicaps including cerebral palsy, mental retardation, and speech or hearing deficits. The children were all three to four years old although each classroom varied by developmental stage, including a classroom of severely delayed, moderately delayed, and minimally delayed children. A developmental sequence was noted, with the severely delayed children exhibiting infant-like peer-interaction behaviors (looking, smiling, snatching toys) and the minimally delayed classroom showing more preschoollike peer-interaction behaviors (offering and sharing toys). In another study the handicapped children were observed playing together with normal children (matching numbers of handicapped and normal children) and playing alone (Field & Roseman, 1979). The frequency of peer-interaction behaviors among the handicapped children increased in the former play situation.

Increasing numbers of mainstreaming studies are suggesting that at least at the preschool stage, when handicapped and normal children are grouped together for play periods, the peer-related behaviors modeled by the normal children are accompanied by increases in the frequency of those behaviors among the handicapped children (Novak, Olley, & Keamey, 1980; White, 1980). It appears, however, that the ratio of handicapped to normal children is a critical factor, as is the introduction of handicapped children into mainstreamed or integrated situations at a very early age.

These data do not support the findings of a number of studies which suggest isolation and strictly self-directed activity among handicapped children (Gregory, 1976; Spradlin & Girardeau, 1966); nor do the data suggest that these children, when matched on developmental ages, show only language differences as suggested by Hulme and Lunzer (1966). Social-development delays of handicapped children may be more marked than developmental lags in other areas. Although some have suggested that social skills may require as much attention as cognitive, motor, and language skills, the focus of most remediation–intervention programs for handicapped children has been cognitive, motor, and language skills. Social gestures which are important for peer relations such as smiling, touching, and offering and sharing toys are not generally built into such curricula. In addition, teacher–child ratios are typically higher and teacher-directed activities more frequent in classrooms of handicapped children, which may provide less opportunity or reinforcement for peer relations (Novak *et al.*, 1980; White, 1980). Tizard (1964) and Mogford (1978) have illustrated that where environments are designed to foster social interactions among handicapped children, the social skills of the handicapped children are appropriate for their developmental age. In addition, social behaviors of handicapped children can be facilitated by integrating handicapped children with normal children (White, 1979). Handicapped children may need to be taught how to socially relate to others, and other children who model social behaviors may be good teachers.

MANIPULATIONS OF PEER SITUATIONS

Context appears to be an important variable in a number of the previously discussed studies on peer relations. Recently a number of investigators have observed variations in preschool environments and their effects on peer interactions and play. These have included variations in the number of children per classroom (Destefano & Lehmann, 1978), teacher–child ratios (Destefano & Mueller, 1978; Field, 1980a; Reuter & Yunik, 1973), degree of structure provided by teachers (Fagot, 1973; Huston-Stein, Friedrich-Cofer, & Susman, 1977), types of curricula (Miller & Dyer, 1975), toys and equipment (Destefano & Mueller, 1978, Pulaski-Spencer, 1970; Scholtz & Ellis, 1975), and types of play areas (Destefano & Lehmann, 1978; Field, 1980a; Harper & Sanders, 1975; Shure, 1963).

The most frequently employed dependent variables in the preschool-environment studies have included the frequency and sex configuration of peer and teacher interactions, the nature of those interactions (fantasy or constructive play), and their emotional tone (positive or negative). A developing picture that emerges from these studies is as follows: The number of children in a classroom has a negligible effect on peer interactions (Destefano & Lehmann, 1978), and peer interactions are more frequent or more sustained in classrooms featuring lower teacher–child ratios (Reuter & Yunik, 1973). Fewer teacher directives (Fagot, 1973), or less structure (Huston-Stein et al., 1977) and free-play-oriented curricula (Miller & Dyer, 1975) contribute to more frequent peer interactions. Less complex toys (Pulaski-Spencer, 1970) and equipment (Scholtz & Ellis, 1975) that are larger and less portable (Destefano & Mueller, 1978) appear to facilitate peer interactions. Finally, more fantasy play occurs in doll areas for girls and block areas for boys (Fagot & Patterson, 1969; Shure, 1963) as well as outdoors for boys (Harper & Sanders, 1975). Although preschool environments are highly variable, the importance of designing environments for early peer play is highlighted by a number of studies.

Teacher–Child Ratios

Teacher–child ratios have been largely determined by legislative regulations, university commitments, or private-school philosophy. For example, high teacher–child ratios have been mandated by federal law for Head-Start schools (Lichtenbert & Norton, 1970) and legislated by state law for day-care centers. University-lab schools, by virtue of their training commitments, feature high teacher–child ratios; whereas a long-standing tradition of Montessori schools dictates a fairly low teacher–child ratio (Standing, 1962). A study by Reuter and Yunik (1973) comparing a Montessori preschool (featuring a teacher–child ratio of 1:12) with a university-lab school (a ratio of 1:4) suggested that peer interactions were more frequent and more sustained in the Montessori classroom, perhaps because of its lower teacher–child ratio. The potential significance of teacher–child ratios is suggested by the Reuter and Yunik study (1973), although their comparison was confounded by other Montessori programmatic features such as heterogeneous age grouping, a factor which also facilitates peer interactions (Lougee, Goldman, & Hartup, 1977).

A comparison of four university-lab schools featuring similar curricula and same-age children, but varying from 1:12 to 1:4 on teacher–child ratios, reported similar findings (Field, 1980a). Several child and teacher behaviors were observed over the course of one year, including the incidence of play behaviors as defined by Parten, peer interactions, and fantasy play in the presence or absence of teachers who did or did not disrupt the interactions. A number of group differences emerged which suggested that the most optimal classroom for facilitating peer interactions and fantasy play was one with a low teacher–child ratio. Lower teacher–child ratios in part resulted in the less frequent presence of teachers in the special play areas. Whether the teachers' less frequent disruption of interaction related to their less frequent presence or their less frequently felt need to disrupt children who were more actively interacting with each other is unclear. The observers anecdotally reported a tendency of teachers in the classrooms with high teacher–child ratios to introduce a number of somewhat competing, prepared activities such as cooking, art, and science projects. Since less interaction and less imaginative play have been observed in highly structured or teacher-organized classrooms (Huston-Stein *et al.*, 1977; Miller & Dyer, 1975), the teachers of the classrooms with high teacher–child ratios may have inadvertently structured teacher-oriented activity into the curriculum and peer-oriented activity out of the curriculum. Although the strikingly higher incidence of peer interactions in the classrooms with a low teacher–child ratio highlights the questionable wisdom of state- and federally mandated high teacher–child ratios, most of the studies on teacher–child ratios have been conducted in classrooms of middle-class children. These findings, therefore, cannot be generalized to classrooms of deprived, lower-class children, who may benefit more from more frequent interactions with teachers.

Teacher-Directed Activity

A number of studies on both normal children (Fagot, 1973; Field, 1980a; Huston-Stein *et al.*, 1977; Miller & Dyer, 1975; Mueller, 1977) and handicapped children (Novak, Olley, & Kearney, 1979; White, 1980) suggest that less teacher-directed activity facilitates peer interactions. Huston-Stein (1977), for example, reported that in highly structured Head-Start classrooms of four- and five-year-old children, in which there was a considerable amount of adult-directed activity, fewer prosocial behaviors were observed toward peers as well as less imaginative play, but also less aggressive play. High levels of adult direction produced conformity when teachers were present but did not facilitate peer interaction on task-oriented behavior. Miller and Dyer (1975) similarly showed that in classrooms of minimal teacher-directed activity, children engaged in more verbal-social interactions, but also in more aggressive activity. Highly controlling teachers were observed to have less interactive, less task-oriented children (Fagot, 1973). It is interesting that in these studies girls were less interactive with peers than were boys. It has been noted that teachers instruct and direct the activities of girls more frequently (Fagot, 1973) to interact in fantasy play and specially planned art and science activities (Field, 1980a), and to reinforce girls' behavior more often than that of boys (Fagot & Patterson, 1969). Thus, the peer-interaction activity of girls may be affected more than that of boys by the amount of interaction, direction, control, and reinforcement provided by teachers.

Integrated classrooms featuring both normal and handicapped children have been compared on the teacher-directed-activity dimension. Observations in classrooms of autistic children (Olley *et al.*, 1979), children with speech and hearing deficits (Novak *et al.*, 1980), and children with physical and emotional problems (White, 1979) suggest that handicapped children appear to interact more with both their handicapped and nonhandicapped peers when there is less teacher-structured activity. These observations are not surprising, since the more time that is spent attending to or interacting with teachers, the less time children have to interact with each other. However, the observations do suggest that if a goal of early preschool programming is the facilitation of peer relations, the reinforcement of peer social behaviors may be provided most effectively by the peers themselves.

Arrangement of Space

The physical layout or arrangement of classroom space may also affect early peer interactions. Preschool classrooms are frequently leased spaces which have not been designed specifically for preschool programs. Although psychologists are growing increasingly sensitive to the effects of physical space on child behavior, most of our current impressions of the effects of physical environments come from teachers' comments. For example, teachers have anecdotally reported that preschoolers "just run about and act hyperactive in large open spaces" while they "tend to play more cooperatively within more enclosed spaces" (Huston-Stein *et al.*, 1977).

A study by Field (1980a) compared classrooms which were large, open spaces featuring special play areas in the corners and similar-size spaces which were partitioned (by short walls) into smaller special play areas including a doll area, block area, reading-puzzles-music area, and art–science–gym area. The curriculum was basically free-play for each classroom. The children of the classrooms featuring partitioned areas engaged in fewer interactions with the teachers, and more interactions (particularly verbal and fantasy interactions) with their peers. The greater frequency of interaction in the smaller, enclosed, or partitioned play areas may have resulted from the children being brought into closer proximity for interaction, physical proximity breeding a kind of intimacy (Shure, 1963). They may have also felt safer about interacting and engaging in fantasy play with the enclosure of their somewhat less public activity. Children's tendency to play within enclosed spaces when presented with a range of options has also been observed by Gramza (1972). Alternatively, they may simply have been less distracted from their peer play by less exposure to goings-on in other areas.

Classroom Materials

The way classrooms and play areas are equipped also appears to affect the nature of peer interactions. For example, the preschool play areas which appear to facilitate the most peer interactions are notoriously the doll corner and block areas (Field, 1979d; Sanders & Harper, 1976; Shure, 1963). Whether these areas are conducive to peer interaction because they are typically smaller areas facilitating closer physical proximity and intimacy of children, or whether the type of activity (playing house or building a house) stimulated by the materials in these areas facilitates closer collaboration is unclear.

Play materials appear to make a difference in the amount and type of peer interaction. Sholtz & Ellis (1975), for example, reported more peer interaction in classrooms featuring less complex objects and structures. Destefano & Mueller (1978) observed low levels of peer interaction when a classroom was stocked with small, portable objects and correspondingly high levels of peer interactions in the same classroom when large, non-portable objects or structures were installed, with the latter serving to partition play areas and reduce the incidence of conflicts of possession. A study involving observations of behaviors pre and post the building of multiple classroom play structures suggested that children related to their peers more frequently and more positively almost immediately following the construction of the play structures (Lubin & Field, 1979). Thus, the mere arrangement of the physical environment appears to have its effect on peer interactions.

Mixed-Age, Same-Age Children

Finally, the effects on peer interactions of mixed-age and of same-age classes have been compared. The literature is inconsistent on the relative advantages of mixed-age and same-age grouping. As mentioned earlier, Konner (1975) notes that children's groups comprised strictly of peers are an artifact of advanced industrial states. Konner claims that the mixed-age group is better equipped than the peer group to transmit cultures, ensure care and protection for younger members, and facilitate the smooth intergration of children into a wider social world. Further, he suggests that mixed-age groups foster the development of communication skills and other abilities among the older children.

In a number of cultures, Whiting (1978) has observed highly competitive and mildly aggressive interactions among same-age groups. Similarly, Bronfenbrenner (1970) expresses concern that "groups of children in the United States are usually composed of a very narrow age range, reducing the possibility for learning culturally established patterns of cooperation and mutual concerns."

A slightly different perspective is provided by Piaget (1932), who claims that there may be adaptational advantages to children interacting with peers of equal status. The combinations of assimilative and accommodative interactions occurring between age-mates may facilitate cognitive decentration as well as sexual, aggressive, and moral development. Taking the interactionist position, Lougee, Grueneich, and Hartup (1977) suggest that social development may be facilitated by both same-age and different-age peer interactions.

The research data are as mixed as the positions expressed above. Interactions between same-age as opposed to different-age peers appear to be both more positive and more negative (Hertz-Lazarowitz, Feitelson, Hartup, & Zahavi, 1978; Whiting & Whiting, 1975). Lewis and colleagues (1975) suggest that more positive affect occurs in interaction between different-age peers, with same-age peers more likely to share but also more likely to take toys and resist peer overtures. A number of preschool studies have reported more frequent peer interactions among mixed-age groups (Bianchi & Bakeman, 1978; Field, 1979d; Lubin & Field, 1980; Reuter & Yunik, 1973). A number of "horizontal-vertical" age-group comparisons in grade schools also suggest advantages for mixed-age grouping. Papay, Costello, Hedl, and Spielberger (1975), for example, reported less anxiety in mixed-age groups. Although another comparison of this kind yielded no differences in anxiety and social adjustment, better work habits, more varied role taking, and closer relationships to teachers in mixed-age groups were noted (Mycock, 1966). This comparison among three types of age groupings (a restricted multiage mix across a three-year span, a complete multiage mix across a seven-year span, and a traditional same-age classroom) suggested that the children had better self-concepts and more interest in the subject matter in the mixed-age settings, most particularly in the complete-multiage setting.

A series of explanations have been offered for the effects of mixed-age grouping. For example, children may prefer to teach children younger than themselves and to be taught by children older than themselves (Allen & Feldman, 1973). Older children are more effective models than younger children (Peifer, 1971). Social reinforcement is more effective when delivered by either an older or a younger child than when delivered by an age-mate (Ferguson, 1965). Children are noted to contribute more to group problem-solving efforts in mixed- than in same-age situations (Graziano, French, Brownell, & Hartup, 1976). Reciprocal imitations occur more frequently among older-younger age dyads (Thelen & Kirkland, 1976); and since imitation is noted to be both a potent initiator and sustainer of interactions (Lubin & Field, 1980) this fact may contribute to the differences in frequency of interactions between mixed-age and same-age groups.

The complexity of comparisons between same- and mixed-age groups is illustrated by some studies which suggest that the mixed-age–same age-effects appear to interact with both the age and sex of the child. For example, Lougee et al. (1977) reported that social interactions and verbal communications were most frequent in five-year-old, same-age dyads, intermediate in mixed-age dyads, and least frequent in three-year-old, same-age dyads. In addition, the Field (1979a) data suggested that while cross-sex peer interactions occurred more frequently in mixed-age than same-age groups, the two-year-old boys and five-year-old girls, seemingly because they were more equivalent in language skills to their same-age, same-sex peers, interacted more frequently with them. Others have suggested that language-matched peer preferences need not be a factor since children are noted to adjust their speech upward or downward in complexity—for example, shortening and simplifying speech in the case of three-year-olds talking to two-year-olds, and speaking in a more adultlike way in the case of three-year-olds to three-year-olds (Shatz & Gelman, 1973). In any case, mean length-of-utterance measures are reputedly similar in mixed- and same-age older dyads (Lougee et al., 1977).

The implication in many of these studies is that the mixed-age situation, either with younger or older children, places greater demands on mature, social accommodations than does same-age interaction. The opportunities for learning modeled by older children accrue to the younger children, and the opportunities for developing empathy and nurturance behaviors may be greater for the older children in the presence of younger children. The assumption that chronological-age difference is equivalent to maturational-age difference runs through these interpretations. It is conceivable, however, that given the wide variability in maturation rate at these early ages, children may have more opportunity to find equal-developmental-status or equal-behavioral-complexity peers in mixed-chronological-age groups. As was noted in the Field (1979d) study, language-cross-sex matches occurred more in mixed-age groups. Girls may play with girls in same-age groups because their language skills are more equivalent than girl–boy peers. But older boys may provide not only a language match but a more rough-and-tumble group-play experience (rough-and-tumble and group play occurring more frequently among boys), thus providing another dimension for the girls that is not available in girl–girl play.

Another confounding factor in comparisons between same- and mixed-age groups relates to teacher activity. Teacher activity was not reported in any of these studies. Since teachers are reputedly more comfortable or feel more competent instructing same-age groups, they may limit the amount of peer interaction in same-age groups by frequent instruction of the entire same-age class. In mixed-age classes, however, they often rotate instructional sessions across same-age subgroups, leaving the other subgroups free to play and engage in peer interactions, artifactually contributing to increases in the rates of peer interaction in mixed-age groups. The long-term effects of mixed-age and same-age groupings are unknown at this point. The old one-room schoolhouses in this country were not investigated prior to the universal move toward graded classes. In Sweden, where family groupings (or mixed-age groups including siblings of multiple families) are an increasingly popular tendency, there may be opportunities to compare the long-term effects of same- and mixed-age classrooms.

PEERS AS BEHAVIOR-CHANGE AGENTS

A growing literature suggests that children might be used as effective agents for behavior changes of their peers via various strategies including modeling, social reinforcement, and tutoring. Since these are the specific subject areas of many chapters in this volume, only a few examples of these techniques will be given.

Peers as Models

The use of modeling or peer imitation as a behavior-change procedure has been noted to have direct effects on affective and cognitive skills as well as children's social relations (Bandura, 1968). An effective demonstration of the use of modeling was provided by R. D. O'Connor (1969), who showed movies to isolated preschool children depicting a gradual increase in peer interactions. Classroom observations subsequently revealed an increased incidence of peer interactions among the isolated children as compared to a control group who saw a film on animals. Films were also effectively used by Bandura, Grusec, and Menlove (1967) to reduce animal phobias by showing the children models who had no fear of animals. The use of live children as effective models has been shown by Debus (1970), who exposed third-grade impulsive problem-solving children to sixth-grade reflective problem solvers. The impulsive problem solvers showed increased latency to responding as a consequence. Live modeling has also been effectively used to increase sharing by altruistic peer models (Hartup & Coates, 1967). In addition, a number of investigators have successfully taught retarded children to imitate nonretarded children with attendant increases in imitative and social behaviors (Apolloni, Cooke, & Cooke, 1977; Cooke, Apolloni, & Cooke, 1977; Devoney, Guralnick, & Rubin, 1974; Guralnick, 1976; Guralnick, this volume).

Peers as Social Reinforcers

Social reinforcement of children by their peers naturally occurs in the classroom. The rewards spontaneously provided by peers appear to both modify and maintain behavior. Reinforcement for aggression and counteraggression, for example, are provided with some frequency by peers (Patterson, Littman, & Bricker, 1967). Patterson observed that among preschool children, physical assaults were positively reinforced approximately 75% of the observation time by the crying or defensive behavior of the victim. Children who were attacked and counterattacked successfully became increasingly aggressive. The direct use of peers as social reinforcers has been demonstrated by training confederate peers, using instructional, role-playing, and reinforcement measures. The most frequent method is a reversal design employing multiple baseline intervention, and withdrawal of intervention procedures (Baer, Wolf, & Risley, 1968).

Prosocial learning was demonstrated by Wahler (1967) using this procedure of peer reinforcement. Baseline rates of several behaviors (cooperation, isolate behaviors, dramatic play) were determined for five preschool children. Response classes associated with high and low rates of peer reinforcement were identified. The experimenters then induced a number of peer confederates to ignore the high- or low-rate subjects when the target behaviors occurred and continue interacting with the subject when he emitted other behaviors. Increases or decreases were observed in these target behaviors during intervention periods, and diminished toward baseline levels during reversal or withdrawal of intervention periods.

Solomon & Wahler (1973) used similar procedures with similar success in reducing disruptive activities among sixth graders. Strain and his colleagues have also employed these training procedures successfully in a series of studies of various age children exhibiting various problems, for example, with withdrawn, autistic children (Ragland, Kerr, & Strain, 1978), with withdrawn preschool children (Strain, 1977; Strain, Shores, & Timm, 1977), and with behaviorally handicapped preschoolers or those with language delays and temper tantrums (Strain, Kerr, & Ragland, this volume; Strain, Shores, & Kerr, 1976). While the immediate effects of training peers as social reinforcers are impressive, there are very little data on whether these effects generalize or persist across time and situations.

Peers as Tutors

Volumes have been written on the use of peers as tutors (Allen, 1976; Gerber & Kauffman, this volume). Although there is a long history of the use of peers as tutors, this practice currently has renewed popularity. The data, in general, suggest that the peer tutoring situation has benefits for both the tutor and the child being tutored. The tutor derives attention and deference from both teachers and other children, receives role-taking experience, and learns nurturant behaviors. The benefits usually ascribed to the tutored child include academic competencies and enhanced motivation to learn. Other generalizations suggested in a review by Allen and Feldman (1973) are that children prefer to be taught by same-sex children and by older children, and tutors conveniently prefer to teach young children and same-sex children.

The complexities of peer tutoring are illustrated in a study by Allen and Feldman (1973) in which low achieving children taught younger children who were average achievers. The tutors and tutees alternated days spent in tutoring and solitary study. Studying alone was initially more efficient for the tutors, but the tutoring experience gradually resulted in better learning than studying alone. The reverse effects of time were noted for tutees, with the tutoring situation being initially more helpful followed by performance gradually showing greater gains from studying alone. Thus, generalizations made about peer tutoring appear to be situation specific. Hartup (1979) further warns that excessive use of peer tutoring may subvert the egalitarian nature of peer relations.

Uniqueness of Peer Relations and Influence

Peer relations are unique or qualitatively different than other relations such as child-adult relations from a very early time in life. Studies of very young infants by Field (1979a) and by Lewis *et al.* (1975) suggest, for example, that proximal behaviors such as touching, hugging, and clinging are more often directed toward parents than peers, as are distress (crying) and comfort-seeking behaviors. Eckermen *et al.* (1975) also observed characteristically different behaviors directed toward parents and peers by older infants. Infant behaviors ordinarily directed toward mothers such as smiling and vocalizing were also directed toward peers, but less frequently. Play materials or toys were more often used as interaction objects in peer play than mother–infant play. As in the Field and Lewis studies, proximal behaviors more often occurred with parents and distal behaviors (e.g., looking) in the presence of peers. Older children similarly direct physical affections, for example, hugging and kissing, more frequently toward adults, while they spend more time following their peers around, engaging them in conversation, and offering to help them (Heathers, 1955).

Different affective responses to adults and children have also been reported in stranger-situations. Infants have been noted to respond more positively to infant strangers than adult strangers in free-play situations (Field, 1979b) and to child strangers than adult strangers in laboratory situations (Greenberg, Hillman, & Crice, 1973). A study by Brooks and Lewis (1976), in which infants showed a preference for midget strangers over adult strangers, suggests that the "stranger who looks more like me" may elicit less negative responses. However, a study in which fear-producing stimuli were presented, suggests that when the child can choose between proximity to a familiar adult or familiar peer, he seeks proximity to the adult (Patterson, Bonvillian, Reynolds, & Maccoby, 1975).

Qualitative differences are also seen in play, with parents and teachers rarely engaging in rough-and-tumble play, fantasy, or object related play. Although parents and teachers may initiate and supervise such modes of play, the child's peers are more often the sustaining forces. Rough-and-tumble play may be less appropriate for child–adult interactions due to mere size and strength differences, and fantasy play may be more difficult due to the greater reality orientation of adults.

The Whitings, in their studies of six cultures (Whiting & Whiting, 1975), suggest that sociable behavior and aggressiveness occur more frequently in peer than adult interaction, while dependency and intimacy occur more frequently in child interactions with adults. These, then, are some of the qualitative differences in behaviors directed toward peers and adults. What qualities intrinsic to children might explain these differential behaviors? The mere physical qualities of children may contribute to the differential behaviors in the presence of children and adults. These features are aspects of both the stimulus and response provided for the peer. Obvious similarities are the size, physiognomy, and behavioral repertoire of peers. The equivalent size and behavioral repertoire may facilitate rough-and-tumble play without injury to the child. Similarly, successful role-playing or imitation may be facilitated by model roles and behaviors of the child already existing in the peer's repertoire (Piaget, 1951). Cognitive equivalence may facilitate peer fantasy play. Affective equivalence, the uninhibited expression of glee, and the repetitive expression of emotion may serve to sustain these bouts of rough-and-tumble and fantasy play. Equivalence in physical characteristics, complexity of behavioral repertoire and cognitive skills, as well as similarities in affective expression and a penchant for repetition are unique features of peers and may contribute to the differences observed in peer and child-adult interactions.

What special functions might these unique qualities and behaviors serve to peers? Hartup (1979) has enumerated some unique peer functions including the development of sociability, the mastery of aggressive impulses, sexual socialization, the development of empathy, and the prevention of social problems. He claims that these functions can be achieved since peer play is egalitarian and reciprocal. The problems of providing evidence for these notions are much greater than citing simple unique stimulus-and-response features of peers. Constructs like empathy and egalitarianism are more difficult to operationalize and quantify. In addition, longitudinal data are missing, and peer deprivation data cannot be provided to answer these questions. That peer relations appear very early and seem to persist may be sufficient evidence for the power of peers as socializing influences.

REFERENCES

Ainsworth, M. D. Attachment and dependency. In J. L. Gewirtz (Ed.), *Attachment and dependency*. Washington, D.C.: Winston, 1972.

Allen, V. L. (Ed.). *Children as teachers: Theory and research on tutoring*. New York: Academic Press, 1976.

Allen, V., & Feldman, R. S. Learning through tutoring: Low achieving children as tutors. *Journal of Experimental Education*, 1973, 42, 1–5.

Apolloni, T., Cooke, S. A., & Cooke, T. P. Establishing a normal peer as a behavioral model for developmentally delayed toddlers. *Perceptual and Motor Skills*, 1977, 44, 231–241.

Baer, D. M., Wolf, M. M., & Risley, T. R. Some current dimensions of applied behavior analysis. *Journal of Applied Behavior Analysis*, 1968, 1, 91–97.

Bakeman, R. Personal communication, 1979.

Bandura, A. Social-learning theory of identificatory processes. In D. A. Goslin (Ed.), *Handbook of socialization theory and research*. Chicago: Rand McNally, 1968.

Bandura, A., Grusec, J. E., & Menlove, F. L. Vicarious extinction of avoidance behavior. *Journal of Personality and Social Psychology*, 1967, 5, 16–23.

Barker, R. G., & Wright, R. *Midwest and its children*. New York: Harper & Row, 1955.

Barnes, K. E. Preschool play norms: A replication. *Developmental Psychology*, 1971, 5, 99–103.

Bell, R. Q. A reinterpretation of the direction of effects in studies of socialization. *Psychological Bulletin*, 1968, *75*, 81–95.

Bianchi, B. D., & Bakeman, R. Sex typed affiliation preferences observed in preschoolers: Traditional and open school preferences. *Child Development*, 1978, *49*, 910–912.

Bowlby, J. *Attachment and loss*. Vol. 1. *Attachment*. New York: Basic Books, 1969.

Bridges, K. M. A study of social development in early infancy. *Child Development*, 1933, *4*, 36–49.

Bronfenbrenner, U. *Two worlds of childhood*. New York: Russell Sage Foundation, 1970.

Bronson, W. C. Competence and the growth of personality. In K. J. Connolly & J. Bruner (Eds.), *The growth of competence*. New York: Academic Press, 1974.

Brooks, J., & Lewis, M. Infants' responses to strangers: Midget, adult and child. *Child Development*, 1976, *47*, 323–332.

Buhler, C. The social behavior of children. In C. Murchinson (Ed.), *Handbook of child psychology*. Worcester, Mass.: Clark University Press, 1933.

Castle, K. S., & Richards, S. *Adult/peer interactions and role taking ability among preschool children*. Paper presented at the Southeastern Conference on Human Development, Atlanta, April 1978.

Charlesworth, R., & Hartup, W. Positive social reinforcement in the nursery school peer group. *Child Development*, 1967, *38*, 993–1002.

Chukovsky, K. *From two to five*. Berkeley: University of California Press, 1963.

Cooke, T. P., Apolloni, T., & Cooke, S. A. Normal preschool children as behavioral models for retarded peers. *Exceptional Children*, 1977, *43*, 531–532.

Cowen, E. L., Pederson, A., Babijian, H., Izzo, L. A., & Trost, M. A. Long-term follow-up of early detected vulnerable children. *Journal of Consulting and Clinical Psychology*, 1973, *41*, 438–446.

Debus, R. L. Effects of brief observation of model behavior on conceptual tempo of impulsive children. *Developmental Psychology*, 1970, *2*, 22–32.

Destefano, C., & Lehmann, L. *Effects of group size on the behavior of preschool children*. Paper presented at the Southeastern Conference on Human Development, Atlanta, April 1978.

Destefano, C., & Mueller, E. *Environmental determinants of peer social behavior and interactions in a toddler play group*. Paper presented at the Southeastern Conference on Human Development, Atlanta, April 1978.

Devoney, C., Guralnick, M. J., & Rubin, M. Integrating handicapped and non-handicapped preschool children: Effects on social play. *Childhood Education*, 1974, *50*, 360–364.

Dolhinow, P. J., & Bishop, L. The development of motor skills and social relationships among primates through play. In J. P. Hill (Ed.), *Minnesota symposia on child psychology* (Vol. 4). Minneapolis: University of Minnesota Press, 1970.

Dragsten, S., & Lee, L. *Infants' social behavior in a naturalistic vs. experimental setting*. Paper presented at the meeting of the American Psychological Association, Montreal, August 1973.

Eckerman, C. O. *Competence in early social relations*. Paper presented at the Symposium on Early Competence: Data and Concepts, meeting of the American Psychological Association, Montreal, August 1973.

Eckerman, C. O., Whatley, J. L., & Kutz, S. L. Growth of social play with peers during the second year of life. *Developmental Psychology*, 1975, *11*, 42–49.

Elkins, D. Some factors related to the choice status of ninety eighth grade children in a school society. *Genetic Psychology Monographs*, 1958, *58*, 207–272.

Emmerich, W., Cocking, R. R., & Sigel, I. E. Relationships between cognitive and social functioning in preschool children. *Developmental Psychology*, 1979, *15*, 495–504.

Fagot, B. I. Influence of teacher behavior in the preschool. *Developmental Psychology*, 1973, *9*, 198–206.

Fagot, B. I., & Patterson, G. R. An in vivo analysis of reinforcing contingencies for sex-role behaviors in the preschool child. *Developmental Psychology*, 1969, *1*, 563–568.

Ferguson, N. *Peers as social agents.* Unpublished Master's thesis, University of Minnesota, 1965.

Field, T. Differential behavioral and cardiac responses of 3-month-old infants to a mirror and peer. *Infant Behavior and Development*, 1979, *2*, 179–184.(a)

Field, T. Infant behaviors directed toward peers and adults in the presence and absence of mother. *Infant Behavior and Development*, 1979, *2*, 47–54.(b)

Field, T. Interaction patterns of high-risk and normal infants. In T. Field, A. Sostek, S. Goldberg, & H. H. Shuman (Eds.), *Infants born at risk.* New York: Spectrum, 1979.(c)

Field, T. *Sex preferences among preschool children as a function of language skills.* Unpublished manuscript, University of Miami, 1979.(d)

Field, T. Preschool play: Effects of teacher/child ratios and organization of classroom space. *Child Study Journal*, 1980.(a)

Field, T. Self, teacher, toy and peer-directed behaviors of handicapped preschool children. In T. Field, S. Goldberg, D. Stern, & A. Sostek (Eds.), *High-risk infants and children: Adult and peer interactions.* New York: Academic Press, 1980.(b)

Field, T., Masi, W., & Ignatoff, E. *Infant-peer interactions in an infant nursery.* Unpublished manuscript, University of Miami, 1979.

Field, T., Goldberg, S., Stern, D., & Sostek, A. (Eds.). *High-risk infants and children: Adult and peer interactions.* New York: Academic Press, 1980.

Field, T., Roseman, S., De Stefano, L., & Koewler, J. H., III. Play behaviors of handicapped preschool children in the presence and absence of nonhandicapped peers. *Journal of Applied Developmental Psychology*, in press, 1981.

Fischer, T. *Peer interactions of infants six- to eight-months-old.* Unpublished manuscript, Tufts University, 1973.

Freud, A., & Dann, S. An experiment in group living. In R. Eisler, A. Freud, H. Hartman, & E. Kris (Eds.), *The psychoanalytic study of the child* (Vol. 6). New York: International Universities Press, 1951.

Furman, W., Rahe, D., & Hartup, W. W. Rehabilitation of socially withdrawn children through mixed-age and same-age socialization. *Child Development*, 1980, *50*, 915–922.

Gewirtz, J. L. *Attachment and dependency.* Washington, D.C.: Winston, 1972.

Gottman, J. M., & Parkhurst, J. *Developing may not always be improving.* Paper presented at the meeting of the Society for Research in Child Development, New Orleans, March 1977.

Goy, R. W., & Goldfoot, D. A. Experimental and hormonal factors influencing development of sexual behavior in the rhesus monkey. In *The neurosciences: Third study program.* Cambridge: MIT Press, 1973.

Gramza, A. F. A measured approach to improvement of play environments. *Johper*, 1972, *3*, 43–41.

Graziano, W., French, D., Brownell, C., & Hartup, W. W. Peer interaction in same and mixed-age triads in relation to chronological age and incentive condition. *Child Development*, 1976, *47*, 707–714.

Greenberg, D. J., Hillman, D., & Grice, D. Infant and stranger variables related to stranger anxiety in the first year of life. *Developmental Psychology*, 1973, *9*, 207–212.

Gregory, H. *The deaf child and his family.* London: Allen & Unwin, 1976.

Guralnick, M. J. The value of integrating handicapped and nonhandicapped preschool children. *American Journal of Orthopsychiatry*, 1976, *42*, 236–245.

Harlow, H. F. Age-mate or peer affectional system. In D. S. Lehrman, R. A. Hinde, & E. Shaw (Eds.), *Advances in the study of behavior* (Vol. 2). New York: Academic Press, 1969.

Harlow, H. F., & Harlow, M. K. The affectional systems. In A. M. Schrier, H. F. Harlow, & F. Stollnitz (Eds.), *Behavior of nonhuman primates* (Vol. 2). New York: Academic Press, 1965.

Harper, L. V., & Sanders, K. M. Preschool children's use of space: Sex differences in outdoor play. *Developmental Psychology*, 1975, *11*, 119.

Hartup, W. W. Peer relations and the growth of social competence. In M. W. Kent & J. E. Rolf (Eds.), *The primary prevention of psychopathology* (Vol. 3) Hanover, N.H.: University Press of New England, 1979.

Hartup, W. W. Peers, play and pathology: A new look at the social behavior of children. In T. Field, S. Goldberg, D. Stern, & A. Sostek (Eds.), *High-risk infants and children: Adult and peer interactions*. New York: Academic Press, 1980.(a)

Hartup, W. W. Two social worlds: Family relations and peer relations. In M. Rutter (Ed.), *Scientific foundations of developmental psychiatry*. London: Heineman, 1980.(b)

Hartup, W. W., & Coates, B. Imitation of peers as a function of reinforcement from the peer group and rewardingness of the model. *Child Development*, 1967, *38*, 1003–1016.

Heathers, G. Emotional dependence and independence in nursery school play. *Journal of Genetic Psychology*, 1955, *87*, 37–57.

Hertz-Lazarowitz, F., Feitelson, A., Hartup, W., & Zahavi, S. *Social interactions and social organization of Israeli five-to-seven-year-olds*. Unpublished manuscript, University of Jaffa, 1978.

Hewett, S. *The family and the handicapped child*. London: Allen & Unwin, 1970.

Holmberg, M. C. *The development of social interchange patterns from 12–42 months: Cross-sectional and short-term longitudinal analyses*. Paper presented at the biennial meeting of the Society for Research in Child Development, New Orleans, March 1977.

Hulme, I., & Lunzer, E. A. Play, language, and reasoning in subnormal children. *Journal of Child Psychology and Psychiatry*, 1966, *7*, 107–115.

Huston-Stein, A., Friedrich-Cofer, L., & Susman, E. J. The relation of classroom structure to social behavior, imaginative play and self-regulation of economically disadvantaged children. *Child Development*, 1977, *11*(4), 411–519.

Jennings, K. D. People versus object orientation: Social behavior and intellectual abilities in preschool children. *Developmental Psychology*, 1975, *11*, 411–519.

Konner, M. Relations among infants and juveniles in comparative perspective. In M. Lewis & L. A. Rosenblum (Eds.), *Friendship and peer relations*. New York: Wiley, 1975.

Langlois, J. H., Gottfried, N. W., & Seay, B. The influence of sex of peers on the social behavior of preschool children. *Developmental Psychology*, 1973, *8*, 93–98.

Lenssen, B. *Infants' reactions to peer strangers*. Unpublished doctoral dissertation, Stanford University, 1973.

Lewis, M., & Rosenblum, L. A. (Eds.) *The effect of the infant on its caregiver*. New York: Wiley, 1974.

Lewis, M., & Rosenblum, L. A. (Eds.). *Friendship and peer relations*. New York: Wiley, 1975.

Lewis, M., Young, G., Brooks, J., & Michalson, L. The beginning of friendship. In M. Lewis & L. A. Rosenblum (Eds.), *Friendship and peer relations*. New York: Wiley, 1975.

Lichtenberg, D., & Norton, D. *Cognitive and mental development in the first five years of life*. Rockville, Md.: National Institute of Mental Health, 1970.

Lieberman, A.F. *The social competence of preschool children: Its relations to quality of attachment and to amount of exposure to peers in different preschool settings*. Unpublished doctoral dissertation, Johns Hopkins University, 1976.

Lougee, M.D., Greuneich, R., & Hartup, W.W. Social interaction in same- and mixed-age dyads of preschool children. *Child Development*, 1977, *48*, 1353–1361.

Lovell, K., Hoyle, H.W., & Siddal, M. Q. A study of some aspects of play and language of young children with delayed speech. *Journal of Child Psychology and Psychiatry*, 1968, *9*, 41–46.

Lubin, L., & Field, T. *Is imitation a sincere form of flattery?: Imitation and its relationship to peer interactions in a mixed age preschool*. Unpublished manuscript, University of Miami, 1980.

Marshall, H. R. Relations between home experiences and children's use of language in play interactions with peers. *Psychological Monographs*, 1961, *75* (5).

Marshall, H. R., & McCandless, B. A study in prediction of social behavior of preschool children. *Child Development*, 1957, *28*, 149–159.

Maudry, M., & Nekula, M. Social relations between children of the same age during the first two years of life. *Journal of Genetic Psychology*, 1939, *54*, 193–215.

Miller, L. B., & Dyer, J. L. Four preschool programs: Their dimensions and effects. *Monographs of the Society for Research in Child Development*, 1975, *40* (112).

Mogford, K. The play of handicapped children. In B. Tizard & D. Harvey (Eds.), *Biology of play*. Philadelphia: J. B. Lippincott, 1978.

Mueller, E. Workshop on peer interactions, presented at biennial meeting of the Society for Research in Child Development, New Orleans, March 1977.

Mueller, E., & Rich, A. Clustering and socially directed behaviors in a play group of one-year-old boys. *Early Child Development and Care*, 1980.

Mundy, P. *The relationship between a measure of cognitive test performance and social style in preschool children*. Unpublished manuscript, University of Miami, 1980.

Mycock, M. A. *A comparison of vertical grouping and horizontal grouping in the infant school*. Unpublished Master's thesis, University of Manchester, 1966.

Novak, M. A., & Harlow, M. Social recovery of monkeys isolated for the first year of life: Rehabilitation and therapy. *Developmental Psychology*, 1975, *11*, 453–465.

Novak, M. A., Olley, J. G., & Kearney, D. J. Social skills of handicapped children in integrated and separate preschools. In T. Field, S. Goldberg, D. Stern, & A. Sostek (Eds.) *High-risk infants and children: Adult and peer interactions*. New York: Academic Press, 1980.

O'Connor, M. Role-taking and social orientation in young children. *The Journal of Psychology*, 1976, *94*, 135–137.

O'Connor, R. D. Modification of social withdrawal through symbolic modeling. *Journal of Applied Behavior Analysis*, 1969, *2*, 15–22.

Olley, G. *Observational study and assessment of social and cognitive development of autistic children*. Paper presented at the meeting of the American Association of Mental Deficiency, Miami, 1979.

Papay, J. P., Costello, R. J., Hedl, J. J., & Spielberger, C. D. Effects of trait and state anxiety on the performance of elementary school children in traditional and individualized multi-age classrooms. *Journal of Educational Psychology*, 1975, *67*, 840–846.

Parten, M. B. Social participation among preschool children. *Journal of Abnormal Social Psychology*, 1932, *27*, 243–269.

Patterson, F. G., Bonvillian, J. D., Reynolds, P. C., & Maccoby, E. Mother and peer attachment under conditions of fear in rhesus monkeys (Macca mulatta). *Primates*, 1975, *16*, 75–81.

Patterson, G. R., Littman, R. A., & Bricker, W. Assertive behavior in children: A step toward a theory of aggression. *Monographs of the Society for Research in Child Development*, 1967, *32*, Serial No. 113.

Peifer, M. R. *The effects of varying age-grade status of models on the imitative behavior of six-year-old boys*. Unpublished doctoral dissertation, University of Delaware, 1971.

Piaget, J. *The moral judgment of the child*. Glencoe, Ill.: Free Press, 1932.

Piaget, J. *Play, dreams and imitation in childhood*. New York: W. W. Norton, 1951.

Pulaski-Spencer, M. A. Play as a function of toy structure and fantasy predisposition. *Child Development*, 1970, *41*, 531–537.

Ragland, E. U., Kerr, M. M., & Strain, P. S. Behavior of withdrawn autistic children: Effects of peer social interactions. *Behavior Modification*, 1978, *2*, 565–578.

Ramey, C. J., Finkelstein, N. W., & O'Brien, C. Toys and infant behavior in the first year of life. *Journal of Genetic Psychology*, 1976, *129*, 341–342.

Reuter, J., & Yunik, G. Social interaction in nursery schools. *Developmental Psychology*, 1973, *9*, 319–325.

Roff, M. Childhood social interactions and young adult bad conduct. *Journal of Abnormal and Social Psychology*, 1961, *63*, 333–337.

Roff, M., Sells, S. B., & Golden, M. M. *Social adjustment and personality development in children*. Minneapolis: University of Minnesota Press, 1972.

Rolf, J. E. The social and academic competence of children vulnerable to schizophrenia and other behavior pathologies. *Journal of Abnormal Psychology*, 1972, *80*, 225–243.

Rosenblum, L. A. Peer relations in monkeys: The influence of social structure, gender and familiarity. In M. Lewis & L. A. Rosenblum (Eds.), *Friendship and peer relations*. New York: Wiley, 1975.

Rubin, K. H., Maioni, T. L., & Hornung, M. Free play behaviors in middle- and lower-class preschoolers: Parten and Piaget revisited. *Child Development*, 1976, *47*, 414–419.

Sackett, G. P. Unlearned responses, differential rearing experiences and the development of social attachment by rhesus monkeys. In L. A. Rosenblum (Ed.), *Primate behavior: Developments in field and laboratory research* (Vol. 1). New York: Academic Press, 1970.

Saltz, E., & Johnson, J. Training for thematic-fantasy play in culturally disadvantaged children: Preliminary results. *Journal of Educational Psychology*, 1974, *66*(4), 623–630.

Sanders, K. M., & Haper, L. V. Free-play fantasy behavior in preschool children: Relations among gender, age season, and location. *Child Development*, 1976, *47*, 1182–1185.

Scholtz, G. J., & Ellis, M. J. Repeated exposure to objects and peers in a play setting. *Journal of Experimental Child Psychology*, 1975, *19*, 448–455.

Selman, R. L. Toward a structural analysis of developing interpersonal relations concepts: Research with normal and disturbed pre-adolescent boys. In A. D. Pick (Ed.), *Minnesota Symposia on Child Psychology* (Vol. 10). Minneapolis: University of Minnesota Press, 1976.

Serbin, L. A., Tonick, T., & Sternglanz, S. H. Shaping cooperative cross-sex play. *Child Development*, 1977, *48*, 924–929.

Shatz, M., & Gelman, R. The development of communication skills: Modification in the speech of young children as a function of listener. *Monographs of the Society for Research in Child Development*, 1973, *38* (152).

Shure, M. B. Psychological ecology of a nursery school. *Child Development*, 1963, *34*, 979–992.

Solomon, R. W., & Wahler, R. J. Peer reinforcement control of classroom problem behavior. *Journal of Applied Behavior Analysis*, 1973, *6*, 49–56.

Spiro, M. *Children of the kibbutz*. Cambridge: Harvard University Press, 1958.

Spradlin, J. E., & Girardeau, F. L. The behavior of moderately and severely retarded persons. In N. R. Ellis (Ed.), *International review of research in mental retardation* (Vol. 1). New York: Academic Press, 1966.

Standing, E. M. *Maria Montessori: Her life and work*. New York: Academy Guild Press, 1962.

Strain, P. S. An experimental analysis of peer social initiations on the behavior of withdrawn preschool children: Some training and generalization effects. *Journal of Abnormal Child Psychology*, 1977, *5*, 445–455.

Strain, P. S., Shores, R. E., & Kerr, M. M. An experimental analysis of "spillover" effects on the social interaction of behaviorally handicapped preschool children. *Journals of Applied Behavior Analysis*, 1976, *9*, 31–40.

Strain, P. S., Shores, R. E., & Timm, M. A. Effects of peer social initiations on the behavior of withdrawn preschool children. *Journal of Applied Behavior Analysis*, 1977, *10*, 289–298.

Suomi, S. J., & Harlow, H. H. Social rehabilitation of isolate-reared monkeys. *Developmental Psychology*, 1972, *6*, 487–496.

Synder, L., Apolloni, T., & Cooke, S. A. Integrated settings at the early childhood level: The role of nonretarded peers. *Exceptional Children*, 1977, *43*, 262–266.

Thelen, M. H., & Kirkland, K. D. On status and being imitated: Effects on reciprocal imitation and attraction. *Journal of Personality and Social Psychology*, 1976, *33*, 691–697.

Tizard, J. *Community services for the mentally handicapped*. London: Oxford University Press, 1964.

Vandell, D. L., Wilson, K. S. & Buchanan, N. R. *Peer interaction in the first year of life: An examination of its structure, content and sensitivity to toys*. Paper presented at biennial meeting of the Society for Research in Child Development, San Francisco, March 1979.

Vincze, M. The social contacts of infants and young children reared together. *Early Child Development and Care*, 1971, *1*, 99–109.

Vygotsky, L. Play and its role in the mental development of the child. *Soviet Psychology*, 1967, *5*, 6–18.

Wahler, R. G. Child-child interactions in a free field setting: Some experimental analyses. *Journal of Experimental Child Psychology*, 1967, *5*, 278–293.

Waters, E., Wippman, J., & Sroufe, A. Social competence in preschool children as a function of the security of earlier attachment to the mother. *Child Development*, 1980, *51*, 208–216.

Werner, H. *Comparative psychology of mental development*. New York: Science Editions, 1948.

White, B. N. Mainstreaming in grade school and preschool: How the child with special needs interacts with peers. In T. Field, S. Goldberg, D. Stern, & A. Sostek (Eds.), *High-risk infants and children: Adult and peer interactions*. New York: Academic Press, 1980.

Whiting, B. B. The dependency hang-up and experiments in alternative life styles. In J. M. Yinger & S. J. Cutler (Eds.), *Major social issues*. New York: Free Press, 1978.

Whiting, B. B., & Whiting, J. W. M. *Children of six cultures*. Cambridge: Harvard University Press, 1975.

Winder, C. L., & Rau, L. Parental attitudes associated with social deviance in preadolescent boys. *Journal of Abnormal and Social Psychology*, 1962, *64*, 418–424.

2

Peer Influences on the Development of Communicative Competence

MICHAEL J. GURALNICK

Eavesdropping on the conversations of young children not only provides the substance for scientific investigations but is a fascinating experience as well. The predictable unpredictability, unpretentiousness, and ingenuous qualities of many of these conversations have a unique and rare capacity for exposing basic assumptions and feelings not found in more sophisticated interactions. This is not to say that these conversations are simple and straightforward or are unaffected by the intricate relationships that exist among speakers, their context, characteristics of listeners, or other complex factors that impinge on a given situation. On the contrary, when our scientific pursuits prevail over the pure enjoyment of listening to the conversations of young children, we are struck by the remarkable communicative competence that characterizes these interactions. Although they are no match for the inveterate and accomplished cocktail-party conversationalist, ample evidence in support of young children's abilities to initiate, maintain, repair, and terminate conversations can be gathered. Similarly, the coherence, balance, reciprocal nature, and sensitivity to many subtle situational variations displayed by their conversations, as well as the application of social "rules" in shaping these interactions, further suggest a well-developed competence.

Consider the following conversations in which normally developing, four-year-old children are attempting to obtain compliance to requests from their companions, some of whom are handicapped. In the first episode, two normally developing children are engaged in play and

MICHAEL J. GURALNICK • The Nisonger Center, The Ohio State University, Columbus, Ohio 43210.

Child R wants Child C to give him one of the toy firemen in the rescue
station that has captured their attention. (Child R: Nonhandicapped;
Child C: Nonhandicapped.)

R: I need him.
c: Not now!
R: I need that man there.
c: They wanna get some rest to see if some fire in there.
R: I need that blue man (*pointing*)!
c: He wants to see if some fire's in there.
R: (*After failing to remove the fireman undetected*) What I'm gonna have
   to do?
c: (*After a twenty-second pause*) You want a man to go up here?
R: Yes, I need it (*pointing*).
c: Okay, here is one.

This sequence's alternating quality and the participants' adjustments to each other's demands reflect the mutual and reciprocal
nature of the interaction. For example, efforts are apparent to clarify and
emphasize the referent ("blue man" and pointing) and, when all fails,
including an attempt to remove the object in the face of rejection, a
question as to how to proceed to obtain compliance is presented ("What
I'm gonna have to do?"). This strategy succeeds with Child C relenting,
even after he had attempted to justify the rejection in earlier statements
("He wants to see if some fire's in there.").
   The next sequence contains an interaction in which a normally developing four-year-old is encouraging a mildly handicapped five-year-
old to put a fish in a bowl during a play episode. (Child B: Nonhandicapped; Child D: Mildly handicapped.)

B: D., do you know what?
D: (*No response.*)
B: You gotta put this thing under here (*demonstrating*).
D: (*No response.*)
B: Okay?
D: Okay. How you do it?
B: (*Demonstrates again.*) See, O.K.?
D: O.K.
B: Go on!
D: (*Attempts, but is not successful.*)
B: D., you gotta pull the thing down (*guiding*).
D: Got it!

In this interaction, the attention-getting initiation of the conversation is apparent, as well as the probes that follow when the initial establishment of communication fails. Moreover, the use of physical prompts and guidance is more pervasive in this episode, as is the increased closeness of the monitoring by the nonhandicapped child of her handicapped companion's behaviors.

Finally, it is instructive to consider the following behavior-request sequence with a severely handicapped, nonverbal companion. (Child N: Nonhandicapped; Child S: Severely handicapped.)

N: S., put this in here.
S: (*Attempts, but is not correct.*)
N: No, S.
N: Wait!
N: Put your hand on it, S.
N: Right here (*guidance*).
S: (*Correctly responds to the simplified request.*)
N: Now, so I could help you.
N: Put it in here (*more guidance*).
S: (*Completes total response correctly with physical guidance.*)
N: There you go.

Clearly, the nature of this interaction differs substantially from the other two as a result of the significant cognitive and linguistic delays of the handicapped child. Close monitoring, the provision of physical guidance, and the simplification of the request do, however, appear to be sufficient to maintain the interaction and even to resolve a difficult problem. The absence of indirect or polite forms of usage is also notable.

These excerpts from encounters among similar-age children at different developmental levels provide some insights into the characteristics of child–child interactions and their degree of communicative competence. It should be noted at the outset that the term "communicative competence" is employed in its very broadest sense in this chapter, and is intended to include influences of peers on the form, content, use, and discourse features of the communications of children (Bloom & Lahey, 1978; Gleason & Weintraub, 1978; Hymes, 1971; McLean & Snyder-McLean, 1978). In addition, this discussion will emphasize the influence of peers on communicative competence related to child–child interactions, that is, communicative interactions of young children when interacting with other young children. Also considered will be any general improvements in communicative skills that may result from interactions with peers. Finally, the deliberate selection of communicative excerpts between nonhandicapped children and companions at different developmental levels was designed to highlight the fact that this chapter will focus on the developmental-educational aspects of communicative interactions occurring among children at different developmental levels. Although interactions among such children have a bearing on a number of important theoretical and developmental issues in the area of peer relations, the impetus for this focus is its importance in relation to programs that mainstream young handicapped children (Guralnick, 1976, 1977, 1978a, in press a). In particular, an effort will be made to establish a theoretical and empirical framework for designing mainstreamed environments that maximize those aspects of communicative competence that can be facilitated through interactions with classmates.

To provide background for this framework, a number of related topics will be discussed. First, a brief review of the emerging concepts of peer–peer social relationships will be presented. Issues generally considered as belonging to the social domain will be included, since social and communicative development are so closely interrelated. In fact, to highlight this relationship, the term "social-communicative" will often be employed. Second, the broad developmental course of communicative competence with peers will be outlined. The growth of interactions among similar-age peers is not only valuable in its own right but also provides an essential framework for understanding interactions among children at different chronological ages and/or developmental levels. The third section will analyze mixed-age interactions, and in the fourth section, those interactions that occur among children at different developmental levels will be examined. Taken together, it is hoped that the concepts and information that emerge from this comprehensive approach will not only establish our present level of understanding regarding peer influences on communicative development, but will provide guidance for practical application to classroom environments that contain both handicapped and nonhandicapped children as well. This issue, along with recommendations for future study, will be addressed in the concluding section of the chapter.

PEERS AS INDEPENDENT CONTRIBUTORS TO SOCIAL-COMMUNICATIVE DEVELOPMENT

The recent resurgence of interest in the study of peer relationships has revealed such interactions to be a potentially powerful source of influence on development. While the contributions of caregiver–child relations remain central to an understanding of development, the concept of a broad social network, which includes peer interactions themselves as important and possibly independent contributors to child–child social development, is finding considerable theoretical and empirical support (Hartup, 1979; Lewis & Feiring, 1979; Lewis & Rosenblum, 1975a; Lewis & Rosenblum, 1975b). Much of the empirical evidence is derived from recent work on children's social development and play. Perhaps most persuasive is the demonstration by Mueller and Brenner (1977) that the development of coordinated, socially directed behaviors and sustained interactions of toddlers with their peers is dependent upon specific inter-actions with those peers, and is not merely an extension of caregiver–child interactions. In the area of play, Rubenstein and Howes (1976, 1979) obtained evidence that toddlers' competence during play is enhanced by the presence of other toddlers. Furthermore, although more indirect in form, the clinical value of peers as agents of change suggests their poten-tial as unique contributors to development. Probably the most dramatic example of the impact of peers in this regard can be found in the work of Furman, Rahe, and Hartup (1979), who were able to obtain substantial and durable improvements in the prosocial behavior of withdrawn chil-dren utilizing peer therapists. Numerous other examples of this strategy can be found in various chapters of this volume. Finally, recent research with primates, which permits experimental manipulations not otherwise possible, offers some additional support for the value of peers. Based on peer-deprivation studies and observational work which noted the existence of differential interaction patterns in relating to peers and to caregivers, Suomi (1979) concluded that peer interactions may well be essential to the proper development of social competence.

A closer analysis of other social-interaction studies has also revealed differences between caregiver–child and child–child interactions which, although not suggesting an autonomous peer–peer system, do indicate areas in which the two domains are not entirely congruent. For example, as summarized by Mueller (1979), the content of the two types of inter-action patterns differs in that more motor behaviors are directed to peers and more verbal behaviors to adults. (Interestingly, peer–peer inter-actions in the primate work cited above more closely resembled future adult–adult relationships than adult–peer interactions.) It also appears that, in contrast to caregiver–child interactions, the context for the origin of peer–peer interactions is primarily object centered. Additional, but highly tentative evidence that the peer–peer system has autonomous aspects can be found in Vandell's dissertation (see Mueller, 1979), which suggested that peer–peer play may be the origin, not the result, of sustained mother–toddler relations.

The importance of peer interactions in relation to social-com-municative development is intriguing, although certainly not com-pelling on either theoretical or empirical grounds. It may well be that the contention that peer–peer relations are powerful developmental factors is derived primarily from speculations regarding the qualities of such inter-actions and the process through which they might contribute to the child's development. The most frequently offered quality is the coequal nature of peer–peer interactions (e.g., Hartup, 1978; Lewis & Rosenblum, 1975a). It is suggested that this characteristic encourages the development of behaviors which require the type of mutuality and reciprocity neces-sary for effective child–child interactions. Furthermore, the novelty and interest afforded by one's peers, as well as the gradual pacing and opportunity to casually explore various components of a social problem, seem to further contribute to the qualities that may make peer–peer interactions essential and unique in promoting various forms of social competence.

RELEVANCE TO COMMUNICATIVE COMPETENCE

What is the relevance of peer–peer social interactions in a chapter devoted to peer influences on the development of communicative compe-tence? At a theoretical level, it should be recognized that, for the most part, social and communicative development are inextricably related. Communication exists to serve social functions; the current inter-disciplinary research in pragmatics and language development amply demonstrates this interdependence (Bloom & Lahey, 1978; McLean & Snyder-McLean, 1978; Moerk, 1977). In a real sense, the study of social development consists of a narrowing of one's focus to one domain, albeit legitimately from a scientific and practical point of view, yet maintaining a recognition of the unified nature of the problems under study (Lewis & Cherry, 1977). Consequently, these social influences will logically extend to what is generally considered the communicative domain.

This relationship between social and communicative development can be understood more clearly by the fact that a close examination of the dependent variables in social-interaction studies actually consists of vari-ables of significance to the study of communicative behavior. For exam-ple, Mueller and his colleagues (Mueller, 1979; Mueller & Brenner, 1977; Mueller & Vandell, 1979) examined social exchanges and their complexi-ty, including length. In the communication literature, closely allied vari-ables such as turn taking (social exchanges) and other surface features of communicative interactions (e.g., complexity) are, of course, highly rel-evant to the study of child–child discourse. Similarly, the extensive work on imitation in peer–peer social interactions may have an important bearing on child language development as well.

If interactions among children at similar ages do, in fact, uniquely contribute to the development of young children, it may be helpful to examine the specific qualities of the interactions that could affect communicative competence.* As suggested earlier, the coequal nature of the interactions may be partially responsible (Hartup, 1978). This quality requires that each participant contribute to a conversation to ensure its initiation and maintenance. Adults are highly responsive and adept at maintaining such interactions, but child–child exchanges often demand equal time and skill from the participants. Accordingly, a very different set of behavior patterns seems to be necessary in this social context, especially since both ambiguity and rejection are common occurrences during these interactions. The development of children's abilities to maintain and repair conversations (that is, ensure mutuality and reciprocity) by effectively utilizing feedback, by recognizing the contributions of the context and listener characteristics to one's conversations, and in clarifying ambiguous referents and concepts all seem essential to adequately solving the communication problem and to fostering communicative competence. It may well be that peer–peer interactions create the appropriate environment for the development of this competence.

The concept of communicative adjustments may be fundamental to an understanding of this process. That is, the ability to effectively modify one's communicative behavior as a function of a complex array of factors may well be at the essence of communicative competence. If this assumption is accurate, then diverse encounters with classmates who provide differential feedback may be needed for this competence to develop. From an educational perspective, since social-communicative competence is so critical a domain in the development of young children, the composition of classrooms in terms of classmates, as well as the design of the structure and curriculum of those classrooms, should reflect an awareness of the importance and potential contributions of peer–peer relationships.

Before turning to analyses of communicative influences among children at different chronological and/or developmental levels, a brief and selective review of the development of communicative competence among normally developing children with age-mates will be presented. It should be noted at the outset that no direct evidence exists demonstrating the unique contributions of peers to the development of communicative competence. However, knowledge of the development of the processes of adjustment, the extent of mutuality and reciprocity, and, in general, the actual communicative skills of young children should provide useful guidelines for assessing indirect evidence. Finally, insight into this proc-

*The fact that age and coequal status are imperfectly correlated is recognized. This variability can, of course, hold for characteristics within individual children, as, for example, when a child is coequal on the playground with gross-motor equipment but not during dramatic play requiring considerable verbal and symbolic behavior. (See the discussion of Lewis, Young, Brooks, & Michalson, 1975, on the definition of "peer" in relation to function.)

cess may be necessary to design effective intervention strategies for children who are delayed in the development of communicative competence.

COMMUNICATIVE COMPETENCE WITH SIMILAR-AGE PEERS

One of the major outcomes of the renewed interest in peer relations is a recognition that the social-communicative abilities of young children have been significantly underestimated. As will be briefly reviewed below, young children appear to be quite capable of successfully initiating exchanges and maintaining interactions through appropriate adjustments with similar-age companions. Moreover, in many respects these adjustments appear to be quite sophisticated, displaying a sensitivity to relevant listener characteristics and feedback as well as to situational factors.

Early studies of developmental changes in communicative development with similar-age peers focused on three- to four-year-old children. Observing two groups composed of dyads in social play, one younger (3½–4⅓ years) and one older (4½–5 years), Garvey and Hogan (1973) analyzed utterance units in terms of the degree of social speech, that is, speech adapted to the children's companions. For the most part, these investigators found that both groups of children were mutually engaged in interactions (an average of 66% of each session) and maintained a balanced interaction in terms of exchanges. Some differences between older and younger dyads were noted, however. Specifically, speech adapted to companion children ranged from 21% to 64% for the younger dyads, and from 48% to 77% for the older groups. In a related study, Garvey and BenDebba (1974) found that the correlation between the number of utterances between same-age dyads increased with age (although utterance length did not), and suggested that this increase reflected improvements in communicative adaptiveness. Additional analyses by Garvey focusing on requests for action (1975) and contingent queries (1977) of three- to five-year-old children also revealed the existence of considerable competence on the part of young children.

Despite the occasional differences that were detected between younger and older dyads, perhaps the most interesting and salient finding of the series of studies reviewed above was that even the younger children had well-developed communicative repertoires. Building upon earlier work with four-year-olds (see Mueller, 1972), in which a substantial degree of mutuality, adaptiveness to listeners, and conversational success was also observed, Mueller, Bleier, Krakow, Hegedus, and Cournoyer (1977) focused on two-year-olds in an effort to track the developmental course of this competence. Examining videotaped records of children's play-group interactions, first at 22 months and again at 30 months, a number of reliable longitudinal changes were observed. First, the percentage of utterances that received a verbal response increased from 27% to 64%. Second, a more detailed analysis of antecedent variables consisting of content (relevant or not relevant), speaker attention (on peer, not on peer), distance (less than three feet, more than three feet), attention getting (present, absent), and listener attention (on speaker, not on speaker) was carried out. This analysis revealed significant changes in all variables across time in the direction of the first behavior in each parenthesis, with the exception of attention getting (toward less of a need to utilize attention-getting techniques). In addition, each antecedent variable was analyzed in terms of its ability to predict responsiveness when it was present. This assessment indicated that the predictive power of each variable remained constant throughout the study, with listener attention being the best predictor in the group. Of equal importance was the fact that these antecedent variables acted in a synergistic fashion, with responsiveness being virtually assured when four or five antecedent variables predicted a verbal response.

The study of Mueller and colleagues (1977) was particularly valuable in that it revealed the growing ability of young speakers to select relevant message content that was adapted appropriately to the listener's needs. In addition, the study underscored the contribution of mutuality in producing successful verbal exchanges, as indicated by the importance of both speaker and listener attention variables. Finally, these findings for younger children are supported by descriptive evidence from psycholinguistic studies which indicated that young children manifest considerable conversational competence and utilize a wide range of conversational devices to maintain interactions (Keenan, 1974, 1977; Keenan & Klein, 1975).

APPROPRIATENESS AND PATTERNS OF COMMUNICATIVE ADJUSTMENT

Adjustments during communicative exchanges to meet multiple-listener and situational contingencies are, of course, essential for effective communication to occur. Since there are numerous strategies speakers can adopt to achieve conversational objectives, any assessment as to whether certain communicative adjustments are, in fact, appropriate must consider those objectives, task demands, and a wide variety of other factors. Although the concept of appropriateness will be discussed in more detail in a subsequent section of this chapter, the relative and flexible qualities of this concept are emphasized at this time.

Assessments of the communicative adjustments of young children in naturalistic settings have consistently demonstrated considerable competence in making appropriate adjustments. For example, Wellman and Lempers (1977) examined the abilities of two-year-old children to have a companion focus on a particular referent during a play-group. Interactions containing referential conversational episodes were identified from videotaped records and then analyzed in terms of the correspondence between the difficulty of the communicative task (e.g., presence or absence of obstacles with regard to the referent) and those aspects of the communicator's behavior that would facilitate referential communication (e.g., removes obstacles, points, uses attention getters). These analyses revealed that, irrespective of the difficulty of the situation, speakers were easily able to elicit adequate responses from companions (nearly 80% of the time). Moreover, the evidence indicated that this success was attributable to young children appropriately adapting the frequency and content of their communicative behaviors to the demands of the situation. This sensitivity is reflected by the fact that most of the speakers' messages concerned companion–referent and companion–speaker relationships. Although messages were directed more to adults than to peers, a rather high degree of overall competence characterized these interactions (see Maratsos, 1973, for a related study).

Utilizing listener feedback and adjusting communications in accordance with that feedback is an additional dimension along which appropriateness can be assessed. Relatively little work has been done exploring these interrelationships, with the investigation by Spilton and Lee (1977) standing as a notable exception. These authors identified sequences of free-play interactions among four-year-old dyads in which a speaker utterance was initially noncommunicative. They then examined the processes that followed in an effort to achieve clarification and mutual understanding of the original statement. Focusing on elaborative sequences (a minimum of five exchanges between the speaker and listener toward resolving the noncommunicative statement), a coding system was devised that analyzed speaker responses in terms of their adaptiveness and listener responses in terms of the type of feedback provided to the speaker. Responses were considered adaptive if they provided any additional information that was relevant to the listener. Clarity of utterances and the use of gestures were also coded. Analyzing the results from many perspectives, it was found that a large proportion of speaker responses following communicative failures were adpative, especially if repetition is included in that category. More detailed, conditional-probability analyses were used to determine if adaptiveness varied as a function of specific listener feedback (e.g., replies, repeats, specific questions, general questions). In general, adaptive speaker responses were most likely to occur in response to specific questions.

From a somewhat different orientation, Garvey (1977) identified and analyzed certain question forms embedded within larger conversations of three- to five-year-old children. Referring to these question forms as "contingent queries," she found that young children have the ability to make such information requests, particularly unsolicited ones, and to respond to rather subtle forms of those requests during child–child discourse. Overall, Garvey demonstrated that nonspecific requests for repetition, as well as specific requests for confirmation, specification, and repetition, received responses considered appropriate by a model of contingent queries.

Further indications of the appropriateness of young children's adjustments to listener needs can be found in Garvey's (1975) work on requests for action. Although sequences of requests for action were analyzed separately for younger (mean 46.3 months) and older (mean 60 months) dyads during play, Garvey found few differences between the groups, as noted earlier. Overall, direct and indirect requests were recognized as such in at least three-fourths of the cases, and actual compliance was noted over half the time. Most interesting, however, were the sequences of adjustments that followed noncompliance. Although limited quantitative data were presented, the use of various strategies and adjustments to requests as well as analyses of the forms of clarification were seen by Garvey as strong indicators that speakers and listeners are able to recognize the relevant factors of a request for action and adjust accordingly.

These studies of adjustments in peer–peer conversations have been particularly instructive. Nevertheless, it may be especially worthwhile for future work to focus more effort on analyzing sequences of events and on identifying patterns of adjustment (see Sackett, 1978, for a detailed discussion of the quantitative issues regarding sequential analyses). This pattern strategy has yielded some preliminary evidence for the existence of structurally formal, but perhaps critical, "routines" that children utilize to both establish and maintain contact during conversations. Such sequences as the summons–answer routine and the rhetorical gambit (Garvey & Hogan, 1973; Schegloff, 1968) may form the building blocks for certain conversational exchanges. These early exchanges may then facilitate the development of longer interactions through variations and elaborations of the successful patterns. Related work by Lee, Brody, Matthews, and Palmquist (1974) also seeks to identify those interactive patterns correlated with success. Taken together, the developmental patterns and adjustment processes discussed in this section may contain sufficient information to form the rudiments of a developmentally based curriculum for children who have delayed or otherwise poorly developed communicative skills with peers.

RECIPROCITY AND MUTUALITY

The concepts of reciprocity and mutuality, briefly noted in earlier discussions, are useful in understanding the general development of social-communicative competence among similar-age children (see Cairns, 1979; Strain & Shores, 1977), and now require elaboration. "Reciprocity" implies a tendency to adjust one's behavior to that of a companion, thereby achieving a more balanced interaction. These adjustments include both qualitative and quantitative components. "Mutuality," as the term is employed here, simply means the ability to maintain contact in an interaction utilizing any number of possible techniques. Corresponding to the development of children's abilities to engage others in communicative interactions, to achieve longer and more complex exchanges, to employ diverse and creative interactive techniques in response to listener and situational factors, and to repair discourse that has failed or is flagging, is the strong tendency to maintain balance in the interaction. In fact, the adjustments that are made and the specific strategies and routines that emerge generally result in ensuring or restoring reciprocity and mutuality—a condition vital for allowing participants to achieve their social-communicative goals.

There are two major aspects of the concepts of reciprocity and mutuality that should be highlighted. First, and most apparent, is that the quality and quantity of one's behavior can be significantly regulated by the quality and quantity of the behavior of one's companion. As such, this is a critical developmental concept and one that has a substantial empirical basis (Cairns, 1979). Second, although only exchanges among peers of similar age and ability have been examined up to this point, it is nevertheless reasonable to suppose that reciprocity and mutuality have limits, particularly when interactions occur among children with wide discrepancies in age and/or developmental levels. The limits of such reciprocity and mutuality and the forms those behaviors might take when pressed to those limits are important concerns of the remainder of this chapter.

Although these comments anticipate forthcoming discussions, it will be argued in this chapter that communicative interactions occurring among children of similar age and developmental level and those occurring among children of different age and/or developmental level can produce important but differing developmental outcomes. The following section examines the details of one of these adjustment patterns—that resulting from interactions occurring among normally developing children who differ widely in chronological age and corresponding developmental levels.

COMMUNICATIVE INTERACTIONS AMONG MIXED-AGE, PRESCHOOL CHILDREN

The ability of four-year-olds to modify their speech when interacting with younger children was a major focus of a systematic series of studies carried out by Shatz and Gelman (1973). In three integrated experiments, these researchers compared the speech of four-year-olds as addressed to two-year-olds, other four-year-olds, and adults in both naturalistic and semistructured settings. Their findings revealed that consistent adjustments occurred as a function of the listener. In general, the speech addressed to two-year-olds was syntactically and semantically less complex and contained a greater number of attention-getting devices. Speech to adults and to four-year-old peers was similar.

It is interesting to note the parallels between the adjustments made by four-year-olds to younger listeners and those of parents. Evidence gathered over the past few years has clearly established that parents provide selective input that apparently is closely matched to the cognitive and linguistic levels of their developing children (Broen, 1972; Gleason, & Weintraub, 1978; Mahoney & Seely, 1976; Snow, 1972; Snow & Ferguson, 1977). Although it is beyond the scope of this chapter to review this evidence in any detail, these extensive efforts point to the fact that the language environment of young children is organized by parents in a manner that tends to facilitate not only the acquisition of language, but communicative competence in general as well.

Certainly, four-year-olds' speech adjustments cannot be equated to adjusted parental or other adult speech; yet similarities in the direction and magnitude of these modifications are quite striking. Commenting on these similarities, Shatz and Gelman (1973) noted that,

> Our results show that 4-year-olds (with and without younger siblings) make similar adjustments [referring to those made by parents] for 2-year-old listeners. They use a preponderance of short utterances and make less frequent use of complex constructions. As illustrated in the protocols ,. . . the speakers often repeat utterances or parts of utterances. Apparently, even 4-year-olds help to produce a restricted and redundant linguistic environment for the early language learner. (p. 33)

Whether or not these adjustments are capable of actually facilitating the communicative development of young children as a supplement to typical adult–child interactions is a question that must await the outcome of experiments that compare communicative development as a function of various degrees of adjusted peer input. More detailed comparisons between adult and child speech for varying task demands would also be valuable. Until such studies are carried out (they will require considerable methodological sophistication and the resolution of extensive practical problems), we must rely on other strategies for evaluating the potential developmental significance of these child–child adjustments. For example, the degree of fine tuning of the adjustments or the extent of the communicative match of mixed-age child–child interactions would be a useful index of the potential value of these interactions. In this regard, Shatz and Gelman observed that not all two-year-old listeners received the same degree of adjusted input from four-year-olds, with the "older" two-year-olds receiving more complex speech than the "younger" ones.

Apart from initial conceptions and expectations of listeners' abilities prior to entry into conversation, the primary mechanism that has been invoked to account for speaker sensitivity to younger listeners is feedback (Bohannon & Marquis, 1977; Gleason, 1977). Apparently, young speakers are capable of closely monitoring the linguistic competence and general comprehension abilities of listeners, although the precise constellation of cues that may produce this effect has not been identified. Certainly, one important factor is sensitivity to the listener's ability to attend (Shatz & Gelman, 1973); however, a recent study by Masur (1978) has demonstrated that even when attention, chronological age, and cognitive ability of two-year-old listeners were held constant, four-year-olds were nonetheless able to adjust the complexity of their speech to both the conversational responsiveness and linguistic levels of the listener. Analyzing communicative interactions during experimental sessions and comparing speech to "high-verbal" and "low-verbal" two-year-olds, Masur found that the discourse feature of conversational responsiveness, given the constancy of other factors, was important in regulating the length and complexity of utterances addressed to the two-year-olds by the four-year-olds.

In a related investigation, Sachs and Devin (1976) found that the speech of four children (CA 3–9 to 5–5 years) was modified in a pattern similar to that noted above when addressed to an adult, peer, baby, and baby doll. An important element of this investigation was the comparison between the latter two categories, since only the former provided feedback. Since this comparison revealed considerable communicative similarities, the authors suggested that even young children have reasonable expectations of age-appropriate speech.

Communicative competence requires the recognition of "rules" that operate in social contexts which, in turn, exert important influences on the selection of communicative strategies as well as the form of individual utterances (Ervin-Tripp & Mitchell-Kernan, 1977; Rees, 1978). Insight into how these subtle and complex factors regulate input in mixed-age interactions can be found in the recent analyses by Gelman and Shatz (1977).

Struck by the differential use by four-year-olds of *that* and *wh* predicate–complement constructions in complex utterances found in their original work (Shatz & Gelman, 1973), they reanalyzed those utterances in terms of their "functional meaning-in-conversation" (Gelman & Shatz, 1977, p. 35). Specifically, those utterances were coded as either directing the interaction, communicating information, clarifying information, or requesting new information; in addition, it was determined whether assertions were marked as to the speaker's certainty of an assertion. Comparing the functional use of these communications by four-year-olds to adults and to two-year-olds in both unstructured and structured tasks, a pattern emerged suggesting that the selection of the form of the predicate complement was consistent with Gelman and Shatz's (1977, pp. 32–33) definition of appropriate speech:

> (a) it shows evidence that the speaker is selecting content that a listener is likely to understand and/or respond to; and (b) it honors conventions about politeness, status, flexibility, and the like that may be relevant for listeners in particular settings.

As an example, *that* complements were rarely addressed to two-year-olds in their structured task, although the form was commonly used with adults. This difference can be understood from the fact that *that* predicate complements were generally employed in this situation as hedging statements or for marking a degree of uncertainty ("I think that's correct"). Given the perceived lower status of the younger children and the different roles adopted by the four-year-olds when relating to two-year-olds, such hedging was not necessary. Other features of the situation, such as the fact that the four-year-olds primarily directed the interaction when interacting with the younger listeners but generally did not request information, also contributed to the variable use of the predicate-complement forms.

Further support for the importance of situational or demand characteristics and listener status on message formulation was found by James (1978) in her analysis of the politeness of children's directives. Even in the absence of feedback (since the task was one of role playing), politeness varied as a function of the listener (adult, same-age peer, younger peer), especially in James's "command" situation. For example, bare imperatives were frequently found in the speech to younger children but rarely addressed to adults. Same-age peers, on the other hand, were provided with modified imperatives that served to mitigate requests. Despite the fact that politeness and utterance length and complexity are confounded in this study, it is likely that the differential adjustments reflect a sensitivity to status-situational relationships.

SUMMARY AND IMPLICATIONS OF MIXED-AGE ADJUSTMENTS

The preceding discussion provides only indirect evidence with regard to the developmental significance of mixed-age interactions on the development of communicative competence of both older speaker and younger listener. Nevertheless, consistent modifications in the syntactic, semantic, pragmatic, and discourse aspects of the speech of older children have been found to occur as a function of a range of listener characteristics and other situational and contextual factors. From both a communications framework and a tutorial perspective, these modifications seem appropriate. Specifically, the adjustments by more advanced children when addressing younger children seem to be organized in a structurally coherent and comprehensible manner, yet appear to contain sufficient diversity so that the input could be considered progressive (e.g., encouraging more advanced language). Similarly, the pragmatic and discourse characteristics of speech, particularly as they affect the use of specific syntactical forms, may even have the capability of transmitting information concerning various social roles associated with age and status factors. Research on the mitigation of directives and modulation of assertive statements that occur when addressing listeners of different age and/or status, as well as correlations between polite syntactical forms, usages, and listener status provide additional support for the fact that modifications in the speech of young children are responsive to social conventions (Gelman & Shatz, 1977; James, 1978). Further indirect support for the possible value of mixed-age interactions for the younger child is based on research that has demonstrated that older and more competent children are imitated more by younger and less competent children (Akamatsu & Thelen, 1974; Lewis, Young, Brooks, & Michalson, 1975), and that even preschool-age older siblings create new interactive patterns that may stimulate important aspects of growth (Lamb, 1978). It should be kept in mind, however, that although the potential developmental implications are clear, the actual effects of this process have not been traced.

Issues for future study include evaluating the correspondence between adult–child and mixed-age child–child adjustments. Although accommodations in important structural features are likely to be similar for these two groups of speakers when overall measures such as mean length of utterance are utilized, other structural characteristics as well as pragmatic and discourse features may, for both overall measures and upon closer analysis, produce very different outcomes. Of course, the responsiveness of the young child to different companions is also a critical variable here. This analysis, and its implications for understanding the potential developmental roles of adult–child and mixed-age child–child adjustments, remain to be clarified. Related to this need is the need for a finer analysis of child–child interactions in particular. As noted earlier, the degree of fine tuning is an important element in determining the appropriateness of interactions. Such a determination would also be facilitated by direct assessment of younger children's immediate and long-term adjustments in response to interactions with older children. Their responsiveness and "code switching" (Gleason, 1973) is another area in need of examination.

Finally, considering possible benefits to older children in a mixed-age situation, the ability to effectively adjust one's social-communicative behavior in accordance with the listener and other relevant factors is an important aspect of social learning (Hartup, 1978; Lougee, Grueneich, & Hartup, 1977). Mixed-age interactions afford opportunities for the development of this competence. The opportunities to practice code switching may prove to be of value from this perspective for the advanced children as well.

COMMUNICATIVE INTERACTIONS AMONG CHILDREN AT DIFFERENT DEVELOPMENTAL LEVELS

As a direct result of the movement generally referred to as "mainstreaming," to integrate handicapped and nonhandicapped children in the classroom environment, opportunities for communicative interactions occurring among children at different developmental levels have increased dramatically. Although the rationale for mainstreaming includes extensive educational and humanistic components, the empirical basis for this educational strategy remains to be clarified (Guralnick, 1978b, in press a). Such a clarification will require an understanding of the nature and potential developmental significance of interactions occurring among children in heterogeneous groups.

Accordingly, with same-age and mixed-age interactions as background, communicative exchanges among similar-age children who are at different developmental levels will be the focus of the remainder of this chapter. A series of experiments focusing on the ability of nonhandicapped children to adjust their interactions to the cognitive and linguistic capacities of a range of handicapped classmates will be reviewed and will form the primary data base for this analysis. These investigations will also provide a framework for developing the concept of appropriateness as a guide for judging the developmental significance of communicative adjustments among children at different developmental levels. In addition, discussions of adjustments made by handicapped children while interacting with more advanced children, as well as a brief review of the use of peers as agents of change for structured, tutorial purposes will be included. This information will then be integrated with our understanding of same- and mixed-age interactions in an effort to identify classroom experiences in mainstreamed environments that would maximize the development of child–child communicative competence.

NONHANDICAPPED CHILDREN'S SPEECH TO HANDICAPPED CHILDREN

In order to be compatible with the intent of the "least-restrictive-environment" principle as mandated by Public Law 94-142 (1975, 1977), it is essential that the ability of mainstreamed environments to promote the developmental growth of all concerned be demonstrable (Guralnick, in press a). Although many proponents of mainstreamed education anticipate that integrated environments will actually be found to be more educationally effective than any other and have a major impact at many levels, integrated environments must, at minimum, be able to meet the diverse needs of all children. As indicated elsewhere (Guralnick, in press a), an evaluation of the feasibility of mainstreamed programs should include measures relating to the developmental potential of interactions occurring in mainstreamed settings as an important element. Accordingly, analyzed from a communications perspective in relation to developmental potential, it is important to determine if the communicative environment provided by nonhandicapped children for handicapped children is sufficiently adapted to the level of the listener to be considered developmentally appropriate.

This issue was investigated in a series of studies conducted by Guralnick and Paul-Brown (1977, 1980, in preparation). The general design of this series was to examine naturally occurring communicative interactions among children at different developmental levels under different task demands. For experimental purposes, four- to six-year-olds participating in an integrated research–service program were divided into groups composed of mildly, moderately, severely, and nonhandicapped children. These classifications were based jointly on the American Association on Mental Deficiency's classification system (Grossman, 1977) as well as the expressive-language measure of mean length of utterance (MLU) in words. Although varying slightly from study to study, the average MLU for the moderately handicapped children was approximately 3.2, whereas the utterance length for severely handicapped children rarely exceeded 1.0. For the mildly handicapped children, mean MLU ranged widely, from 4 to 7 words, but averaged slightly below that of the nonhandicapped children. None of the children showed evidence of any major orthopedic or sensory handicaps. These categorizations were carried out with full recognition of the problems inherent in omnibus classification systems, and the fact that in all instances clinical decisions must be made on an individualized basis. Nevertheless, it was felt that, since no previous data on the issues under study were available, such a grouping was justifiable in order to determine the existence of general trends and patterns. Should clear patterns emerge, a more detailed examination of the effects on individual children's behaviors would follow.

The initial investigation centered primarily on assessing adjustments of nonhandicapped children as a function of the listener's developmental level (four different listener groups including other nonhandicapped children) in terms of speech productivity, grammatical complexity, and semantic diversity. For both a dyadic setting (which was instructional in nature in that the nonhandicapped child was asked to "teach" the companion child a drawing task) as well as a free-play setting, analyses revealed the occurrence of a number of important adjustments. In general, the speech of nonhandicapped children was syntactically more complex, occurred more frequently, and was more diverse when addressed to the more advanced children. Moreover, this pattern held for both the instructional and free-play settings.

Inspection of the distribution of utterance lengths revealed that, although the average MLU of the nonhandicapped children varied as a function of the listener's developmental level, a range of utterance lengths was addressed to all children. In addition, many of the linguistic parameters, despite varying as a function of listener level on an absolute basis, maintained a proportional relationship across developmental levels. For example, although more diverse speech was addressed to the more advanced children, the type–token ratio, that is, the ratio of the number of different words to the total number of words spoken, remained constant. Taken together, a reasonable interpretation of these findings is that the speech addressed to handicapped by nonhandicapped children was adjusted in a manner that increased the probability of being understood, yet was sufficiently diverse as to press for the development of more complex linguistic forms.

In the second study, a larger group of subjects participated in a dyadic instructional situation in which nonhandicapped children were asked to instruct various companion children to operate a particular toy. Analyses of these data permitted a replication of the findings of the first study with respect to measures of productivity and complexity, but were primarily designed to gather information on the function of utterances as well as selected features of discourse. Specifically, each utterance was classified as functioning as either a behavior request, an informational statement, or an informational request. Utterances were also classified in terms of their mutuality. Discourse features that were included in the analysis consisted of the quantitative distribution of utterances between different developmental level pairs, the degree of turn taking, the use of repetitions, and the extent to which nonverbal assistance was employed to facilitate the interaction. The intent of the analysis of these nonstructural categories of speech was to assess those aspects of communicative competence that include an ability to achieve the communicative goals of the speaker as well as reflect a sensitivity to the specific roles, and perhaps status, of the participants.

Analyses of the measures of syntactic complexity, including MLU, the proportion of long utterances, and the proportion of complex utterances, replicated earlier work in that more complex speech was addressed to the more advanced children. Informational statements accounted for over half of the total number of utterances. Differential use of this functional category was primarily responsible for the finding that speech occurred more frequently to the more advanced children. With respect to the proportional use of the functional categories, a number of adjustments were observed in relation to the listener's developmental level. Specifically, the proportion of informational statements increased (as did the tendency for informational requests), whereas the proportion of behavior requests decreased when more advanced children were addressed. Discourse measures indicated that repetition of behavior requests was considerably greater to the less advanced children and nonverbal assistance occurred at a very high level for all listener groups (nearly 50% of the time). As expected, the instructional interaction was dominated by the nonhandicapped child when interacting with less advanced companions, but this dominance faded when interacting with nonhandicapped or mildly handicapped children. Taken together, it appeared that when addressing more significantly handicapped companions, nonhandicapped children adopted an instructional strategy that utilized compliance with behavior requests (as opposed to informational requests) both to probe for comprehension and as a primary instructional device. In conjunction with a reduced information exchange to these children as well as the structural simplifications that occurred, these adjustments were interpreted by Guralnick and Paul-Brown (1980) as constituting reasonable communicative strategies. This interpretation considered a wide range of factors, including the limited cognitive and linguistic abilities of the children's companions and the role responsibility of the nonhandicapped children to provide instruction in that setting.

A different analytic technique was employed in the third study of this series (Guralnick & Paul-Brown, in preparation) which provided an alternative perspective on the problem of communicative adjustments among children at different developmental levels. One concern of the previous research was that the experimental approach required post-hoc interpretations of appropriateness using data aggregated over subjects for each of the four listener groups (see the discussion of appropriateness in the next section). In contrast, analyses in this investigation were centered on speaker–companion *sequences* within each developmental-level pairing, and definitions of adaptiveness were developed prior to examining each interaction (see below). This analysis was further delimited by focusing solely on what was considered to be an important and ecologically meaningful communicative episode—that is, those interactions in which the nonhandicapped child attempted but initially failed to obtain compliance to a behavior request from his or her companion. Accordingly, nonhandicapped speaker–companion sequences, in which efforts to resolve this compliance problem were identified, formed the basis for analysis.

In order to assess the adaptiveness of the communicative interactions within each of these sequences more directly, adaptive communication was broadly defined in this situation as an attempt to clarify a behavior request to better enable the listener to comprehend what was requested, to clarify the basis for the request, or to assist or encourage the listener in carrying out the request. Following the work of Spilton and Lee (1977), this concept was further operationalized by identifying an extensive number of specific adaptive categories such as adding demonstration or exemplification, seeking the listener's knowledge level, or making syntactical adjustments. These categorizations of adaptiveness were all carried out in relation to specific listener responses and other context factors.

Although the results of this study were somewhat complex, a number of important patterns emerged. First, the sequential analyses supported earlier work in that a large preponderance of communicative interactions were classified as adaptive, with the proportion of adaptive utterances tending to increase when the listeners were more severely handicapped. In addition, a wider range and more extensive use of adaptive strategies were employed by the nonhandicapped children when interacting with the less advanced listeners which, in turn, appeared to be appropriately tied to the specific feedback provided by individual children. Success at resolving the problem of achieving compliance did vary, however. For approximately half the sequences, nonhandicapped children switched the topic without achieving a successful resolution when interacting with the severely handicapped children, although they were quite persistent in their efforts. Often a form of compliance was achieved through the use of additional supports or cues. A considerably greater degree of success was achieved when companions were moderately, mildly, or nonhandicapped children.

THE APPROPRIATENESS OF ADJUSTMENTS BY ADVANCED CHILDREN IN CHILD–CHILD SPEECH

The series of studies just reviewed centering on communicative adjustments of nonhandicapped children when addressing handicapped children, as well as those cited in an earlier section concerned with adjustments to younger, normally developing children in mixed-age interactions have all taken the position that, in general, the nature and form of those adjustments were "appropriate." For mixed-age interactions, arguments in support of this interpretation ranged widely. Included were Shatz and Gelman's (1973) analysis indicating that adjustments appeared to be formed so that the "young speaker and very young listener interact to produce a linguistic environment favorable to the process of language acquisition" (p. 34), as well as those analyses that suggested that not only were syntactic simplifications and modifications in certain discourse features, such as repetitions and use of attentionals, also favorable in this regard (i.e., language to younger child consisted of progressive input), but that the final form of the utterance reflected a sensitivity to social and task constraints (Gelman & Shatz, 1977). Other research has correlated adult judges' ratings of "politeness" with young children's use of directives to different listener types (James, 1978), and has concluded that young children adjusted the form of their requests in accordance with expectations based on their responsiveness to situational and status variables; consequently, these adjustments were considered to be appropriate.

For the most part, the body of knowledge based on adult–child adjustments to normally developing children (e.g., Broen, 1972; Snow, 1972; Snow & Ferguson, 1977), or adult perceptions of appropriate child–child speech, has been utilized as a framework for interpreting the meaning of adjustments that occur in mixed-age interactions. Although not without a high degree of face validity, especially where syntactic simplification is concerned, alternative interpretations not confined to this framework should be considered in mixed-age situations. Since numerous variables of potential interest exist and multiple outcomes and patterns of child–child interactions are possible, many of which may be reasonable from a particular perspective, extreme care must be exercised to avoid selective examination and interpretation of the evidence.

The problems of selection of variables for study and interpretation of results are related to constraints inherent in each of the experimental approaches that have been adopted. Specifically, three general types of strategies can be identified, each providing a different yet necessary perspective on the concept of appropriateness. The first, which can be referred to as the distribution-category design, selects communicative categories in advance from syntactic, semantic, functional, or discourse domains. These measures are then counted and aggregated within groups and distributed across listener groups or tasks. Although listener groups are considered in the analysis, specific speaker–listener relationships on an utterance-by-utterance basis are not analyzed. Rather, overall differences as a function of listener or task characteristics are compared and judgments of appropriateness are determined by a post-hoc search for patterns. Unfortunately, this search is often guided by only incomplete developmental models.

Because of its static nature, the distribution-category design cannot tell us very much about the closeness of the communicative match between individual children within individual sequences. This is a major concern since it is quite possible that analyses of individual sequences at this more detailed and dynamic level may reveal that overall reductions in complexity across different listener groups, for example, should actually be considered inappropriate in many instances when a broader context and a variety of other factors are considered. Consequently, some investigators have adopted what can be referred to as a sequence strategy (the second approach). This design considers individual speaker–listener exchanges as the unit of analysis. Moreover, instead of identifying communicative categories, counting, and then seeking to determine if the patterns that are obtained are compatible with one or another interpretation, each exchange is evaluated in terms of appropriateness or adaptiveness by some predetermined criterion. This criterion generally tends to be some form of "connectedness" (such as whether a response was elicited), and data are reported in terms of the proportion of adaptive interactions. The nature of the connectedness criteria and the adaptiveness criteria must be carefully delineated in this approach. The approach works well if specific types of sequences are chosen (e.g., contingent query), but frequently adaptiveness is so broadly defined that it loses much of its conceptual meaning.

A third approach, which can be referred to as the pattern strategy, also focuses on individual sequences, and shares many characteristics in common with the two previously discussed approaches. More specifically, sequences of exchanges as a function of listener or task variables are examined to identify the primary patterns of exchange and whether these patterns (and their distribution) differ across the variables being studied. With respect to appropriateness, post-hoc considerations are important, but it is also possible to identify "successful patterns," that is, those that achieved the goals of the speaker, and to subject them to a review for appropriateness by experienced clinicians and teachers. It is at this level that the data must be gathered in order to design future curricula for promoting communicative competence.

As can be seen, each of these three general approaches provides an important perspective on the possible appropriateness of communicative interactions. The first provides a taxonomy and distribution of categories across relevant variables. For sequences, a more dynamic form of data analysis is needed that considers specific speaker–listener interactions. A priori definitions of appropriateness are also required of this approach.

Finally, the analysis of patterns goes beyond the distribution of communicative categories and the connectedness of discourse and considers subunits of the interactions—their frequency, diversity, creativity, and so on. Once identified, these patterns can be subjected to post-hoc interpretations of appropriateness as well as being distributed across listener groups or task demands and correlated with successful outcomes.

For those studies that have evaluated the appropriateness of the speech of nonhandicapped children as addressed to handicapped companions, many of the same limitations exist regarding the type of experimental approach selected and its relation to the concept of appropriateness. In fairness, the strong and consistent patterns that have emerged suggest that, certainly as a first approximation, the interpretations that have been put forth utilizing both the distribution-category and sequence designs are plausible. Nevertheless, despite the potential value of the framework provided by typical parent–child and child–child adjustments, a more comprehensive approach to appropriateness is needed to adequately evaluate nonhandicapped children's communicative adjustments to handicapped children.

It seems reasonable to propose that such a comprehensive approach should include a series of general factors or criteria that can serve as organizing frameworks for assessing appropriateness, a procedure for evaluating communicative interactions in relation to these criteria, and, in view of the multifaceted nature of the appropriateness concept, a process for validating the concept through various converging operations. Accordingly, despite the relatively limited empirical research available and the tentative nature of relevant developmental models with respect to communicative competence, it is suggested that four general factors be considered when judging the appropriateness of a particular communicative unit when nonhandicapped children address handicapped children:

1. *The communicative goals of the speaker in relation to task and situational demands are being effectively pursued or accomplished.* This evaluation requires an identification of the interpersonal goals of the interaction, an analysis of the consistent and persistent efforts to accomplish those goals, and an assessment of the outcomes of the interaction.

2. *Mutuality and reciprocity are being maintained.* That is, there is evidence for conversational contact, including a shared focus and topic, with adjustments being made in accordance with listener feedback. In addition, there should be evidence that interactions are being repaired when they are failing, and that varied discourse devices are being utilized to maintain contact and conversational balance whenever possible. Maintaining mutuality and reciprocity in this sense implies that an effective communicative match is being achieved. This match may occur at seman-

tic or syntactic levels, and is designed to maximize comprehension among participants.

3. *Social conventions are being honored.* To assess this factor, task demands and perceived roles and status must be considered. The way language is formed (e.g., bare or indirect imperatives), what strategies are used (e.g., persuade or demand), and related functions that are employed will vary with a variety of socially based factors.

4. *Diverse and developmentally progressive input is being provided.* The evaluation of progressive input applies to the form, content, and function of the communicative units. Input must be adjusted to the listener's level, but be sufficiently complex and diverse to challenge the child's current developmental skills. Within the parameters of form, content, and function, nonprogressive input, such as narrow and often needlessly repetitive interactions, should occur only on a limited basis.

When analyzing communicative units in relation to these general criteria, it is important that all factors be considered simultaneously. Certainly, they are all interrelated to some degree, but a careful analysis will reveal that each retains an aspect of independence from all the others. It is suggested here that appropriateness fails when any one of these factors fails.

Unquestionably, such judgments will be difficult and will depend, in part, upon the size of the communicative unit selected for analysis and the type of experimental design. With respect to the type of design, a complete evaluation of these four factors clearly requires multiple approaches. In some instances a sequential design will be necessary (e.g., maintaining mutuality and reciprocity), whereas some form of distribution of categories and a pattern analysis may be needed to determine whether or not diverse and developmentally progressive input is being provided. Moreover, achieving agreement for the division of a complex conversation into a series of "chunks" is very difficult to accomplish. One strategy is to identify episodes with a clear interpersonal purpose (e.g., tutorial), or those which share a common characteristic or function (e.g., resolving an initially noncommunicative statement). The significance of the selection of such a unit can be made more apparent when it is recognized that different communicative-unit lengths may be needed for each of the four factors even within a particular episode. For example, although the existence of mutuality and reciprocity can be evaluated on an utterance-by-utterance basis within a sequence, a larger unit is required to determine whether or not input is developmentally progressive.

The translation of these four general factors into an operational strategy can only be outlined in this chapter. Essentially, the first step would be to specify the interpersonal purpose (Wells, 1975) for a given situation and the salient characteristics of the participants. These identifications would form the basis for many other decisions. Next, a series of "if-then" propositions or rules regarding the types of interactions which would be considered appropriate could be formulated. These general statements could initially use the parent–child, child–child, and clinician–handicapped child research as an evaluation base. Such propositions or rules would be general in form, permitting a wide range of behaviors to be incorporated within a particular classification. The key here is that the generation of each rule must consider all four of the factors that have been described. Accordingly, highly detailed statements, identifying a clear rationale, would be required and should strengthen analyses for the sequence and pattern designs. Despite the fact that this approach still requires considerable interpretation with respect to the appropriateness of a particular communicative unit, the prior establishment of potentially appropriate outcomes should ensure a higher level of agreement among investigators and, ultimately, a clearer definition of the concept of appropriateness in general.

To further validate the concept of appropriateness, particularly when it consists of an assessment of nonhandicapped children's speech to handicapped children, a variety of converging methods should be employed. One possibility would be to have expert clinicians and teachers judge the appropriateness of actual communicative units in accordance with the four factors noted above. This approach is not constrained by prior "if-then" propositions and allows for the possibility that a wide range of communicative interactions, many of which may not previously have been considered as such, can be classified as appropriate. This information, in turn, could be used to modify the investigators' initial models and propositions. Such social validation (Kazdin, 1977) is an essential component in validating a concept such as appropriateness.

A companion approach would be to develop a series of scripts comprised of simulations that closely resemble actual circumstances occurring in child–child interactions. By carefully selecting vignettes and asking experienced clinicians and teachers how they *would* interact, important and probably different information can be gained. For example, since numerous strategies are possible for each situation, this more open-end approach may identify communicative units not previously considered as appropriate. The importance of such a converging strategy is that it is capable of generating an interplay between models and data.

The need for such a comprehensive approach also relates to the problems in establishing the degree of "fine tuning" or synchrony of the communicative match. This concern is perhaps most apparent in some of the work by Guralnick and Paul-Brown discussed earlier. They noted that although reasonable communicative adjustments did appear to result during interactions between nonhandicapped and handicapped children, it was also observed that the adjustments were quite similar to those of severely and moderately handicapped children on the one hand, and of mildly and nonhandicapped children on the other. Certainly, more detailed studies are needed to achieve a more complete understanding of the appropriateness of nonhandicapped children's speech to handicapped children.

Once again, it must be understood that this effort to define appropriateness is capable only of determining whether the communicative environment provided by nonhandicapped children to handicapped children is *potentially* of developmental significance or, at minimum, supportive of effective communication. The provision of a supportive environment relates to the essential issue of the feasibility of mainstreamed environments, and is discussed in detail elsewhere (see Guralnick, in press a). Nevertheless, as suggested in the following section, if developmental potential can be established, it is not unreasonable to expect that properly designed, integrated environments may prove to be more effective than segregated ones in promoting the competence of all participants, although a set of experimental designs quite different from those typically employed to evaluate feasibility would be required to test this possibility.

The Potential Role of Mainstreamed Environments in Facilitating the Communicative Development of Handicapped Children

In a chapter devoted to peer influences, the fact that parents, teachers, and clinicians retain the central role in promoting the communicative competence of handicapped children can be easily overlooked. Yet, even with this fact in mind, it would certainly be shortsighted for individuals responsible for the communicative development of handicapped children to place those children in environments in which their classmates were either unresponsive, provided little stimulation, or created an environment that was virtually incomprehensive. Moreover, young children spend considerable portions of their daily activities in the company of other young children, and the important role peer relations may play in fostering many aspects of communicative competence has been discussed in detail. Consequently, the design of classroom environments that support the communicative development of handicapped children must take into account the composition of peers and their skills.

In order to place the potential value of communicative interactions in mainstreamed environments in perspective, it is important to consider the entire range of exchanges possible in those environments as well as the potential contributions of each type of exchange. Up to this point, the contributions of advanced classmates to the development of handicapped children have been the focus of discussion, and analogies to adult–child and mixed-age child–child interactions have been drawn. Nevertheless, as pointed out in earlier sections, it is likely that important aspects of child–child communicative competence develop as outgrowths of peer interactions with age-mates of similar developmental levels. It was noted that the qualities thought to mediate peer–peer communicative skills included the existence of reciprocity, as well as opportunities to practice initiating interactions and to develop successful strategies when communicative failures occur. Certainly, these qualities, many of which require coequal status, do not characterize adult–child interactions nor, for that matter, many of the interactions occurring among handicapped and nonhandicapped children. One issue, then, is to identify the conditions under which interactions of nonhandicapped children when addressing handicapped children are peerlike, adultlike, or reflect some combination of characteristics. Corollary questions concern the possible functions and developmental significance of peerlike or adultlike communicative interactions, as well as the role of factors such as situational specificity.

For children with significant handicaps, it appears that advanced children, even if somewhat younger than their handicapped classmates, behave in a fashion similar to that of older children in mixed-age situations—that is, more adultlike. It seems that the limited repertoires of the handicapped children elicit forms of behavior on the part of the advanced children that are generally instructional in order for meaningful communication to be achieved. Status factors also encourage a form of communication that seems to be more adultlike. Although interactions between adults and handicapped children (be the adult a parent, teacher, or clinician) and between advanced children and handicapped children certainly cannot be equated with each other,* they often appear to serve

*Of course, in contrast to adults, nonhandicapped children will not be nearly so sensitive to the communicative intent of their younger or handicapped classmates (see Bates, 1975), nor as persistent in their interactions. Similarly, we would not expect to see the conversational coherence and specialized efforts common to constructive parent–child and clinician–child interactions that are designed to teach important communication skills. Moreover, nonhandicapped children are not likely to be as resourceful in facilitating communicative interactions as adults, despite the potential for interacting in novel and probably attention-getting play-type circumstances. Finally, although it appears that reasonable adjustments to the level of the listener occur when children at different developmental levels do interact, there are concerns regarding the frequencies of occurrence of those interactions (see Guralnick, 1980, in press a). Similarly, additional information concerning the responsiveness of children to one another when grouped heterogeneously is needed to obtain a more complete understanding of the value of peer relations in comparison to adult interactions.

similar instructional or tutorial purposes for the more severely handi-capped child. In fact, casual observations indicate that even play situa-tions among children with widely dissimilar behavioral repertoires rapidly tend to take on a directive or tutorial form. In the mainstreamed preschool setting, this type of interaction is even more likely to occur as advanced children adopt the role models of teachers. Of course, this instructional role contrasts sharply with the form and possible contribu-tions of interactions common to more truly peerlike experiences.

With regard to the possible function of these adultlike interactions, it appears that when nonhandicapped children interact with handicapped children manifesting relatively severe handicaps, the handicapped chil-dren receive simplified yet adequately diverse input. These adjustments in the syntactic and semantic aspects of speech, in conjunction with those in the functional and discourse domains, suggest that the potential for promoting language and communicative development certainly exists. Of course, as discussed earlier, the problem of appropriateness, the degree of fine tuning, and related issues remain to be clarified.

An often overlooked potential benefit of having classmates heterogeneous with respect to communicative ability is the opportunity for the handicapped children, even children with relatively severe delays, to adjust their own communicative interactions to the level of the listener. If complexity begets complexity, as the reciprocity literature suggests, then interactions with advanced children may have important develop-mental implications that extend beyond the input provided by advanced classmates. It is also possible that even "talking down" to children with greater delays may be an important element in developing communica-tive competence. In fact, research in social development indicates the value of providing opportunities for socially withdrawn young children to test out the effectiveness of a variety of social-communicative be-haviors (Furman et al., 1979). Less advanced children may play a similar role, although a minimal level of responsiveness of the companion, as well as a minimal level of development of skill on the part of the hand-icapped children, would be necessary for this to be feasible.

When the developmental levels of children are more similar, in addition to a reasonable similarity in chronological age and associated physical-growth characteristics, the peerlike qualities of interactions are likely to be more apparent. If this is true, the handicapped child may have the best of both worlds. That is, conditions fostering the development of peer–peer competencies may exist (coequal status) in addition to the advanced communicative interactions provided by more advanced classmates. Research is needed to evaluate where the balance lies in these interactions.

Additional but presently unanswered questions relate to the types of children who should be encouraged to interact for peerlike purposes. For example, would the form, nature, and potential value of interactions between two handicapped children of similar chronological ages and developmental levels differ when compared with interactions between a handicapped child and a younger, normally developing child who are also at similar developmental levels? Would responsiveness vary in these two circumstances, and to what degree would any differences be dependent upon the absolute levels of development of the participants? For preschool children, this comparison can only be useful for children with less extensive handicaps, since the matching of normally developing and severely handicapped children according to developmental levels would require much too great an age discrepancy. Future research is needed to examine this matching issue.

STRUCTURED INTERACTIONS

Up to this point, the analyses and the possible value of interactions among children at different developmental levels have focused on situations that are primarily unstructured. That is, although opportunities for interactions may have been modified by manipulating group composition or by arranging for tutorial interactions between selected dyads, no specific or systematic training related to communicative variables was provided. Essentially, the value of peers as agents of change for a given situation was permitted to develop as a function of the skills and behavioral patterns manifested by the participants.

Nevertheless, the use of advanced peers as agents of change in a direct and systematic manner is a potentially significant educational strategy that is unique to mainstreamed settings. Although most of the work employing this strategy has focused on social-emotional variables (Guralnick, 1978c; Strain, 1977; Strain, Kerr, & Ragland, this volume), some research has been conducted in relation to language and communicative development. For example, Guralnick (1976) utilized peer modeling and reinforcement of an advanced peer's correct usage of a linguistic form in a multiple-baseline design to increase the use of that form by a mildly handicapped child. The essentials of this study were replicated and expanded by Goosen (1977). In that study, mildly developmentally delayed children's use of descriptive adjectives, their generalization, and the use of complete sentences were increased through the use of nonhandicapped models in a structured situation. Additional work on nonverbal (Apolloni, Cooke, & Cooke, 1977; Nordquist, 1978), and verbal imitation (Raver, Cooke, & Apolloni, 1978) has also demonstrated the potential value of modeling and reinforcement by advanced peers in the development of language or language-related behaviors of handicapped children.

This research has established what "can" happen in structured settings, but it is not known if similar processes operate in more typical situations; that is, whether they "do" happen (see McCall, 1977). Our assessment of this question is hampered by the absence of information regarding observational learning in naturalistic settings.

SUMMARY AND CONCLUSIONS

It seems that the more young children are probed with respect to communicative competence with similar-age peers in naturalistic settings, the more competent they appear. Not only are young children capable of initiating and maintaining meaningful discourse, but they display a remarkable range of sensitivity to situational and listener cues. Analyses of the internal structure of their conversations have also revealed the existence of a rather agile communications system, with children easily shifting strategies and conversational forms in an effort to accomplish their goals.

One of the most interesting aspects of this field of study is that peers not only form the necessary context for assessing peer social-communicative interactions, but that these interactions themselves may be necessary conditions for the adequate development of the interactions that are being assessed. Put another way, one impact of the recognition of the role of peer interactions has been to shift the focus of study from peer interactions as dependent variable to that of independent variable. It must be admitted that, despite evidence from the area of social development (Mueller, 1979; Mueller & Vandell, 1979), the empirical base for establishing the independent contribution of similar-age peers to the development of peer social-communicative competence is not very substantial. As noted earlier, more compelling have been the arguments related to certain qualities unique to peer relations, such as those associated with balanced interactions, that make them likely candidates for facilitating the development of at least certain aspects of communicative competence.

Research centering on mixed-age interactions has further contributed to our understanding of the potential importance of peer relations. First, this work has reinforced the view that young children are effective communicators. Adjustments to even younger children in particular have revealed considerable competence, including a recognition of social factors in guiding message selection. Second, an intriguing possibility has emerged that older children, through these adjustments, are able to provide a communicative environment for the younger listener that can facilitate communicative development. Once again, no direct evidence to support this contention is available, but the parallels to adult–child adjustments and their implications suggest that this is a strong possibility.

Certainly mixed-age interactions do not share many qualities associated with same-age interactions (e.g., dominance is usually clearly established in mixed-age interactions), so they cannot be expected to serve similar functions. Similarly, the occurrence of interactions among children relatively close in chronological age but varying in developmental level pose different problems for the communicators and, consequently, may also serve different functions. In fact, it has been suggested that the severity of a child's handicap determines whether "peerlike" or "adultlike" interactions will develop.

If communicative interactions with different age and developmental level children serve different functions, yet are each potentially significant from a developmental point of view in their own right, then mainstreamed environments should be designed to ensure the occurrence of these diverse experiences. From the perspective of the handicapped child in a mainstreamed program, the following types of interactions are recommended as valuable.

First, the involvement of advanced peers in mainstreamed settings provides a potentially important stimulus to the development of communicative competence of their handicapped classmates. As we have seen, the adjusted communicative interactions as a function of the listener's developmental level appear to be appropriate, in accordance with the definition discussed earlier. This definition included the provision of progressive input, one outcome of which may be the promotion of the development of advanced communicative or language skills. The point should be emphasized that, for children with more severe handicaps, the significant dissociation between age (and its correlates, such as physical size and strength) and the cognitive and linguistic abilities of companion handicapped children has not resulted in grossly discrepant nor consistently inappropriate interactions on the part of nonhandicapped classmates. On the contrary, adjustments seem to parallel the adult–child and mixed-age child–child communicative interactions. In addition, interactions with advanced peers may encourage the use of advanced language forms and communicative styles by handicapped children adjusted to the level of their more sophisticated companions.

Second, in order to have the opportunity to practice developing abilities and to experience qualities associated with children with similar communicative skills, considerable interactions with such peers must be fostered. It is not clear at this time whether the functions associated with peers at this level can be accomplished by companions who are somewhat younger but equivalent in developmental level (usually normally developing children), or whether handicapped peers could be of equal value to one another. Some form of direct intervention and facilitation is likely to be needed in the latter situation. In any event, the key here is to ensure that the qualities that characterize peer–peer interactions occur during these exchanges.

Third, and perhaps most speculative, is the possible developmental value of the availability of younger and/or less advanced children as companions for classmates with significant social-communicative deficiencies (Furman *et al.*, 1979). Arranging opportunities for children to test their emerging skills with companions who are likely to provide only supportive feedback is a potential strategy that can be readily utilized when children are grouped heterogeneously.

Issues for Future Study

Increasing the heterogeneity of children in classrooms creates major organizational problems for teachers, clinicians, and administrators. Although this heterogeneity can potentially be of educational and developmental significance, like any resource it must be properly utilized. It is quite likely that, in many instances, teachers will need to *directly arrange* circumstances to maximize the likelihood of occurrence of specific forms of interaction. Recent research has clearly demonstrated that social-communicative interactions among similar-age advanced and less advanced children (those classified as severely and moderately handicapped) occur at relatively low rates (Guralnick, 1980), although mildly and nonhandicapped children are well integrated with one another (Guralnick, 1980; Ispa & Matz, 1978). In addition, heterogeneous groupings of children, in and of themselves, are not sufficient to increase the frequency of communicative interactions (Guralnick, in press, b). Consequently, considerable planning and perhaps even training of peers may be necessary to encourage specific interactions to occur.

Ideally, gatherings of small groups of children, for particular developmental purposes carefully selected in terms of age and/or developmental level and associated behavioral characteristics, would be recommended. The context could be one of play or one with a specific didactic focus. In addition, the advanced children could be enlisted to assist teachers in providing a more naturalistic method for testing for generalization of various behaviors (Guralnick, 1978b). The question of which techniques could be utilized in this endeavor is important, but has not yet been systematically studied.

In the clinical domain, relevant assessment instruments are needed in order to design an environment for handicapped children that yields appropriate "communicative matches," in the broad sense of the term. Unfortunately, instruments that assess social-communicative competence in relation to peers are highly limited (Guralnick & Weinhouse, in preparation). In particular, the assessment of skills related to conversational competence, such as the various routines children utilize to engage and maintain contact discussed earlier, have simply not received adequate attention. Such assessment and program-planning instruments should be designed to assist in decision making with respect to "what types" and "how much" of each type of peer experience would be valuable. In fact, such assessments may even assist in determining the most effective chronological age–developmental level matches.

The corresponding development of curricula and training programs designed to foster communicative competence with peers is another major issue for future study. Despite the fact that the simple provision of peer play-group activities for normally developing children may be sufficient to promote peer–peer social-communicative development, this is certainly not likely to be the case for handicapped children. As in other areas of delayed development, it will be necessary to provide specialized programs and educational strategies. The implementation of a developmentally based curriculum here should benefit significantly from the presence of children with a range of developmental skills.

Many of these issues are directly linked to the concept of the appropriateness of the communicative interaction. Future research must seek to clarify and refine this concept in the context of the fine tuning of communicative adjustments. This problem is further complicated by the fact that the feedback mechanisms and information-gathering strategies of handicapped children also appear to be deficient (Mahoney, 1975; Snyder-McLean & McLean, 1978). The impact of the degree of discrepancy between children's chronological ages and/or developmental levels and the identification of specific behavioral sequences associated with these global variables on communicative effectiveness and development must also be more adequately understood. In relation to individual behavioral characteristics, most of the research to date has involved handicapped children manifesting general developmental delays. Unfortunately, we know very little about adjustments that may occur for children with other handicaps, such as emotional, orthopedic, or sensory problems.

Finally, it is essential that an assessment of the value of classroom peers with respect to the communicative development of handicapped children be conducted within a developmental context. As new information and concepts emerge from the domains of developmental psychology and communicative and language development, their potential application to problems discussed in this chapter should be considered.

REFERENCES

Akamatsu, T., & Thelen, M.H. A review of the literature on observer characteristics and imitation. *Developmental Psychology*, 1974, *10*, 38–47.

Apolloni, T., Cooke, S.A., & Cooke, T. P. Establishing a normal peer as a behavioral model for developmentally delayed toddlers. *Perceptual and Motor Skills*, 1977, *44*, 231–241.

Bates, E. Peer relations and the acquisition of language. In M. Lewis & L.A. Rosenblum (Eds.), *Friendship and peer relations*. New York: Wiley, 1975.

Bloom, L., & Lahey, M. *Language development and language disorders*. New York: Wiley, 1978.

Bohannon, J., & Marquis, A. L. Children's control of adult speech. *Child Development*, 1977, *48*, 1002–1008.

Broen, P. A. The verbal environment of the language-learning child. *American Speech and Hearing Association Monograph*, 1972, *17*.

Cairns, R. B. *Social development: The origins and plasticity of interchanges*. San Francisco: W. H. Freeman, 1979.

Ervin-Tripp, S., & Mitchell-Kernan, C. (Eds.). *Child discourse*. New York: Academic Press, 1977.

Furman, W., Rahe, D. F., & Hartup, W. W. Rehabilitation of socially withdrawn preschool children through mixed-age and same-age socialization. *Child Development*, 1979, *50*, 915–922.

Garvey, C. Requests and responses in children's speech. *Journal of Child Language*, 1975, *2*, 41–63.

Garvey, C. The contingent query: A dependent act in conversation. In M. Lewis & L. A. Rosenblum (Eds.), *Interaction, conversation, and the development of language*. New York: Wiley, 1977.

Garvey, C., & BenDebba, M. Effects of age, sex, and partner on children's dyadic speech. *Child Development*, 1974, *45*, 1159–1161.

Garvey, C., & Hogan, R. Social speech and social interaction: Egocentrism revisited. *Child Development*, 1973, *44*, 562–568.

Gelman, R., & Shatz, M. Appropriate speech adjustments: The operation of conversational constraints on talk to two-year-olds. In M. Lewis & L. A. Rosenblum (Eds.), *Interaction, conversation, and the development of language*. New York: Wiley, 1977.

Gleason, J. B. Code switching in children's language. In T. E. Moore (Ed.), *Cognitive development and the acquisition of language*. New York: Academic Press, 1973.

Gleason, J. B. Talking to children: Some notes on feedback. In C. E. Snow & C. A. Ferguson (Eds.), *Talking to children: Language input and acquisition*. Cambridge: Cambridge University Press, 1977.

Gleason, J. B., & Weintraub, S. Input language and the acquisition of communicative competence. In K. Nelson (Ed.), *Children's language* (Vol. 1). New York: Gardner Press, 1978.

Goosen, J. *The effects of a normal peer model on verbal production of descriptive adjectives by handicapped children*. Unpublished Master's thesis, University of Kansas, 1977.

Grossman, H. J. *Manual on terminology and classification in mental retardation*. Washington, D.C.: American Association on Mental Deficiency, 1977.

Guralnick, M. J. The value of integrating handicapped and nonhandicapped preschool children. *American Journal of Orthopsychiatry*, 1976, *46*, 236–245.

Guralnick, M. J. Early childhood intervention: Nonhandicapped peers as educational and therapeutic resources. In P. Mittler (Ed.), *Research to practice in mental retardation: Care and intervention* (Vol. 1). Baltimore: University Park Press, 1977.

Guralnick, M. J. (Ed.). *Early intervention and the integration of handicapped and nonhandicapped children*. Baltimore: University Park Press, 1978.(a)

Guralnick, M. J. Integrated preschools as educational and therapeutic environments: Concepts, design, and analysis. In M. J. Guralnick (Ed.), *Early intervention and the integration of handicapped and nonhandicapped children*. Baltimore: University Park Press, 1978.(b)

Guralnick, M. J. *Promoting social interactions among children at different developmental levels: Process and problems*. Paper presented at annual meeting of the Council for Exceptional Children, Kansas City, April 1978.(c)

Guralnick, M. J. Social interactions among preschool children. *Exceptional Children*, 1980, *46*, 248–253.

Guralnick, M. J. Mainstreaming young handicapped children. In B. Spodek (Ed.), *Handbook of research on early childhood education*. New York: Free Press/MacMillan, in press.(a)

Guralnick, M.J. The social behavior of preschool children at different developmental levels: Effects of group composition. *Journal of Experimental Child Psychology*, in press.(b)

Guralnick, M. J., & Paul-Brown, D. The nature of verbal interactions among handicapped and nonhandicapped preschool children. *Child Development*, 1977, *48*, 254–260.

Guralnick, M. J., & Paul-Brown, D. Functional and discourse analyses of nonhandicapped preschool children's speech to handicapped children. *American Journal of Mental Deficiency*, 1980, *84*, 444–454.

Guralnick, M. J., & Paul-Brown, D. Sequential analyses of communicative episodes among children at different developmental levels, in preparation.

Guralnick, M. J., & Weinhouse, E. An analysis of the available assessment instruments for peer-peer social/communicative interactions, in preparation.

Hartup, W. W. Peer interaction and the process of socialization. In M. J. Guralnick (Ed.), *Early intervention and the integration of handicapped and nonhandicapped children*. Baltimore: University Park Press, 1978.

Hartup, W. W. Peer relations and the growth of social competence. In M. W. Kent & J. E. Rolf (Eds.), *Primary prevention of psychopathology* (Vol. 3). Hanover, N.H.: University Press of New England, 1979.

Hymes, D. Competence and performance in linguistic theory. In R. Huxley & E. Ingram (Eds.), *Language acquisition: Models and methods*. New York: Academic Press, 1971.

Ispa, J., & Matz, R. D. Integrating handicapped preschool children within a cognitively oriented program. In M. J. Guralnick (Ed.). *Early intervention and the integration of handicapped and nonhandicapped children*. Baltimore: University Park Press, 1978.

James, S. L. Effect of listener age and situation on the politeness of children's directives. *Journal of Psycholinguistic Research*, 1978, *7*, 307–317.

Kazdin, A. E. Assessing the clinical or applied importance of behavior change through social validation. *Behavior Modification*, 1977, *1*, 427–452.

Keenan, E. O. Conversational competence in children. *Journal of Child Language*, 1974, *1*, 163–183.

Keenan, E. O. Making it last: Repetition in children's discourse. In S. Ervin-Tripp & C. Mitchell-Kernan (Eds.), *Child discourse*. New York: Academic Press, 1977.

Keenan, E. O., & Klein, E. Coherency in children's discourse. *Journal of Psycholinguistic Research*, 1975, *4*, 365–380.

Lamb, M. E. Interactions between eighteen-month-olds and their preschool-aged siblings. *Child Development*, 1978, *49*, 51–59.

Lee, L. C., Brody, L., Matthews, W. S., & Palmquist, W. *The development of interpersonal competence: Strategies of social exchange*. Symposium presented at annual convention of the American Psychological Association, New Orleans, September 1974.

Lewis, M., & Cherry, L. Social behavior and language acquisition. In M. Lewis & L. A. Rosenblum (Eds.), *Interaction, conversation, and the development of language*. New York: Wiley, 1977.

Lewis, M., & Feiring, C. The child's social network: Social object, social functions, and their relationship. In M. Lewis & L. A. Rosenblum (Eds.), *The child and its family*. New York: Plenum Press, 1979.

Lewis, M., & Rosenblum, L. A. Introduction. In M. Lewis & L. A. Rosenblum (Eds.), *Friendship and peer relations*. New York: Wiley, 1975.(a)

Lewis, M., & Rosenblum, L. A. (Eds.). *Friendship and peer relations*. New York: Wiley, 1975.(b)

Lewis, M., Young, G., Brooks, J., & Michalson, L. The beginning of friendship. In M. Lewis & L. A. Rosenblum (Eds.), *Friendship and peer relations*. New York: Wiley, 1975.

Lougee, M. D., Grueneich, R., & Hartup, W. W. Social interaction in same- and mixed-age dyads of preschool children. *Child Development*, 1977, *48*, 1353–1361.

Mahoney, G. J. An ethological approach to delayed language acquisition. *American Journal of Mental Deficiency*, 1975, *80*, 138–148.

Mahoney, G. J., & Seely, P. B. The role of the social agent in language acquisition: Implications for language intervention. In N. R. Ellis (Ed.), *International review of research in mental retardation* (Vol. 8). New York: Academic Press, 1976.

Maratsos, M. P. Nonegocentric communication abilities in preschool children. *Child Development*, 1973, *44*, 697–700.

Masur, E. F. Preschool boys' speech modifications: The effect of listeners' linguistic levels and conversational responsiveness. *Child Development*, 1978, *49*, 924–927.

McCall, R. B. Challenges to a science of developmental psychology. *Child Development*, 1977, *48*, 333–344.

McLean, J. E., & Snyder-McLean, L. K. *A transactional approach to early language training*. Columbus, Ohio: Charles E. Merrill, 1978.

Moerk, E. L. *Pragmatic and semantic aspects of early language development*. Baltimore: University Park Press, 1977.

Mueller, E. The maintenance of verbal exchanges between young children. *Child Development*, 1972, *43*, 930–938.

Mueller, E. Toddlers + toys = an autonomous social system. In M. Lewis & L. A. Rosenblum (Eds.), *The child and its family*. New York: Plenum Press, 1979.

Mueller, E., & Brenner, J. The growth of social interaction in a toddler playgroup: The role of peer experience. *Child Development*, 1977, *48*, 854–861.

Mueller, E. C., & Vandell, D. Infant-infant interaction. In J. D. Osofsky (Ed.), *Handbook of infant development*. New York: Wiley, 1979.

Mueller, E., Bleier, M., Krakow, J., Hegedus, K., & Cournoyer, P. The development of peer verbal interaction among two-year-old boys. *Child Development*, 1977, *48*, 284–287.

Nordquist, V. M. A behavioral approach to the analysis of peer interactions. In M. J. Guralnick (Ed.), *Early intervention and the integration of handicapped and nonhandicapped children*. Baltimore: University Park Press, 1978.

Public Law 94-142. The Education for All Handicapped Children Act, 1975: 20 U.S.C. 1401 et. seq.: Federal Register 42(163): 42474–42518, August 23, 1977.

Rauer, S. A., Cooke, T. P., & Apolloni, T. Developing nonretarded toddlers as verbal models for retarded classmates. *Child Study Journal*, 1978, *8*, 1–8.

Rees, N. S. Pragmatics of language: Applications to normal and disordered language development. In R. L. Schiefelbusch (Ed.), *Bases of language intervention*. Baltimore: University Park Press, 1978.

Rubenstein, J., & Howes, C. The effects of peers on toddler interaction with mother and toys. *Child Development*, 1976, *47*, 597–605.

Rubenstein, J. L., & Howes, C. Caregiving and infant behavior in day care and in homes. *Developmental Psychology*, 1979, *15*, 1–21.

Sachs, J., & Devin, J. Young children's use of age-appropriate speech styles. *Journal of Child Language*, 1976, *3*, 81–98.

Sackett, G. P. Measurement in observational research. In G. P. Sackett (Ed.), *Observing behavior: Data collection and analysis methods* (Vol. 2). Baltimore: University Park Press, 1978.

Schegloff, E. A. Sequencing in conversational openings. *American Anthropologist*, 1968, 70, 1075–1095.

Shatz, M., & Gelman, R. The development of communication skills: Modifications in the speech of young children as a function of listener. *Monographs of the Society for Research in Child Development*, 1973, 38 (5).

Snow, C. E. Mothers' speech to children learning language. *Child Development*, 1972, 43, 549–565.

Snow, C. E., & Ferguson, C. A. (Eds.). *Talking to children: Language input and acquisition*. Cambridge: Cambridge University Press, 1977.

Snyder-McLean, L. K., & McLean, J. E. Verbal information gathering strategies: The child's use of language to acquire language. *Journal of Speech and Hearing Disorders*, 1978, 43, 306–325.

Spilton, D., & Lee, L. C. Some determinants of effective communication in four-year-olds. *Child Development*, 1977, 48, 968–977.

Strain, P. S. An experimental analysis of peer social initiations on the behavior of withdrawn preschool children: Some training and generalization effects. *Journal of Abnormal Child Psychology*, 1977, 5, 445–455.

Strain, P. S., & Shores, R. E. Social reciprocity: A review of research and educational implications. *Exceptional Children*, 1977, 43, 526–530.

Suomi, S. J. Differential development of various social relationships by rhesus monkey infants. In M. Lewis & L. A. Rosenblum (Eds.), *The child and its family*. New York: Plenum Press, 1979.

Wellman, H. M., & Lempers, J. D. The naturalistic communicative abilities of two-year-olds. *Child Development*, 1977, 48, 1052–1057.

Wells, G. *Coding manual for the description of child speech*. Unpublished manual, University of Bristol, Bristol, England, 1975.

3

Utilization of Peer Imitation in Therapeutic and Instructional Contexts

CHARLES A. PECK, THOMAS P. COOKE,
AND TONY APOLLONI

The importance of imitation in the social development of young children has been so widely emphasized as to become axiomatic in the literature of psychology and education (Baer & Sherman, 1964; Bandura & Walters, 1963; Gewirtz & Stingle, 1968; N.E. Miller & Dollard, 1941; Mowrer, 1960; R.F. Peterson, 1968; Piaget, 1951). Recently, increased attention has been directed toward investigating the role of *peer* imitation during early childhood (Apolloni & Cooke, 1975; Hartup, 1970, 1978). Much of this work has been motivated by a conceptualization of peer imitation as a potentially powerful instructional resource which educators have yet to fully utilize in a systematic manner (Guralnick, 1976; Snyder, Apolloni, & Cooke, 1977). Peer imitation may be valuable along both quantitative and qualitative dimensions. Quantitatively speaking, it is clear that utilizing children as teachers represents a means of increasing the available instructional personnel in the classroom (V.L. Allen, 1976). Qualitatively, there is evidence that under some conditions children may be more effective instructional models than adults (Barry & Overman, 1977; Becker & Glidden, 1979; Nordquist, 1978; Rubenstein & Howes, 1976). The purpose of our chapter will be to delineate the major findings of the basic and developmental research on peer imitation, and to review the efforts of

CHARLES A. PECK ● Department of Special Education, University of California at Santa Barbara, Santa Barbara, California 93430.   THOMAS P. COOKE ● California Institute on Human Services, Sonoma State University.   TONY APOLLONI ● California Institute on Human Services, Sonoma State University.

69

several researchers, including ourselves, to develop therapeutic techniques based on peer imitation for use in instructional contexts. Additionally, we will suggest further steps in the development of an instructional technology based on peer imitation, and relate the importance of such a technology to current trends in educational-service delivery.

BASIC AND DEVELOPMENTAL RESEARCH ON PEER IMITATION

Basic research on peer imitation has served as a foundation for much of the later work of a more directly therapeutic emphasis. Broadly outlined, this research has explored the control of peer imitation in laboratory settings, the relationship of age and developmental status to rates of peer imitation, and contextual variables affecting the likelihood of children imitating their peers. We will highlight findings from each of these areas.

REINFORCEMENT CONTROL OF PEER IMITATION

A series of early laboratory studies by N.E. Miller and Dollard (1941) demonstrated that peer imitation could be increased through the contingent application of positive reinforcement. Forty-two first-grade subjects were divided into two experimental groups of 20 each. Two children served as peer models for the other subjects on a simple box-selection task. One experimental group was rewarded with candy for imitating the box choice of the peer model; the other group was rewarded for avoiding the peer model's choice. Results of the procedure demonstrated that children could be systematically trained to imitate or to avoid imitating the responses of a peer. In a generalization probe involving four box choices, it was observed that the imitative and avoidance of imitative behavior established under training conditions generalized to similar responses never directly trained.

A second experiment demonstrated that contingencies of reinforcement could control whether an adult or a peer model would be imitated. Twelve fourth-grade boys were divided into two groups: one group was rewarded for imitating an adult model and the other group was rewarded for imitating a peer model. Subsequently, each group was rewarded for avoiding imitation of the other group's model. Subjects learned to imitate only the model associated with reward for imitation. Generalization probes conducted with the same subjects revealed that they imitated models similar to those previously associated with reward for imitation (i.e., children trained to imitate peer models subsequently imitated other peers and children trained to imitate adult models subsequently imitated other adults).

A final investigation in the Miller and Dollard report demonstrated that through peer imitation, children may learn strategies for obtaining reinforcement that they continue to use when the model is no longer present. Employing the same subjects and box-selection task as in the earlier experiment, the experimenters arranged the appearance of a flashlight beam from within one of the boxes as a relevant cue for correct box selection. Experimental subjects were rewarded when they imitated a peer model's choice, which was paired with the flashlight cue. Control subjects were also rewarded for imitating a peer model's choice, but were not exposed to the flashlight cue. Posttraining assessment of subjects' success on the same task was made with the peer models absent. The flashlight was retained as a relevant cue for box selection. Results showed that subjects who had previously been exposed to the flashlight cue were significantly more successful on the task than those who had not been exposed.

The role of extrinsic reinforcement in the acquisition and maintenance of imitation remains a subject of controversy (Flanders, 1968; Parton, 1976). Whatever the relative merits of contiguity (Bandura & Walters, 1963), reinforcement (Baer & Sherman, 1964), or cognitive (Piaget, 1951) interpretations of imitative behavior, the work of Miller and Dollard demonstrates the potential value of direct reinforcement as a means of increasing and maintaining peer imitation in young children. For older individuals who have not developed a generalized imitative repertoire, direct reinforcement of imitative behavior may be a particularly effective (Baer, Peterson, & Sherman, 1967; Lovaas, Freitas, Nelson, & Whalen, 1967) or even necessary (Bry & Nawas, 1972) instructional strategy.

Vicarious-reinforcement effects (Bandura & Walters, 1963) similar to those reported with adult models (Bandura, 1965; Ross, Bandura, & Ross, 1963) have been noted using peers as models for observing children. Clark (1965) investigated the influence of vicarious reinforcement of peer models on the button-pressing responses of boys 9–11 years old. Results indicated significantly more imitation of rewarded peer models than of nonrewarded peer models. Vicarious-reinforcement effects have also been demonstrated for kindergarten and first-grade boys (Geshuri, 1972). In this study, filmed peer models who were verbally reinforced for play responses were imitated more than models not reinforced. Similar vicarious-reinforcement effects were reported by Ditrichs, Simon, and Greene (1967). Junior-high-school subjects listened to a tape recording of a peer model being given approval or disapproval contingent upon certain word choices in a sentence-construction task. Results indicated that vicarious reinforcement and punishment affected the subjects' subsequent acquisition rates when they were later trained on the same task.

A study by Morris, Marshall, and Miller (1973) focused more specifically on vicarious-punishment effects. Studying first-, second-, and third-grade girls, these investigators found that punishment of a peer model for failing to share increased sharing behavior by observing children. Interestingly, increased sharing was also reported when peer models were punished noncontingently. The authors report data from a second experiment which replicated both findings. It was suggested that vicarious punishment in an ambiguous situation may result in increases in behaviors which have avoided punishment in the past.

Film Mediation of Peer Models

Several research efforts have demonstrated that film-mediated peer models may produce significant changes in the behavior of observing children. Extending the findings of Debus (1970), who used live models, Ridberg, Parke, and Hetherington (1971) altered the "impulsive" cognitive style of fourth-grade children using a film-mediated peer model. In this study, 50 "impulsive" and 50 "reflective" children were exposed to a filmed model demonstrating behavior characteristic of either the reflective or impulsive cognitive style. Each subject viewed a film depicting a style opposite his own. Results showed the impulsive group to be more reflective after viewing the reflective film. Effects were unclear for the reflective group. Investigating peer imitation in children with mental retardation, Fechter (1971) reported changes in "friendly" and "aggressive" behavior subsequent to exposure to a film-mediated peer model demonstrating either friendly or aggressive behavior. Previously nonaggressive subjects became more friendly after the "friendly" film and more aggressive after the "aggressive" film. Previously aggressive subjects became more aggressive after viewing the "aggressive" film and slightly more friendly after viewing the "friendly" film. Similar findings have been reported by Talkington and Altman (1973) and Hicks (1965). Results of these investigations are essentially congruent with those of research utilizing film-mediated adult models (Bandura, 1965; Bandura *et al.*, 1963), and provide additional support for the efficacy of film-mediated modeling procedures.

Effects of Being Imitated

Although research on the subject has not been extensive, it appears to be clear that children are affected by being imitated (Hartup, 1978).

Studies of children whose responses on a marble-drop task were imitated by adults indicate that being imitated may have reinforcing effects (Fouts, 1972; R.S. Miller & Morris, 1974). Studying reciprocal peer imitation in third- and fourth-grade children, Thelen and Kirkland (1976) reported that being imitated by an older child led to more reciprocal imitation than being imitated by a younger child. Additionally, results indicated that children imitated by older children later chose imitators over non-imitators on a measure of personal attraction. In contrast, children imitated by younger peers did not show a preference for imitators or nonimitators. Changes in social attraction as an effect of being imitated were also reported by V.L. Allen and Devin-Sheehan (1974). They found that sixth-grade girls reported increased liking for younger children who imitated them, while sixth-grade boys reported less liking of younger children who imitated them. As noted by Hartup (1978), it appears that the reinforcing effects of being imitated may be mediated by the perceived status of the imitator. It is clear that this issue warrants additional investigation, particularly in the context of establishing behaviorally sophisticated peers as models for children with behavior problems or developmental delays.

Developmental Age and Peer Imitation

The precise role of developmental variables in the emergence and maintenance of peer imitation in young children remains largely unknown (Hartup & Coates, 1970; Parton, 1976). However, some developmental investigators have observed the phenomenon of peer imitation at early age levels. In a descriptive study, Bridges (1933) arranged daily interaction sessions in a playpen for infants 9–12 months old. Observations in dyad and triad groupings over a three-month period revealed that infants at this early age did imitate one another. Other studies have verified the occurrence of peer imitation at the toddler age level. Apolloni and Tremblay (1978) investigated peer imitation between children two years old or younger in group settings comprised of four or five children. After training of one of the children outside the group in correct use of novel materials, the trained child returned to the peer group. Spontaneous imitation of the material-use behaviors of the trained child was demonstrated by at least one peer in each of four groups observed. Rubenstein and Howes (1976) investigated changes in the social and play behaviors of toddlers (19 months old) observed at home with their mothers. When another toddler was introduced into the setting, the imitative behavior of the subjects was observed to increase. Concomitant increases in the sophistication of toy play were also observed. Also studying peer imitation at the toddler level, Eckerman, Whatley, and

Kutz (1975) observed differential rates of social interaction (including peer imitation) in 30 pairs of normal children from 10 to 24 months old. They reported increases in social interaction (and peer imitation) as the children approached the 24-month age level.

Research conducted with children who have developmental delays due to mental retardation has indicated differences in peer imitation associated with mental age level. Forehand, Robbins, and Brady (1973) studied differences in imitative responses to tape recordings of a peer made by 32 handicapped and 32 nonhandicapped primary-age children. The handicapped children's IQs ranged from 50 to 80. Mental ages for all of the children were determined on the Stanford-Binet and the WISC. Results showed differences in the type and quantities of imitative responses associated with the mental ages of the children—handicapped and nonhandicapped. Other studies have supported the notion that peer imitation may be affected by variables associated with mental age (Litrownik, 1972) but that IQ is not directly correlated with peer imitation (Cullinan, 1976; Forehand *et al.*, 1973; Litrownik, 1972). These results emphasize similarities in the way handicapped and nonhandicapped children acquire increasingly sophisticated skills despite obvious differences in learning rates (Bijou & Baer, 1965; W.A. Bricker & Bricker, 1974).

Research on early-childhood development has suggested that reciprocal imitation (wherein the child's imitative responses are imitated by the model) may play an important part in the development of generalized imitative repertoires (Parton, 1976; Piaget, 1951). Extrapolating from these findings, it might be expected that reciprocal imitation would foster the development of generalized imitation in children with developmental delays. This possibility was investigated by Kauffman, Snell, and Hallahan (1976), who studied children labeled severely or profoundly retarded. They compared the effects of imitation training under two procedural conditions: (a) shaping plus imitation of the imitator (reciprocal imitation), and (b) shaping only. Results supported the superiority of the reciprocal-imitation procedure in that fewer trials were required to achieve criterion levels of correct imitative responses. This phenomenon was explained both in terms of Piaget's theories regarding the role of reciprocal imitation and in terms of research demonstrating the reinforcing effects of being imitated carried out with other populations (Fouts, 1972; G.J. Miller, 1974; Piaget, 1951).

Some research has indicated that vicarious reinforcement may affect peer imitation differently at several age levels. Barnwell and Sechrest (1965) studied 240 first- and third-grade children divided into model and observer dyads. Observing children viewed positive or negative consequences delivered to peer models playing one of two available games. First-grade observers' subsequent choice of games was found to be affected by the vicarious reinforcement or punishment of the peer models. However, these vicarious effects were not observed for third-grade subjects. Other research conducted with a similar population did not show vicarious reinforcement effects with primary-age children, including first graders (Elliott & Vasta, 1970). Differences in the effects of vicarious punishment at two age levels were observed by Morris (1973). Studying first- and second-grade children, it was found that vicarious punishment effects were greater for the older children. While it appears that vicarious reinforcement and punishment may differentially affect peer imitation by children at various age levels, insufficient evidence exists as yet to allow delineation of specific conditions under which vicarious effects may be expected. One of the reasons for this difficulty is the multiplicity of contextual variables which have been shown to influence peer imitation, and which may be assumed to interact with the effects of vicarious reinforcement and punishment. Some of these variables are reviewed below.

Contextual Variables and Peer Imitation

In addition to contingencies of reinforcement and developmental status, a number of variables have been shown to influence peer imitation in specific contexts. One of the most important of these is the competency of the peer model. Andrews (1966) studied differential rates of peer imitation by three- and four-year-olds under three conditions of model competency. Sixty-four children matched for sex and age were divided into three experimental groups comprised of observer–model dyads. Data were collected on rates of peer imitation exhibited during a simple game under three conditions: (1) Neither the model nor the observer had previous experience with the game, (2) both the model and the observer had experience with the game, and (3) the model, but not the observer, had experience with the game. Results indicated that the three conditions of task familiarity differentially affected rates of peer imitation. It was found that naïve subjects imitated task-familiar peer models significantly more than naïve peer models.

Related findings were reported by Luchins and Luchins (1961) in studies of 120 elementary students (mean CA 11-6) and 60 high-school students (mean CA 16-0). Both experiments examined the effects of knowledgeable or unknowledgeable peer models on observers' solutions to a two-choice maze problem. Knowledgeable models were informed by the experimenter of the correct choices in the maze problem; unknowledgeable models were not informed. Although no consistent effects on observers' acquisition of the maze task were shown for the different modeling conditions, the authors interpreted portions of the data to suggest that knowledgeable models may facilitate observers' acquisition of a task when the task is particularly difficult or when its solution involves discovery of an underlying principle.

A similar hypothesis has been suggested by Barry and Overman (1977) on the basis of their study of children labeled "educably mentally retarded" (EMR). Research reported by Becker and Glidden (1979) further demonstrated the effects of model competency on peer imitation by children with mild mental retardation. Subjects were 80 boys (mean age 12.2 years) labeled EMR. They viewed film-mediated adult or peer models who were of high or low competence on a motor task. Results showed that high-competence models were imitated more than low-competence models—whether they were adults or peers. The off-task behavior of high-competence peers was imitated more than the off-task behavior of adult models and low-competence peer models.

Akamatsu and Thelen (1974), reviewing literature on observer characteristics and imitation (primarily with adult models), have concluded that observer competency as well as model competency affect the likelihood of imitation.

Another contextual variable which may affect peer imitation is the nature and length of the child's social history with the peer model. A report on children labeled "mentally retarded" found that previous positive social contact with the peer model increased subsequent peer imitation (Kindberg, 1971). These results are supported by earlier research with normally developing children (Grossner, Polansky, & Lippitt, 1951). In a related study of normally developing preschool children, Hartup and Coates (1967) showed rates of peer imitation to be functionally related to reinforcement history within the peer group. Initial observations were made under naturalistic conditions to determine the level of reward (i.e., positive social responses) exchanged among the subjects. Next, observations under controlled conditions were made of the extent to which subjects with various histories of peer rewards imitated rewarding vs. nonrewarding peers. It was found that subjects with histories of frequent social reinforcement from peers imitated rewarding peer models significantly more often than they imitated nonrewarding peer models. Subjects with histories of infrequent reinforcement from peers imitated less-frequently rewarding models significantly more often than rewarding models. These results parallel those of laboratory studies employing adult models (Bandura & Huston, 1961; Mischel & Grusec, 1966). Hartup (1970) hypothesizes that the tendency of children with histories of infrequent reinforcement from the peer group to imitate nonrewarding models may be a function of a perceived similarity to nonrewarding children.

This hypothesis has been subjected to empirical scrutiny in a study of peer imitation in preadolescent boys as a function of perceived similarity to a model (Rosekrans, 1967). In this investigation, 90 boy scouts aged 11 to 14 were divided into nine experimental groups exposed to a film of either a highly similar peer model or a highly dissimilar model. Additional assessment was made of vicarious reinforcement effects with both peer models by including three different endings to the film depicting positive, negative, or neutral consequences to the model for his play in a war-strategy game. After viewing one of the three films, subjects were given an opportunity to play the game themselves. Observation of the subjects' imitative behavior indicated that peer models whom the subjects perceived as highly similar to themselves were imitated more often than those perceived as dissimilar. Vicarious reinforcement effects were not shown at significant levels.

Kornhaber and Schroeder (1975) have investigated the effects of perceived similarity to the model in reducing the avoidance behavior of elementary-school girls who showed fear of snakes. Exposure to filmed models showed that child models produced a greater reduction in avoidance than adult models, even when the child models were depicted as fearful of snakes. Other research has indicated that models may be imitated more frequently in some contexts when they are of the same sex as observers (Hartup, 1964; Madsen, 1968).

Verbal cues related to the behavior of the model have been shown to increase peer imitation in some cases. In the Elliot and Vasta (1970) report noted earlier, three types of peer-modeling tactics were involved: (1) modeled sharing, (2) modeled sharing plus reward to the model, and (3) modeled sharing plus reward, plus provision of a rule to the model explaining why he was rewarded. The third condition resulted in significantly more peer imitation by observing subjects. Similar effects of verbalizing task-relevant information were reported by Rosenbaum (1967). Studying 148 elementary-school children divided into model–observer pairs, Rosenbaum tested observers on retention of relevant data from a multiple-choice maze task. Three modeling conditions were evaluated: (1) The peer model verbalized data relevant to his response, (2) the observer verbalized data relevant to the response of the peer model, and (3) the observer simply viewed the peer model's response. Results showed that observers retained most when the peer model verbalized task-relevant information. Similar results supporting the importance of verbalizations related to the behavior of the model have been found by Cullinan (1976) with children labeled EMR. Here, nine- to 12-year-old boys who were required to verbally describe the behavior of a peer model were subsequently able to imitate more accurately than those who did not verbalize the model's behavior.

Taken together, the results of research on the reinforcement, developmental, and contextual factors affecting peer imitation represent a substantial body of information upon which educators and psychologists may base strategies for therapeutic intervention. Some research has also been reported describing procedures for employing peer imitation to achieve specific therapeutic and instructional goals.

Peer Imitation in Therapeutic and Instructional Settings

Applied research on peer imitation has focused on the identification of strategies for promoting therapeutic behavioral gains for clients in natural settings. Some of the findings of basic and developmental research have been utilized in applied settings. Therapeutic contexts in which peer-imitation strategies have been successfully employed include modification of avoidance behavior and social withdrawal, instruction in appropriate classroom behaviors, and development of simple social responses.

One of the earliest therapeutic applications of peer imitation procedures utilized peer models to reduce toddler-age children's fear of a rabbit (Jones, 1924). The author reported that the procedure of "social imitation [consisting of placing a nonfearful child in the same play area with the subject and the rabbit] was one of the first to show signs of yielding results" (p. 389). The absence of an experimental assessment of control (Sidman, 1960) over the fear responses of the subjects and the lack of a more objective index of the fear responses obscure the specific effects of peer imitation in this study. More rigorous experimental controls were later employed to substantiate the efficacy of peer-modeling procedures in reducing children's fear and avoidance responses to animals (Bandura & Menlove, 1968; Bandura, Grusec, & Menlove, 1967). In the first study (Bandura *et al.*, 1967), 48 preschool children manifesting fear-and-avoidance behavior toward dogs were divided into three matched groups. The experimental group viewed a film depicting a peer model playing with a dog in a progressively more active manner; a non-experimental group viewed a film of a dog without a model present; and a control group played without the model or a dog present. Posttest observations one day and one month after treatment revealed a significant reduction in fear and avoidance behavior for the group of children exposed to the peer model film. In an extension of these findings, Bandura and Menlove compared the effectiveness of two peer modeling procedures for reducing fear and avoidance behavior in dog-phobic preschoolers. Subjects viewed a film depicting either (a) one peer model playing with a dog, (b) several peer models playing with different dogs, or (c) a control film without animals in it. Results showed reductions in fear and avoidance behavior under both peer-modeling conditions. Additionally, children who viewed the multiple peer model film subsequently demonstrated such substantial reduction in avoidance responses as to allow them to interact with dogs in an intimate manner.

Social withdrawal has also been successfully treated using peer-modeling procedures. O'Connor (1969) utilized film-mediated peer models to increase the social participation of withdrawn preschoolers. Studying 13 children identified as "isolates" by teacher ratings and direct observation, O'Connor exposed a six-child experimental group to a film depicting six peer models socially interacting in a positive manner. A control group, comprised of the remaining seven children, viewed a neutral film containing no human characters. Pretest and posttest assessment showed increases in social interaction for the experimental group beyond the "isolate" level. However, data for individual subjects revealed that social interaction was not increased beyond the "isolate" level for the two most socially deficient children. Moreover, large increases in social interaction were evidenced for only two of the six experimental children. Even with these limitations, the author notes that social gains made subsequent to one viewing of a 23-min peer-modeling film support the cost-effectiveness of this procedure as a means of treating young children manifesting extremely low rates of social behavior. An effort to assess specific variables that might account for the large inter-subject variability of O'Connor's (1969) results was reported by Evers-Pasquale and Sherman (1975). These researchers hypothesized that the effects of peer modeling appropriate social behavior may be mediated by the observing child's value of contact with peers. They studied the responses of 16 social-isolate preschoolers to a film similar to that used by O'Connor. The subjects were divided into two groups according to their preference for play (1) with peers or (2) with adults and/or solitary play. Results indicated that the peer-play-preference group demonstrated significantly larger increases in social interaction after viewing the film than did the adult- and/or solitary-play-preference group.

In an extension of this line of research, O'Connor (1972) examined the relative effects of modeling, shaping, and modeling plus shaping in increasing social interaction of isolate preschoolers. This investigation employed 33 children (identified as in the 1969 study) who were divided into four matched treatment groups accordingly exposed to (1) a peer-modeling film identical to the one used in the 1969 study, (2) a peer-modeling film plus shaping (consisting of adult social reinforcement of social responses), (3) shaping only, and (4) a control film identical to that used in the 1969 study. Between-group comparisons were made based on direct observational data. Results of three comparisons between experimental groups (one immediately following treatment and two at subsequent three-week intervals) indicated that (1) modeling and modeling plus shaping conditions resulted in more rapid increases in social interaction than shaping alone, (2) modeling, modeling plus shaping, and shaping all resulted in temporary increases in social interaction beyond the isolate level, and (3) increases in social interaction resulting from modeling procedures were maintained over time whereas gains made utilizing shaping procedures eroded to pretreatment levels. O'Connor hypothesized that modeling procedures may be particularly effective in adding new social responses to the repertoire of the young, isolated child. The insufficiency of data on the effects of the modeling procedure on individual subjects warrants a conservative interpretation of these results, particularly in view of the variability in previously obtained results of this procedure (O'Connor, 1969).

The work of O'Connor (1969, 1972) in modifying social withdrawal via film-mediated peer-modeling procedures was extended by Keller and Carlson (1974). These investigators observed 19 socially isolated preschool children on measures of social interaction, giving positive reinforcement, and receiving positive reinforcement. Experimental-group children saw four videotapes of five min each depicting peer models engaging in imitation, smiling and laughing, giving tokens, and giving positive physical contact to each other. The videotape depicted peers responding positively to these behaviors. Control children viewed a nature film. Posttreatment, direct-observational data collected immediately after the videotapes and three weeks later revealed significant increases in all three social-behavior categories. The authors noted that, after treatment, experimental children no longer received significantly less positive reinforcement from peers than nonisolate children. Control children continued to receive significantly less positive reinforcement from peers. These results support other research indicating the importance of reciprocity in social interaction (Strain & Timm, 1974; Strain, Cooke, & Apolloni, 1976; Strain, Shores, & Timm, 1977). Keller and Carlson (1974) also noted that their intervention resulted in increases in experimental children imitating behaviors after treatment that were never directly modeled on the videotapes. This finding suggests the possible use of this strategy for developing generalized peer imitation by socially deficient children.

Peer-modeling strategies have also been used to change social behavior in classroom situations. Hansen, Niland, and Zani (1969) reported using a peer-model-reinforcement procedure as a means of increasing the social skills of children who rate low on sociometric measures of peer acceptance in elementary classrooms. Subjects were divided into counseling groups which were exposed to one of three experimental conditions: (1) inclusion of a highly accepted peer model, who received reinforcement for appropriate social behaviors during group sessions, (2) a social-skills training program based on social-learning principles, or (3) a no-treatment control in which children had an unrelated activity together. The authors reported that the peer-model-reinforcement condition produced the greatest increases in sociometrically measured peer acceptance. Unfortunately, no direct-observation data were presented and the procedures followed during treatment conditions were not described in sufficient detail to permit replication.

Other classroom applications of peer modeling and imitation have been more thoroughly described and validated. Peer modeling was employed in a study of primary children labeled EMR as part of a training package to increase listening skills (Ross & Ross, 1972). The efficacy of the training package (consisting of intentional teaching; peer modeling; and tangible, social, and symbolic rewards) was evaluated using a criterion-referenced listening test. Examples of subtest categories were "following directions at table," "repeating sentences," and "imitating sounds." Results showed significant increases in eight of 10 subtests. Although results supported the training procedure as a package, the experimental design did not include a component assessment of individual tactics, including peer modeling, which comprised the procedure. The investigators hypothesized that vicarious reinforcement effects were partially responsible for observed gains in listening skills.

In another study of EMR preschool and primary-age children, Ross (1970) extended the findings of the earlier laboratory research on the importance of the observing child's social history with a peer model (Hartup & Coates, 1967). A "psychological attachment" was established by exposing each experimental-group child to a series of positive, vicarious interactions with a peer model. These interactions consisted of social and tangible rewards from an adult experimenter who presented himself to the child as the agent of the peer model. Control-group subjects were exposed to similar vicarious interactions with another peer who was never employed as a model. Results of comparisons between experimental and control groups revealed that children with psychological attachment (i.e., histories of positive reinforcement) with the peer model imitated the model's responses on a preacademic task significantly more than did children without psychological attachment to the model. Findings of the Ross study were interpreted as supporting the efficacy of establishing a positive social history between observing children and peer models as a method of maximizing benefits of the peer-modeling procedure.

PEER IMITATION BY INDIVIDUALS WITH SEVERE HANDICAPS

The work by O'Connor (1969, 1972), Ross (1970), and Ross and Ross (1972) has demonstrated that peer modeling may be an effective tool for promoting behavioral gains in mildly handicapped children. A similar approach to remediating more severe behavioral deficits in children with moderate to profound mental retardation has been investigated by a few researchers (Berkowitz, 1968; Talkington, Hall, & Altman, 1973; Whalen & Henker, 1969, 1971). These studies have employed children with mild or moderate retardation as models for peers manifesting less developmentally sophisticated behavior. Berkowitz taught profoundly retarded children from nine to 12 years old to imitate simple motor responses modeled by a moderately retarded peer. Results of the study showed that imitative behavior generalized during reinforcement conditions to responses never directly reinforced. It was noted that all imitation decreased during extinction phases of the investigation. After a retraining phase using a continuous reinforcement schedule, imitative behavior was maintained on reduced schedules of reinforcement (fixed ratios of 1:1, 1:2, and 1:3) and maintained without reinforcement through follow-up probes conducted three and six weeks after training. Findings of the Berkowitz investigation of peer modeling resemble those of research on the use of other modeling procedures employing direct reinforcement of imitative behavior with children labeled retarded (Baer *et al.,* 1967) and autistic (Metz, 1965), as well as nonhandicapped subjects (Baer & Sherman, 1964; Brigham & Sherman, 1968).

Two additional studies that focused on employing retarded peers as behavioral models for children with severe retardation were reported by Whalen and Henker (1969, 1971). In the earlier work, three severely retarded children from six to 12 years old were taught to imitate simple motor and verbal responses modeled by moderately retarded peers. The peer models were given training in operant conditioning techniques to teach them how to demonstrate the reinforce the desired responses of the severely retarded subjects. Peer models then conducted the imitation training with target subjects under the supervision of the experimenter. Although no direct-observational data were reported, the authors state that imitative responses were acquired by all three target subjects who received training from peer models. Informal observation indicated that the imitative repertoires of the peer models maintained over time. The authors reported that this procedure of "pyramid therapy" appeared to be a viable means for augmenting instruction in institutional settings.

Another application of peer-modeling procedures with children with severe handicaps was conducted by Talkington and colleagues (1973). Assessment was made of the differential effects of (1) peer modeling plus verbal instructions and praise, (2) verbal instructions and praise, and (3) a no-treatment-equal-activity time on the acquisition of simple receptive-language skills in 75 children with severe mental retardation (mean CA 10 years). The peer models employed in the study were moderately retarded adolescents. The results of pre- and postassessment on criterion-referenced and standardized receptive-language tests indicated the modeling group acquired significantly more language skills than did the verbal-instruction or control group. The verbal-instruction group scored significantly higher than the no-treatment control group on the tests. The authors suggested that use of modeling procedures may be particularly appropriate with retarded children who may be highly dependent upon cues from others.

Recent investigations have extended these demonstrations of the value of employing peer-modeling procedures in therapeutic or instructional contexts for people with severe handicaps. Mansdorf (1977) utilized peer models as a means to rapidly token-train 20 women labeled severely retarded on an institution ward. These women were divided into two groups which each received one training session, one week apart. Training consisted of asking one typically compliant member of the group to perform a simple task. This woman received verbal and token reinforcement for completing the task and was immediately sent to a staff member to exchange the token for tangible, back-up reinforcers. This procedure was observed by the other members of the group, who each then had an opportunity to perform tasks as the peer model had. All observers in both groups performed the task, received the token, and exchanged the token correctly after observing the peer model. Follow-up data collected two and three weeks later revealed that rates of compliance had increased from a mean of 4% at pretreatment to a mean of 100%. The author noted the relative efficiency of this procedure for conducting token training over those previously reported in the literature.

Increases in instructional efficiency were also reported by Biberdorf and Pear (1977) when opportunities for peer imitation were available to retarded children. This research found two-to-one student-to-teacher ratios more efficient than one-to-one during simple language instruction involving separate tasks for each child. It was noted that each of the children learned some of the appropriate language responses modeled by the other child during the lesson.

Demonstrations of increased instructional efficiency through use of peer models are particularly valuable when considered in the context of the recent trend in educational-service delivery toward accommodating wider diversities of learner needs within classroom settings. This trend is singularly evident at the preschool level, where integration of handicapped and nonhandicapped children is an increasingly familiar arrangement (D. A. Bricker & Sandall, 1979; Guralnick, 1978). A few researchers have directed attention to developing procedures utilizing peer imitation as an instructional resource in integrated classrooms.

PEER IMITATION IN INTEGRATED CLASSROOMS AT THE EARLY CHILDHOOD LEVEL

Recent ideological, legislative, and judicial developments in the field of special education mandate the inclusion of handicapped children in "normalized" classroom settings whenever appropriate (Birch, 1974; Langstaff-Pasanella & Volkmor, 1976; Wolfensberger, 1972). Purported advantages of integrated classrooms are that nonhandicapped peers may serve as models for handicapped children and that integrated settings may provide opportunities for "normalized" social interaction at an early age (D.D. Bricker, 1978; Guralnick, 1976; Snyder *et al.*, 1977; Wolfensberger, 1972). However conceptually appealing integrated classrooms may be, there is a need for gathering empirical evidence to guide educators in ensuring that purported benefits do indeed accrue to handicapped and nonhandicapped preschoolers in such settings (Scriven, 1976; Wynne, Ulfelder, & Dakof, 1975). Existing studies on integrated settings at the preschool level indicate that little cross-group imitation or social interaction takes place without specific programming (K.E. Allen, Benning, & Drummond, 1972; Devoney, Guralnick, & Rubin, 1974; Feitelson, Weintraub, & Michaeli, 1972; Guralnick, 1976; Karnes, Teska, & Hodgins, 1970; Palyo, Cooke, Peck, & Apolloni, 1977; Ray, 1974).

Recently educators have begun to directly address the need for an empirically based instructional technology for integrating handicapped and nonhandicapped children. An early study directed toward this goal was reported by Csapo (1972). Six primary-age children referred by classroom teachers as "emotionally disturbed" and demonstrating disruptive classroom behavior were integrated into a classroom with 12 peer models selected for their appropriate classroom behavior. Six of the peer models were instructed to demonstrate appropriate classroom behavior to the target subjects and to reinforce target subjects with tokens for appropriate responses. Target subjects self-recorded the number of tokens they received and self-evaluated their progress. The author reported that rates of disruptive behavior declined for all target subjects. Unfortunately, the correlational design of this investigation did not permit a conclusive analysis of specific peer-modeling effects.

Other investigations of peer imitation in integrated settings have been carried out at the preschool level. In a study by Devoney and colleagues (1974), nonhandicapped children were integrated into a preschool classroom with handicapped children in hopes of increasing the social play of the handicapped group. Time sampling of social-play behavior indicated that there was little substantial change in rates of social play of handicapped children subsequent to placing nonhandicapped peer models in the same setting. A systematic structuring of the environment to promote imitation of the peer models and social interaction between the two groups resulted in further increases in social play. Some of the limitations cited for the Csapo (1972) study are also apparent in this report—that is, failure to describe dependent and independent variables in replicable detail, and absence of a functional analysis of the effects of the independent variable. Nevertheless, these investigations provided early evidence that integrated classroom environments could be arranged to achieve therapeutic goals through use of peer imitation.

In a more recent investigation, Guralnick (1976) utilized peer-modeling procedures in two experiments, one designed to increase social play and one designed to increase appropriate language usage by handicapped preschool children. Both experiments involved integrating a developmentally delayed preschooler with normally developing peer models. In the experiment on social play, one handicapped child and two peer models were placed in a free-play environment containing three toys for 15-min play sessions. During this condition the handicapped child engaged in very little social interaction. In an initial attempt to increase peer-modeling effects, the handicapped subject was requested to watch the play of the nonhandicapped children for the first five min of each play session. No increases in subsequent social play were observed. The experimenters then implemented structured training sessions "using role-playing and verbal descriptions to instruct the nonhandicapped children how to attend selectively to the handicapped child's appropriate behaviors and how to encourage him to interact with them" (p. 240). Concomitantly the experimenters instructed the nonhandicapped children to play only with the toy most preferred by the handicapped child. These procedures were associated with increases in social play for the handicapped child. Similar results were obtained when the procedure was replicated with another handicapped child.

In the experiment on language intervention, the author employed one developmentally delayed child and one nonhandicapped peer model. The introduction of the nonhandicapped child into a 15-min language session in which he modeled appropriate language responses did not result in increases in appropriate language usage for the handicapped subject. However, the addition of a vicarious-reinforcement component, in which the peer model was socially reinforced for appropriate language usage resulted in large increases in the observing subject's emission of correct language forms. Probes of untrained language responses indicated that training effects generalized.

Our own research has been directed toward developing instructional techniques for increasing rates of generalized imitation of nonhandicapped peers by handicapped children in integrated preschools (Apolloni, Cooke, & Cooke, 1977; Cooke, Apolloni, & Cooke, in press; Cooke, Cooke, & Apolloni, 1978; Peck, Apolloni, Cooke, & Raver, 1978). We have collectively termed these procedures Peer Imitation Training (PIT). In the Apolloni *et al.* (1977) study, three toddler-age children with moderate mental retardation were taught to imitate the motor and material use responses of a nonhandicapped peer model. This was accomplished by placing the peer model and one handicapped subject at a time in a highly structured training environment. An adult experimenter was seated behind each child and prompted the child to imitate the peer model. Peer models were verbally prompted to demonstrate one of several specific motor or material use behaviors. Social reinforcement was delivered by the adult experimenter to the handicapped child contingent upon imitation of the peer model's responses. Results on directly trained responses indicated that the handicapped children did learn to imitate the motor and material-use behavior of the nonhandicapped peer model. Data collected on untrained imitative responses and data collected in a setting somewhat dissimilar to the training environment revealed some stimulus-and-response generalization effects.

In a related experiment focusing on verbal behavior (Cooke *et al.*, 1978), we employed the same training procedure—with the exception that verbal responses were modeled by the nonhandicapped peer. In this study, data were collected under two generalization conditions: one structured similarly to the training environment and the other a relatively unstructured, free-play setting. Results of the peer imitation training showed clear training effects for each of the subjects. Stimulus and response generalization were observed for each subject in the structured setting, but were not observed in the free-play setting. Increases in spontaneous, nonimitative verbalizations to peers in the free-play setting were observed subsequent to peer imitation training. The failure of gains in imitative behavior to generalize to the free-play situation may have been caused by the large disparity in environmental conditions between the two settings. Consequently, large disparities between highly structured training settings and unstructured free-play settings may have to be reduced incrementally before training gains may be expected to generalize. Alternatively, PIT might be carried out directly in the free-play setting.

Our next study explored the latter strategy (Peck *et al.*, 1978). Thus, conducting the training within a typically unstructured preschool environment offered a twofold advantage. Problems inherent in transferring behavioral gains made in highly structured settings to minimally structured, more naturalistic settings were eliminated. Moreover, the implementation of PIT procedures in a situation typical of those commonly found in preschools served as a preliminary test of the clinical viability of PIT procedures under naturalistic conditions.

Two experiments were reported in this study. In Experiment 1, dyadic social-interaction data (Strain *et al.*, 1976) were collected under training and nontraining conditions regarding the extent to which: (a) retarded children (mean CA 36 months) imitated and socially interacted with nonretarded peers (mean CA 53 months), and (b) nonretarded children imitated and socially interacted with retarded peers. Additionally, in Experiment 2, dyadic data were collected on the affective nature (positive or negative) of the social interaction between the children with retardation and the nonretarded peer models.

Experiment 1 was carried out in a large-group, free-play situation. The PIT procedure consisted of delivering instructions to a retarded child when the child was within three feet of a peer model engaged in an appropriate material-use activity: "Look! See what he is doing? You do it." The teacher then pointed to the peer model and gave additional prompts as necessary to the retarded child until the child engaged in the modeled behavior. Each imitative response during training was rewarded with praise and a pat or other positive physical contact. Following a three-min training period, the teacher left the free-play setting and the children were observed under nontraining conditions. Results clearly showed immediate increases in peer imitation when training was applied, with some generalization of the imitative behavior to nontraining conditions.

Experiment 2 was carried out with slightly younger handicapped children ($N = 2$, mean CA 29 months) and one nonhandicapped child (CA 44 months). The handicapped children manifested developmental delays due to moderate mental retardation similar to the children who participated in Experiment 1. Training and generalization data were collected in a free-play situation where only the peer model and the handicapped child were present. Intervention was similar to that carried out in Experiment 1, except that specific toys were introduced one at a time by the teacher, who prompted both children to play with them. The handicapped child was prompted to imitate the peer model and received praise and positive physical contact for imitative responses.

As in Experiment 1, the imitative responses of the handicapped children increased immediately when training began. In this experiment, substantial generalization of increases in imitation were observed under nontraining conditions. Notable increases in social interaction between handicapped and nonhandicapped children were observed during the course of PIT during both of these studies (these data are graphically presented in Peck et al., 1978). Negative social interaction was very seldom observed.

Another strategy for developing generalized peer imitation was reported by Nordquist (1978). An initial training phase established a high percentage of correct imitative responses by a four-year-old boy labeled "autistic" to adult-modeled, nonverbal behaviors. Subsequently, two confederate peers were trained to model and reinforce imitation of the same behaviors in a nursery-school classroom. During this phase adult-imitation training was discontinued. Assessment of spontaneous imitation during free-play across all training phases showed that increases in generalized, spontaneous peer imitation were systematically associated with the peer-imitation condition. Increases in the boy's autisticlike behaviors were also noted during PIT, however, as well as some decreases in sustained peer interactions. These results suggest the potential value of teaching confederate peers to prompt and reinforce peer-imitation behavior by less sophisticated classmates, as well as the need for assessment of possible side effects of PIT with individual children.

The body of literature on peer imitation in early-childhood educational settings reviewed herein and elsewhere (Guralnick, 1978) demonstrates clearly that classroom environments may be arranged to increase the instructional benefits of integrating handicapped and nonhandicapped children. The available research suggests several contextual variables which merit consideration for program planners and researchers.

Several studies have reported differential rates of social interaction (including imitation) between handicapped and nonhandicapped children when various options for type of playmate (i.e., handicapped or nonhandicapped) are available (Porter, Ramsey, Tremblay, Iaccobo, & Crawley, 1978). N.L. Peterson and Haralick (1977) report data demonstrating that, although handicapped children did play with nonhandicapped children, the nonhandicapped children preferred to play with other nonhandicapped peers. These findings support our own data collected in a similar investigation (Cooke, Apolloni, & Cooke, in press) with a smaller number of children. In this study we observed that introducing a second nondelayed child into an ongoing free-play situation with one delayed and one nondelayed child resulted in decreases in imitative and social responses between the original playmates, and a predominance of social responding between the nondelayed children. These findings are similar to those from studies of older children (Goodman, Gottlieb, & Harrison, 1972; Gottlieb & Davis, 1973), and suggest the need for specific programming to maximize opportunities for handicapped children in integrated classrooms to socially interact with nonhandicapped peers. One strategy that seems worthy of investigation is systematic manipulation of the ratios of handicapped to nonhandicapped children in order to identify conditions facilitative of desirable social play in both quantitative and qualitative aspects (N.L. Peterson & Haralick, 1977).

Another contextual variable which may affect peer imitation in integrated classrooms is that of age matches between handicapped and nonhandicapped children. Anecdotal evidence from our work in integrated preschools suggests that selecting peer models of the same or younger chronological age as the handicapped children may facilitate positive social interaction and imitation between them. This notion is consistent with that of observers of similar settings (D.D. Bricker, 1978). Some of the child-development literature on cross-age peer interaction (Hartup, 1976) has indicated that peer conflict may be reduced when age dissimilarities are minimal.

Considerations in utilizing peer imitation in integrated classrooms must include possible effects on normally developing children who will usually function as peer models. Scriven (1976) has argued forcefully for increased attention to the needs of nonhandicapped children in integrated settings. This is clearly a largely overlooked issue, although data are emerging on the developmental outcomes of integrated preschools which indicate that nonhandicapped children are not adversely affected (D.D. Bricker & Sandall, 1979; Ispa & Matz, 1978; Peck, Cooke, Ruskus, & Apolloni, 1980). One of the most common fears of parents and educators is that "reverse imitation" will occur, that is, that nonhandicapped children will imitate the less adaptive behaviors of the handicapped children. Data we collected in one of our studies (Peck *et al.*, 1978) revealed only three instances of reverse imitation during 246 min of observation. This may have been an effect of the large disparity in developmental sophistication between the peer models and the handicapped children in this study. During the second experiment in that report (in which peer models and handicapped children were closer in age), we observed substantially more reverse imitation. We did not observe any imitation of maladaptive behavior on the part of the peer models. In a direct investigation of this issue, C. Peterson, Peterson, and Scriven (1977) assessed the rates at which handicapped or nonhandicapped children were imitated by each other. Their results showed that both handicapped and nonhandicapped children imitated nonhandicapped peers significantly more often than they imitated handicapped peers. Although model competency was not assessed in this study, the results are consistent with findings previously reviewed on the effects of model competency on peer imitation.

An investigation by Toner and Moore (1978) has demonstrated the possibility that serving as a peer model may increase the appropriate behavior of the model. First- and second-grade boys who had opportunities to be peer models of instruction-following behaviors subsequently followed rules better than children who did not serve as models. Although we agree with Scriven (1976) that the effects of integrated educational programming must be rigorously assessed for nonhandicapped as well as handicapped children, we are confident that instructional arrangements can be made to effectively serve all participating children.

Summary and Conclusions

Peer imitation may have a facilitative effect on learning with young children (Apolloni & Cooke, 1975; Rubenstein & Howes, 1976) as well as with older individuals (Bandura & Walters, 1963). Researchers have described some of the factors influencing peer imitation which have relevance to its development as a therapeutic and instructional resource.

Peer imitation may be controlled by arranging contingencies of reinforcement and/or punishment of the behavior of the model or the observer. Similar contingencies may affect whether peer or adult models are imitated. Findings from both clinical and laboratory investigations have supported the notion that direct reinforcement may be necessary to develop generalized peer imitation repertoires in individuals demonstrating extremely low rates of spontaneous imitation (Bry & Nawas, 1972).

Film or video mediation of peer models has been demonstrated successfully in laboratory research (Ridberg *et al.*, 1971) and applied in therapeutic contexts to reduce avoidance behavior (Bandura & Menlove, 1968; Bandura *et al.*, 1967) and social withdrawal (O'Connor, 1969, 1972).

The question of what effects being imitated may have on the peer model is as yet largely unanswered. It appears that although being imitated often has reinforcing effects upon the model, these effects may be substantially mediated by the age, sex, or perceived status of the imitator (Hartup, 1978). Similarly, the role of reciprocal peer imitation remains unclear (Parton, 1976). However, at least one study (Kauffman *et al.*, 1976) indicated that reciprocal imitation may have value as a programmed instructional event for developmentally young children.

The factors of chronological and developmental age have been shown to have clear effects on peer imitation, although these effects have not yet been precisely delineated (Hartup, 1978). Existing studies suggest that developmental or mental age is more closely associated with differential rates of peer imitation than is IQ (Forehand *et al.*, 1973; Litrownik, 1972). Other research indicates that contextual variables influencing rates of peer imitation, such as the relative competency of the peer model and observer, the observer's social history with the peer model, and the presence of verbal cues may interact with age variables (Akamatsu & Thelen, 1974; Hartup, 1978).

An important area of research and application of strategies for utilizing peer imitation for instructional purposes has focused on the integration of handicapped and nonhandicapped children in the classroom, particularly at the early childhood level (Snyder, Apolloni, & Cooke, 1977). Applied research has demonstrated that instructional strategies based on peer imitation can be an effective means of increasing language skills (Cooke *et al.*, 1978; Guralnick, 1976), social behavior (Csapo, 1972; Devoney *et al.*, 1974), and material-use skills (Apolloni *et al.*, 1977; Peck *et al.*, 1978). Additionally, some studies have shown generalization of behavioral increases achieved through PIT to settings in which there was little or no active instruction by adults (Guralnick, 1976; Nordquist, 1978; Peck *et al.*, 1978). Evidence was reported suggesting that PIT may have a beneficial side effect of increasing social interaction between handicapped and nonhandicapped children (Peck *et al.*, 1978). Although negative side effects of PIT have been reported with one child labeled autistic, the predominance of evidence from our own research indicates that neither the observing children nor peer models are harmed by these procedures. This position is supported by anecdotal, observational, and developmental evidence from other investigators of integrated classroom settings (D.D. Bricker & Sandall, 1979; W.A. Bricker & Bricker, 1974; Guralnick, 1978; C. Peterson *et al.*, 1977). Therapeutic and instructional gains achieved through use of peer imitation support the value of continued research in this domain. Some specific issues warrant rigorous scientific investigation if intervention strategies based on peer imitation are to be maximally beneficial.

One issue which has clearly not received sufficient research to date is that of defining the effects of being imitated on developmentally sophisticated peers. Results of presently available research indicate that being imitated may affect social relationships between children in either a positive or a negative fashion (V.L. Allen & Devin-Sheehan, 1974; Hartup, 1978; Thelen & Kirkland, 1976). Additional work is required to more clearly specify the conditions under which specific effects accrue and how these effects may interact with intervention variables such as PIT.

Another research issue concerns the generalization of behavioral gains generated via peer imitation which have been observed by some researchers. These have most often been instances of stimulus generalization—in which children have demonstrated previously trained, imitative responses outside the direct training environment (Nordquist, 1978; Peck *et al.*, 1978). Other studies have reported limited response generalization—wherein children have imitated behaviors topographically dissimilar to those directly trained (Apolloni *et al.*, 1977; Nordquist, 1978). The social significance of these generalized gains in peer-imitative behavior is not clear. It seems crucial that researchers devote increased efforts to assessing the generalized effects of PIT. The intent of such efforts would be two-fold: (a) to increase the durability and generalization of PIT effects, and (b) to ensure that PIT is indeed making a worthwhile contribution to the achievement of therapeutic and instructional goals. An important goal for integrated classroom settings is the development of peer imitation as a generalized learning strategy employed by handicapped children to learn new skills as well as to increase previously learned adaptive responses (D.D. Bricker, 1978; Guralnick, 1978, Snyder *et al.*, 1977).

Other research conducted in integrated classrooms should be directed toward identifying ratios and age matches of handicapped to nonhandicapped children which foster peer imitation and social interaction. Initial investigation of these issues indicates that the availability of other nonhandicapped peers as playmates may reduce the inclination of nonhandicapped children to interact with handicapped peers (Cooke, Apolloni, & Cooke, in press; N.L. Peterson & Haralick, 1978). However, it also appears that handicapped children may engage in more sophisticated play behaviors when placed in settings including large numbers of nonhandicapped playmates (N.L. Peterson & Haralick, 1977). Hartup (1976) has suggested that large discrepancies between age levels may be associated with increased conflict between young children. This is supported by anecdotal evidence in our own research (Peck *et al.*, 1978), which indicated that behaviors such as taking toys, pushing, and crying occurred more often when there were large age differences between handicapped and nonhandicapped children. Additional investigation is needed to clarify the effects of integrating handicapped and nonhandicapped children at various ratios and age levels.

Additional research is needed to broaden the application of PIT procedures. There is some evidence that peer imitation may operate to increase the effectiveness of small-group instruction of preacademic responses (Biberdorf & Pear, 1977). Further investigations utilizing PIT in academic instruction would be valuable. Although the predominance of research to date has focused on peer imitation in young children or in individuals with developmental delays, PIT intervention may be useful with other groups as well. For example, Stumphauzer (1972) successfully utilized a PIT procedure to increase delay of gratification by adult prison inmates. Additionally, PIT may be useful with components of social-behavior-training procedures characterized as "role playing" (Meerbaum, Apolloni, & Shores, 1976).

Finally, it seems likely that research may be most valuably carried out in the context of broader evaluation efforts based upon indices of developmental gain and social validity (Wolf, 1978). Research of this type would be directed toward generating information regarding not only whether PIT worked to produce targeted behavior change, but also whether that change itself contributed substantially to positive developmental and social outcomes.

We have noted the potential value of an empirically developed instructional technology based on peer imitation for addressing some of the educational challenges associated with the mainstreaming movement. It also seems that teaching individuals to imitate competent peers may have relevance to other trends in educational- and developmental-service delivery. The recently increased attention to developing community-based semiindependent and independent living arrangements (Apolloni, Cappuccilli, & Cooke, 1980) as alternatives to institutionalization of people with developmental disabilities represents one likely area of application for instruction based on peer imitation. In this context, the utilization of high-competence peers may be practical in teaching independent-living skills (Westaway & Apolloni, 1978).

Another recent service trend has been toward consumer self-advocacy. This movement is most clearly exemplified by the People First organization. People First is comprised of primary consumers of special developmental and educational services. One of the important challenges before this group is the development of personal-advocacy skills for its members. Promoting peer imitation of individuals highly competent in advocacy behaviors would appear to be an instructional strategy with desirable qualities of low cost, simplicity, and flexibility.

As a result of policy changes aimed at reintegrating people with special developmental needs into more generic service-delivery agencies (e.g., Public Law 94-142; Section 504, Rehabilitation Act of 1973; Wolfensberger, 1972), educators and other therapeutic-service providers are faced with increasing responsibility for responding to wider diversities of learning needs. It is clear that additional programmatic resources must be identified and developed to meet this challenge. We anticipate that PIT may serve as an important means of increasing therapeutic and instructional resources available to service providers attempting to broaden the accommodative capacity of their settings.

REFERENCES

Akamatsu, T.J., & Thelen, M.H. A review of the literature on observer characteristics and imitation. *Developmental Psychology*, 1974, *10*, 38–47.

Allen, K.E., Benning, P.M., & Drummond, T.W. Integration of normal and handicapped children in a behavior modification preschool: A case study. In G. Semb (Ed.), *Behavior analysis and education*. Lawrence; University of Kansas Press, 1972.

Allen, V.L. (Ed.), *Children as teachers: Theory and research on tutoring*. New York: Academic Press, 1976.

Allen, V.L., & Devin-Sheehan, L.D. The tutor as a role model: Effects of imitation and liking on student tutors. Madison: Wisconsin Research and Development Center for Cognitive Learning, 1974.

Andrews, M.G. Peer imitation by three and four year old children as a function of three conditions of task familiarity. *Dissertation Abstracts*, 1966, *26*, 4802.

Apolloni, T., & Cooke, T.P. Peer behavior conceptualized as a variable influencing infant and toddler development. *American Journal of Orthopsychiatry*, 1975, *45*, 4–17.

Apolloni, T., & Tremblay, A. Peer modeling between toddlers. *Child Study Journal*, 1978, *8*, 243–251.

Apolloni, T., Cooke, S.A. & Cooke, T.P. Establishing a nonretarded peer as a behavioral model for retarded toddlers. *Perceptual and Motor Skills*, 1977, *44*, 231–241.

Apolloni, T., Cappuccilli, J., & Cooke, T.P. (Eds.). *Achievements in living arrangements for the developmentally disabled: Toward excellence.* Chicago: University Park Press, 1980.

Baer, D.M., & Sherman, J.A. Reinforcement control of generalized imitation in young children. *Journal of Experimental Child Psychology*, 1964, *1*, 37–49.

Baer, D.M., Peterson, R.F., & Sherman, J.A. The development of imitation by reinforcing behavioral similarity to a model. *Journal of the Experimental Analysis of Behavior*, 1967, *10*, 405–416.

Bandura, A. Influence of models' reinforcement contingencies on the acquisition of imitative responses. *Journal of Personality and Social Psychology*, 1965, *1*, 589–595.

Bandura, A., & Huston, A.C. Identification as a process of incidental learning. *Journal of Abnormal and Social Psychology*, 1961, *63*, 311–318.

Bandura, A., & Menlove, F.L. Factors determining vicarious extinction of avoidance behavior through symbolic modeling. *Journal of Personality and Social Psychology*, 1968, *8*, 99–108.

Bandura, A., & Walters, R.H. *Social learning and personality development.* New York: Holt, Rinehart & Winston, 1963.

Bandura, A., Ross, D., & Ross, S. Vicarious reinforcement and imitative learning. *Journal of Abnormal and Social Psychology*, 1963, *6*, 601–607.

Bandura, A., Grusec, J.E., & Menlove, F.L. Vicarious extinction of avoidance behavior. *Journal of Personality and Social Psychology*, 1967, *5*, 16–23.

Barnwell, A., & Sechrest, L. Vicarious reinforcement in children at two age levels. *Journal of Educational Psychology*, 1965, *56*, 100–106.

Barry, N.J., & Overman, P.B. Comparison of the effectiveness of adult and peer models with EMR children. *American Journal of Mental Deficiency*, 1977, *82*, 33–36.

Becker, S., & Glidden, L. Imitation in EMR boys: Effects of model competency and age. *American Journal of Mental Deficiency*, 1979, *83*, 360–366.

Berkowitz, S. *Acquisition and maintenance of generalized imitative repertories of profound retardates with retarded peers functioning as models and reinforcing agents.* Unpublished doctoral dissertation, University of Maryland, 1968.

Biberdorff, J.R., & Pear, J.J. Two-to-one versus one-to-one student/teacher ratios in an operant verbal training of retarded children. *Journal of Applied Behavior Analysis*, 1977, *10*, 506.

Bijou, S., & Baer, D. *Child development.* New York: Appleton, Century, Crofts, 1965.

Birch, J.W. *Mainstreaming: Educable mentally retarded children in regular classes.* Reston, Va.: Council for Exceptional Children, 1974.

Bricker, D.D. A rationale for the integration of handicapped and nonhandicapped preschool children. In M.J. Guralnick (Ed.), *Early intervention and the integration of handicapped and nonhandicapped children.* Baltimore: University Park Press, 1978.

Bricker, D.D., & Sandall, S. Mainstreaming in preschool programs: Why and how to do it. *Education Unlimited*, 1979, *1*, 25–29.

Bricker, W.A., & Bricker, D.D. An early language training strategy. In R.L. Schiebelmusch & L.L. Lloyd (Eds.), *Language perspectives: Acquisition, retardation, and intervention.* Baltimore: University Park Press, 1974.

Bridges, K.M. A study of social development in early infancy. *Child Development*, 1933, *4*, 36–49.

Brigham, T.A., & Sherman, J.A. An experimental analysis of verbal imitation in preschool children. *Journal of Applied Behavior Analysis*, 1968, *1*, 151–160.

Bry, P.M., & Nawas, M.M. Is reinforcement necessary for the development of a generalized imitation operant in severely and profoundly retarded children? *American Journal of Mental Deficiency*, 1972, 76, 658–667.

Clark, B.S. The acquisition and extinction of peer imitation in children. *Psychonomic Science*, 1965, 2, 147–148.

Cooke, S.A., Cooke, T.P., & Apolloni, T. Developing nonretarded toddlers as verbal models for retarded classmates. *Child Study Journal*, 1978, 8, 1–8.

Cooke, T.P., Apolloni, T., & Cooke, S.A. The effects of a second nondelayed playmate on the free-play imitation and interaction of delayed and nondelayed children. *Mental Retardation*, in press.

Csapo, M. Peer models reverse the 'one bad apple spoils the barrel' theory. *Teaching Exceptional Children*, 1972, 4, 20–24.

Cullinan, D. Verbalization in EMR children's observational learning. *American Journal of Mental Deficiency*, 1976, 81, 65–72.

Debus, R.L. Effects of brief observation of model behavior on conceptual tempo of impulsive children. *Developmental Psychology*, 1970, 2, 22–32.

Devoney, C., Guralnick, M.J., & Rubin, H. Integrating handicapped and nonhandicapped preschool children: Effects on social play. *Childhood Education*, 1974, 50, 360–364.

Ditrichs, R., Simon, S., & Greene, B. Effects of vicarious scheduling on the verbal conditioning of hostility in children. *Journal of Personality and Social Psychology*, 1967, 6, 71–78.

Eckerman, C.O., Whatley, J.L., & Kutz, S.L. Growth of social play with peers during the second year of life. *Developmental Psychology*, 1975, 11, 42–49.

Elliot, R., & Vasta, R. The modeling of sharing: Effects associated with vicarious reinforcement, symbolization, age, and generalization. *Journal of Experimental Child Psychology*, 1970, 10, 8–15.

Evers-Pasquale, W., & Sherman, M. The reward value of peers: A variable influencing the efficacy of timed modeling in modifying social isolation in preschoolers. *Journal of Abnormal Child Psychology*, 1975, 3, 179–189.

Fechter, J.V. Modeling and environmental generalization by mentally retarded subjects of televised aggressive and friendly behavior. *American Journal of Mental Deficiency*, 1971, 76, 266–267.

Feitelson, D., Weintraub, S., & Michaeli, O. Social interactions in heterogeneous preschools in Israel. *Child Development*, 1972, 43, 1249–1259.

Flanders, J.P. A review of research on imitative behavior. *Psychological Bulletin*, 1968, 69, 316–337.

Forehand, R., Robbins, B., & Brady, C.P. Effects of IQ and mental age on verbal imitative performance of children. *Journal of Psychology*, 1973, 84, 353–358.

Fouts, G.T. Imitation in children: The effect of being imitated. *JSAS. Catalogue of Selected Documents in Psychology*, 1972, 2, 105.

Geshuri, Y. Observational learning: Effects of observed reward and response patterns. *Journal of Educational Psychology*, 1972, 63, 374–380.

Gewirtz, J.L., & Stingle, K.G. The learning of generalized imitation as the basis for identification. *Psychological Review*, 1968, 75, 374–397.

Goodman, A., Gottlieb, J., & Harrison, R.H. Social acceptance of EMR's integrated into a nongraded elementary school. *American Journal of Mental Deficiency*, 1972, 76, 412–417.

Gottlieb, J., & Davis, J.E. Social acceptance of EMR children during overt behavioral interactions. *American Journal of Mental Deficiency*, 1973, 78, 141–143.

Grossner, D., Polansky, N., & Lippitt, R. A laboratory study of behavioral contagion. *Human Relations*, 1951, 4, 115–142.

Guralnick, M.J. The value of integrating handicappped and nonhandicapped preschool children. *American Journal of Orthopsychiatry*, 1976, 42, 236–245.

Guralnick, M.J. (Ed.) *Early intervention and the integration of handicapped and nonhandicapped children.* Baltimore: University Park Press, 1978.

Hansen, J.C., Niland, T.M., & Zani, L.P. Model reinforcement in group counseling with elementary school children. *Personnel and Guidance Journal,* 1969, *47*, 741–744.

Hartup, W.W. Friendship status and the effectiveness of peers as reinforcing agents. *Journal of Experimental Child Psychology,* 1964, *1*, 154–162.

Hartup, W.W. Peer interaction and social organization. In P.H. Mussen (Ed.), *Carmichael's manual of child psychology Vol. 1 (3rd ed.).* New York: Wiley, 1970.

Hartup, W.W. Cross-age versus same-age peer interactions: Ethological and cross-cultural perceptives. In V.L. Allen (Ed.), *Children as teachers: Theory and research on tutoring.* New York: Academic Press, 1976.

Hartup, W.W. Peer interaction and the process of socialization. In M.J. Guralnick (Ed.), *Early intervention and the integration of handicapped and nonhandicapped children.* Baltimore: University Park Press, 1978.

Hartup, W.W., & Coates, B. Imitation of a peer as a function of reinforcement from the peer group and rewardingness of the model. *Child Development,* 1967, *38*, 1003–1016.

Hartup, W.W., & Coates, B. The role of imitation in childhood socialization. In R.A. Hoppe, G.A. Milton, & E.C. Simmel (Eds.), *Early experiences and the processes of socialization.* New York: Academic Press, 1970.

Hicks, D.J. Imitation and retention of film-mediated aggressive peer and adult models. *Journal of Personality and Social Psychology,* 1965, *2*, 97–100.

Ispa, J., & Matz, R.D. Integrating handicapped preschool children within a cognitively oriented program. In M.J. Guralnick (Ed.), *Early intervention and the integration of handicapped and nonhandicapped children.* Baltimore: University Park Press, 1978.

Jones, M.C. The elimination of children's fears. *Journal of Experimental Psychology,* 1924, *7*, 383–390.

Karnes, M.B., Teska, J.A., & Hodgins, A.S. The effects of four programs of classroom intervention on the intellectual and language development of four-year-old disadvantaged children. *American Journal of Orthopsychiatry,* 1970, *40*, 58–76.

Kauffman, J.M., Snell, M., & Hallahan, D.P. Imitating children during imitation training: Two experimental paradigms. *Education and Training of the Mentally Retarded,* 1976, *11*, 324–332.

Keller, M.F., & Carlson, P.M. The use of symbolic modeling to promote social skills in preschool children with low levels of social responsiveness. *Child Development,* 1974, *45*, 912–919.

Kindberg, M.N. Imitation of a peer model by severely retarded institutionalized boys. *Dissertation Abstracts,* 1971, *31*, 56,056–56,065.

Kornhaber, R.C., & Schroeder, H.E. Importance of model similarity on extinction of avoidance behavior in children. *Journal of Consulting and Clinical Psychology,* 1975, *43*, 601–607.

Langstaff-Psanella, A., & Volkmor, C. *Coming back (or never leaving).* Columbus, Ohio: Charles E. Merrill, 1976.

Litrownik, A.J. Observational learning in retarded and normal children as a function of delay between observation and opportunity to perform. *Journal of Experimental Child Psychology,* 1972, *14*, 117–125.

Lovaas, O.I., Freitas, L., Nelson, K., & Whalen, C. The establishment of imitation and its use for the development of complex behavior in schizophrenic children. *Behavior Research and Therapy,* 1967, *5*, 171–181.

Luchins, A.S., & Luchins, E.H. Intentional and unintentional models in social learning. *Journal of Social Psychology,* 1961, *54*, 321–325.

Madsen, C. Nurturance and modeling in preschoolers. *Child Development,* 1968, *39*, 221–236.

Mansdorf, I.J. Rapid token training of an institution ward using modeling. *Mental Retardation*, 1977, *15*, 37–39.

Meerbaum, M., Apolloni, T., & Shores, E.R. Role-playing to increase the social interaction of adult psychiatric day treatment patients. *Corrective and Social Psychiatry and Journal of Behavior Technology Methods and Therapy*, 1976, *22*, 28–32.

Metz, J.R. Conditioning generalized imitation in autistic children. *Journal of Experimental Child Psychology*, 1965, *2*, 389–399.

Miller, G.J. An on-campus community living center for the mentally retarded. *Training School Bulletin*, 1974, *71*, 112–118.

Miller, N.E., & Dollard, J. *Social learning and imitation*. New Haven: Yale University Press, 1941.

Miller, R.S., & Morris, W.N. The effects of being imitated on children's responses in a marble-dropping task. *Child Development*, 1974, *45*, 1103–1107.

Mischel, W., & Grusec, J. Determinants of the rehearsal and transmission of neutral aversive behaviors. *Journal of Personality and Social Psychology*, 1966, *3*, 197–205.

Morris, W.N., Marshall, H.M., & Miller, R.S. The effect of vicarious punishment on prosocial behavior in children. *Journal of Experimental Child Psychology*, 1973, *15*, 222–236.

Mowrer, O.H. *Learning theory and the symbolic process*. New York: Wiley, 1960.

Nordquist, V.M. A behavioral approach to the analysis of peer interactions. In M.J. Guralnick (Ed.), *Early intervention and the integration of handicapped and nonhandicapped children*. Baltimore: University Park Press, 1978.

O'Connor, R.D. Modification of social withdrawal through symbolic modeling. *Journal of Applied Behavior Analysis*, 1969, *2* 15–22.

O'Connor, R.D. Relative efficacy of modeling, shaping, and combined procedures for modification of social withdrawal. *Journal of Abnormal Psychology*, 1972, *79*, 327–334.

Palyo, W., Cooke, T.P., Peck, C.A., & Apolloni, T. *An observational study of social interaction in an integrated preschool*. Unpublished manuscript, Sonoma State University, 1977.

Parton, D.A. Learning to imitate in infancy. *Child Development*, 1976, *47*, 14–31.

Peck, C.A., Apolloni, T., Cooke, T.P., Raver, S.A. Teaching retarded preschoolers to initiate the free-play behavior of nonretarded classmates: Trained and generalized effects. *Journal of Special Education*, 1978, *12*, 195–207.

Peck, C.A., Cooke, T.P., Ruskus, J., & Apolloni, T. *Developmental gains of children in integrated preschools: A two year study*. Unpublished manuscript, California Institute on Human Services, 1980.

Peterson, C., Peterson, J., & Scriven, G. Peer imitation by nonhandicapped and handicapped preschoolers. *Exceptional Children*, 1977, *43*, 223–225.

Peterson, N.L., & Haralick, J.G. Integration of handicapped and nonhandicapped preschoolers: An analysis of play behavior and social interaction. *Education and Training of the Mentally Retarded*, 1977, *12*, 235–245.

Peterson, R.F. Imitation: A basic behavioral mechanism. In H.M. Sloane, Jr., & B.P. MacAulay (Eds.), *Operant procedures in remedial speech and language training*. New York: Houghton Mifflin, 1968.

Piaget, J. *Play, dreams, and imitation in childhood*. New York: W.W. Norton, 1951.

Porter, R.H., Ramsey, B., Tremblay, A., Iaccobo, M., & Crawley, S. Social interaction in heterogeneous groups of retarded and normally developing children: An observational study. In G.P. Sackett & H.C. Haywood (Eds.), *Application of observational/ethological methods to the study of mental retardation*. Baltimore: University Park Press, 1978.

Public Law 94–142. Education for All Handicapped Children Act, 1975, 88 Stat. 733 (Codified at 20 U.S.C. 1232–1453).

Ray, J.D. *Behavior of developmentally delayed and nondelayed toddler-age children: An ethological study*. Unpublished doctoral dissertation, George Peabody College, 1974.

Rehabilitation Act of 1973, Section 504. *Federal Register,* 1977, *42,* No. 86, 22676–22702.

Ridberg, E.H., Parke, D., & Hetherington, E.M. Modification of impulsive and reflective cognitive styles through observation of film mediated models. *Developmental Psychology,* 1971, *5,* 369–377.

Rosekrans, M.A. Imitation in children as a function of perceived similarity to a social model and vicarious reinforcement. *Journal of Personality and Social Psychology,* 1967, *7,* 307–315.

Rosenbaum, M.E. The effect of verbalization of correct responses by performers and observers on retention. *Child Development,* 1967, *38,* 615–622.

Ross, D.M. Effect on learning of psychological attachment to a film model. *American Journal of Mental Deficiency,* 1970, *74,* 701–707.

Ross, D.M., & Ross, S.A. The efficacy of listening training for educable mentallyretarded children. *American Journal of Mental Deficiency,* 1972, *77,* 137–142.

Rubenstein, J., & Howes, C. The effects of peers on toddler interaction with mother and toys. *Child Development,* 1976, *47,* 597–605.

Scriven, M. Some issues in the logic and ethics of mainstreaming. *Minnesota Education,* 1976, *2,* 61–67.

Segal, R. Current trends in the pattern and delivery of services to the mentally retarded. *Mental Retardation,* 1971, *9,* 44–47.

Sidman, M. *Tactics of scientific research: Evaluating experimental data in psychology.* New York: Basic Books, 1960.

Snyder, L., Apolloni, T., & Cooke, T.P. Integrated settings at the early childhood level: The role of nonretarded peers. *Exceptional Children,* 1977, *43,* 262–266.

Strain, P.S., & Timm, M.A. An experimental analysis of social interaction between a behaviorally disordered preschool child and her classroom peers. *Journal of Applied Behavior Analysis,* 1974, *7,* 583–590.

Strain, P.S., Cooke, T.P., & Apolloni, T. *Teaching exceptional children: Assessing and modifying social behavior.* New York: Academic Press, 1976.

Strain, P.S., Shores, R.E., & Timm, M.A. Effects of peer imitation on social behavior of withdrawn preschool children. *Journal of Applied Behavior Analysis,* 1977, *10,* 289–298.

Stumphauzer, J.S. Increased delay of gratification in young prison inmates through imitation of high delay peer models. *Journal of Personality and Social Psychology,* 1972, *21,* 10–17.

Talkington, L.W., & Altman, R. Effects of film-mediated aggressive and affectual models on behavior. *American Journal of Mental Deficiency,* 1973, *77,* 420–425.

Talkington, L.W., Hall, S.M., & Altman, R. Use of a peer modeling procedure with severely retarded subjects on a basic communication response skill. *The Training School Bulletin,* 1973, *69,* 145–149.

Thelen, M.H., & Kirkland, K.D. On status and being imitated: Effects on reciprocal imitation and attraction. *Journal of Personality and Social Psychology,* 1976, *33,* 691–697.

Toner, S., & Moore, L. The effect of serving as a model of self-control on subsequent resistance to deviation in children. *Journal of Experimental Child Psychology,* 1978, *26,* 85–91.

Westaway, A., & Apolloni, T. *Becoming independent: A living skills system.* Bellevue, Wa.: Edmark, 1978.

Whalen, C.K., & Henker, B.A. Creating therapeutic pyramids using mentally retarded patients. *American Journal of Mental Deficiency,* 1969, *74,* 331–337.

Whalen, C.K., & Henker, B.A. Pyramid therapy in a hospital for the retarded: Methods, program evaluation, and long-term effects. *American Journal of Mental Deficiency,* 1971, *75,* 414–434.

Wolf, M.M. Social validity: The case for subjective measurement or how applied behavior analysis is finding its heart. *Journal of Applied Behavior Analysis,* 1978, *11,* 203–214.

Wolfensberger, W. *The principle of normalization in human services*. Toronto: National Institute on Mental Retardation, 1972.

Wynne, S., Ulfelder, L.S., & Dakof, G. *Mainstreaming and early childhood education for handicapped children: Review and implications of research*. Washington, D.C.: Division of Innovation and Development, BEH-USOE, 1975.

4

The Use of Peer Social Initiations in the Treatment of Social Withdrawal

PHILLIP S. STRAIN, MARY MARGARET KERR, AND
ELIZABETH U. RAGLAND

INTRODUCTION

In the 1920s, 1930s, and 1940s, the social interactions of young children were the subject of extensive observational study. However, none of these early naturalistic investigations was aimed at remediating social withdrawal. Also, from the 1940s to the 1970s, only sporadic attention was paid to the assessment and treatment of children's social behavior. Strain, Cooke, and Apolloni (1976) characterized the information base for improving the social behaviors of withdrawn children as neglectful. In addition to their review, other recent commentaries on the assessment and modification of social withdrawal (Hops, in press; Hops & Greenwood, in press) have concluded that the lack of attention to children's peer relations resulted from the Piagetian and Freudian theories that dominated psychological conceptions of development for many years.

In this chapter, we will highlight one of the principal peer-mediated intervention techniques developed to remediate social isolation—namely, the use of social initiations delivered by peers. Before examining the empirical research evaluating this treatment approach and discussing issues of clinical application, a brief review of the importance of remediat-

PHILLIP S. STRAIN ● Western Psychiatric Institute and Clinic, University of Pittsburgh School of Medicine, Pittsburgh, Pennsylvania 15261.   MARY MARGARET KERR ● Western Psychiatric Institute and Clinic, University of Pittsburgh.   ELIZABETH U. RAGLAND ● Nashville-Metro Public Schools, Nashville, Tennessee 37215.

ing social withdrawal and other peer-mediated intervention paradigms will be provided.

The Importance of Remediating Social Withdrawal

Why be concerned about peer relations in the first place? This is a question frequently asked by individuals who are primarily responsible for children's education and mental health. More often than not educators and mental-health professionals are exclusively involved with academic-skills development, controlling aggressive, acting-out behavior, and developing better parent–child and teacher–child interactions. Notwithstanding the secondary role that peer social relations have played, an ever-increasing literature points to the critical importance of child–child interaction in the development of a broad array of competencies. To answer the question, "Why be concerned with peer relations," it is necessary to examine those functional skills that develop during the course of social interaction among children and also to explore the consequences of not developing satisfactory relationships with peers.

Development of Behavioral Competencies during Peer Interaction

First of all, it is important to note that the behavioral competencies that are displayed and apparently acquired during children's peer interactions are independent of similar skills that are associated with adult–child interaction. This separation of skill development is particularly pronounced from the age of two onward.

Prior to the child's second birthday, it is clear that a series of complex behaviors have emerged that the infant uses to communicate with and control the social environment. In the area of auditory functioning, the newborn displays an exceptional ability to discriminate between such fine phonemic differences in adult speech as "b" and "d." Similarly, newborns of either sex exhibit a consistent physical-orientation response toward the direction of female as opposed to male voices that are both unfamiliar or familiar.

In the area of verbal behavior, the social contacts between infants as young as three months and their caretakers closely match the structure of verbal exchanges between adults. That is, infant and caretaker engage in vocal dialogues characterized by a talk-listen, listen-talk sequence with few interruptions of one another's speech (Anderson, Vietze, & Dokecki, 1977). Even at three months, infant speech is carefully regulated to the vocal behavior of social partners.

As early as one month, social attention has been shown to be a powerful and consistent reinforcing stimulus. In studies using both familiar and unfamiliar adults' contingent social attention, infants' vocalizations, activity level, and manipulative responses have been altered systematically (see Rheingold, Gewirtz, & Ross, 1959; Weisberg, 1963).

As the infant's babbling becomes more frequent, rather distinct differences emerge in the complexity of these vocalizations across social and nonsocial settings. For example, most of the vocal behaviors exhibited by infants as they examine a part of their anatomy or a toy are redundant (for example, "ba, ba, ba, ba," or "oh, oh, oh") and contain few alterations in pitch or volume. In contrast, the vocal behavior of the infant can be very complex when a caretaker is present, particularly in a face-to-face orientation. Not only do fluctuations in the content of speech (for example "ba, da, ga") occur, but the infant changes the pitch and volume of utterances such that "exclamatory" or "interrogatory" babbles are produced.

Toward the end of the first year of life, infants may exhibit a stress response when they are removed from the presence of one caretaker (usually mother) with whom they have developed a primary attachment (Bowlby, 1969). The literature on infant attachment has been characterized by considerable theoretical and methodological debate; however, few would argue that this transitory social-response pattern does not regularly occur across child-rearing situations that include both singular- and multiple-caretaking traditions (Ainsworth, 1963).

Although the opportunities for peer interaction during the first two years of life are often limited by social convention and the social partners provided to infants, these early social encounters do represent quite regularized events. In one of the first studies of interaction among infants, Buhler (1931) found that children from six to 18 months engaged in frequent, positive interaction when they participated in daily play sessions. The majority of the positive contacts were composed of sharing responses involving a toy or material. It is important to note that the children were not encouraged by adults in any way to play with each other. In a later study of interaction among infants, Maudry and Nekula (1939) observed a developmental change in the number of positive and negative interactions across nine- to 25-month-old youngsters. Specifically, dyads of children from nine to 13 months often quarreled over ownership of a toy, whereas interactions among children from 19 to 25 months were largely positive. Recently, Meighan and Birr (1979) have observed infants up to 12 months touching each other several hundred times a day in a free-play setting with no adult involvement.

The social-behavior developments during the first two years of life are indeed remarkable. The child's auditory and vocal functioning are keenly attuned to the behavior of social partners; interactions with peers are sought out, and they become quite positive; a sophisticated system of verbal communication is rapidly developing; and social attention has a profound influence on the child's entire behavior repertoire (Strain, 1980). When these developments are contrasted with the isolate child's generalized avoidance and rejection of social stimuli, one can readily understand the clinical and developmental significance of social withdrawal.

As play among toddlers becomes more regularized, a number of social, manipulative, and cognitive skills can be observed. For example, children's social interactions develop a reciprocal quality (Mueller, 1972; Strain & Shores, 1977). That is, when a child initiates a positive social behavior toward another (e.g., says "Hi"), it is most likely that the social partner will reciprocate in a positive fashion. By age three the probability of a positive response has been found to be as high as .97 (Greenwood, Walker, & Hops, 1977). Also, cooperation between children can be enhanced by increasing the number of social encounters between them (Cook & Stingle, 1974).

In other areas of behavioral development, toddlers' object manipulations are more functionally appropriate and mature during social as opposed to solitary play (Rubenstein & Howes, 1976). There is also some evidence that preschool children's verbal behaviors with younger peers serve to stimulate more elaborate verbal utterances by the latter (Garvey & Hogan, 1973). Hops (in press) has observed that many of the positive effects of participating in social interaction may result from the prerequisites for successful peer relations. Several of these prerequisites include appropriate toy use, ability to discriminate between playful approaches and physical assaults, ability to discriminate between fantasy and real situations, and ability to abstract and conform to rules of organized play (see Garvey, 1976).

Negative Consequences of Social Withdrawal

Hartup (1979) and Strain, Cooke, and Apolloni (1976) have proposed that socially withdrawn children are at risk in the areas of language acquisition, moral values, and socially acceptable methods of expressing sexual and aggressive feelings. Moreover, the negative consequences of withdrawal may persist into adolescence and adulthood (Bronson, 1968; Strain, 1980). In fact, Strain (1980) has noted that childhood social withdrawal is the single most powerful behavioral predictor of adult social-adjustment problems.

Researchers have consistently identified withdrawal as a primary dimension of behavioral disorders during childhood and adolescence (Becker, 1960; Walker, 1970). Hops (in press) has noted that social withdrawal has been established as a unique clinical disorder regardless of whether parents, teachers, or peers have furnished the data on problematic behaviors.

There is also an increasing amount of evidence that problems associated with social isolation are relatively stable phenomena. For example, Waldrop and Halverson (1975) conducted a longitudinal study of the quality and quantity of social behaviors exhibited by children 2½ to 7½ years old. Group and individual-subject data revealed only minor fluctuations in overall social responsiveness.

Not only does social withdrawal represent a stable pattern of behavior during childhood, but it also may set the occasion for more extended negative consequences. Using a retrospective research paradigm, Birren (1944), Frazee (1953), and O'Neal and Robins (1958) demonstrated that a large proportion of adults requiring psychiatric care were described by parents and teachers as shy, withdrawn young children. The results of longitudinal research also indicate that the effects of childhood social withdrawal may persist into adolescence and adulthood. Roff, Sells, and Golden (1972) found that children described as "loners" during the elementary grades were represented disproportionately in groups of juvenile delinquents, school dropouts during adolescence, and adults who required mental-health services. Similarly, Robins (1966) observed that socially withdrawn children were more likely than socially skilled children to be referred for psychiatric treatment as adults.

In summary, social withdrawal represents a response pattern that inhibits the child's acquisition of many adaptive behaviors and thus may set the occasion for marginal adjustment throughout the life span.

OTHER PEER-MEDIATED INTERVENTIONS

Besides peer social initiations, three rather distinct peer-mediated interventions have been validated with socially isolate children: (a) prompting and reinforcement, (b) modeling, and (c) incidental peer influence. Each of these procedures and available treatment data will be briefly summarized.

PROMPTING AND REINFORCEMENT

Of the several peer-mediated strategies, prompting and reinforcement requires the most continuous teacher management of peer behavior. Here, the teacher utilizes the same procedures (prompting and reinforcement) as are used in adult-mediated interventions with an isolate child, but instead applies them to a peer (or peers) to increase approach behaviors to withdrawn children. The teacher may verbally and/or physically cue the peer(s) to approach and interact with the isolate child, repeating these prompts whenever the isolate child is engaged in solitary behaviors. Nordquist and Bradley (1973) used this technique to increase a peer's cooperative-play behavior with a nonverbal, socially withdrawn preschool girl. The peer confederate's later absence forced these investigators to employ direct teacher-reinforcement procedures. Nevertheless, Nordquist and Bradley's data show that prompting and reinforcement of the peer was critical to establishing cooperative-play behavior with the target youngster.

Other reports on the prompting and reinforcement strategy (*SCIP Year End Report,* 1979) indicate that the technique can itself reduce social withdrawal. Six preschool- and elementary-age boys and girls participated in studies using this strategy. Teachers initially taught peers to emit several social-approach behaviors which had been empirically identified (Tremblay, Strain, Hendrickson, & Shores, in press) as having a high probability of setting the occasion for reciprocal interaction. The teachers then provided verbal instructions to the peers to interact with a withdrawn child and occasionally praised the peers' approach behaviors. These prompting and reinforcement procedures resulted in substantial increases in the overall social responsiveness of the withdrawn children.

The above-mentioned studies show that a teacher's direct involvement in altering withdrawn behavior can be effectively limited to intermittently observing and assessing the level of target children's social behavior. If the withdrawn child is engaging in isolate activity, then prompts and occasional reinforcement can be directed toward a trained peer for initiating play with the target child.

PEER MODELING

As applied to managing social withdrawal, peer modeling consists of having withdrawn children view a peer or peers engaging in specific, positive social behaviors or view peers engaged in ongoing interaction. Subsequent performance of the modeled behaviors may (e.g., O'Connor, 1972; Walker & Hops, 1973) or may not (e.g., O'Connor, 1969; Keller & Carlson, 1974) be reinforced directly. The medium through which modeling is effected may be live demonstration (e.g., Apolloni, Cooke, & Cooke, 1977) or pictorial/filmed presentation (e.g., O'Connor, 1969, 1972).

In an initial, filmed-peer-modeling approach, O'Connor (1969) studied 13 preschool children, nominated by their teachers as isolate and observed to interact with peers less than 15% of the baseline observation intervals. These children were randomly assigned to experimental and control groups in which they watched either a nature film or a peer-interaction film. The experimental film showed several peer models engaging in sequences of cooperative, social activities. The audio portion of the film was designed to draw the viewer's attention to the positive, cooperative aspects of the interaction. Immediate posttreatment change in social interaction was then assessed in the children's regular classrooms. Two clear results emerged: (a) only the peer-modeling group's social interaction increased significantly above their baseline levels; and (b) not only was the peer-modeling group significantly more social than the control group following exposure to the film, but they also closely approximated social-interaction levels of children identified by the teacher as socially competent. In a later replication effort, O'Connor (1972) reported that the peer-modeling film alone was as effective as a peer-modeling and direct-shaping package for increasing the amount of time that isolate children interacted with peers. Also, the film alone produced superior results at a six-week follow-up.

In a replication of the peer-modeling and peer-modeling-plus-shaping approach, Evers and Schwartz (1973) found peer modeling alone to be superior to the modeling-plus-shaping procedure at an immediate posttest. However, no differences across the two groups were evident at a later follow-up assessment. Evers and Schwartz propose that direct shaping of social behaviors may have disrupted ongoing child–child interactions. Recently, this notion has received increased support. Strain and Hill (1979) reanalyzed data from the Strain and Timm (1974) and Strain, Shores, and Kerr (1976) studies of direct prompting and reinforcement of social interaction and found that positive interactions between children had a reduced likelihood of occurrence immediately following teacher reinforcement of social interaction.

In contrast to earlier studies which employed a single showing of a 20-min peer-modeling film, Jakubcheck and Smeriglio (1976) and Keller and Carlson (1974) used four four-min peer-modeling films which were shown once a day for four days. Jakubcheck and Smeriglio also employed two different types of peer models which were associated with differential levels of posttreatment social-behavior change. A "coping" peer model who narrated the film in a first-person voice was associated with significantly greater increases in positive behavior than a peer model who narrated the same action in a third-person voice. Keller and Carlson found that peer modeling which focused on specific social behaviors (imitation, smiling-laughing, token giving and affection) increased only those behaviors (smiling, imitation, and verbalization) which were of relatively higher frequency during baseline.

Live peer models also have been found to have a positive influence on withdrawn children. Apolloni and Cooke (1978) have described a series of studies (Apolloni et al., 1977; Cooke, Apolloni, & Cooke, 1976; Cooke, Cooke, & Apolloni, 1977; Peck, Apolloni, Cooke, & Cooke, 1976) in which developmentally delayed children were taught to imitate various play behaviors by a nondelayed peer. The live-modeling procedure differs from the filmed-model tactic in one important way. Adult-mediated prompting and reinforcement of the delayed child for imitation of the peer's behavior is an integral part of the live-modeling procedure. For example, Peck *et al.* (1976) required the delayed child to observe free-play behaviors of the peer model during a regular free-play period. Performance of similar free-play behaviors by the delayed child was prompted and praised by an adult. When both delayed and normal peer models were prompted and praised for imitating each other, appropriate, reciprocal imitation and interaction between the normal and delayed children increased. As Apolloni and Cooke (1978) pointed out, this finding is especially noteworthy since previous research has documented that natural rates of interaction and imitation between handicapped and nonhandicapped children are typically low (Allen, Benning, & Drummond, 1972; Devoney, Guralnick, & Robin, 1974; Guralnick, 1976; Ray, 1974).

It appears that both filmed and live peer models can facilitate the performance of discrete social behaviors and of more complex interactions (e.g., O'Connor, 1969). However, peer modeling by itself may not be sufficient to teach new or low-incidence behaviors (Keller & Carlson, 1974). Also, Apolloni and Cooke (1978) have shown that bidirectional modeling between withdrawn children and their peers increases the likelihood of reciprocal social interaction between handicapped and nonhandicapped children.

INCIDENTAL PEER INFLUENCE

Peer prompting and reinforcement and peer modeling constitute rather distinct intervention techniques. However, several other techniques have been reported which in some way involve the use of peers but do not fit easily into well-defined categories. This final, loosely associated group of techniques includes vicarious-reinforcement processes, group contingencies, and sociometric pairings. These tactics include procedures which have been implemented to effect changes in withdrawn children's behavior (e.g., sociometric pairing), and of "side effects" accruing to one withdrawn child when directly intervening with another youngster (e.g., vicarious reinforcement).

Vicarious reinforcement is said to occur when a withdrawn child's social behavior increases as a function of observing another child being reinforced for positive social behaviors. Thus, in a classroom where one withdrawn child is the target of a reinforcement-based intervention, side effects on other withdrawn children may occur although they are not direct recipients of that intervention. This phenomenon was termed "spillover" by Strain, Shores, and Kerr (1976), who investigated its effects on three socially withdrawn children. Direct teacher prompting and reinforcement of positive social behaviors was introduced sequentially for the preschool boys. This intervention increased the positive social behaviors of the subjects to whom it was applied, and smaller, though consistent, increases were observed for two of the three subjects when they were not receiving prompts and reinforcement. In a replication of Strain, Shores, and Kerr's prompting and reinforcement procedure with a more severely handicapped (autistic) population, Strain, Kerr, and Ragland (1979) were able to increase the positive social behaviors of these socially withdrawn children only when the intervention package was applied directly to each child.

It would appear, then, that vicarious-reinforcement effects are not a predictable outcome (Strain & Fox, 1981). Analyses sufficient to isolate the factors which result in spillover effects have yet to be conducted. At this point, vicarious reinforcement should be viewed as a supplemental intervention tactic to reduce social withdrawal.

Another peer technique which has had incidental effects on socially withdrawn children was reported by Walker and Hops (1973). Each of three withdrawn youngsters was involved in one of three different interventions. In the peer-mediated tactic, an elementary-school girl who made few approaches to classroom peers was selected as the target of a group "peer-intervention." All children in the classroom, except the target child, saw one presentation of O'Connor's (1969, 1972) social-interaction-modeling film. Next, the class peers were informed that a group contingency was to be instituted in which they could earn points by getting the withdrawn classmate to initiate interactions with them. Points could be exchanged for a back-up consequence when the target child had made 25 initiations to her peers. Following implementation of this group contingency, initiations by peers to the isolate child and by the isolate child showed a substantial increase. The classroomwide effects obtained by Walker and Hops argue that this modeling and group-contingency package may improve both the social behavior of withdrawn children and the social system of which that child is a part.

All of the peer-mediated techniques presented thus far have involved the application of well-delineated antecedent and/or consequent events to alter withdrawn behavior. The impact of these environmental-change tactics has been assessed by directly observing changes in specific social behaviors of the withdrawn child and peers. A conceptually different peer-mediated approach derives from sociometry (Gronlund, 1959), which is concerned primarily with sociometric standing and accompanying interventions that include a variety of treatment tactics.

Chennault (1967) reported the successful use of a sociometric-pairing technique. Children from 16 intermediate- and junior-high-school classes completed sociometric questionnaires measuring peer acceptance and perceived peer acceptance. The four lowest-rated children in each class were selected as target subjects and randomly assigned to experimental and control groups. The experimental subjects then participated with the two highest-rated students from each class in the planning, rehearsing, and presenting of a skit. Control subjects received no intervention. Post-test measurement indicated that the experimental subjects increased their sociometric standing and were now rated much higher than control subjects.

In a similar study, Lilly (1971) grouped low-achieving, low-status children with high-status peers in making a movie for later presentation to the entire class. The planned interactions occurred twice weekly for five weeks. Results showed that the target children received more favorable social-acceptance scores immediately after treatment. However, the gains washed out over a six-week period.

The same basic pairing tactic has been used to improve the social status of mainstreamed, mildly retarded children (Ballard, Corman, Gottlieb, & Kaufman, 1977). Target children and their regular classmates were placed together in a group whose goal was to create a multimedia project. The groups met 40 min each day for eight weeks. Each child was rated by peers as being "liked," "disliked," or "neutral." The target children received significantly more "liked" ratings as compared to a nontreatment control group. These gains were maintained at a two-week follow-up assessment. Although the number of students rating the handicapped children as acceptable increased, the number of rejection ratings was not altered. Hops (in press) has commented that these data indicate the independence of peer acceptance and rejection, and that it is difficult to know at what stage of acceptance-rejection the child becomes liked by class peers.

Peer Social Initiations

In an initial study, Strain, Shores, and Timm (1977) trained two four-year-old age peers to serve as intervention agents with six severely handicapped preschool boys. The target children ranged in IQ from 30 to 58, and each boy displayed a wide variety of inappropriate and bizarre behaviors. Four 20-min training sessions were conducted with each of the normally functioning age peers. During these sessions the age peers learned and rehearsed a number of verbal and motoric behaviors to engage the target children in social play. First, the peers learned to initiate play by emitting phrases such as, "Come and play," "Let's play ball." Next, the children were taught to engage in those motor behaviors that would naturally accompany the verbal play overtures. For example, the peers would say "Let's play ball," and then roll a ball to the experimenter. Each session contained 30 discrete opportunities to practice appropriate initiations. On half of these occasions the experimenter would ignore the child's overture for 10 sec and then say, "Sometimes children will not want to play at first, but you need to keep asking them to play." During an initial baseline period the target subjects rarely engaged in any positive interaction, and their age peers initiated only occasional social behaviors toward the six youngsters. When the peers were first instructed to play with the target subjects, two results were obtained. First, each target subject's responses to initiations immediately increased; and second, the positive initiations of all but one child also increased. Treatment effects were replicated during subsequent return to baseline (low levels of initiations) and intervention phases. The one subject whose level of initiations did not increase was more severely language-delayed than his peers. This child had a three-word vocabulary, "Yes," "No," and "Mommy." However, he did not necessarily use these words on appropriate occasions.

In order to determine whether the effects produced by this peer-mediated intervention would generalize to another setting and maintain across a short time span, Strain (1977) conducted a systematic replication of the Strain, Shores, and Timm (1977) study. Three preschool-age boys were treated by one normally developing age peer. The target children had IQs of 55, 47, and 50 and ranged in age from 43 to 51 months. The children's expressive-language development was at a one-year-old level and they were observed to be extremely oppositional to adults' requests. Two of the boys were echolalic and self-stimulatory. A peer-training approach identical to that used by Strain, Shores, and Timm was employed. The intervention sessions in the withdrawal-of-treatment design took place in a small playroom. Generalization to another setting was assessed by observing the subjects in a regular free-play period in their classroom (the peer trainer was absent from this setting). Maintenance of behavior change across time was assessed by conducting observations in the subjects' classroom immediately or 23 hr after intervention. Data from both intervention and generalization sessions showed an increase in social responding when intervention was in effect. For two of the subjects, a fivefold increase in the frequency of positive social behavior obtained during treatment sessions. The remaining child's level of positive social behavior increased from an average of one positive behavior per five-min session to an average of four per session. For the first two children, an increase in positive social behavior was noted in the generalization session. Here, the children were responding at twice the level observed during baseline. The child who was affected minimally in the treatment setting showed no sign of generalized behavior change. Maintenance effects were found also for the first two children, as no differences in performance were noted for generalization sessions that occurred immediately after treatment or 23 hr later.

The differential responsiveness of these subjects to the intervention procedures highlights the need for more extensive and fine behavioral assessments of social withdrawal. From the present data system it is only possible to say that the child who showed little improvement had a lower baseline level of positive social behavior than his peers. However, other behavioral characteristics may have operated to diminish treatment effects with this child. For example, this youngster engaged in a high rate of self-stimulatory activity and on occasion he would scream loudly when a peer interrupted his behavior.

More direct evidence of the interaction between the inappropriate behaviors of autistic children and the impact of peer social intiations has been provided by Ragland, Kerr, and Strain (1978). When compared to children treated in earlier studies of peer social initiations, the subjects in this investigation engaged in more active withdrawal from peers and adults and more extensive forms of bizarre behavior. The first subject, Sally, had a measured IQ of 35. She was echolalic, frequently avoided eye contact, and engaged in lint picking, object twirling, and scratching of herself. The second child, Darrin, was a nine-year-old boy who obtained a Vineland Social Maturity Scale score of 36 months. His speech was unintelligible and he continually engaged in some form of self-stimulation, including thumb sucking, twirling objects, finger tapping, and tongue clicking. The final subject, Dennis, was a nine-year-old boy who obtained an IQ score of 64. He had a history of petit-mal seizures and bizarre verbalizations. At the time he participated in the peer-mediated treatment, Dennis's primary verbal behavior involved his fantasy of being a car. Also, Dennis was observed to bite and pinch himself when adults made requests of him. The peer trainer in this study was a ten-year-old boy who was enrolled in a class for children with learning and behavior problems. He had a long history of academic failure and disruptive classroom behavior. However, he was a child with exceptional social skills and he got along well with his peers. A peer-training approach similar to that used in earlier studies was employed. One important change was made. When the experimenter did not respond positively to initiations by the peer trainer, she exhibited some of the self-stimulatory and avoidance behavior typical of the target subjects. The design employed was a withdrawal-of-treatment tactic with multiple baseline procedures. In other words, intervention was begun and terminated at different times for each child. The initial baseline phase indicated that Sally engaged in no positive or negative social behaviors. Darrin participated in approximately three times the number of negative as opposed to positive behaviors during the initial baseline. Dennis, on the other hand, engaged in an equal number of positive and negative behaviors. The onset of peer social initiations produced an immediate increase in positive social behavior by each subject. In return to baseline and subsequent intervention conditions the treatment effect was replicated. Besides an increase in positive responding, the social-initiation treatment had a tendency to increase negative interactions by Sally and Darrin, especially during the first several days of each intervention phase. Observers in the play setting reported that the peer trainer often interrupted Sally and Darrin while they were engaging in some self-stimulatory activity. When this happened, these children would often scream, run away, or push the peer aside. After the first day in which this situation occurred, the experimenter made sure to remind the peer after each session that sometimes children would respond in this way.

In a final study using peer-mediated treatment, Strain and colleagues (1979) attempted to compare the effectiveness of two treatment tactics: (a) peer social initiations, and (b) peer prompting and social reinforcement. Four elementary-age children served as target subjects. Earl was a nine-year-old boy who obtained an IQ score of 38. He was first seen at a psychiatric facility at age three. At the time of the study he was not toilet trained, he often cried for long periods of time, and was observed to engage in a high rate of self-stimulatory activity. Most of his verbal behavior was composed of calling his own name. Sue was a 10-year-old girl who was echolalic and extremely oppositional to adults' requests. She was also observed to tantrum when approached by peers. Tom was a 10-year-old boy who engaged in a high rate of self-stimulatory behavior and unintelligible verbalizations. He obtained an IQ score of 44. The final subject, Carl, was a 10-year-old boy who was described as hyperactive, and nonresponsive to adults' requests. During a typical free-play period he would pull fabric from the carpet, slap a ball against the wall, and giggle. One-half of the peer training was identical to that employed by Ragland et al. (1978). During the remaining portion, the peer was taught a prompting and reinforcement strategy. The experimenter told the peer that he would be getting two of the children at a time to play with each other. The peer was instructed to rehearse such prompting statements as: "Roll the ball to————", "Give————a block," "Push the truck to————." Later, the peer began to practice such praise statements as: "Good,————," "That's the way to play," "Very nice,————," The study employed two separate withdrawal-of-treatment designs (ABAC and ACAB), with two subjects exposed to each order of treatment. Sue and Carl composed one dyad for treatment while Tom and Earl were paired together during intervention periods. During the first intervention phase, the prompting and reinforcement treatment was applied to Sue and Carl. The initial intervention for Tim and Earl was composed of peer social initiations. These treatments were later reversed for the two dyads. A generalization assessment was conducted each day 23 hr after intervention. The findings suggest that: (a) both treatment procedures resulted in an immediate increase in the level of positive social behavior by each child; (b) a comparable behavior change was associated with the two treatment procedures; and (c) no generalized behavior change was associated with either treatment procedure.

It has been well established that peer-mediated interventions can alter the frequency of positive social behaviors emitted by seriously disturbed and autistic children. However, it would be unreasonable to expect peer-mediated initiations to be equally effective with every child. It seems likely that a child's entry-level behavior repertoire may inhibit or enhance the effects of intervention. Although sufficient research into the precise nature and function of mediating subject variables has yet to be done, it seems important to note them nonetheless.

Several studies using the social-initiation treatment have found a direct relationship between initial baseline performance and the effectiveness of treatment (Strain, 1977; Strain et al., 1977). Specifically, withdrawn children who displayed lower baseline levels of positive social behavior were less responsive to treatment than youngsters with a relatively higher baseline performance. However, when the social-initiation treatment was applied to children who engaged in a high level of self-stimulatory activity, no relationship was noted between subjects' initial baseline performance and treatment outcomes (e.g., Ragland et al., 1978; Strain et al., 1979). One possible explanation for these divergent findings is that self-stimulatory behavior may compete with or mask children's existing social repertoire.

Other components of a child's nonsocial repertoire may also affect the degree of behavior change associated with peer social initiations. For example, Guralnick (1976) has suggested that imitative skills represent a critical prerequisite for successful peer-mediated treatment. Also, a number of investigators have indicated that appropriate toy and material use can impact significantly on intervention effectiveness (Apolloni & Cooke, 1978).

Assessment and Treatment Evaluation

In the vast majority of intervention research, rate or frequency of global-interaction categories has been used to identify withdrawn children and monitor the effects of treatment. Typical categories of interaction include "positive motor-gestural," "positive vocal-verbal," and "positive social behavior." While it is true that global-response categories have proven to be sensitive to treatment effects, they provide little information for on-line personnel regarding what to teach.

Recently, a number of attempts have been made to specify those positive social behaviors of preschool children that set the occasion for reciprocal social interaction. Tremblay, Strain, Hendrickson, and Shores (in press) studied the social interactions of 61 preschool children over a two-month period. Each child was observed for a total of 60 min. Using a 14-category system of observation, these authors report that the following social initiations were followed more than 50% of the time by a positive response from an interacting peer: (a) rough-and-tumble play, (b) share, (c) play organizer (e.g., "Let's play ball"), (d) physical assistance, (e) affection, and (f) question.

These same authors also conducted a follow-up observational study on the 10 highest- and lowest-level interactors among the original group of 61 children (Tremblay et al., in press). The primary aim of this study was to provide a thorough assessment of the behaviors engaged in by preschool children following positive social initiations. Once again, a total of 60 min of data was collected for each child. The results indicated that the overwhelming majority of responses to initiations was composed of two categories of activity. The first category was described as "responding in kind." That is, if a child received a "share" initiation it was quite likely that he or she would reciprocate with a "share" behavior. The other frequently occurring response category was described as "compliance." For example, if a youngster initiated a "play organizer," such as "Let's play trucks," the peer might say "O.K.," and proceed to collect several trucks.

The results from these two observational studies have been employed in recent treatment studies as both target behaviors for severely handicapped children and as components of a social-initiation intervention. Data from these efforts indicate that social initiations such as play organizer, share, rough-and-tumble play, and physical assistance can set the occasion for positive social behavior by withdrawn preschool children (Strain, 1980). Moreover, generalization data on several of the youngsters show across-setting and across-time treatment gains when the above-mentioned social initiations were used by normally developing children as approach behaviors.

Whereas some data are now available to empirically select treatment targets and intervention procedures, only anecdotal reports now address the critical treatment-evaluation issue of intervention effects on peer trainers. This issue is certainly brought into focus when target children may engage in negative, possibly threatening behavior toward peer trainers. In one study, Ragland et al. (1978) indicated that the peer trainer was reported by his teachers to engage in improved classroom and bus-riding behavior during the course of the study.

MAINTENANCE AND GENERALIZATION OF BEHAVIOR CHANGE

The maintenance of social-behavior change across time and the generalization of effects to new social partners, play objects, and settings have been most difficult to achieve. It would appear that the peer-mediated social-initiation treatment is more likely to result in behavior maintenance and generalization than adult-mediated treatment. Yet it is doubtful that the positive social behavior exhibited during follow-up or in generalization settings represents a clinically acceptable level of inter-action. A number of environmental and treatment-related variables seem important to understanding the minimal maintenance and generalization demonstrated by target children.

First, the social environments in which maintenance and generalization have been assessed did not provide socially responsive partners. Most often, the withdrawn children were returned to nonintegrated settings with peers who could be expected to ignore, overtly punish, and quickly extinguish any positive overtures by treated children. Not only is this situation a severe test of maintenance and generalization, it may also be an inappropriate assessment technique. However, the mere integration of socially competent children with isolate youngsters will not automatically result in any posttreatment behavior change. A considerable body of research has established that in settings where socially withdrawn and socially competent children are integrated, the socially skilled children do not interact with less skilled peers (Porter, Ramsey, Tremblay, Iacobbo, & Crawley, 1978; Ray, 1974; Strain, 1977). Even when socially competent children have participated in the training of withdrawn classmates, they tend not to interact with these youngsters when socially skilled children are available in the setting (Peck et al., 1976). Strain and Fox (1981) have noted that the isolation of handicapped children in integrated settings is not necessarily the result of overt rejection but more often represents a choice made by nonhandicapped children to interact with established friends. Thus, it may be necessary to alter the entire social ecology and friendship network in a classroom if maintenance and generalization of treatment gains are to obtain (Strain, 1980).

The lack of maintenance and generalization may also be attributed in part to the limited range of social behaviors targeted for change with isolate children. Intervention efforts have been limited to: (a) increasing children's responsiveness to social initiations; (b) increasing various motor and verbal responses relevant to cooperative play; and (c) setting the occasion for imitation of positive social behaviors. A recent review of social-skills training (van Hasselt, Hersen, Whitehall, & Bellack, 1979) indicates that isolate children will likely not exhibit long-term behavior change without systematic training of multiple social skills. The observational studies by Tremblay *et al.* (in press) have provided some initial information on critical social behaviors by preschool children. With elementary-age youngsters, Reardon, Hersen, Bellack, and Foley (1978) have identified six social skills that characterize the behaviors of highly competent as opposed to less competent children. These social skills include: (a) shorter latency to respond to social initiations; (b) use of more lengthy utterances; (c) display of more appropriate affect; (d) more spontaneous social initiations to social partners; (e) more lengthy responses to social initiations; and (f) more requests for information from social partners. Obviously, those social skills identified by observational research represent a significant programming challenge. Considerable task analyses must precede the incorporation of multiple social skills into intervention efforts.

CLINICAL-APPLICATION ISSUES

"How on earth did you get the peer trainer to do that?" This is one of the most common questions asked by the readers of the peer-initiation literature. Indeed, it is paradoxical that such a young paraprofessional can accomplish significant change in behaviors of a long and durable history. In answer to the question, the following sections address how a peer trainer is prepared; how the setting is selected and equipped; and how the whole process is observed and recorded.

SETTING VARIABLES

Remarkable uniformity characterizes the research settings for the peer-social-initiation studies. In each investigation, carefully selected toys became the tools of the peer trainer. Quilitch, Christophersen, and Risley (1977) assisted this area of inquiry by documenting those play materials which held the greatest promise for cooperative play. Their list—that used by peer-initiation researchers—includes toy telephones; blocks; trucks and cars; doll houses and dolls; puppets; and balls. Successful additions to the original list are "Nerf" toys and "Frisbees." Toys were selected according to the target students' play skills and interests rather than their chronological ages. (For a more detailed discussion of toy selection for social-skill development, see Wehman, 1979.) In each study these toys alone were placed in an area of the classroom or in an adjacent playroom, measuring approximately 10 feet by 10 feet.

Several questions remain unanswered with regard to setting variables:

1. Can the peer-initiation procedures be extended to outdoor settings? To date, all studies have been conducted indoors, in relatively small areas.

2. Should the play setting be varied to promote generalization of cooperative-play behaviors? Thus far, the setting has remained constant within small areas.

3. What specific features predict a toy or play activity's usefulness in promoting cooperative play? A recent investigation (Tremblay *et al.*, in press) showed that in doll, block, and ball play, normal preschoolers are most likely to reciprocate social initiations. However, toys have not received such systematic examination with handicapped students.

4. How might *new* toys or activities best be introduced to isolate children? Many autistic children develop narrow interests in play activities, participating in only one or two games. It is important for clinicians to be able to expand this interest to other games and toys; yet in most of the previous research, data on the number of different play activities were not reported.

Selection of Peer Trainer

An ex post facto analysis of the peer-social-initiation literature suggests a few distinct criteria for selection of the peer trainer:

1. The student must attend school regularly, to ensure uninterrupted training.

2. The student must display positive social initiations during free-play periods.

3. The student must follow adult directions reliably.

Unlike many job descriptions, this one does not include minimum age (peer-trainer ages ranged from three to 12 years), previous experience (only one had prior training as a confederate), or a certain type of education (several of the peer trainers were themselves enrolled in classes for the behaviorally disordered).

In one study, data collected during five prebaseline free-play sessions supported the choice of peer trainer (Young & Kerr, 1979). This child exhibited the greatest vocabulary and played for longer periods of time than others in his class. In other investigations, teachers simply nominated the peers as trainers. Despite such an informal selection procedure, none of the peer trainers was replaced and all proved successful at their task.

In some areas, more examination of the selection of peer trainers is warranted:

1. What are the minimal social-cognitive abilities of an effective peer trainer? In only one study was a mentally retarded student used to train others (Young & Kerr, 1979). Most of the peer trainers were described as normal in terms of intellectual functioning.

2. What is the optimal ratio of trainers to target children? In all studies, the trainer worked with one child at a time (with the exception of the prompting and reinforcement phases of the Strain *et al.*, 1979 study), and with a total of three or four students. Although these seem to be satisfactory ratios, further examination of this question is needed.

3. Is it possible to engage more than one trainer for the same target children? As stated earlier, peer trainers were never replaced during these studies. In some school settings, however, it might prove more practical for a pair of peer trainers to be employed interchangeably. Furthermore, such a process might foster across-child generalization of social skills.

SELECTION OF TARGET CHILDREN

Teacher nominations augmented by formal observations led to the inclusion of specific isolate children in these studies. In general, teachers were asked to select students who were rarely observed to interact with other students during free-play times. The observational procedure described in a later section substantiated these evaluations.

Target children ranged in age from three to 10 years, with diagnostic labels of developmentally delayed, autistic, behaviorally disordered, or moderately mentally retarded. Specific behavioral patterns of these children also varied, as is partially evidenced by baseline observational data and by Table 1.

Some areas of future inquiry might include:

1. Can older students benefit from social-initiation training? How should the play-based procedures be modified to be more appropriate for the older subject? One specific medium for social training might be prevocational tasks requiring cooperation (e.g., assembly tasks).

2. Can the isolate behavior of severely handicapped students be altered by such tactics? This population frequently exhibits behaviors which are incompatible with social cooperation (e.g., self-stimulation, self-mutilation). Some research has begun on the modification of social behaviors of severely retarded preschoolers *(SCIP, Year End Report* 1979).

3. What is the most efficient way for parents, pediatricians, and teachers to identify children at risk for social isolation? In each of the studies cited, the students had been thoroughly assessed and formally

TABLE 1.
Overview of Subject Characteristics in Peer-Initiation Studies

Study	Subjects	Age	Problem behaviors
Ragland, Kerr, & Strain, 1978	Sally	8 yr.	Echolalic; had limited eye contact; had frequent temper tantrums; twirled paper and other objects; engaged in no cooperative play
	Darrin	9 yr.	Continuously self-stimulated; echolalic; engaged in no cooperative play
	Dennis	9 yr.	Hyperactive; self-destructive
Strain, 1977	Jim Tom Rob	Ranged in age from 43–51 mos.	Were considered the most isolate youngsters in class; had delayed lanugage; extremely oppositional
Strain, Kerr, & Ragland, 1979	Earl	9 yr.	Self-stimulated; cried inappropriately; not toilet trained
	Sue	10 yr.	Echolalic; engaged in temper tantrums whenever social bids were made toward her; self-stimulated frequently
	Tom	10 yr.	Frequently made bizarre verbal statements; majority of interactions with other children consisted of confiscating toys; oppositional to requests
	Carl	9 yr.	Engaged in unintelligible speech; excessively active; destroyed toys through self-stimulating with them
Strain, Shores, & Timm, 1977	Mark Ted Al Tommy Dicky Steve	Ranged in age from 39–53 mos.	Rarely engaged in cooperative play; were language-delayed; frequently engaged in temper tantrums
Strain & Timm, 1974	Martha	3 yr.	Was language-delayed; had no appropriate interactions with siblings or peers; did not seem to recognize danger; rarely obeyed commands; only interacted with adults
Young & Kerr, 1979	Linda Mark	10 yr. 6 yr.	Had no expressive speech; responded to only 10% of verbal instructions; never played with other children

identified as exceptional. Their teachers—trained in special education—were sensitive to social-behavior deficits. But many regular classroom teachers, parents, and other professionals are not systematically trained to consider social withdrawal as a serious problem.

PREPARATION OF PEER TRAINER

Teaching a student to modify the isolate behavior of others seems like a major undertaking. Yet the previous studies relied upon a rather simple training format which took place before any actual play sessions.

> 1. The child was given an explanation of the task, such as "Try hard to get the others to play with you."
>
> 2. "Training to expect rejection" was accomplished through a role-play in which the adult ignored every other initiation by the peer trainer, explained this behavior and, finally, encouraged the peer trainer, "Keep trying, even when children don't play at first," (Strain *et al.*, 1977, p. 291)

The training steps were repeated in 20-min daily sessions (usually four) until the peer trainer could reliably make social bids to the occasionally reluctant adult. (A puppet, "Scippy," enacted isolate behavior during peer training conducted in the Social Competence Intervention Project developed by Shores, Strain, and Stowitschek, *SCIP Year End Report*, 1979.) In one study involving a mildly retarded trainer (Young & Kerr, 1979), the initial training required more time and structure. A verbal request to play was trained first. Then, the confederate was trained to make this request while handing the adult a toy. These practice sessions continued until the peer trainer initiated appropriately on 80% of the role plays.

In all studies, the peer trainer rehearsed in the actual play setting and used toys that were selected for the isolate children. The adult frequently praised the peer trainer's efforts during this practice. Praise was supplemented during some of the studies by tangible rewards. One peer trainer received a weekly hamburger as well as a certificate of merit and trophy at the end of the study (Ragland *et al.*, 1978). When a moderately retarded student served as a peer trainer, he received edibles during each intervention session (Young & Kerr, 1979).

A great deal remains to be examined in peer-trainer preparation:

1. Can the training procedures be packaged for maximum replicability? The initial attempt in this area was designed primarily for preschoolers (*SCIP Year End Report*, 1979). Additional development is needed for older and/or more severely handicapped students.

2. Is it possible for a peer tutor to train the confederate?

3. How do the peer-training strategies need alteration to accommodate peer trainers with different entry skills?

OBSERVATION PROCEDURES

The observation system introduced by Strain and Timm (1974) was used in several of the peer-social-initiation studies (e.g., Ragland *et al.*,

1978; Strain *et al.*, 1977; Strain *et al.*, 1979). This system relied upon the following behavioral categories (Strain, Shores, & Kerr, 1976, p. 33):

I. Motor-Gestural: All movements emitted that cause a child's head, arms, or feet to come into direct contact with the body of another child; that involve waving or extending arms directly toward another child; or that involve placing of hands directly upon a material, toy, or other movable apparatus that is being touched or manipulated by another child.

  A. Positive:
     touch with hand or hands; hug; holding hands; kiss; wave; all cooperative responses involved with sharing a toy or material.

  B. Negative:
     hit; pinch; kick; butt with head; "nonplaying" push or pull; grabbing object from another child; destroying construction of another child.

II. Vocal-Verbal: All vocalizations emitted while a child is directly facing any other child within a radius of 0.9 m or all vocalizations that by virtue of content (e.g., proper name, "hey you," etc.) and/or accompanying motor-gestural movements (e.g., waving, pointing) clearly indicate that the child is directing the utterance to another child within or beyond a 0.9 m radius.

  A. Positive:
     all vocalizations directed to another child excluding screams, shouts, cries, whines, or other utterances that are accompanied by gestures that indicate rejecting, oppositional behavior.

  B. Negative:
     screams, shouts, cries, whines, or other utterances that are accompanied by gestures that indicate rejecting, oppositional behavior.

Figure 1 displays a sample observation form. Letters indicate the children emitting the coded behaviors.

Interobserver reliability for this system was calculated by this formula:

$$\frac{\text{Agreements}}{\text{Agreements plus Disagreement}} \times 100$$

Summary and Conclusions

Behavioral research on the treatment of children's social withdrawal is rapidly growing. However, the available technology for choosing behavioral targets and implementing effective interventions is still most limited. In this final section we will summarize our view of the current "state of the art" in social-behavior modification and the use of peer social initiations in particular. Because new information is continuously being presented in this area, the following conclusions are offered and should be considered as tentative:

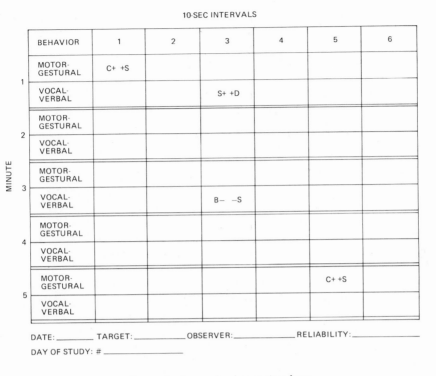

FIGURE 1. A sample observation form.

1. Social withdrawal represents a response pattern that is pervasive in its incidence and developmental significance. The literature on handicapped children indicates that withdrawn behavior is a commonly observed characteristic among mentally retarded, behaviorally disordered, learning-disabled, autistic, and sensory-impaired children (Strain, 1980). For these youngsters as well as those shy, withdrawn children who have no accompanying handicaps, social withdrawal appears to be a stable and persistent behavior pattern. Several authors (Hartup, 1979; Strain, Cooke, & Apolloni, 1976) have considered socially withdrawn children to be "at risk" in the areas of language development, moral values, and socially appropriate methods of expressing anger, affection, and sexual feelings. These children are "at risk" for the simple reason that they are excluded from that seemingly informal yet powerful network of peer influence through which youngsters typically develop such interpersonal and communication skills. Both longitudinal and retrospective research indicate that withdrawn children tend to grow up to be withdrawn adolescents and adults who experience mental-health and adjustment problems.

2. The various peer-mediated strategies (modeling; prompting and reinforcement; incidental influence; and social initiations) have produced direct treatment gains equivalent to those associated with adult-mediated strategies. Moreover, the level of behavior generalization and maintenance resulting from peer-mediated interventions seems to be superior to that accompanying adult-mediated tactics (Strain & Fox, 1981). This differential effectiveness favoring peer-mediated tactics probably results from: (a) the closer match between peer interventions and the social context of generalization settings; and (b) the tendency for direct adult prompting and reinforcement to encourage frequent yet brief social contact between children.

3. The immediate and substantial behavior change that has characterized the effects of peer-social-initiation studies strongly suggests that the withdrawn behavior of handicapped children is partially a function of the socially unresponsive, developmentally segregated settings in which many of these youngsters are educated. Likewise, the limited generalization and maintenance associated with the social-initiation intervention (and all other strategies) may be explained, in part, by the lack of appropriate social stimuli available in the developmentally segregated settings in which posttreatment effects are often assessed.

4. While a good deal of research attention has been paid to developing intervention strategies for remediating social withdrawal, relatively little attention has been devoted to the systematic study of target-behavior selection. To date, the a priori selection of target behaviors has not resulted in the kind of spontaneous behavioral entrapment that one would logically expect if functional, socially valid behaviors are taught (Strain & Fox, 1981). The naturalistic literature on children's social encounters is a likely source for the needed behavior targets. However, much of the current data is of limited utility because of the global behavioral categories employed and the brief, monadic sampling of individual children's social encounters (Tremblay *et al.*, in press). What seems to be needed at this point is naturalistic study which focuses on discrete social behaviors and which samples interaction in a continuous fashion such that it is possible to analyze the effects of one child's behavior on social partners and vice versa.

5. Anecdotal reports indicate that peer trainers who have participated in the social-initiation procedures have both enjoyed and, in one instance, profited from this experience (Ragland *et al.*, 1978). However, ethical considerations and a good empirical sense dictate more in-depth and long-term study of peer trainers. Specific issues for study might be: (a) does the social status of peer trainers change following participation as intervention agents; (b) do peer trainers tend to assume an instructional role with their peers; (c) do peer trainers exhibit any positive or negative

collateral behavior change during intervention; and (d) how do peer trainers describe their experience as intervention agents?

6. Finally, the demonstrations of peer-initiation effectiveness have involved relatively few target children. Significant questions remain to be answered concerning the exportability of the procedure and its efficacy with children exhibiting severe developmental delays and aberrant behaviors. Presently, it can be said that the social-initiation procedure represents one viable and resource-efficient alternative for remediating social withdrawal.

REFERENCES

Ainsworth, M. D. The development on infant-mother interaction among the Ganda. In B. M. Foss (Ed.), *Determinants of infant behavior* (Vol. 2). London: Methuen, 1963.

Allen, K. E., Benning, P. M., & Drummond, T. W. Integration of normal and handicapped children in a behavior modification preschool: A case study. In G. Semb (Ed.), *Behavior analysis and education.* Lawrence: University of Kansas Press, 1972.

Anderson, B. J., Vietze, P., & Dokecki, P. R. Reciprocity in vocal interaction of mothers and infants. *Child Development*, 1977, *48*, 1969–1981.

Apolloni, T., & Cooke, T. P. Integrated programming at the infant, toddler, and preschool levels. In M. Guralnick (Ed.), *Early intervention and the integration of handicapped and nonhandicapped children.* Baltimore: University Park Press, 1978.

Apolloni, T., Cooke, S. A., & Cooke, T. P. Establishing a nonretarded peer as a behavioral model for retarded toddlers. *Perceptual and Motor Skills*, 1977, *44*, 231–241.

Ballard, M., Corman, L., Gottlieb, J., & Kaufman, M. J. Improving the social status of mainstreamed retarded children. *Journal of Educational Psychology*, 1977, *69*, 605–611.

Becker, W. C. The relationship of factors in parental ratings of self and each other to the behavior of kindergarten children as rated by mothers, fathers, and teachers. *Journal of Consulting Psychology*, 1960, *24*, 507–527.

Birren, J. W. Psychological examinations of children who later become psychotic. *Journal of Abnormal and Social Psychology*, 1944, *39*, 84–96.

Bowlby, J. *Attachment and loss.* Vol. 1. *Attachment.* London: Hogarth Press, 1969.

Bronson, W. C. Stable patterns of behavior: The significance of enduring orientations for personality development. In J. P. Hill (Ed.), *Minnesota symposia on child psychology* (Vol. 2). Minneapolis; University and Minnesota Press, 1968.

Buhler, C. The social behavior of children. In C. Murchinson (Ed.), *Handbook of child psychology.* Worcester, Mass.: Clark University Press, 1931.

Chennault, M. Improving the social acceptance of unpopular educable mentally retarded pupils in special classes. *American Journal of Mental Deficiency*, 1967, *72*, 455–458.

Cook, H., & Stingle, S. Cooperative behavior in children. *Psychological Bulletin*, 1974, *81*, 918–933.

Cooke, T. P., Apolloni, T., & Cooke, S. A. The effects of a second nondelayed playmate on the free-play imitation and interaction of delayed and nondelayed children. *Mental Retardation*, 1980, in press.

Cooke, S. A., Cooke, T. P., and Apolloni, T. Developing nonretarded toddlers as verbal models for retarded classmates. *Child Study Journal*, 1978, *8*, 1–8.

Devoney, C., Guralnick, M. J., & Rubin, H. Integrating handicapped and nonhandicapped preschool children: Effects on social play. *Childhood Education*, 1974, *50*, 360–364.

Evers, W. L., & Schwartz, J. C. Modifying social withdrawal in preschoolers: The effects of filmed modeling and teacher praise. *Journal of Abnormal Psychology*, 1973, *1*, 248–256.

Frazee, H. E. Children who later become schizophrenic. *Smith College Studies in Social Work*, 1953, *23*, 125–149.

Garvey, C. Some properties of social play. In J. S. Bruner, A. Jolly, & K. Sylva (Eds.), *Play: Its role in development and evolution*. New York: Basic Books, 1976.

Garvey, C., & Hogan, R. Social speech and social interaction: Egocentrism revisited. *Child Development*, 1973, *44*, 562–568.

Greenwood, C. R., Walker, H. M., & Hops, H. Some issues in social interaction/withdrawal assessment. *Exceptional Children*, 1977, *43*, 490–499.

Gronlund, N. E. *Sociometry in the classroom*. New York: Harper, 1959.

Guralnick, M. J. The value of integrating handicapped and nonhandicapped preschool children. *American Journal of Orthopsychiatry*, 1976, *42*, 236–245.

Hartup, W. W. Peer relations and the growth of social competence. In M. W. Kent & J. E. Rolf (Eds.), *Primary prevention of psychopathology* (Vol. 3). Hanover, N.H.: University Press of New England, 1979.

Hops, H. Social skills training for socially isolated children. In P. Karoly & J. Steffen (Eds.), *Intellectual and social deficiencies*. New York: Gardner Press, in press.

Hops, H., & Greenwood, C. R. Social skills deficits. In E. J. Mash & L. G. Terdal (Eds.), *Behavioral assessment of childhood disorders*. New York: Guilford Press, in press.

Jakubcheck, Z., & Smeriglio, V. The influence of symbolic modeling on the social behavior of preschool children with low levels of social responsiveness. *Child Development*, 1976, *47*, 838–841.

Keller, M. F., & Carlson, P. M. The use of symbolic modeling to promote social skills in preschool children with low levels of social responsiveness. *Child Development*, 1974, *45*, 912–919.

Lilly, M. S. Improving social acceptance of low sociometric status, low achieving students. *Exceptional Children*, 1971, *37*, 341–348.

Maudry, M., & Nekula, M. Social relations between children of the same age during the first two years of life. *Journal of Genetic Psychology*, 1939, *54*, 193–215.

Meighan, M., & Birr, K. *The infant and its peers*. Unpublished manuscript. Kansas City, Kansas: University of Kansas Medical Center, 1979.

Mueller, E. The maintenance of verbal exchanges between young children. *Child Development*, 1972, *43*, 930–938.

Nordquist, V. M., & Bradley, B. Speech acquisition in a nonverbal isolate child. *Journal of Experimental Child Psychology*, 1973, *15*, 149–160.

O'Connor, R. D. Modification of social withdrawal through symbolic modeling. *Journal of Applied Behavior Analysis*, 1969, *2*, 15–22.

O'Connor, R. D. Relative efficacy of modeling, shaping and combined procedures for modification of social withdrawal. *Journal of Abnormal Psychology*, 1972, *79*, 327–334.

O'Neal, P., & Robins, L. N. Childhood patterns predictive of adult schizophrenia: A follow-up study. *American Journal of Psychiatry*, 1958, *15*, 385–391.

Peck, C. A., Apolloni, T., Cooke, T. P., & Cooke, S. A. *Teaching developmentally delayed toddlers and preschoolers to imitate the free play behavior of nonretarded classmates: Trained and generalized effects*. Unpublished manuscript, Sonoma State University, 1976.

Porter, R. H., Ramsey, B., Tremblay, A., Iacobbo, M., & Crawley, S. Social interactions in heterogeneous groups of retarded and normally developing children: An observational study. In G. P. Sackett (Ed.), *Observing behavior: Theory and application in mental retardation*. Baltimore: University Park Press, 1978.

Quilitch, H. R., Christophersen, E. R., & Risley, T. R. The evaluation of children's play materials. *Journal of Applied Behavior Analysis*, 1977, *10*, 501–502.

Ragland, E. U., Kerr, M. M., & Strain, P. S. Effects of peer social initiations on the behavior of withdrawn autistic children. *Behavior Modification,* 1978, 2, 565–578.

Ray, J. S. *Ethological studies of behavior in delayed and nondelayed toddlers.* Paper presented at annual meeting of the American Association on Mental Deficiency, Toronto, May 1974.

Reardon, R. C., Hersen, M., Bellack, A. S., & Foley, J. M. *Measuring social skills in grade school boys.* Unpublished manuscript, University of Pittsburgh, 1978.

Rheingold, H., Gewirtz, J. L., & Ross, H. W. Social conditioning of vocalizations in the infant. *Journal of Comparative and Physiological Psychology,* 1959, 52, 68–73.

Robins, L. N. *Deviant children grown up: A sociological and psychiatric study of sociopathic personality.* Baltimore: Williams & Wilkins, 1966.

Roff, M., Sells, S. B., & Golden, M. M. *Social adjustment and personality development in children.* Minneapolis: University of Minnesota Press, 1972.

Rubenstein, J., & Howes, C. The effects of peers on toddler interaction with mother and toys. *Child Development,* 1976, 47, 597–605.

SCIP Year End Report. Document submitted to the Bureau of Education for the Handicapped by George Peabody College (R. E. Shores, Principal Investigator), 1979.

Strain, P. S. Effects of peer social initiations on withdrawn preschool children: Some training and generalization effects. *Journal of Abnormal Child Psychology,* 1977, 5, 445–455.

Strain, P. S. Social behavior programming with severely emotionally disturbed and autistic children. In B. Wilcox and A. Thompson (Eds.), *Critical issues in educating autistic children and youth.* Washington, D.C.: Bureau of Education for the Handicapped, 1980.

Strain, P. S., & Fox, J. E. Peers as therapeutic agents for isolate classmates. In A. E. Kazdin & B. B. Lahey (Eds.), *Advances in child clinical psychology* (Vol. 4). New York: Plenum Press, 1981.

Strain, P. S., & Hill, A. D. Social interaction. In P. Wehman (Ed.), *Recreation programming for developmentally disabled persons.* Baltimore: University Park Press, 1979.

Strain, P. S., Shores, R. E. Social interaction development among behaviorally handicapped preschool children: Research and educational implications. *Psychology in the Schools,* 1977, 14, 493–502.

Strain, P. S., & Timm, M. A. An experimental analysis of social interaction between a behaviorally disordered preschool child and her classroom peers. *Journal of Applied Behavior Analysis,* 1974, 7, 583–590.

Strain, P. S., Cooke, T. P., & Apolloni, T. *Teaching exceptional children: Assessing and modifying social behavior.* New York: Academic Press, 1976.

Strain, P. S., Shores, R. E., & Kerr, M. M. An experimental analysis of "spillover" effects on the social interaction of behaviorally handicapped preschool children. *Journal of Applied Behavior Analysis,* 1976, 9, 31–40.

Strain, P. S., Shores, R. E., & Timm, M. A. Effects of peer initiations on the social behavior of withdrawn preschool children. *Journal of Applied Behavior Analysis,* 1977, 10, 289–298.

Strain, P. S., Kerr, M. M., & Ragland, E. U. Effects of peer-mediated social initiations and prompting/reinforcement procedures on the social behavior of autistic children. *Journal of Autism and Developmental Disabilities,* 1979, 9, 41–54.

Tremblay, A., Strain, P. S., Hendrickson, J. M., & Shores, R. E. Social interactions of normally developing preschool children: Using normative data for subject and target behavior selection. *Behavior Modification,* in press.

van Hasselt, V. B., Hersen, M., Whitehall, M. B., & Bellack, A. S. Social skill assessment and training for children: An evaluative review. *Behavior Research and Therapy,* 1979, 17, 413–437.

Waldrop, M. G., & Halverson, C. F. Intensive and extensive peer behavior: Longitudinal and cross-sectional analyses. *Child Development,* 1975, 46, 19–26.

Walker, H. M. *The Walker problem behavior identification checklist.* (Test and manual.) Los Angeles: Western Psychological Services, Inc., 12031 Wilshire Blvd., 1970.

Walker, H. M., & Hops, H. The use of group and individual reinforcement contingencies in the modification of social withdrawal. In L. A. Hamerlynck, L. C. Handy, & E. J. Mash (Eds.), *Behavior change: Methodology, concepts, and practice.* Champaign, Ill.: Research Press, 1973.

Wehman, P. (Ed.). *Recreation programming for developmentally disabled persons.* Baltimore: University Park Press, 1979.

Weisberg, P. Social and nonsocial conditioning of infant vocalizations. *Child Development,* 1963, *34,* 377–388.

Young, C. C., & Kerr, M. M. The effects of a retarded child's social initiations on the behavior of severely retarded school-aged peers. *Education and Training of the Mentally Retarded,* 1979, *14,* 185–190.

5

Vicarious Reinforcement and Punishment Processes in the Classroom

ALAN E. KAZDIN

People can be greatly influenced by observing the behaviors of their peers. Indeed, psychological treatments based upon modeling capitalize on the behavior-change capacities of observing others. Carefully planned modeling experiences can be arranged in which clients observe others engaging in behaviors the clients wish to develop. Modeling has been effective in altering a variety of problems, including fears, social withdrawal, and aggressiveness, in both child and adult treatment (e.g., Kirkland & Thelen, 1977; Rosenthal & Bandura, 1978).

Evidence suggests that people are especially influenced when they see their peers receive rewarding or punishing consequences for their performance. The effects of behavior changes that result from seeing others receive consequences are referred to as *vicarious processes*. Depending upon the nature of the consequences that are administered to the peer, the processes usually are referred to as *vicarious reinforcement* and *punishment*. As usually defined, vicarious reinforcement (or punishment) refers to an increase (or decrease) in behavior of individuals who see others receive consequences for behavior. Although "vicarious" processes may inadvertently imply a particular interpretation of how the effects of consequences delivered to one individual extend to others, the term is employed in the present context merely to denote that contingency effects occasionally spread beyond those who receive direct consequences for performance.

ALAN E. KAZDIN • Department of Psychiatry, Western Psychiatric Institute and Clinic, University of Pittsburgh School of Medicine, Pittsburgh, Pennsylvania 15261. Preparation of this chapter was facilitated by a grant (MH31047) from the National Institute of Mental Health.

Ambiguity in defining vicarious processes occasionally arises from assumptions about the changes that are made in the performance of the model and observer, and the assumption that these changes are similar. However, the changes in the person who receives reinforcing consequences and in the peer who observes delivery of the reinforcing consequences may depart considerably. Vicarious effects may be evident when the behavior of the observer changes in a direction opposite to the change of the peer model (e.g., Sechrest, 1963). Thus, for present purposes, it is useful to adopt a description of vicarious effects that is relatively neutral with regard to the changes that occur in the model's or observer's behavior. Providing consequences to selected persons in a situation such as a classroom has led to all sorts of changes in the behaviors of other children who do not receive these consequences. These changes are viewed generally as vicarious processes.

Examination of vicarious reinforcement and punishment is important for several reasons. First, vicarious processes are a potentially important source of influence on a child in the classroom or other situations. Opportunities for vicarious reinforcement or punishment are much more prevalent than are opportunities for direct reinforcement. For example, in a classroom, a child is likely to receive relatively few instances of direct reinforcement or praise. However, the cumulative number of opportunities for vicarious reinforcement is much greater because the child can observe every other individual receive consequences.

Second, vicarious processes are frequently neglected and uncontrolled in the classroom, which can create or exacerbate existing problems. For example, teachers may inadvertently reinforce inappropriate behavior (e.g., by attending to disruptiveness). The problem of accidental reinforcement for inappropriate behavior extends beyond the child who received the attention; if there are vicarious effects of reinforcement of inappropriate behavior, that behavior may increase among others. Hence, uncontrolled vicarious reinforcement may create classroom problems.

A third reason that the study of vicarious processes is important pertains to concerns about the effects of behavioral programs. In many situations, only one or a few children need to be placed on a special program to improve their behavior. Placing one or a few persons on a program raises the prospect that other children who are not included may respond adversely. Perhaps because the more deviant children receive the benefits of a behavioral program (i.e., increase in reinforcers), others who are not included in the program will behave poorly in order to earn access to the program (Kazdin, 1980). Actually, vicarious reinforcement would suggest that persons who are not included in the contingencies may show improvements as a function of seeing others receive consequences. The investigation of vicarious processes is critical in examining the side effects of programs aimed at a few persons.

Finally, investigation of vicarious processes is important because the vicarious effects can interfere with evaluating the effects of direct reinforcement. For example, in some reinforcement programs in the classroom, comparisons may be made between the behaviors of students who receive reinforcement and of those who do not. The comparison appears to test reinforcement against no-treatment control children who do not receive direct consequences. However, the operation of vicarious reinforcement has been reported in a few studies showing that children may improve without receiving the intended treatment (Bolstad & Johnson, 1972; Patterson, 1974). Hence, in evaluating direct effects of reinforcement has been reported in a few studies showing that children not included in the contingency but who can observe others receive direct consequences must be considered.

Investigation of vicarious processes has important implications for understanding peer influences and for developing techniques that may improve performance. The present chapter examines vicarious reinforcement and punishment among children and adolescents in classrooms and, in a few instances, other applied settings. The chapter reviews the current findings, examines the characteristics of effects of vicarious reinforcement and punishment and the dimensions that promote vicarious effects, and evaluates interpretations of vicarious reinforcement. In addition, recommendations are provided for utilizing vicarious processes.

EVIDENCE FOR VICARIOUS REINFORCEMENT

A large number of demonstrations exist reporting the spread of effects of direct reinforcement. Vicarious reinforcement has been demonstrated across several settings, populations, and situations.

CLASSROOM APPLICATIONS

The bulk of the evidence of vicarious reinforcement has emerged from classroom research. An important investigation that stimulated much of the research was reported by Broden, Bruce, Mitchell, Carter, and Hall (1970), who examined the effects of praise on two disruptive, retarded boys in a second-grade classroom. When teacher attention was provided to only one of the boys, both boys increased in their attentiveness to their lessons. This effect was demonstrated for both boys when one of them received direct praise. This initial study provided evidence suggesting that vicarious reinforcement could influence behavior.

The evidence for vicarious effects in this study was somewhat ambiguous. During the phases in which one child was supposed to receive consequences vicariously, direct reinforcement inadvertently increased as well. In addition, teacher proximity, known in other classroom research to be a positive reinforcer (Goetz, Holmberg, & LeBlanc, 1975), may have directly reinforced attending behavior of the nontarget subject. Hence, the vicarious reinforcement effect may have resulted from changes in the direct consequences delivered to the children, a possibility acknowledged by the authors.

Replication of the study in a special-education class of trainable retardates ruled out the influence of extraneous factors (Kazdin, 1973a). Proximity and attention were controlled by placing an aide equidistant from the target and nontarget students and by allowing only pre-scheduled consequences to occur. As in the Broden (1970) study, nontarget subjects who did not receive direct attention for behavior improved in deportment when target subjects received praise for appropriate behavior.

Christy (1975) examined the vicarious effects of reinforcement with remedial preschool children in two classrooms. In-seat behavior in selected target subjects in each group was reinforced with edible rewards (e.g., candies, nuts). In separate phases, different children served as the target subject. In general, when one child received reinforcing consequences in the classroom, peers who did not receive these consequences tended to show similar increases in behavior.

Drabman and Lahey (1974) evaluated the effects of reinforcement delivered to a disruptive child on the behaviors of her peers in a fourth-grade classroom. Periodically, the teacher provided ratings from 1 to 10 that reflected the degree to which the target child performed appropriate classroom behavior. The ratings provided feedback for the child's performance and could not be exchanged for other reinforcers. Feedback not only altered the behavior of the target subject but also the behavior of her classmates as well.

Not all of the classroom demonstrations of vicarious reinforcement have been restricted to deportment. Strain and Timm (1974) altered the social interaction of a three-year-old girl in a classroom for behaviorally handicapped children. Social interaction consisted of motor behaviors such as touching, hugging, or sharing something with another child. These behaviors were reinforced with verbal and physical praise by an adult in the classroom. Initially, the girl's peers received direct reinforcement for their social interaction with her. This reinforcement increased social behavior of both the class and the girl, although she did not receive direct consequences herself. The increases in social behavior included responses to acts initiated by the peers as well as initiations of social behavior on her part. In a later phase, the girl received direct-reinforcing consequences and her peers did not. Yet, both she and her classmates increased their social interactions. Thus, this study demonstrated vicarious effects in two fashions.

In a later demonstration in the same facility, the teacher increased social interaction during a free-play period by using prompts and praise (Strain, Shores, & Kerr, 1976). The reinforcement program increased social interaction of three children. Peers in class also increased and decreased in social behaviors as a function of presenting and withdrawing conditions for the target subjects.

Aside from attentiveness and social behavior, vicarious reinforcement has been demonstrated in the area of academic productivity. Aaron and Bostow (1978) provided reinforcement to children in a classroom for educable mentally handicapped children. Reinforcement consisted of free time at the end of the class and was provided contingent upon completion of academic tasks. Three target children who received contingent free time showed increased productivity in academic tasks as well as improved on-task behavior. Interestingly, the productivity of others in the class who were not directly included in the free-time contingency also increased. These results suggested vicarious reinforcement effects, although measures of direct praise and punishment were not included to rule out the possible influence of direct consequences for nontarget children.

Several other classroom studies have been conducted attesting to the presence of vicarious reinforcement effects (Bolstad & Johnson, 1972; Kazdin, 1977; Kazdin, Silverman, & Sittler, 1975; Patterson, 1974; Strain & Pierce, 1977). The effects have been demonstrated among a wide range of ages and levels of intelligence. And, in most of the demonstrations, the effects of direct consequences that would provide the most plausible explanation of effects attributed to vicarious reinforcement have been ruled out. Specifically, such teacher behaviors as proximity, praise, and physical contact delivered to the nontarget subjects cannot explain findings in the investigations.

OTHER SETTINGS

Although the majority of demonstrations of vicarious reinforcement have been reported in the classroom, demonstrations in the home have also been provided. Contingencies implemented in the home for one child appear to influence the behaviors of that child and siblings. Resick, Forehand, and McWhorter (1976) developed compliance in the home with two brothers. Praise for compliance and time out for noncompliance for one boy across different household tasks led to changes in the nontarget sibling, who was not exposed to the contingencies until much later in the program. Interestingly, the behaviors in the nontarget sibling improved only on those tasks that resembled those that had been assigned to the target child and were scheduled to be performed at the same time. Similarly, Arnold, Levine, and Patterson (1975) reported that training parents to alter behaviors of their conduct problem children in the home was reflected in decreases in deviant behavior of these children and their siblings. Possibly, the contingencies implemented for the target children were responsible for the changes in the nontarget siblings, that is, vicarious effects of the contingencies.

Although the results of the above studies suggest operation of vicarious processes, data were not gathered on the behavior of the parents who implemented the contingencies. Changes in the nontarget siblings may have resulted from the direct operation of some contingency (e.g., differential attention, praise, physical contact) that was not assessed in this report. The plausibility of this interpretation is attested to by Lavigueur, Peterson, Sheese, and Peterson (1973), who implemented contingencies in the home to control the disruptive behavior of a three-year-old boy. However, collection of data on the mother who implemented the contingencies revealed that her behavior changed in relation to both the target child and his five-year-old sister. Essentially, change in the "nontarget" child's behavior could be accounted for by the mother's increased direct attention to that child.

Vicarious reinforcement has been demonstrated in a number of settings other than the classroom or the home. Brown and Pearce (1970) reported vicarious reinforcement effects in a simulated workshop setting at a public school with mentally retarded persons ranging in age from 12 to 20 years. The clients worked on piece-rate production jobs (filling envelopes) and were exposed to conditions in which they saw others receive approval and feedback on the number of envelopes filled. Observation of others receiving reinforcing consequences led to increases in performance of two of the three nontarget subjects.

Similarly, Kazdin (1973b) examined the effects of vicarious effects of praise on mentally retarded adults who attended a sheltered workshop. In each of two pairs of workers, one was selected as a target subject as they worked on various tasks (assembling taillights, counting metal rings). For each pair of clients, praise was given to one of the clients for increased production (increased unit-per-min performance over mean rate). Production increased for the nontarget client as well. Thus, observing a peer receive praise appeared to result in vicarious reinforcement.

Weisberg and Clements (1977) investigated vicarious reinforcement at a day-care center for children from 1½ to three years of age. Reinforcement, consisting of prizes and approval, was provided for instruction-following behavior while the children were in the dining area of the facility. Providing consequences to a few of the children had little impact on others. However, after a phase in which all persons received direct reinforcement, merely providing reinforcement to one child maintained high levels of performance of others as well. Thus, vicarious effects of reinforcement had minimal impact on developing behavior but helped maintain behavior once that behavior was established.

Hauserman, Zwebeck, and Plotkin (1972) examined the effects of reinforcement on altering verbalizations in group-therapy sessions among hospitalized adolescents. Token reinforcement, which could be exchanged for back-up reinforcers, was provided to selected members of the group for initiating verbalizations. The results indicated that direct reinforcement increased verbalizations of those who received tokens directly as well as of those who only observed reinforcement delivery.

EVIDENCE FOR VICARIOUS PUNISHMENT

Vicarious punishment in applied settings has received very little attention. The paucity of research is unfortunate because punishment in such settings as the classroom or at school is often justified on the basis of the deterrent effect it is likely to have on others. The absence of systematic work on vicarious punishment leaves open the question of the spread of effects among nontarget clients.

An initial study that suggested the vicarious effects of punishment was reported by Kounin and Gump (1958). This was a naturalistic investigation of 26 kindergarten classes and was designed to evaluate the effects of reprimands delivered to select children on the behaviors of their peers. Observers simply noted incidents in which a child watched the teacher reprimand another child for misbehavior, and reported the behavior of the child who observed the reprimand for 2 min after the reprimand. In general, teacher punishment of one child tended to influence the behavior of other children, a phenomenon the authors termed a "ripple effect."

In the above study the investigators did not attempt to control delivery of teacher reprimands, and it is difficult to rule out extraneous influences that may have had direct impact on the nontarget children. However, the observation of a large number of classes involving many children and teachers suggests the importance of vicarious punishment.

The effects of vicarious punishment were experimentally demonstrated by Wilson, Robertson, Herlong, and Haynes (1979), who focused upon aggressive behavior of a five-year-old kindergarten boy. The boy frequently engaged in aggressive behavior including kicking, throwing things, hitting, and blocking others with his body or arms. Time out from reinforcement, which consisted of placing the child in a booth in the classroom for 5 min, was used to punish aggressive behavior. The time-out procedure was shown to suppress aggressive acts. Interestingly, the aggressive acts of the child's classmates also decreased during the period in which time out was applied, even though none of the peers was included in the time-out contingency.

CHARACTERISTICS OF VICARIOUS EFFECTS

Vicarious reinforcement has been demonstrated in a variety of classroom and other settings. Although vicarious punishment has not been well studied, the available evidence suggests that seeing others receive aversive consequences has suppressive effects on behavior. Apart from demonstrating the spread of reinforcement and punishment effects, studies have yielded important and relatively consistent information about the characteristics of vicarious effects.

TRANSIENCE OF BEHAVIOR CHANGE

Several studies have shown that vicarious reinforcement produces relatively short-term changes in performance. For example, Strain and Pierce (1977) observed the effects of vicarious reinforcement among mentally retarded children. The phases in which reinforcement effects were observed were relatively long (20 days), which permitted evaluation of the course of change among children who did not receive direct reinforcement. The results showed improvements in attentive behavior at the beginning of each phase for children who saw a partner receive reinforcing consequences. However, a consistent pattern showed that at the beginning of the phase, vicarious effects were obvious. The effects consistently diminished over time, and in some cases the long-term effect of vicarious reinforcement was not clearly above baseline performance levels.

The transient effects of vicarious processes sometimes are evident relatively early in the program. For example, Christy (1975) observed that vicarious effects of reinforcement often disappeared among students within a brief period of only a day or two. Similarly, Kounin (1970) found that the strongest effects of vicarious punishment in kindergarten classes were evident on the first day of the contingency and diminished thereafter. In several other studies, the effects of vicarious reinforcement have been short-lived (Budd & Stokes, 1977; Okovita & Bucher, 1976).

GENERALITY AMONG SUBJECTS

Another characteristic of the studies of vicarious effects is the inconsistency of behavior change among subjects. Several investigations have examined only a small number of children, such as pairs of children, rather than larger groups such as entire classes (Broden *et al.*, 1970; Kazdin, 1973a; Kazdin, 1977; Strain & Pierce, 1977). When such small numbers of subjects are studied, it is difficult to interpret the lack of responsiveness of one or two of the subjects. Lack of responses might be idiosyncratic or reflect a larger problem that might be more pervasive if larger numbers of subjects were studied.

In studies where several subjects are included, vicarious effects appear to be evident for some children but not for others. For example, Budd and Stokes (1977) found that only three of 10 nontarget subjects in a classroom of preschool children showed clear increases in attending behavior. Other children showed no evidence of vicarious reinforcement, or only minimal and transient effects. Similarly, Ward and Baker (1968) evaluated the effects of a reinforcement program for three children in three different classrooms. In each of the classrooms, control children were identified who did not receive direct consequences. These latter children did not improve as a function of reinforcement delivered for behavior of the target children.

In a study of vicarious punishment, Kounin (1970) attempted to extend his work from the classroom to a summer camp with preadolescent boys. The study was terminated because vicarious effects were not found in sufficient numbers to continue. This finding is consistent with several others showing that some subjects do not show vicarious effects of reinforcement and punishment, even in studies where such demonstrations are regarded as successful (Brown & Pearce, 1970; Christy, 1975).

STRENGTH OF VICARIOUS EFFECTS

The magnitude of vicarious effects is obviously an important issue. The fact that vicarious effects of reinforcement and punishment are often transient addresses the issue of magnitude to some extent. Whatever the changes that may occur initially, the likelihood exists that the effects will diminish over time, as noted earlier. Hence, over the course of time ranging from one or a few to several days, the magnitude of vicarious effects is not likely to be large. The magnitude of vicarious effects has at least initially been large. Indeed, a few studies have shown relatively dramatic changes in performance in classroom attentive behavior when target subjects receive praise from the teacher (Kazdin, 1973a; Strain & Pierce, 1977).

A question that often arises is whether vicarious effects are as marked as those produced by direct reinforcement. Evidence culled from different applied studies suggests that the direct operation of reinforcement and punishment as a general rule is much more effective than vicarious effects. Indeed, in some of the vicarious reinforcement studies, direct reinforcement is resorted to when vicarious effects have been weak or nonexistent. For example, Brown and Pearce (1970) found that direct reinforcement greatly increased performance on a production task when added to vicarious reinforcement, which had no influence on performance for a mentally retarded adolescent. For another case, where vicarious reinforcement alone produced change, the effects of adding direct reinforcement could not be discerned.

Similarly, Weisberg and Clements (1977) found that young children in a day-care center increased their instruction-following behaviors only slightly when selected peers received direct reinforcement for the behavior. When reinforcement was provided directly, albeit intermittently, to each subject, instruction following for all subjects markedly increased.

Broden (1970) compared direct and vicarious reinforcement with two subjects in the classroom study. Teacher praise was first given to one subject directly and then only vicariously by delivering praise to an adjacent peer. For the other child, the conditions were in the opposite order. In both children, seeing another child receiving praise improved performance. However, the magnitude of the change from baseline was not as great as the effects of direct praise for performance.

Christy (1975) provided contingent reinforcement for children in a classroom. In different phases, children received direct reinforcement for in-seat behavior or saw a peer receive reinforcement. For each of the six children who received these conditions, direct reinforcement led to greater changes in performance over baseline levels than did vicarious reinforcement. Similarly, Kazdin (1973b) examined the effects of vicarious reinforcement among retarded adults working on jobs in a sheltered workshop. Performance was higher when clients received direct reinforcement for behavior than when they saw a peer receive reinforcing consequences. Finally, in the study by Hauserman (1972), individuals among hospitalized adolescents participating in group therapy received tokens for initiating verbalizations. At some point, the adolescents either received direct reinforcement or saw others receive reinforcement for verbalizing. Although vicarious effects of reinforcement were evident, performance was higher when direct reinforcement was administered.

GENERAL COMMENTS

The characteristics of vicarious reinforcement and punishment suggest that the effects are not particularly generalizable among persons, durable, or invariably large when they occur. The tendency might be to discount these characteristics by looking at inadequacies within individual studies on how reinforcement or punishment effects might have been studied. However, the characteristics reviewed above cannot be easily discounted on the basis of procedures peculiar to one or a few studies. Investigators occasionally have reported diverse characteristics using the same procedures across subjects within the same investigation. For example, Brown and Pearce (1970) studied three adolescent or young-adult retarded subjects in separate experiments. Of the three subjects, one showed no vicarious effects at all; another showed strong effects initially but these diminished quickly (within a few sessions); a third showed relatively consistent effects of vicarious reinforcement. Thus, the highly variable results among three subjects exposed to similar procedures within the same study reflect the pattern evident across several other studies.

The characteristic findings of vicarious processes in applied settings raise questions about the pervasiveness and importance of the phenomena. The inconsistency of the effects suggest that vicarious processes may not be very useful for changing behavior. However, the inconsistency of the effects suggests another possibility. Perhaps the conditions that contribute to vicarious effects are not well understood, and variables that moderate vicarious effects remain to be identified.

FACTORS THAT MAY PROMOTE VICARIOUS EFFECTS

Relatively few studies have evaluated variables that influence vicarious reinforcement or punishment effects, at least in such settings as the classroom, home, or institution. However, a few variables have been examined that suggest procedures which may be used to enhance vicarious processes. The variables include the conspicuousness of reinforcement delivery, exposure to the target subject, the manner of delivering direct consequences, and others. Because of the paucity of studies evaluating these variables, the conclusions about their effects must be regarded as only suggestive.

CONSPICUOUS DELIVERY OF REINFORCEMENT

One variable that might be expected to influence vicarious effects is the conspicuousness of the delivery of the consequences to persons in the situation who are not receiving consequences directly. For example, at one extreme, reinforcement in the form of praise might be delivered quietly to one child in a way that is undetectable to others. Other persons in the situation might be unaware that reinforcement was delivered and, of course, not affected by it. On the other hand, reinforcement could be delivered in a highly conspicuous fashion so that it is quite noticeable to others. Indeed, in most of the studies in the classroom setting, vicarious effects of verbal reinforcement are evaluated. Verbal reinforcement delivered aloud to one child is likely to influence other children's behaviors because it is readily detected.

The importance of conspicuousness of reinforcer delivery was suggested in research that examined the effects of nonverbal and verbal approval for selected children on the behavior of their peers. In a special-education classroom, Kazdin (1975) found that nonverbal approval in the form of contingent physical contact (patting a child, nodding, smiling) increased attentive behavior of the children who received these consequences directly but did not produce behavior change in their adjacent peers. On the other hand, verbal approval, when added to physical contact in the same situation, produced vicarious effects. Essentially, whether vicarious effects of reinforcement were evident depended upon whether verbal approval was included as part of the reinforcement. One possible interpretation of the effects of the role of verbal approval is that it was more readily detectable to the classmates of the target children. Of course, other interpretations might be advanced, such as the greater familiarity with verbal rather than nonverbal approval, greater clarity of verbal approval, or the ambiguity that might be associated with nonverbal approval alone as a reinforcer.

The possible importance of conspicuousness of reinforcer delivery in enhancing vicarious reinforcement effects was suggested further by examining the role of verbal prompts. The demonstration that nonverbal approval alone was not associated with improvements in the performance of adjacent peers led to the use of verbal prompts delivered either to the class as a whole or to an adjacent student (Kazdin *et al.*, 1975). When the target child behaved appropriately and was scheduled for reinforcing consequences, children other than the target children were instructed to look at the target subject. The instruction drew attention to the target subject. This prompt was immediately followed by delivery of nonverbal approval to the target subject. Prompts combined with nonverbal approval led to vicarious effects that were not evident with verbal approval alone.

Actually, the role of prompts and conspicuousness of the reinforcer is only suggestive. It is possible that the delivery of prompts to individual children or the class as a whole increased performance of appropriate classroom behavior of students who did not receive direct reinforcement. The purpose of using prompts was to allow children to see others receive direct nonverbal reinforcement. The prompting procedure may have enhanced performance because it facilitated this observational procedure. On the other hand, the mere delivery of a verbal prompt to peers or a class as a whole might have had an effect in its own right rather than enhancing vicarious effects. The prompts were never given alone without direct reinforcement, so their independent effects on performance were not evaluated.

EXPOSURE TO THE TARGET PEER

Exposure to the target peer consists of several related variables pertaining to the opportunities for children who do not receive direct consequences to observe the consequences delivered to their peers. As one might expect, evidence suggests that the greater exposure one has to a model who receives reinforcing consequences for behavior, the more likely vicarious effects are to occur and the greater the behavior change when these effects do occur.

Much of the work on vicarious effects has focused directly on the performance of children who are adjacent to the target child who receives direct consequences. Perhaps depending upon the conspicuousness of the reinforcer, the proximity of the nontarget child to the target child may influence vicarious effects. To evaluate this prospect, Okovita and Bucher (1976) investigated vicarious effects in two nursery-school children who were sitting adjacent to another child who received direct consequences. Each child received token reinforcement, which consisted of points registered on an electrically operated counter. Only the target subject received back-up reinforcers (e.g., toys, small candies) at the end of the session. The reinforcement procedure showed that when the target child received tokens and back-up reinforcers for appropriate classroom behavior, performance improved for the target child and the other students sitting to either side of him. In a subsequent phase, the seating was changed. The two other students alternated in their position so that they were next to the target child on one day and separated by one child from the target child on the next. Results suggested that the nontarget's attending behavior was greater when the child was sitting next to the target subject than when away from that subject. Thus, proximity to the person receiving direct consequences appeared to influence performance, an effect that might be viewed as another aspect of conspicuousness of the reinforcer delivery.

Exposure to the target child who receives direct consequences has been examined in other ways. The number of opportunities to observe others receiving reinforcing consequences can enhance vicarious effects. The opportunities for vicarious reinforcement can be increased by increasing the number of persons who serve as target subjects. For example, Strain *et al.* (1976) demonstrated that behavior of classroom peers who did not receive direct reinforcement of behavior showed higher levels of social behavior when two rather than one child received direct consequences. Thus, applying direct consequences to a larger number of children increased the amount of changes in nontarget peers.

MANNER OF DELIVERY

Vicarious reinforcement and punishment may depend upon the manner in which the consequences are delivered and the specific consequences that are delivered to target peers. Unfortunately, little evidence is available on the delivery of consequences and its effects on others. The importance of the topic, however, is suggested by the naturalistic study of vicarious punishment by Kounin and Gump (1958). In the study of kindergarten classes, the effects of teacher reprimands to one child were observed on other children.

The vicarious effects of reprimands depended upon characteristics of the reprimand and the behavior of the nontarget subjects. Reprimands had been classified according to the extent to which they were clear (i.e., explicit in specifying the problem), firm (i.e., expressed the teacher's resolve), and rough (i.e., angry). Children who witnessed a teacher make a clear reprimand that identified the problem behavior showed greater conformity with the desired behavior than those exposed to unclear reprimands. Firm reprimands tended to be associated with a broader spread of effects than those which were less firm. Interestingly, roughness or anger was not related to vicarious effects. However, the more anger expressed by the teacher, the more adverse reactions (side effects) there were among the children, including anxiety, apprehension, restlessness, and interference with ongoing activities.

Additional comparisons in the Kounin and Gump investigation suggested that what the nontarget subject was doing at the time punishment was delivered to a peer partially influenced the ripple effects. The nontarget child who was misbehaving at the time punishment was delivered to the target child was more influenced by the punishment than were children who were not misbehaving at this time. Interactions between the type of reprimand and what nontarget children were doing indicated that firmness of the reprimand only affected children who were engaging in misbehavior. On the other hand, clarity of the reprimand affected nontarget subjects independently of what they had been doing at the time punishment was delivered to a peer (Kounin, 1970).

The findings by Kounin and Gump suggest the need for research on the topic of the manner in which consequences are delivered in terms of their vicarious, or for that matter direct, effects. In a naturalistic study where consequences are observed as they occur normally, it is possible that uncontrolled features of the situation might be systematically confounded with the delivery of punishment. For example, the type of punishment (e.g., clear, firm, or angry reprimands) may systematically vary as a function of the person who administers or receives the punishing consequences, the behaviors they are performing, their location in the classroom and in relation to the teacher, the relative social standing of the punished child among his or her peers, and so on. These latter features may contribute to vicarious reinforcement processes as well. Perhaps most important in evaluating naturalistic research on vicarious punishment is the possibility that vicarious effects might be confounded with direct reinforcement to the nontarget subjects. Teacher behavior in relation to nontarget subjects has not been assessed in the naturalistic study of vicarious punishment (Kounin & Gump, 1958).

ADDITIONAL VARIABLES

Several variables other than those enumerated above are likely to influence the extent to which vicarious effects occur. The reinforcement history of the nontarget persons and the level of their performance may be important. For example, Weisberg and Clements (1977) found that young children in a day-care center only slightly increased their instruction-following behavior when a few of their peers received positive consequences for that behavior. Later, reinforcement was provided intermittently to each subject, which markedly accelerated instruction-following behavior for all subjects. Once instruction following was high, providing reinforcing consequences to select peers was sufficient to maintain high levels of instruction following in children who no longer received direct consequences themselves. The authors suggested that vicarious reinforcement effects might result from a history of intermittent reinforcement and establishing a high level of behavior.

The influence of history was further suggested by Strain et al. (1976), who noted that subjects with a history of responsiveness to social reinforcers were likely to show vicarious effects of reinforcement when praise was delivered to peers. In contrast, one subject who had not responded previously to direct social approval did not show vicarious effects when a peer received approval. Of course, these latter conclusions are tentative because of the small number of subjects.

Several variables can be extrapolated from the laboratory findings on observational learning to suggest areas for research in applied settings.

For example, research on modeling has suggested that several characteristics of the model such as similarity to the observer (nontarget subjects), the prestige and competence of the model, the number of models,
and similar factors can influence the extent to which the behavior is
imitated by observers (Bandura, 1971; Rosenthal & Bandura, 1978). Research on vicarious reinforcement has yet to examine these factors systematically.

INTERPRETATIONS OF VICARIOUS EFFECTS

Reasons why vicarious effects occur in applied settings have been
proposed, although few specific tests of alternative interpretations have
been provided (see Bandura, 1971; Gewirtz, 1971). It is useful to consider
various interpretations. Alternative interpretations point to features of
the situation that may contribute to performance and that need to be
controlled for evaluating the basis for behavioral changes.

INTERDEPENDENCE OF BEHAVIORS OF TARGET AND NONTARGET SUBJECTS

One reason that providing consequences to one individual may
influence others might be that the behaviors of the target and nontarget
subjects are somehow interdependent. That is, the behavior of one person may be a direct function of how others are performing. Providing
consequences to one person may change the network of behaviors among
persons in the situation.

Interpreting vicarious effects on the basis of interdependency among
behaviors of target and nontarget subjects is feasible in many studies of
classroom settings where the target and nontarget subjects are adjacent or
within close proximity. In such cases, providing consequences to one
child might be expected to influence the behaviors of others.

For example, if a target child becomes more attentive in class, others
may have less opportunity to be disruptive. Essentially, the target subject
may have served as a direct source of the distraction or as an impetus for
the deviant behavior of the peer group. Once the behavior of the target
subject is controlled, the behavior of others may improve because of the
reduction in opportunities to misbehave (e.g., no one to talk with). The
inappropriate behavior of an adjacent child may be extinguished by the
target subject's lack of reactions to overtures of disruptiveness. Broden
(1970) provided data bearing on this interpretation and found that target
and nontarget subjects tend to glance at each other less when consequences are provided to one of them. Thus, interaction may be reduced
by the effects of the contingency, an effect that is evident in improved
behavior on the part of both subjects.

Aside from distraction, the interdependence of behaviors of target subjects may be evident in other ways. Perhaps the increase of the target person's behavior may entail changes in the behaviors of others who are implicitly part of the contingency. For example, in studies showing vicarious reinforcement with social interaction, providing reinforcement for social interaction of one subject means that other subjects will increase their social interaction with the target subject (e.g., Strain & Timm, 1974; Strain et al., 1976). The contingency is actually for cooperative or interactive responses, and changes on the part of the target subject and nontarget subjects might be expected. It is not possible in such situations to separate the effects of vicarious reinforcement from the direct effects of reinforcing complex and reciprocally interrelated behaviors.

The effects of reinforcing interdependent behaviors alone, independently of vicarious reinforcement, were evident in a study by Cooke and Apolloni (1976), who developed such behaviors as smiling, sharing, positive physical contact (e.g., hugging, patting), and providing compliments among learning-disabled children in a classroom. As behaviors of the target subjects increased with training, changes in the behaviors were also evident in untrained peers with whom the target subjects interacted. However, training of the target subjects was conducted outside of the presence of the untrained subjects. Special periods of interaction between trained and untrained children were observed in order to assess whether training effects generalized to an unstructured situation free from programmed reinforcement contingencies. Untrained subjects improved in the target behaviors even though they did not observe direct reinforcement for these behaviors. Hence, the specific behaviors that are developed in some persons may, by their very nature, encompass or result in changes in the performance of others.

When behaviors of target and nontarget subjects are highly interrelated and the subjects are within close proximity, "vicarious effects" might be expected. Although interdependence of behaviors may occur in some of the research, it does not readily account for the bulk of the evidence. In addition, demonstrations of vicarious reinforcement are available where nontarget subjects showed improvements in behavior as target subjects received reinforcing consequences for inappropriate behavior, as outlined below (Kazdin, 1973a, 1977). Thus, improvements in children who are adjacent to the target children are sometimes unrelated to the target child's behavior.

CUE PROPERTIES OF DIRECT CONSEQUENCES

Another reason that providing consequences to one individual influences the behavior of others may pertain to the cue properties of reinforcement delivery. The delivery of reinforcers such as praise to a target child may serve as a cue to adjacent children that other events are likely to follow. For example, in a classroom situation, teacher praise to one child may function as a discriminative stimulus (S^D) for other children because it often precedes direct, contingent reinforcement or punishment for these other children. After such experiences, hearing the teacher deliver praise or seeing the teacher nearby may serve as a cue that direct consequences are likely to follow. If these cues have been paired with such consequences in the past, the children are likely to perform the desired behaviors as a function of hearing or seeing the relevant cues associated with delivery of reinforcement or punishment.

An interpretation of vicarious effects that stresses the cuing functions of direct consequences relies upon stimulus control rather than a modeling or imitation explanation. Essentially, the *act* of delivering reinforcing or punishing consequences may prompt behavior of persons who do not receive direct consequences. The actual behaviors that the target subjects are performing may not be crucial to obtain vicarious effects since nontarget subjects may be responding to the cues.

This interpretation has been utilized plausibly in a few studies in explaining the initial basis for vicarious reinforcement effects. For example, (Kazdin (1973a) demonstrated the effects of vicarious reinforcement by providing teacher praise to target subjects for attentive behavior in a special education classroom with retarded children. When the target children received praise for *attentive* behavior, this behavior increased for both target and nontarget children. After a return to baseline conditions, the target children received praise contingent upon *inattentive* behavior. Although this tended to decrease attentive behavior of the target children, attentive behavior of the nontarget children increased markedly. Improvements in the behavior of nontarget children did not depend upon the specific behaviors that were reinforced in the target children. The delivery of reinforcement to the target children per se seemed to control behavior of the nontarget children.

One explanation of these results is that a phase where teacher praise was contingent upon *appropriate* behavior preceded the phase where praise was associated with *inappropriate* behavior of the target subject. The nontarget subject may have only observed reinforcement of the target subject's appropriate behavior early in the investigation, and thus did not make the discrimination in a later phase. Yet the order in which the phases are given does not seem to be crucial. Reinforcing inattentive behavior in a target child during the first reinforcement phase was still associated with improvements in performance of a nontarget subject (Kazdin, 1977).

These results might be accounted for by a stimulus control explanation of vicarious reinforcement. A difficulty with this explanation is that subjects would be expected to learn relatively quickly that delivering reinforcers to the target subject is not in fact associated with consequences for the nontarget subject. Eventually, priase to the target subject should lose its discriminative properties and vicarious effects of reinforcement should diminish. This explanation would account for the transitory effects of vicarious reinforcement in many of the studies reviewed earlier. However, in the situations in which the stimulus-control explanation was proposed, vicarious effects did not diminish quickly (Kazdin, 1973a, 1977). The failure of vicarious effects to diminish over time (up to three or four weeks) might have resulted from direct, intermittent reinforcement delivered to nontarget subjects during periods of the day not included in the research. The discriminative properties of praise might have been maintained by direct praise to peers followed by indirect (vicarious) praise at these other times (cf. Weisberg & Clements, 1977).

In any case, the stimulus control interpretation may account for some of the initial effects of vicarious reinforcement, particularly when behavior change in the nontarget child is independent of those changes made in the target child. When behavior of the nontarget children is influenced independently of the direction of change of the target children who receive direct consequences, a number of other variables may be particularly important. For example, the influence of either direct reinforcement of the nontarget child's behavior prior to the implementation of the vicarious-reinforcement project or the concurrent reinforcement of the behavior at times other than those observed might account for behavior.

INFORMATIVE FUNCTION OF DIRECT CONSEQUENCES

Vicarious effects might be accounted for by the information that is provided to nontarget children—one of the interpretations noted by Bandura (1971). The consequences that are delivered to select individuals convey information to others. Different kinds of information can be provided. Each of these alone or in conjunction might influence behavior and account for vicarious processes.

The initial source of information that might account for vicarious effects is information about the desired behaviors in the setting. By providing consequences to a target subject, information is conveyed to others about the situation-appropriate or desired behaviors. Another, certainly related, aspect is the information conveyed about the consequences that are available for the desired behaviors in the setting. Individuals may be able to perform the desired behavior but are unfamiliar with the consequences with which the behaviors are associated. Reinforcement or punishment following peer behavior can convey the information about the available consequences.

Information about both the desired behaviors and the available consequences suggest that individuals who do not receive direct consequences observe the behavior of the target subjects. The nontarget subjects may imitate those behaviors which they observe to be followed by reinforcing consequences in order to increase their own chances for these consequences. This interpretation is especially pertinent to situations in which the contingencies are not already familiar to all individuals and direct consequences have not been provided frequently. Yet, research mentioned earlier has shown that vicarious effects can and do occur without imitation of the behavior of a target subject who receives reinforcing consequences. Individuals who see others receive direct consequences do not always perform the behaviors they see reinforced in the target children (Kazdin, 1973a, 1977; Resick *et al.*, 1976).

Individuals in the setting may already be fully informed of the desired behaviors and the consequences with which they are associated. Direct observation of the target child who receives reinforcing consequences may convey information about the immediate availability or delivery of reinforcers. The information provided is not that there are contingencies or that particular behaviors are desired. Rather, the information is that the contingencies are in effect or being executed at a particular point in time. Expressed in this fashion, the information conveyed corresponds to that elaborated under the stimulus control interpretation of vicarious effects.

GENERAL COMMENTS

The overview of potential influences mediating vicarious effects provides implicit suggestions for maximizing the spread of effects of direct reinforcement or punishment contingencies. Providing consequences to a target subject is likely to influence others if the behavior of these other individuals is somehow incorporated into the contingency. Requiring target subjects to speak or interact with others is the primary example of this tactic, because social behavior of the target subject encompasses interactions with others whose behaviors are likely to be altered without directly programmed contingencies.

Also, the practice of occasionally following direct consequences for one child with immediate consequences intermittently administered to others is likely to help sustain the stimulus control value of reinforcer delivery. Finally, the delivery of direct consequences should be designed in such a way as to provide maximum information to nontarget subjects about the desired behaviors, the available consequences, and the times that these consequences can be provided. Variables mentioned earlier, such as conspicuousness of reinforcer delivery, may maximize the informative value of reinforcer delivery to nonreinforced peers.

LIMITATIONS AND RECOMMENDATIONS

Even though considerable evidence for vicarious reinforcement effects exists, particularly in the classroom, the findings need to be evaluated critically before making definitive recommendations about the use of vicarious processes. Several characteristics of the experiments may limit the generality of the results to ordinary classroom situations. In most experiments on vicarious reinforcement, investigators have controlled or eliminated all sources of direct reinforcement to evaluate the effects of vicarious reinforcement on select children (e.g., Kazdin, 1973a; Strain *et al.*, 1976). Although this technique may be necessary for isolating vicarious reinforcement in initial studies, vicarious effects probably do not operate this way under ordinary circumstances. The effects of vicarious reinforcement and punishment when isolated experimentally may be very different from ordinary situations where direct and vicarious effects operate in conjunction.

Another characteristic that may limit generality of the findings is the placing of children in relatively contrived situations that depart from the normal situation in which vicarious effects are likely to occur. For example, in some investigations children are placed into pairs that depart from the usual seating arrangement (e.g., Kazdin, 1973a), or receive reinforcing consequences on a rich schedule that departs from the usual conditions (e.g., Kazdin, 1973a; Okovita & Bucher, 1976). Also, children may be given tasks that totally depart from the usual situation so that the effects that are obtained may depart from those evident in more naturalistic interactions.

Finally, the range of behaviors studied has been relatively narrow. Classroom investigations have been devoted primarily to the alteration of on-task, attentive, or disruptive behavior. A few studies on social behavior and academic productivity suggest that vicarious effects are not limited to deportment, but additional work is needed to evaluate the generality of vicarious processes across classes of behavior.

Additional work elaborating the conditions that contribute to vicarious processes would provide a valuable base from which specific recommendations could be drawn. In advance of additional information, several tentative recommendations seem appropriate for maximizing the effects of vicarious processes.

To begin with, reinforcement delivery to children in the classroom should probably be increased in most classrooms. This recommendation is important because of evidence suggesting that teachers rarely deliver contingent approval in the classroom (Thomas, Presland, Grant, & Glynn, 1978; White, 1975). Aside from the obvious benefits of direct reinforcement, vicarious reinforcement effects are likely to be increased with more frequent reinforcement occasions in the classroom.

Aside from increased frequency, evidence suggests that delivery of direct reinforcement should be conspicuous. Preceding reinforcer delivery with a prompt to the class or to adjacent peers is likely to increase performance of the behavior among nontarget children. Of course, there may be a point at which conspicuous reinforcement to one child interrupts the behaviors of others and hence competes with the goal of the particular contingency.

The number of persons who receive direct consequences should be increased in a classroom. Evidence reviewed earlier suggested that direct consequences to several persons in a classroom lead to greater vicarious effects than do direct consequences to only one individual. For a given child whose behavior is being developed slowly under direct contingencies, additional opportunities for learning might be programmed by trials of several other children receiving consequences for the target behaviors.

Vicarious effects of reinforcement might be increased when children receive direct consequences for imitating appropriate behavior. The direct delivery of reinforcement to one child may produce vicarious effects in others. These vicarious effects may become more pronounced or consistent if they are immediately followed up with direct reinforcement for imitation of appropriate behavior.

Perhaps the major recommendation that can be culled from the available evidence pertains to how vicarious reinforcement is used. Vicarious reinforcement may have its greatest value in prompting the occurrence of behavior. The effects produced by vicarious reinforcement often are relatively weak and short-lived. Thus, vicarious reinforcement alone is not likely to develop high levels of sustained performance. Vicarious reinforcement may increase the likelihood that the behavior occurs among persons who did not receive direct consequences. However, evidence suggests that direct consequences should be given to all of the persons for whom change is desired. Thus, vicarious reinforcement may facilitate utilization of direct contingencies.

CONCLUSION

Vicarious processes have been shown to influence performance in the classroom settings across different age groups and populations. Although vicarious processes have been demonstrated in many programs with children, the effects have not been as consistent or potent as the direct operation of contingencies. Yet, the findings suggest that vicarious effects may enhance existing programs. Vicarious effects have rarely been explicitly programmed in the classroom. Factors that are likely to enhance these vicarious processes have not been maximized, so the potential influence of these processes cannot really be assessed.

Even if vicarious processes do not prove to produce potent effects in their own right, they may still be useful to add to an intervention. Vicarious processes might be incorporated explicitly with direct contingency manipulations to help gradually wean individuals from direct to more social control over behavior. To accomplish this goal, schedules of reinforcement might combine direct and vicarious consequences in such a way that at the beginning of a program, the control over behavior is almost exclusively based upon direct consequences. As behavior develops, direct consequences to the child and to the child's peers may be interspersed. Eventually, direct consequences to any particular individual may be very rare, although opportunities for vicarious consequences continue to be present. Future research needs to examine the utility of vicarious processes in effecting behavior change, facilitating the operation of direct contingencies, and enhancing sustained performance.

REFERENCES

Aaron, A.A., & Bostow, D.E. Indirect facilitation of on-task behavior produced by contingent free-time for academic productivity. *Journal of Applied Behavior Analysis*, 1978, *11*, 197.

Arnold, J.E., Levine, A.G., & Patterson, G.R. Changes in sibling behavior following family intervention. *Journal of Consulting and Clinical Psychology*, 1975, *43*, 683–688.

Bandura, A. Vicarious and self-reinforcement processes. In R. Glaser (Ed.), *The nature of reinforcement*. New York: Academic Press, 1971.

Bolstad, O.D., & Johnson, S.M. Self-regulation in the modification of disruptive behavior. *Journal of Applied Behavior Analysis*, 1972, *5*, 443–454.

Broden, M., Bruce, C., Mitchell, M.A., Carter, V., & Hall, R.V. Effects of teacher attention on attending behavior of two boys at adjacent desks. *Journal of Applied Behavior Analysis*, 1970, *3*, 199–203.

Brown, L., & Pearce, E. Increasing the production rates of trainable retarded students in a public school simulated workshop. *Education and Training of the Mentally Retarded*, 1970, *5*, 15–22.

Budd, K.S., & Stokes, T.F. *Cue properties of praise in vicarious reinforcement with preschoolers.* Paper presented at the 85th Annual Meeting of the American Psychological Association, San Francisco, August 1977.

Christy, P.R. Does use of tangible rewards with individual children affect peer observers? *Journal of Applied Behavior Analysis*, 1975, *8*, 187–196.

Cooke, T.P., & Apolloni, T. Developing positive social-emotional behaviors: A study of training and generalization effects. *Journal of Applied Behavior Analysis*, 1976, *9*, 65–78.

Drabman, R.S., & Lahey, B.B. Feedback in classroom behavior modification: Effects on the target and her classmates. *Journal of Applied Behavior Analysis*, 1974, *7*, 591–598.

Gewirtz, J.L. The roles of overt responding and extrinsic reinforcement in "self-" and "vicarious-reinforcement" and in "observational learning" and imitation. In R. Glaser (Ed.), *The nature of reinforcement*. New York: Academic Press, 1971.

Goetz, E.M., Holmberg, M.C., & LeBlanc, J.M. Differential reinforcement of other behavior and noncontingent reinforcement as control procedures during the modification of a preschooler's compliance. *Journal of Applied Behavior Analysis*, 1975, *8*, 77–82.

Hauserman, N., Zweback, S., & Plotkin, A. Use of concrete reinforcement to facilitate verbal initiations in adolescent group therapy. *Journal of Consulting and Clinical Psychology*, 1972, *38*, 90–96.

Kazdin, A.E. The effect of vicarious reinforcement on attentive behavior in the classroom. *Journal of Applied Behavior Analysis*, 1973, *6*, 71–78.(a)

Kazdin, A.E. The effect of vicarious reinforcement on performance in a rehabilitation setting. *Education and Training of the Mentally Retarded*, 1973, *8*, 4–11.(b)

Kazdin, A.E. Vicarious reinforcement and direction of behavior change in the classroom. *Behavior Therapy*, 1977, *8*, 57–63.

Kazdin, A.E. *Behavior modification in applied settings* (2nd ed.). Homewood, Ill: Dorsey, 1980.

Kazdin, A.E., Silverman, N.A., & Sittler, J.L. The use of prompts to enhance vicarious effects of nonverbal approval. *Journal of Applied Behavior Analysis*, 1974, *8*, 279–286.

Kirkland, K.D., & Thelen, M.H. Use of modeling in child treatment. In B.B. Lahey & A.E. Kazdin (Eds.), *Advances in clinical child psychology* (Vol. 1). New York: Plenum Press, 1977.

Kounin, J.S. *Discipline and group management in classrooms*. New York: Holt, Rinehart & Winston, 1970.

Kounin, J.S., & Gump, P.V. The ripple effect in discipline. *Elementary School Journal*, 1958, *59*, 158–162.

Lavigueur, H., Peterson, R.F., Sheese, J.G., & Peterson, L.W. Behavioral treatment in the home: Effects on an untreated sibling and long-term follow-up. *Behavior Therapy*, 1973, *4*, 431–441.

Okovita, H.W., & Bucher, B. Attending behavior of children near a child who is reinforced for attending. *Psychology in the Schools*, 1976, *13*, 205–211.

Patterson, G.R. Interventions for boys with conduct problems: Multiple settings, treatments, and criteria. *Journal of Consulting and Clinical Psychology*, 1974, *42*, 471–481.

Resick, P.A., Forehand, R., & McWhorter, A.Q. The effect of parental treatment with one child on an untreated sibling. *Behavior Therapy*, 1976, *7*, 544–548.

Rosenthal, T.L., & Bandura, A. Psychological modeling: Theory and practice. In S.L. Garfield & A. Bergin (Eds.), *Handbook of psychotherapy and behavior change* (2nd ed.). New York: Wiley, 1978.

Sechrest, L. Implicit reinforcement of responses. *Journal of Educational Psychology*, 1963, *54*, 197–201.

Strain, P.S., & Pierce, J.E. Direct and vicarious effects of social praise on mentally retarded preschool children's attentive behavior. *Psychology in the Schools*, 1977, *14*, 348–353.

Strain, P.S., & Timm, M.A. An experimental analysis of social interaction between a behaviorally disordered preschool child and her classroom peers. *Journal of Applied Behavior Analysis*, 1974, *7*, 583–590.

Strain, P.S., & Shores, R.E., & Kerr, M.M. An experimental analysis of "spillover" effects on the social interaction of behaviorally handicapped preschool children. *Journal of Applied Behavior Analysis*, 1976, *9*, 31–40.

Thomas, J.D., Presland, I.E., Grant, M.D., & Glynn, T.L. Natural rates of teacher approval and disapproval in grade-7 classrooms. *Journal of Applied Behavior Analysis*, 1978, *11*, 91–94.

Ward, M.H., & Baker, B.L. Reinforcement therapy in the classroom. *Journal of Applied Behavior Analysis*, 1968, *1*, 323–328.

Weisberg, P., & Clements, P. Effects of direct, intermittent, and vicarious reinforcement procedures on the development and maintenance of instruction-following behaviors in a group of young children. *Journal of Applied Behavior Analysis*, 1977, *10*, 314.

White, M.A. Natural rates of teacher approval and disapproval in the classroom. *Journal of Applied Behavior Analysis*, 1975, *8*, 367–372.

Wilson, D.D., Robertson, S.J., Herlong, L.H., & Haynes, S.N. Vicarious effects of time-out in the modification of aggression in the classroom. *Behavioral Modification*, 1979, *3*, 97–111.

6

Peer Tutoring in Academic Settings

Michael Gerber and James M. Kauffman

The Historical Basis for Peer Tutoring

In the early years of the nineteenth century, before public education existed, Joseph Lancaster founded a school for working-class children in London (Kaestle, 1973; Lancaster, 1803). Lancaster's belief that basic education would discipline and morally shape working-class children, together with his dislike for corporal punishment, attracted some financial supporters and hundreds of children. Faced with severe economic constraints, Lancaster devised a system of peer-mediated instruction which had immediate and dramatic international impact upon educational practice (Charconnet, 1975; Kaestle, 1975; Reigert, 1916/1969).

Lancaster's "monitorial system" consisted of a hierarchy of children who, under the guidance of a single teacher, managed the basic learning of hundreds of students. The overnight success of Lancasterian methods is attributable to: (a) treatment of the working-class school as a "system" or "machine" analogous in its organization to the industrial-production schemes which dominated that era; (b) systematic use of behavior-management techniques based on principles that have been formally described only within the past two decades (Kazdin & Pulaski, 1977); and (c) use of basic reading-, spelling-, and arithmetic-skill hierarchies similar to modern-day task analyses and behavioral objectives. For most of the first half of the nineteenth century, the Lancasterian system was the most acclaimed innovation in the organization of mass education in every Western country, some East European countries (including Russia), and

MICHAEL GERBER AND JAMES M. KAUFFMAN • Department of Special Education, University of Virginia, Charlottesville, Virginia 22903.

in Western territorial possessions around the world (Charconnet, 1975; Kaestle, 1973; Reigert, 1916).

The monitorial system was initially effective because of the manner in which instruction was organized and programmed. Levels (graded classes) were formed for each of the three academic areas—reading, spelling/writing, and arithmetic. A child's placement in a given class was entirely dependent upon his demonstrated (i.e., tested) proficiency in the skills taught at that level. Mastery of the instructional objectives for a given class meant automatic promotion to the next class in the sequence for that subject. For example, there was a class for learning to recognize and say the alphabet, followed by a class for recognizing and saying two-letter words and syllables, which was in turn followed by a class for learning three-letter words and syllables, and so on.

Each class consisted of a monitor and about 10 students. The monitor was equipped with proficiency in those skills being taught for the given class, plus a set of simple commands to be used in drills and testing, and, on occasion, a visual aid, such as a poster containing material to be learned. The students—"scholars," as they were called—sat in rows or stood in a semicircle according to their rank in the class. That is, the child who performed best was entitled to stand (or sit) in the first position and wear a badge identifying him as first in the class. The lesson proceeded by the monitor's prescribed commands (e.g., cues for attention, for respond-ing, or for displaying work). The scholars were required to give written or oral responses which the monitor immediately checked for correctness. Opportunities to respond were given to the class in order of their ranks. If students responded incorrectly, the monitor continued questioning others in rank order until the correct response was obtained, whereupon the child who was correct moved to the position (and rank) of the first child who responded incorrectly.

Lancaster established monitors to control noninstructional aspects of school management as well. For instance, there were monitor inspectors who ascertained whether or not a given student was to be promoted. There were monitors for attendance and monitors for supplies. In addi-tion, there was a "monitor general" who served as the monitor of all other monitors, thereby assuring that the monitors themselves were working appropriately.

The monitorial system worked well, in part because Lancaster had created a system of reward and punishment (also administered by monitors) which assured that every child was continually on-task, includ-ing the monitors themselves. Toward this end, Lancaster used what we would today describe as a token economy (Kazdin & Pulaski, 1977). Not only did a child's performance in his class competition provide the possi-bility of improving his rank and status, but also exchangeable tokens, merit badges, and toys could be earned for exemplary achievement both within the class and in the school as a whole. Lancaster insisted upon the liberal dispensing of rewards such as these, but also meted out punishment for tardiness, inattention, poor work, and other breaches of school conduct. Opposed as he was to corporal punishment, Lancaster relied on public humiliation and loss of honors or privileges as his most potent punishers. Some of his punishments strike the modern educator as somewhat bizarre or even cruel, but it must be remembered that the usual and accepted form of punishment in Lancaster's day was a beating. Moreover, Lancaster understood the reinforcing and corrective potential of permitting boys with behavior problems to act in the role of monitor.

> Lively, active-tempered boys, are the most frequent transgressors of good order, and the most difficult to reduce to reason; the best way to reform them is by making monitors of them. (quoted in Kaestle, 1973, p. 79)

Over a century and a half after Lancaster founded the Borrough Road School, Melaragno and Newmark (1969/1970) proposed a peer-tutoring solution to the problems of underachievement and of the public schools' failure to individualize instruction which occupied national attention in the 1960s.

> The ultimate objective . . . is the development of a functioning, operational "tutorial community," involving an entire elementary school. It will serve as a prototype model where people can observe a totally innovative school in operation and can gain experience in developing and operating a tutorial community. (Melaragno & Newmark, 1969/1970, p. 34)

Melaragno and Newmark's tutorial community, like Lancaster's Borrough Road School, was structured around the ideas of: (a) systematic and universal use of peers as mediators of instruction, (b) teachers serving as managers of instruction through their role in managing and training tutors, (c) a programmed curriculum based on task-analyzed behavioral objectives, (d) a model school to train other personnel in implementing similar programs, and (e) economy of teaching resources through the use of peers as teachers. Moreover, the target children toward which Melaragno and Newmark directed their "innovation" were ethnic-minority students who, like Lancaster's working-class children, were not being successfully educated under the existing system. They were predominantly from low-income families, and were the focus of political agitation and advocacy as part of larger movements of social reform.

Both the Lancasterian and Melaragno–Newmark innovations enjoyed initial successes and inspired much interest and imitation. Ultimately, neither program was sustained, probably because of the political turmoil which inevitably accompanies educational change. Despite the differences in time, motive, and geography, the similarities in the two programs are striking indeed. However, important distinctions can and should be made. Whereas Lancaster was intuitive, morally driven, and somewhat prescient in developing the monitorial system, Melaragno and Newmark were methodical and deliberate in their program development, implementation, and evaluation. This scientific approach to educational problems and the study of peers as instructional mediators heralded a new era in understanding education both as an institution and as a process. Such an understanding of the potential and problems of peer tutoring is the concern of this chapter.

The Pacoima, California project of Melaragno and Newmark (Melaragno, 1976) was not the first or sole rediscovery of the peer tutoring concept originated by Lancaster. Gartner, Kohler, and Riesman (1971) described the development of modern peer tutoring in the context of the broad educational reforms of the 1960s. The various early attempts at implementing peer-tutoring strategies were intimately associated with antipoverty and compensatory-education politics and, as such, were focused on the perceived need of minority youth for dramatic and radical educational interventions designed to correct underachievement and improve life outcomes (Gartner et al., 1971; Strodtbeck, Ronchi, & Hansell, 1976). Moreover, these programs departed from the Lancasterian tradition in their interest in: (a) the affective and attitudinal results which might accrue from peer tutoring, and (b) beneficial *tutor* outcomes as well as benefits for the tutee.

In the late 1960s through the 1970s, interest in peer tutoring was heightened by an abundance of testimonial evidence and a few empirical reports of both academic and emotional growth in tutor and tutee (Cloward, 1967; Gartner et al., 1971). For example, Gartner et al. (1971) reported on, or referred to, hundreds of local programs following the "learning-through-teaching" principle, which emphasized mutual benefits in tutoring. The earliest, and most cited, of these was the Youth Teaching Youth (YTY) program, which established large-scale, structured, after-school tutorials near ghetto schools in Philadelphia and Newark, New Jersey in 1967–1968. Reflecting a concern for adolescent unemployment as well as for underachievement, the YTY programs hired and trained academically underachieving teenagers to act as tutors for elementary-school students of the same socioeconomic background. By 1970, more than 200 school districts had adopted some type of after-school tutoring program. Other programs, based on some type of within-school or after-school peer tutoring, were also implemented throughout the 1970s. Melaragno (1974) claims that over 10,000 elementary schools attempted some form of peer-tutoring program.

Years of experimentation have yielded important information which can serve to guide the implementation of programs of peer tutoring or methods for using peers to mediate changes in their classmates' social or academic behaviors (Devin-Sheehan, Feldman, & Allen, 1976; Feldman, Devin-Sheehan, & Allen, 1976; McGee, Kauffman, & Nussen, 1977; Stainback, Stainback, & Lichtward, 1975; Strain, Cooke, & Apolloni, 1976). However, despite these many years of experience and an accumulating body of empirical research, several questions concerning the implementation of peer tutoring in school settings have not yet been satisfactorily answered. Different projects have used different evaluation instruments, many of the instruments having questionable reliability. Clear and unequivocal empirical evidence supporting the programmatic, as opposed to limited and incidental, use of peer tutoring as a valid instructional strategy is not abundant. Furthermore, the few controlled, experimental studies that have been published must be interpreted with caution. In addition, studies have not always adequately addressed questions of importance to educational administrators, practitioners, and other researchers. For example:

1. Historically, peer-tutoring schemes have been defended by arguments claiming greater efficiency in instruction and economy of resources (e.g., teacher time), but what reliable evidence supports or challenges these assertions?

2. Is there a normal, naturally occurring type of interpersonal "teaching" which peer-tutoring strategies may exploit in classroom environments?

3. Is there sufficient evidence to permit specification of a behavioral technology of peer tutoring?

4. What guidelines derived from empirical research can assist decision makers in selecting, training, and supervising tutors or choosing tutees?

5. What are the ethical considerations implied by the use of peers as mediators of instruction?

Each of these questions is addressed in the following sections of this chapter.

Peer Tutoring as an Instructional Resource

The underlying motivation and conceptualization of Lancaster's innovation arose out of economic necessity and the prevailing economic theory of his time. Not only could many children be taught despite scarce resources, but also, by applying the principles of industrial organization, Lancaster could provide instruction to great numbers of children. One teacher with appropriately managed monitors could teach 1,000 children!

In many ways the motivation and conceptualization of peer-tutoring schemes in the modern era, such as those which emerged from the school-reform movement of the 1960s, have been similar to Lancaster's. In both the nineteenth and twentieth centuries, the underachievement of children from low-income families was believed to threaten not only the children themselves, but also was perceived as threatening the social good. The solution offered by government-subsidized programs in the 1960s was a more individualized educational program supported by additional educational resources. Viewing peers as an instructional resource in an enterprise plagued by scarcity of teacher time per pupil naturally seemed promising. That is, teacher time, an expensive and relatively fixed resource in the classroom, could in effect be multiplied by training peers as mediators of instruction. If this premise was accepted, it was further argued that as more individualization was realized by the use of peer tutors, improved academic outcomes for more pupils could be achieved.

Several studies attempted to compare the effectiveness of various peer-tutoring plans to either teacher-led instruction or some form of self-instruction. These studies can be taken as at least a basis for exploring the proposition that peers as tutors constitute an instructional resource (Barry & Overman, 1977; Duff & Swick, 1974; Epstein, 1978; Jenkins, Mayhall, Peschka, & Jenkins, 1974; Oakland & Williams, 1975; Stainback & Stainback, 1972). In general, the results indicated that peer tutoring may be at least as effective as teacher-led instruction under certain specified conditions, and that tutoring as a supplement to teaching may be better than teaching alone.

For example, Jenkins et al. (1974) conducted a series of short experiments using an applied-behavior-analysis methodology comparing various outcomes of teacher-instructed small groups to mutual, structured tutoring among elementary special-education students. One of the skills taught in these experiments was word recognition. The number of correctly recognized words per minute was greater in the tutorial group than in the teacher-instructed group. The same result was replicated in other schools with different students and teachers. Similar results favoring tutoring over teacher-led instruction of small groups were reported for experiments using upper-elementary exceptional children who learned spelling lists, multiplication facts, and higher rates or oral reading. In the experiment comparing tutoring with self-instruction of math facts, the tutoring condition was related to greater gains and higher mean facts correct per minute. Jenkins argued that individualized instruction by the teacher in special-education resource rooms is expensive and that the teacher's role should shift to that of instructional manager. Various instructional resources, including tutors, could be organized and used to individualize instruction more economically.

In another comparison study, Oakland and Williams (1975) used a randomized group design to compare gain scores in word recognition and comprehension achieved by third- and fourth-grade students who were assigned to one of the three learning groups: (a) tutoring only (i.e., no teacher), (b) supplementary tutoring, and, (c) teaching only (i.e., no tutoring). They found that the supplementary-tutoring group made greater gains than the teaching-only group, followed by the tutoring-only group. However, the differences in gains were not statistically significant.

A similar finding emerged from a study by Stainback and Stainback (1972) which compared the performances of upper-elementary students assigned to either a tutorial or self-study condition on measures of arithmetical skills. Again, no statistically significant differences were found between the experimental and control groups. Since the experimental group received tutoring as a *supplement* to regular teaching, the authors concluded that peer tutoring plus teaching was shown to be no worse than teacher-led instruction and independent study.

Duff and Swick (1974) did find that students in lower elementary grades who were randomly assigned as tutees showed significantly greater gains in reading achievement than students in a teacher-led contrast group. They also found that the tutees' achievement was correlated with the skill level of their randomly assigned upper-elementary tutors. To understand the apparent contradiction presented by these studies, it is important to note that Duff and Swick and the Stainbacks used significantly different criteria in creating their tutor and tutee subject pools. Duff and Swick identified possible tutees from those students exhibiting a pretutorial performance that was near grade level. Their prospective tutors were relatively low-achieving. In contrast, the Stainbacks' tutees were in the bottom third of their grade in tested arithmetic achievement and their tutors were selected from among high achievers. Interestingly, neither study found significant gains in tutor achievement.

However, Epstein (1978) found that both tutors and tutees in an experimental group of learning-disabled, primary-grade children achieved reading scores that were significantly higher than those obtained by children assigned randomly to four control groups: (a) peer tutoring in math (i.e., a Hawthorne control), (b) self-instruction, (c) teacher-led instruction, and (d) no additional instruction (i.e., blind control). Epstein stressed that this outcome was attributable to several "structural" factors. These factors included a thorough pretutoring orientation for the students, easy-to-follow, step-by-step directions for the students, programmed material which prevented student error and maximized consistency, and careful selection of tutors based on their knowledge of the subject matter.

Unfortunately, however encouraging these findings seem, it cannot be assumed that the utilization of trained and competent tutors is without any real cost. The peer tutor is not a *free* resource. Existing school resources must be allocated so as to create and sustain peers as teaching mediators. Few proponents of peer tutoring offer evidence to support the implementation of programs on the grounds that it is cost-effective or has a favorable benefit–cost ratio. Moreover, an implicit assumption is often made that peer tutoring represents the use of a *new* resource. That assumption is not quite valid. The use of peers as tutors simply represents a *different allocation of existing resources* which may or may not result in greater productivity (i.e., better academic outcomes).

If teacher time is the most expensive and most critical resource in the classroom, it can be seen that the teacher can "invest" time in creating instructional materials, arranging the classroom environment, conducting instruction, or keeping records according to whatever trade-off between short-term and long-term outcomes is deemed most desirable. For example, a teacher might choose in a planning hour to: (a) arrange materials and notes for a group lesson, (b) prepare and organize materials for a self-instructional package, or (c) train students to perform as peer tutors. The teacher's choice, assuming all else is equal, involves a complex distribution of direct-teacher-instruction time across children in the classroom in a manner that achieves an array of short-term and long-term outcomes with the students. To do this the teacher must also choose teaching methods and instructional technologies which increase the productivity of each teaching hour beyond the productivity obtainable if the teacher were to divide his or her time among the students.

Therefore, the choice to train one or more students as peer tutors is rational *if* the resulting educational outcomes are improved with the expenditure of the same amount of teacher time, or *if* the educational outcomes remain the same with an investment of less time. Consequently, research that seeks to compare peer-tutoring outcomes with teacher-led outcomes, such as that of Oakland and Williams (1975), must not be content to find no significant difference in learning without also comparing the investment in time and materials that underlies the particular teacher- or peer-led instruction being considered. Clearly, if many hours of training, extensive material preparation, and time-consuming monitoring are required to achieve the same educational objectives attainable with fewer hours of direct, teacher-led instruction (or the use of other, alternative methods), then a peer-tutoring program is an option to be weighed very carefully.

The studies that claim to have investigated the comparative benefits of peer tutoring as an instructional resource have not been rigorous in accounting for these considerations. Many studies fail to report in detail the amount of instructional resources required for training or maintenance of peer tutors. Others neglect to provide clear information concerning the range of educational objectives the tutor is prepared to implement or the amount of time the tutor can be productive without further investment of teacher time. These concerns must be addressed more adequately before peer tutors can be conceptualized as instructional resources comparable to others under the teacher's control.

Aside from assertions of economic efficiency, the proponents of peer tutoring sometimes argue that the cultural similarities between tutor and tutee may independently enhance learning. Holliday and Edwards (1978), for example, have argued that peer tutoring may be especially effective with black students because of its similarity to existing cultural practices which stress the responsibility of older siblings for younger children. Fourth- and sixth-grade tutors were assigned to low-achieving third-grade students once each week over a seven-month period. After six months, Holliday and Edwards reported that the average gain for tutees in tested vocabulary and comprehension skills was 23 and 16 months, respectively, for those having fourth- and sixth-grade tutors. However, it is not clear from the published report what portion of the gain scores was attributable to tutoring and what portion resulted from the ongoing teaching program.

A similar cultural rationale was given for a tutoring program reported by Gardiner (1978). Inner-city third- and fourth-graders were assigned to tutor first- and second-graders. The tutors and tutees participated in 11 weeks of ongoing "guidance" sessions, including meetings, field trips, and other activities designed to encourage close tutor–tutee relationships. Though Gardiner claims that the program benefited both tutor and tutee, a statistical analysis of the data is not provided, thereby precluding inferences.

Patterson (1976) reported on a peer-tutoring program for all black sixth- and seventh-graders in one Dallas school who were low achievers. The program failed to reach criterion levels of improvement within eight months for at least 60% of the students. It is therefore difficult to find support for the hypothesis that peer tutoring is especially suitable for minority students.

In another inner-city study, however, Luckner, Rosenfield, Sikes, and Aronson (1976) assigned rotating tutoring responsibilities to fifth- and sixth-graders over a two-week period and found that the statistically significant treatment effect of increased social studies test scores was largely due to large increases in minority students' posttest scores, whereas the gain for white students was not significant. The authors did not report whether or not there were significant pretest differences between racial groups, nor did they contrast the tutoring effect with any specific teacher-instruction model (i.e., the control was simply described as "traditional"). Consequently, it is difficult to determine to what degree the reported gains for the minority students were the product of peer tutoring.

Studies such as these, which have attempted to demonstrate the effectiveness of peer tutoring based on cultural affinity, are marred by serious methodological flaws and inadequate data analysis. Furthermore, even those studies which report significant gains have not demonstrated that peer tutoring (either alone or as an instructional supplement) is more effective than alternative strategies. Since the rediscovery of peer tutoring coincided with compensatory-education concerns in the 1960s, many of the anecdotal and testimonial reports of successful peer-tutoring programs have emanated from researchers or practitioners working in schools with large numbers of underachieving minority students (Gartner *et al.*, 1971; Lippit, 1976; Strodtbeck *et al.*, 1976). More empirical research is necessary to support the notion that peer tutoring is especially suited for use as an instructional resource in educational programs for minority students.

PEER TUTORING IN THE NATURAL CLASSROOM ENVIRONMENT

Peer tutoring may refer to large-scale programmatic efforts in the Lancasterian tradition or to one-time, limited instructional strategies such as designs reported in the experimental literature (e.g., Devin-Sheehan *et al.*, 1976). Another concept of peer tutoring supposes that various helping and cooperative behaviors are natural concomitants of group endeavor, such as in classrooms, under certain specifiable conditions. These normal helping behaviors are seen as part of a natural socialization processes that classroom environments either encourage or suppress (Allen, 1976; Bronfenbrenner, 1970; Hartup, 1976). Unfortunately, it is often the case, as Strodtbeck (1976) has pointed out, that

> . . . there is no disposition in our schools, in the ghetto or elsewhere, to encourage a collective responsibility for the performance of one's peers. (p. 215)

Of course, in situations in which resource scarcity is particularly severe, cooperation is often encouraged for other than educational reasons. For example, at the beginning of this century there were an estimated 200,000 "one-room" schools in this country (Devin-Sheehan &

Allen, 1975). In 1970, there were still over 2,000 such schools with six to eight grades per school. Devin-Sheehan and Allen conducted a survey of these schools in Nebraska to investigate the degree to which peer-tutoring strategies had emerged by necessity. Of the 110 teachers surveyed, 77% justified the use of peers as tutors as a method of individualizing instruction; 35% said that tutoring had benefits for the tutee, and 26% thought it had benefits for the tutor. Approximately one-third of the schools used some form of informal, occasional tutoring on a one-to-one basis. Another third of the schools used more formalized strategies of same-age or cross-age tutoring.

Damico and Watson (1976) conducted an ethological study of peer-helping behaviors and relationships which occurred naturally among third- and fifth-graders attending a laboratory school. They were able to observe various categories of peer interactions which could be considered mutually helpful. Children spontaneously sought the help of peers to obtain specific task information, to clarify instructions, or to acquire necessary materials. Likewise, children responded helpfully contingent upon a fellow student's or the teacher's request. However, Damico and Watson reported that most behaviors observed were not peer-interactive, that there were no instances of cross-sex helping interactions, and that observed patterns of relationship remained stable throughout the school year, despite the fact that the teacher verbally encouraged and rewarded (verbally) helping behaviors.

Blaney, Stephan, Rosenfield, Aronson, and Sikes (1977) hypothesized that cooperative interactions in the classroom resulted from mutually advantageous outcomes and that, similarly, the creation of interdependencies should foster positive peer relations and desirable academic outcomes. They placed 245 fifth-graders in learning groups and assigned them the role of peer teacher in rotation. The groups were equated on the basis of sex, ethnicity, and ability. The children were instructed to master part of the assigned material and to teach what they learned to the other members of their group. When contrasted with a control group receiving traditional instruction, the investigators found that the academic performance of the learning-group members was "as good or better" compared to that of the controls.

Slavin (1977) and De Vries and Slavin (1978) reported several studies which attempted to create group interdependency as a means of achieving targeted academic and behavioral outcomes. Group interdependency is created by the use of the "teams-tournaments-games" (TTG) concept introduced by Slavin (1977), in which competition between groups fosters cooperation within groups. A special system permits the scoring of both individual-effort and team totals. Most importantly, individuals' scores are weighted in such a way as to allow relatively low-achieving students to make as large a contribution as their high-achieving peers to their teams' totals. De Vries and Slavin noted that effort toward group goals spontaneously produced increased rates of peer tutoring for which both the tutee and tutor received reinforcement.

Feshbach (1976) reported a series of studies investigating the natural teaching styles of young children when assigned to teach a peer a simple task. Feshbach found that even when they are as young as four years old children's patterns of reinforcement of others may be a function of their sociocultural background. When good and poor readers were assigned to teach a simple maze task to either good or poor readers, Feshbach found that: (a) poor readers tended to be more negative toward tutees who were good readers, (b) competent female readers tended to be more negative toward tutees who also were good readers, and (c) competent male readers tended to be more negative toward tutees who were not similarly competent. There was also a tendency for competent male readers to positively reinforce other competent readers, whereas competent female readers tended to reinforce problem readers more often. Feshbach argued that the differential reinforcement patterns observed in her studies ultimately reflected different histories of reinforcement in the home. That is, children whose cognitive and behavioral successes have been rewarded by parents will tend to be more successful in school and be more responsive to the intrinsic reward system of the classroom. However, an interesting divergence in the patterns of reinforcement while tutoring was noted between boys and girls who were good readers. While boys tended to reward competence and punish poor performance more often, girls displayed the reverse pattern when tutoring.

The issue of natural reward structures at work among children was clarified by research reviewed by Buckholdt and Wodarski (1978). The results of a series of experiments appeared to indicate that either direct reinforcement of tutoring or specific structures of group contingencies could promote and maintain tutoring and other helping behaviors among school-age children in classrooms. The term "group contingencies" in Buckholdt and Wodarski's review refers to social and tangible rewards that are delivered to individuals contingent upon some measure of the performance of their group. For example, they described group contingencies based upon the average performance of the group, the average of the highest performances, or the average of the lowest performances. In all cases, though the academic output varied under different contingencies, the frequency of peer-tutoring interactions reliably increased.

Slavin and Wodarski (1977) attempted to analyze the learning-team phenomenon into two component structures—a cooperative-task structure and a cooperative-reward structure. In their experiment, four of 11 classes of fourth-graders were organized into learning teams, given assignments, encouraged to help one another, and assigned scores based upon both individual and group performance. This group of classes was designated as the "team-with-tutoring" group. The remaining seven classes were designated as follows: (a) "team only" (i.e., they were asked not to help one another), (b) "tutor only" (i.e., no team membership, but encouragement to find others to work with), and (c) "no team or tutoring" (i.e., a control group). Slavin and Wodarski found that for all groups that had teams, peer tutoring and on-task behavior were significantly more frequent than for no-team groups, for all groups that included tutoring, less time was spent on-task than for groups that did not include tutoring. The researchers argued that some fundamental opposition may exist in a team-learning-plus-tutoring condition because the increased time spent tutoring to meet team goals may counter the expected individual increases derived from having access to peer tutoring.

However, Hamblin, Hathaway, and Wodarski (1971) showed that manipulation of group contingencies can increase group and individual academic performance, especially in inner-city schools where large numbers of students may be underachieving. In two experiments, the researchers compared academic performance in reading, math, and spelling under two different group contingencies—reinforcement based upon the average of the highest performances, and reinforcement based upon the average of the lowest performances. The higher-achieving pupils tended to perform better under the high-performance contingency, while the low-achieving pupils improved most under the low-contingency condition, even though each of the experimental subjects was exposed to the various contingency conditions in random order (i.e., there were not order effects).

In the second study, Hamblin (1971) investigated the effect of varying the proportion of reward that was earned contingent upon group vs. individual performance. As the proportion of reward based upon group effort increased, disruptive behavior decreased and peer tutoring increased markedly. Even the high-achieving students performed better under the increasing-return-to-group contingency arrangements. Clearly, the increases in academic performance of the lower-achieving students were related to the dramatic increase in peer tutoring which accompanied an increasing portion of reward contingent upon group effort.

McCarty, Griffin, Apolloni, and Shores (1977) have reported similar findings with behavior-disordered adolescents in a hospital classroom; group-performance contingencies were functionally related to increases in arithmetic problem solving as well as associated improvements in social behavior, including increased positive verbalizations and peer tutoring. Ulman and Sulzer-Azaroff (1975) compared individual contingencies with group contingencies with a similar population and found that the percentage of correct arithmetic problems was higher under individual contingency arrangements. However, rewards were delivered to the subjects by first pooling the individually earned token reinforcers and then equally dividing the pool among the subjects. Though in the Hamblin (1971) experiments the amount of reward was fixed by the performance of some or all of the individuals, the amounts were calculated at the end of the task without any intermediate reinforcement of individuals. When individuals in the Ulman and Sulzer-Azaroff study earned rewards based upon their individual effort and then suffered a possible loss in the ultimate division of the aggregated reward, their performance showed a preference of reward contingent upon individual effort only.

Nevertheless, it is not entirely clear from Hamblin *et al.* (1971) and McCarty (1977) to what extent high-achieving students were responding to the tangible reward and to what extent their motivation stemmed from peer interaction and the intrinsic reward of high performance. It is possible that they or other, more average students preferred more individualized contingencies under different circumstances. In fact, Hamblin reported that students initially objected to reward contingent upon the performance of low-achieving classmates. However, they concluded that the students seemed to share "a cultural bias towards individual contingencies," which was apparently overcome without difficulty.

These various studies suggest that perhaps more spontaneous helping behavior and peer tutoring is not observed in the natural classroom environment because prevailing instructional philosophy, administrative barriers, or systematic social reinforcement for competitiveness prevent the arrangement of those group contingencies which would foster collective responsibility for one's peers. If peer tutoring in its various forms were available as part of a comprehensive instructional technology, its use could be made dependent upon specific instructional needs. It would not have to be pitted against "regular" teacher-led instruction, but rather could become part of a system of alternative teaching techniques and strategies (Bronfenbrenner, 1970; Sowell, Candler, Blackburn, & Blackburn, 1978).

PEER TUTORING AS AN INSTRUCTIONAL TECHNOLOGY

The concept of an instructional technology is different from the Lancasterian adaptation of an industrial technology for use in education. In the Lancasterian system, the organization of the school and its activities required the homogenization of the students, their monitors, and the mode of learning. For example, in 1818, Joseph Hammel described the monitorial system to the Russian Czar as follows:

> This method owes its excellence to the distribution of tasks, a principle which in England has already produced marvellous effects in all branches of industry. After it had been tried out with signal success in connection with mechanical work, the idea occurred of applying it to the cultivation of the mind—with equally gratifying results. (quoted in Charconnet, 1975, p. 7)

Instructional technology differs from the nineteenth-century technology of commodity production both in its historical origins and its mode of application. It is the systematic application of methods derived from empirical investigations of learning. It is designed and applied with the objectively defined needs of the learner in mind. In the hands of a knowledgeable and capable teacher, an instructional technology based upon principles of learning is a powerful tool for achieving educational goals for individual students.

Presently, the historically noted and naturally occurring phenomenon described as "peer tutoring" can be subjected to scientific scrutiny. Its internal dynamics can be analyzed and explicated and its beneficial features may be included within an effective instructional technology for a wide range of educational purposes.

Since the first large-scale experiments with peer tutoring in the 1960s, scores of programs have been implemented and somewhat fewer empirical investigations undertaken (Allen, 1976; Allen & Feldman, 1976; Cloward, 1967; Devin-Sheehan et al., 1976; Gartner et al., 1971; Sowell et al., 1978; Stainback et al., 1975; Wagner, 1974). However, only recently, with the widespread use of applied behavior-analysis techniques, have the variables controlling the behavioral interaction during peer tutoring been investigated empirically (Apolloni, 1977; Buckholdt & Wodarski, 1978; Conrad, 1975; Dineen, Clark, & Risley, 1977).

One of the central principles of an applied science of education is that children's behaviors, be they academic performances or social interactions, tend to occur more predictably when they are reinforced by immediate consequences. If responding in a given circumstance results in praise from the teacher or attention from an admired or respected peer, the probability of that same response occurring in the next similar circumstance increases. Over the past 15 years, researchers and practitioners have accumulated a wealth of evidence indicating the potency of reinforcement emanating from children's peers (McGee et al., 1977).

Reinforcement techniques in peer-tutoring studies fall into three general categories. The simplest and least intrusive method for eliciting peer-tutoring behaviors involves changes in the classroom reward structure by the setting of group contingencies (Hamblin et al., 1971; McCarty et *al.*, 1977). When individuals are rewarded for mutual effort toward a common goal, peer-tutoring behaviors occur spontaneously. It is not yet known whether intergroup competition will increase this effect (De Vries & Slavin, 1978) or if group contingencies that carry a risk of loss contingent upon a peer's lack of achievement will produce smaller academic gains and more negative peer interactions (Axelrod, 1973; Frankosky & Sulzer-Azaroff, 1978; Ulman & Sulzer-Azaroff, 1975). Under group contingencies arranged to reward individuals for group effort but not to punish them for the failures of other members, positive social behaviors have been seen to increase (Hamblin *et al.*, 1971; Harris & Sherman, 1973; Harris, Sherman, Henderson, & Harris, 1972; McCarty *et al.*, 1977). Unfortunately, very few studies of peer tutoring induced by group contingencies have directly measured the positiveness of student interaction or described the topographies of the behaviors that constitute "tutoring."

A second category of reinforcement involves rewarding the peer tutor for appropriate tutoring behaviors (Buckholdt & Wodarski, 1978; Dineen *et al.*, 1977; Johnston & Johnston, 1974; Sanders & Glynn, 1977). For example, Johnston and Johnston and Sanders and Glynn provided reinforcement to tutors for correct monitoring of the target behaviors of another child. Fourth-grade children assigned to monitor misbehavior in the Sanders and Glynn study paid less attention to nontarget behaviors and monitored more accurately under reinforcement contingencies. The behavior of the target child improved as the peer monitoring improved. Johnston and Johnston modified articulation problems in a target child by reinforcing a peer monitor with tokens. Generalization to nonintervention settings was accomplished by continued reinforcement of the peer monitoring.

In a carefully designed study, Dineen *et al.* (1977) trained three children to play a rotating role as spelling tutor for the remaining two pupils. Both tutee and tutor were rewarded based on the tutee's performance on a postsession spelling test. An observing teacher also intermittently praised both the tutor's and tutee's on-task behavior and fined inappropriate responding by loss of tokens. The results showed that the spelling gains of the tutors were almost as great as those of the tutees, and both were significantly greater than performances under a nontutoring control condition.

A third category of reinforcement technique applied to peer tutoring includes direct reinforcement of the tutee for appropriate or improved performance. This reinforcement either occurs naturally as a result of the social encounter (Feshbach, 1976) or is manipulated by a trained tutor (Collins & Calevro, 1974; Conrad, 1975; Jenkins *et al.*, 1974). In the studies using trained tutors to administer praise or token reinforcement, very little is reported concerning the nature, duration, or success of the training methods used. In most cases, it is simply noted that the tutors were taught to discriminate correct responses, to reinforce the tutee contingent upon a correct response, and to record instances of correct or incorrect responding. Conrad provided second graders in the Follow Through project with tutor training in reinforcement and correction procedures. The performance of tutees on a test of sight words was compared according to whether the tutees received teaching from a trained or untrained tutor. The performance of tutees being taught by trained tutors was significantly better than that of tutees taught by untrained tutors. In general, experience with children as tutors or behavior-change agents has supported some kind of training when the intervention procedure requires peer-delivered reinforcement (McGee et al., 1977). However, it is clear that the type of behavior the tutor must teach as well as the complexity of the behavior expected of the tutor must be considered.

The nature of the child being tutored does not seem to be a critical matter. Successful peer-tutoring schemes have been used with preschoolers (Stokes & Baer, 1976), developmentally delayed toddlers (Apolloni, 1977), economically disadvantaged students (Hamblin et al., 1971), mentally retarded children (Barry & Overman, 1977; Wagner, 1974; Wagner & Sternlicht, 1975), profoundly retarded adolescents (Snell, 1979), learning-disabled children (Collins & Calevro, 1974; Epstein, 1978; Jenkins et al., 1974), speech-impaired students (Evans & Potter, 1974; Johnston & Johnston, 1974), and emotionally or behaviorally disordered children (McCarty et al., 1977; Slavin, 1977; Strain et al., 1976).

Likewise, the characteristics of the tutor may vary considerably. Tutors have been low achievers (Cloward, 1967, 1976; Duff & Swick, 1974), preschoolers (Apolloni, 1977; Feshbach, 1976; Stokes & Baer, 1976), learning-disabled (Epstein, 1978; Jenkins et al., 1974), mentally retarded (Snell, 1979; Wagner & Sternlicht, 1975), male or female, highly preferred or not preferred by the tutee, expecting good or poor performance from the tutee (Conrad, 1975; Ehly & Larsen, 1977), and with or without specific training (Conrad, 1975). What appears to be important to the success of peer tutoring is mutual reward, some of which may be instrinsic to the tutoring process (Allen & Feldman, 1976) and some of which derives from the reward structure imposed by the classroom or experimental environment.

A second factor which seems critical is the organization and structure of the material to be tutored and the responses expected from the tutees. Peer tutors have taught their classmates social studies (Luckner et al., 1976), math skills (Collins & Calevro, 1974; Harris & Sherman, 1973; Jenkins et al., 1974; McCarty et al., 1977), reading skills (Duff & Swick, 1974; Epstein, 1978; Feldman, Towson, & Allen, 1975; Hamblin et al., 1971; Harris et al., 1972; Jenkins et al., 1974; Oakland & Williams, 1975), phoneme articulation (Evans & Potter, 1974; Johnston & Johnston, 1974), spelling (Dineen *et al.*, 1977; Ehly & Larsen, 1977; Harris *et al.*, 1972; Jenkins *et al.*, 1974), and motor skills (Apolloni, 1977). In most cases, though, the material was organized in a programmed format or in some other clear hierarchical and sequential arrangement which the tutor could easily follow. Moreover, the responses to be obtained from the tutee were consistently simple and unambiguous, such as writing the solution to an arithmetic problem, reading a word, articulating a sound, or spelling a word. This type of structure aided the tutors in discriminating correct responses which were to signal them to deliver reinforcement or correction. Additionally, the programmed arrangement of the material permitted the tutor to work unassisted over many tutoring sessions. Clear behavioral objectives also made it possible for the teacher to integrate tutoring and other instructional methods so that peer tutoring facilitated and did not compete with the overall instructional program (Melaragno, 1976; Melaragno & Newmark, 1969/1970).

With programmed instructional material and an adequate reward structure, the trained tutor can function quite independently in most settings (Rosenbaum, 1973). Unlike the single large hall in which Lancaster's monitors worked, the modern peer tutor can be effective in the regular classroom at all grade and ability levels (Devin-Sheehan *et al.*, 1976; Harris & Sherman, 1973). The tutor, in fact, can assist the tutee in transferring a learned behavior to new settings once the tutor is established as the source of reinforcement for certain target behaviors (Stokes & Baer, 1976).

Unfortunately, the applied research does not yet answer all the questions of concern to practitioners. For example, in the studies that manipulated group contingencies, direct measurement of the tutoring behaviors elicited was seldom reported. It is important to know what specific behaviors both tutor and tutee exhibit and how they are related over the period of tutoring interaction. Tutoring obviously refers to a class of behaviors requiring further elucidation. For example, Allen and Feldman (1976) investigated the relationship between the tutee's performance and the tutor's attitude toward tutoring a specific student. The tutor's reactions to the tutee (i.e., attributions about intelligence, liking, enjoyment of the interaction, etc.) were related to the *initial* success or failure of the tutee regardless of the tutee's performance in subsequent sessions.

This finding is especially interesting in light of Conrad's (1975) data showing that pretutorial expectancy does not significantly affect the tutorial outcome. Furthermore, Ehly and Larsen (1977) have shown that pretutorial liking of the tutee or the tutor does not affect outcomes either. Moreover, although the tutor's reactions to the tutee may be based on initial experiences, there is evidence indicating that the tutee's reaction to tutoring depends on whether or not a trend toward improvement is perceived. For instance, Sanders and Glynn (1977) found that tutors who initially were not highly preferred by their tutees were more highly regarded following improvements in the tutee's target behavior. Since the tutor is a source of reinforcement when target behaviors improve, it is reasonable to suppose that the tutee's liking for the tutor will increase as the rate of reinforcement increases. The research further shows that children who have a history of being reinforced by their peers will be more susceptible to peer modeling and instruction (McGee et al., 1977).

Consequently, it can be seen that the initial success of the tutor is as important as the eventual success of the tutee. Both participate in a complicated interaction during which each is capable of affecting the behavior of the other. The empirical research reviewed thus far does not assess the variable long-term effects of such reciprocal relations, nor does it attend directly to those factors that may contribute to maintenance or generalization of behaviors evolving out of the tutoring encounter. The most highly controlled of the studies reported in the research literature tend to involve few subjects in stable laboratory environments for relatively brief periods of time. Similar studies need to be conducted in less controlled natural environments for longer periods to investigate the effects of alterations in the normal behavioral ecology of the classroom when peer tutoring is made routine.

For example, Rosen, Powell, Shubot, and Rollins (1978) have raised some serious questions concerning the relationships among perceived performance, actual performance, and role satisfaction when the relative abilities of tutor and tutee, the equity of their roles, relationship over time, and changes in role assignment are manipulated. Their findings indicated that when the differences between tutor and tutee were relatively small, satisfaction with role did not correlate significantly with actual performance. Tutors resisted changes in their status roles as tutors when the differences between tutor and tutee were relatively great. The implications of these data for understanding the long-term development of tutorial relationships in a classroom are not clear, but they suggest that assignment of status as tutor may interfere with tutoring in terms of cooperative and helpful behavior.

These various findings suggest that peer tutoring may play a significant, even powerful, part in an overall instructional technology. Clearly, the control of contingency arrangements, the organization of material, and the monitoring of both tutor and tutee performance are mandatory in future research if the technology is to be advanced. However, it has been seen that control of contingency arrangements involves significant control over the peer-interaction behaviors identified with peer tutoring. Part of this control will derive from careful planning of instructional sequences, adequate pretutorial training for the tutor, and active monitoring of peer-interaction behaviors. In addition, the congruence of behavior-management procedures, such as the contingent arrangement of positive reinforcement, can provide a unified context in which peer tutoring can contribute to the general program of behavior management and instruction. Finally, the use of clearly defined, hierarchically arranged behavioral objectives makes peer tutoring a useful extension of and not an alternative to normal instructional processes.

GUIDELINES FOR THE USE OF PEER TUTORING

Guidelines based mainly on user experience have been available for many years for those desiring to implement programs of peer tutoring (Ehly, 1977; Gartner et al., 1971; Lippitt, 1976; Melaragno, 1974, 1976, 1977; Niedermeyer, 1976; Sowell et al., 1978; Vacc, 1978). It is now possible to begin constructing technical as well as programmatic guidelines based on empirical research. The recent experimental literature which has analyzed peer tutoring within a framework of instructional technology provides the data base for instructional as well as administrative decision making and planning.

WHEN TO TUTOR

The persisting argument in favor of peer tutoring stems from the perception of classroom programs as resource-scarce in the face of ever greater pressures to individualize instruction. It has been proposed in a previous section of this chapter that peers do not represent a new resource, but rather a different use of existing resources. Teacher planning, training, and management are critical and continuing factors in peer-tutoring implementation, even when relatively simple, unstructured tutoring is to be encouraged by the arrangement of various group contingencies. To the extent that teacher time must be devoted to implementation of tutoring procedures, the decision to use peer tutors must take into account the *real* costs and benefits of tutoring compared to alternative uses of the same teacher time.

Those who would use peer-tutoring procedures should also consider the prevailing modes of instruction and behavior management as well as the reward structure of the given classroom. A precisely targeted use of peers as tutors requires that the tutoring complement, not subvert, the normal instructional program. It has been shown that peer tutoring is successful when the supporting classroom environment: (a) encourages cooperative behaviors by its reward structure; (b) provides clearly defined, hierarchically arranged learning objectives; and, (c) maintains a systematic congruence and consistency between its behavior management and instructional procedures. If any of these elements is missing in a classroom, it would be advisable to instate it prior to any large-scale efforts involving peer tutoring.

Lastly, if peer tutoring is to be a controlled and directed technique of enhancing academic outcomes, the same thoroughness and clarity in assessing the academic needs of prospective tutees must be evident as when any other instructional approach is used. This means that the specific aims of tutoring, be they informal, of limited duration, or comprehensive, must be specified in measurable terms in advance. Furthermore, these aims must derive from the observable array of skills the pupil has and has not mastered. Moreover, the teacher considering peer tutoring must be equally cognizant of goals for the prospective tutor's academic and social learning. As far as possible, the learning goals of the tutor must be either accounted for within the peer-tutoring structure or provided through alternative means.

How to Implement Peer Tutoring

The selection of tutors and tutees will depend, among other considerations, on instructional goals and existing methods of instruction. The competence of the tutor cannot be expected to exceed that of the teacher, nor can the expected learning of the tutee exceed the range of instructional objectives provided in the normal instructional plan.

In general, three principles may serve to guide in the selection and matching of tutor and tutee. The research literature has shown that personal characteristics are not, in themselves, critical to this decision.

Assuming that instructional goals are clear and peer tutoring is compatible with alternative methods of instruction in the classroom environment, the teacher should investigate the susceptibility of prospective tutees to peer modeling and peer-delivered reinforcement. The teacher can directly observe either naturally occurring interactions or those contrived, for example, by imposing specific but limited group contingencies. From this type of observational record, the teacher can derive objective guidance concerning the likelihood of success with a given individual. If an unstructured and informal sort of peer tutoring is being considered, such as team competition or reinforcement contingencies for group effort, the teacher can observe target children and record in an experimental fashion their rates of responding in an academic task under both tutoring and nontutoring conditions. Ideally, multiple measures should be obtained in addition to academic rates of responding, including frequency of giving or receiving positive reinforcement, frequency and types of inappropriate behaviors, and the degree to which the peer's effect on an individual "carries over" to other settings, times, and tasks.

A second consideration in selecting tutors and tutees involves the trainability of the prospective tutor. Depending upon the complexity of anticipated tutoring behaviors, the teacher must choose tutors who can be effectively and efficiently trained. Again, careful pretutorial observation and recording will assist the teacher in objectifying the selection process. It will be important to know, for instance, the natural rate with which the "tutor" delivers positively reinforcing comments to others, the events antecedent to the reinforcement, and response of the children receiving the reinforcement. Training can often capitalize on naturally occurring behaviors and circumstances (e.g., peer assistance during competitive games) if the teacher is aware of them. To obtain this sort of information, the teacher may have to contrive experimental situations (as discussed previously) if opportunities for observing peer interactions are not ordinarily available or are inadequate.

The teacher should be particularly observant of the prospective tutor's behaviors, such as approach, avoidance, helpfulness, and persistence, when the tutor encounters slow learners, handicapped individuals, behavior-problem children, or others of a different culture or sex. It will be recalled that research indicated: (a) high rates of naturally occurring negative behavior toward poor performers or poor performance in some circumstances (Feshbach, 1976), and (b) increasingly negative attitudes and decreasing satisfaction when initial tutee performance is poor (Allen & Feldman, 1976). Therefore, a record based on objective observation will facilitate matching individuals as well as providing the foundation for effective training. Also, the teacher may wish or need to directly assess the prospective tutor's ability to learn the necessary discriminations, methods for administering reinforcement, and a system for keeping tutoring records.

The third major consideration in selecting tutors and tutees is either to assure in advance that there is an absence of mutual or unilateral aversive behaviors or to have an effective plan for controlling and modifying such behaviors should they occur. In line with previously discussed research findings, the teacher can increase the positiveness of peer contacts by maintaining high rates of consistently delivered reinforcement to both the tutor and the tutee contingent upon their appropriate performance. One fairly simple approach is to reward the tutor contingent upon his or her accurate and consistent reinforcement of correct *tutee* responses. Additionally, extra reward might be provided for the tutor contingent upon tutee improvement. The responsiveness of the prospective tutor to these procedures can be directly assessed by the teacher before committing time and material to further training.

From the available empirical research, several general principles of training for children designated to be tutors emerge. First, the child selected to be a tutor needs to be familiar with the materials to be used for instruction, with their organization, and with their behavioral requirements. In particular, the tutor must be taught by the trainer to discriminate correct from incorrect responses. If the tutor does not already demonstrate this ability (e.g., on a test), then the necessary discriminations must be taught. An alternative technique is to provide the tutor with a set of acceptable responses that could then be compared in match-to-sample fashion with those produced by the tutee. None of the studies reviewed investigated the use of one trained tutor to train other tutors, though such an arrangement would be possible within the limitations previously discussed and desirable in terms of obtaining an optimal benefit from the investment of teacher time.

Second, once the tutor can reliably discriminate correct responses, he or she must be taught that such responses are to signal the delivery of appropriate reinforcement. The precise nature of the reinforcement is to be determined by consideration of: (a) the prevailing reward structure of the classroom, (b) the observed effect of various contingencies on the target behavior of the tutee, and (c) the ability of the tutor to master the mechanics of contingent reinforcement with a given consequence (e.g., points, stars, praise, etc.). Some children may not spontaneously deliver verbal praise contingent upon correct responses from the tutee and must be specifically trained and motivated to do so.

Third, the tutor should, of course, be taught to perform any of the particular actions demanded by the tutoring task, such as exposing cards, reading from lists, or positioning materials. Additionally, the tutor should be instructed in how to correct faulty responses appropriately. For example, Rosenbaum's (1973) spelling procedure explicitly directs the tutor to draw a vertical line after the last correctly sequenced letter and to cross out the incorrect letters. Following the tutee's second attempt, the tutor must write the word in a prescribed manner as a model for the tutee. Though all correction procedures need not be complicated, they must not be left to chance. They should serve the purpose of efficiently teaching the correct response. In particular, it is important to avoid overly negative responses from the tutor following a tutee's error. Sanders and Glynn (1977) were able to reduce the attention their tutors gave to inappropriate behaviors by simply rewarding the tutors for the accuracy with which they monitored targeted behaviors. Such record keeping is also subject to training.

When tutoring has begun, the teacher must have a system for monitoring its progress so that problems can be swiftly identified and solved. As has been discussed, the keeping of records by the tutor can increase tutor attention to task and obtain better outcomes from the tutee, especially when the tutor is rewarded for accurate record keeping. Of course, the accuracy of records can only be determined by comparing the records with those of an independent observer. This role can be filled by another student, similarly trained, but not assigned to tutor the child in question. Otherwise, the teacher must arrange to observe. Even with tutor-kept records, the teacher should have access to information other than the mere correctness of the tutee's responses. The teacher should also know how efficient the tutoring is; without evidence to support its efficiency, it is incumbent upon the teacher to use alternative, more efficient instructional methods. The teacher will also want to monitor the degree to which tutoring is mutually satisfying for the participants. Efficiency is not to be purchased at the children's expense; if tutoring is aversive to either party, teacher intervention is required, though it is entirely possible that dissatisfaction may not in itself preclude some academic gains (Rosen *et al.*, 1978). Again, it will be necessary for the teacher to weigh alternatives to obtain the most satisfactory outcomes in the least aversive way. However, careful consideration of the foregoing guidelines should eliminate the possibility that tutoring will be aversive. Nevertheless, ongoing monitoring is necessary to assist in making this and all other relevant instructional decisions.

In addition to decision making and progress monitoring, records from direct observation signal the teacher to deliver positive reinforcement to either or both of the participants. The observations may be accomplished by a time-sampling method in which the teacher records observable behaviors in categories chosen at predetermined (though not necessarily equal) intervals.

INTEGRATION OF TUTORING WITH ONGOING INSTRUCTION

There is a need for more research to clarify what type of integration can be made between peer tutoring and the ongoing instructional program of the classroom, of several classrooms (e.g., in cross-age tutoring projects), and of large-scale, schoolwide programs. The natural fit between peer tutoring and the instructional program when both make use of similar reinforcement contingencies and learning-objectives hierarchies has been discussed. However, questions still remain concerning long-term or large-scale use of peer tutoring. Naturally, the greater the number of decision makers involved in implementation, the more complex administration becomes. Though it is clear that peer tutoring has broad applications in the elementary-school curriculum, the best methods for extending and elaborating small-scale efforts await more research.

It is perhaps important to reiterate the need to extend tutoring programs only so far as they remain more beneficial for the increased cost than available alternative methods. If an equal expenditure of teacher time can produce better results, the precise benefits obtainable from peer tutoring must be carefully evaluated with respect to overall program goals. Instructional planning is a process of continually searching for the best mix of procedures with respect to a given array of objectively defined desirable outcomes.

Periodic reevaluation of peer tutoring may suggest a need to recompose the tutoring roles. For example, there may be good reason to assign tutees to act as tutors with the same material, with different material, or in different settings after they have mastered the tasks. Another factor to consider is the probability that each trained tutor has a finite "tutoring life," after which he or she must be retrained, reoriented, or reassigned. Definitive research is lacking on these long-term issues, but it is important to attend to the possibility that tutors will tend to "run down" unless their tutoring continues to be reinforcing. Although simple responses are easier to submit to tutors for purposes of peer instruction, tutoring activities that are highly repetitive and mechanical might be expected to induce fatigue and boredom.

One further caution is offered. The availability of children willing to tutor, the incessant pressure of classroom learning problems, and the apparent simplicity of the peer-tutoring solution have encouraged some to treat its implementation with perhaps too much casualness. When a too-casual approach is taken the results are almost always dissatisfying for everyone. For example, Weiner, Goldman, Lev, Toledano, and Rosner (1974) described a study undertaken with the assumption that tutoring is therapeutic for the tutor. In this study, four children with emotional and behavioral problems were selected to tutor younger children with learning (but no behavioral) difficulties. Three social-work students acted as trainers. The trainers explained the mechanics of tutoring, the possible problems, and the methods to be used, and role-played tutoring sessions. Although the investigators found that the children acting as tutors initially displayed improvement in their own behavior, over time their behavior deteriorated. Only subjective, anecdotal evidence was presented to support improvements, but it is clear that the project eventually disintegrated. Unfortunately, one can only speculate about the reasons for such failures of generally successful techniques. Undoubtedly, the report shows that some of the difficulty arose from the prolonged dependency of tutors on the presence of their trainers. It appears that little attention was paid to problems in using reinforcement contingencies that secured a general behavioral compliance but failed to sustain the disturbed students as tutors—the presence of the trainers, who provided much unconditional attention, had become more reinforcing than the tutoring process itself.

By way of contrast, Jorgensen (1978) reported an equally nonempirical study of peer tutoring but one that illustrates the logic and benefit of the guidelines discussèd in this section. The teacher of a special-education resource room managed a reinforcement system to control the inappropriate behavior of six upper-elementary students. When six lower-elementary students were added to the class, the older students were hostile, aggressive, and abusive toward the younger ones. The teacher decided to let the older students tutor the younger ones, an approach similar to that of Weiner (1974). What sets the Jorgensen narrative apart from the Weiner report is not only the fact that there was an existing, previously successful behavior-management system under which the tutors had worked, but also the fact that the teacher had the insight to provide additional reinforcement for the older students equal to that which was earned in a token economy by the younger students during tutoring. Although Jorgensen's report lacks empirical data, its findings are intuitively appealing in light of the other evidence reviewed in this chapter. In a short time, Jorgensen reported, the hostile behaviors ceased and both groups showed academic gains.

In the field of education, the recent mastery of an embryonic science of behavior and the accompanying development of a technology of teaching have fostered enthusiasm for attempts to solve all problems endemic to a massive, bureaucratic system of schooling by technological means. It is therefore important in this discussion of peer tutoring to emphasize a fundamental, undisputed, but occasionally circumvented ethical issue. Technologies must serve human needs, not the other way around. A headlong rush to adopt materials and methods without a concomitant improvement in teacher competence represents a serious abrogation of responsibilities. It should be recalled that the enormous amount of money connected with the schooling enterprise cannot be transformed into any product which, in itself, will make learners successful in attaining academic or social goals. Nor can any technique, no matter how valid and useful, be safely and effectively applied without (a) an educational process that is responsive to the needs of individual learners, and (b) basic competence and professionalism among practitioners. Educators must be alert, in this new era of instructional technology, to the need "to close the distance between the push-button order and the human act" (Bronowski, 1973, p. 374).

Peer tutoring must, then, be considered an instructional method that is part of a more comprehensive technology of teaching. It requires the same attention to potential benefits and detriments for the children involved as any other approach to instruction. It is a method of choice in some but not all classroom situations. In general, it is preferred when: (a) competence in its application is assured by teacher ability and knowledge; (b) prevailing goals and modes of classroom instruction will support its use; (c) clear and definable benefits for both tutor and tutee can be specified; (d) the benefit–cost relationship is superior to that obtainable with available alternatives; and (e) its processes and outcomes are planned, monitored, and controlled in a professional and responsible manner.

The research reviewed in this chapter supports the *probable* effectiveness of peer-tutoring schemes that are well planned and carefully integrated within the ongoing instructional process. Although tutees have been seen to benefit, at least in the short run, from peer tutoring, some questions remain concerning the long-term effects on motivation and performance (Rosen *et al.*, 1978; Strodtbeck *et al.*, 1976). Nevertheless, close monitoring by the teacher and clear specification of goals will help protect against any unknown, but negative, side effects.

Of more substantial ethical importance is the need to ascertain that tutoring provides for the tutor's learning needs. It will not suffice to prove that some benefit, either social or academic, accrues to the tutor. Rather, it must be demonstrated that the tutor benefits in a way that serves his or her learning needs specifically. Some research has addressed the issue of designing the tutoring assignment with the tutor as well as the tutee in mind (e.g., Cloward, 1967, 1976; Dineen *et al.*, 1977; Strodtbeck *et al.*, 1976), but apparently no one has conducted research concerned with specifically targeting benefits for the tutor by means of an instructional plan or needs assessment. It is of considerable ethical concern that a tutor's participation advance his or her own academic or social development at least as well as alternative uses of the tutor's time. The Lancasterian expropriation of children's learning time to solve the teacher's problems of resource scarcity cannot be justified in the 1980s.

Another frequently heard criticism of behavioral technology may also apply to abuses of peer tutoring. The criticism concerns powerful procedures, the use of which bolsters the operation of inefficient, corrupted, or harmful institutions. As stated previously, educators must accept a measure of responsibility for the technology under their control. The decision to use behavior-management techniques to support an irrelevant or harmful classroom (or school) program must be seen as unethical. If peer tutoring is used in this manner, short-term or incidental benefits to the children must be weighed against their long-term interests. The use of effective procedures cannot correct institutional flaws and social-policy failures.

A final ethical consideration concerns the long-term or side effects potentially created by interferences in natural behavioral ecologies. These effects, if present, are not immediately obvious or even evident, but prudent practice would include a wary alertness to their possibility. To be sure, the classroom is not a natural ecological system in the sense that its children would choose, given the option, to come together with the same peers and teacher and interact in the same way. The classroom is already, for better or worse (though, it is hoped, for better), an engineered environment. Consequently, the application of new techniques may disturb that environment, but cannot be any more artificial or premeditated than those procedures already in use. In fact, it has been argued throughout this chapter that premeditation and systematic, deliberate control are exactly the prerequisites necessary to attain desirable educational outcomes.

Education, in this final analysis, is not merely a consumer good. Society has a vested interest in the attainment of academic and social competence by its children. However, procedures which stress peer tutoring introduce reinforcement for cooperative behaviors which may not be available outside the classroom. The teacher must be sensitive to the need for students to learn appropriate and adaptive responses to competitive situations. Despite the existence of some such discrepancy between cooperative classroom and competitive societal environments, it will probably be widely agreed that a greater sense of mutual respect, concern, and responsibility in our society would be welcome and beneficial for all. If peer tutoring provides an educationally valid route to this end, then it is worthy of attention.

CONCLUSIONS

Peer tutoring is a technique that may provide educational benefits to both the tutor and the tutee. Historically, it has been proposed as a solution to the persistent problem of resource scarcity and the accompanying need for individualized instruction. The Lancasterian system of the early nineteenth century emphasized the mechanistic fascination of the times in its use of disciplined groups of children as peer teachers. Efficiency was more important than either individual learning needs or the social needs of the working-class children who constituted the target population for the monitorial system.

In the 1960s, peer teaching was again emergent as part of an educational ideology as well as an instructional technology. The notion that peers acting as tutors constituted a new resource is fundamentally incorrect. Educational resources must be committed to select, train, monitor, and program children who will be involved in peer-tutoring schemes. There is a need to understand the rationale for implementing tutoring, especially in the case of large-scale projects. Only when such implementation can be objectively shown to hold potential benefit superior to that obtainable from alternative methods, or to yield equal benefits at smaller real cost than alternatives, is it fully justified.

Since a certain amount of spontaneous helping behaviors can be observed among children in natural classroom settings, the environmental variables controlling these behaviors can be subjected to direct analysis. A given classroom environment may either encourage or suppress cooperation among students by the structure of reward contingencies it maintains. It is possible that a lack of group-contingency arrangements in classrooms discourages peer tutoring and encourages competitive learning instead. Research has clearly demonstrated that simple arrangements of reinforcement contingent upon group effort will result in spontaneous, academically and socially productive helping behaviors.

Experimental studies derived from learning theory and applied behavior analysis provide strong support for the potential effectiveness of peer-tutoring arrangements, especially when included within a comprehensive instructional technology. Such a technology includes systems of positive reinforcement for appropriate learning behaviors as well as instructional material arranged into objectively defined, hierarchically sequenced learning goals. The power of these and other management elements has been repeatedly demonstrated when used in conjunction with peer tutoring. The greatest benefit from peer tutoring may be obtained when it is viewed as one of a number of techniques that the teacher commands. It cannot be proposed as an alternative to teacher-led instruction until or unless the effectiveness of direct instruction and other teacher-managed learning is given full and fair opportunity to prove itself.

Since technologies are neutral, whereas its users must make ethical decisions, peer tutoring can be used ethically or abused. Its implementation should be based on reliable data indicating probable benefit to both tutor and tutee when compared with alternative methods. The personal, ethically responsible decisions of educators using peer tutoring or any other powerful technology should reflect an awareness of the basic inability of society to solve social and institutional problems solely by technical means. Finally, information is lacking about the evolution of the tutor–tutee relationship over extended periods of time. Neither the long-term effects upon the children nor upon the classroom ecology are known. Though the ecological relationships in classrooms are inherently the product of social engineering, the use of peer tutoring, or any other technical procedures, requires thoughtful planning and carefully specified controls.

REFERENCES

Allen, V.L. The helping relationship and socialization of children: Some perspectives on tutoring. In V.L. Allen (Ed.), *Children as teachers.* New York: Academic Press, 1976.

Allen, V.L., & Feldman, R.S. Studies on the role of tutor. In V.L. Allen (Ed.), *Children as teachers.* New York: Academic Press, 1976.

Apolloni, T. Establishing a normal peer as a behavioral model for developmentally delayed toddlers. *Perceptual and Motor Skills, 1977, 44,* 231–241.

Axelrod, S. Comparison of individual and group contingencies in two special classes. *Behavior Therapy, 1973, 4,* 83–90.

Barry, N.J., Jr., & Overman, P.B. Comparison of the effectiveness of adult and peer models with EMR children. *American Journal of Mental Deficiency, 1977, 82,* 33–36.

Blaney, T., Stephan, C., Rosenfield, D., Aronson, E., & Sikes, J. Interdependence in the classroom: A field study. *Journal of Educational Psychology, 1977, 69,* 121–128.

Bronfenbrenner, U. *Two worlds of childhood.* New York: Russell Sage Foundation, 1970.

Bronowski, J. *The ascent of man.* Boston: Little, Brown, 1973.

Buckholdt, D., & Wodarski, J. Effects of different reinforcement systems on cooperative behaviors exhibited by children in classroom contexts. *Journal of Research and Development in Education, 1978, 12,* 50–68.

Charconnet, M. Peer tutoring: Operational description of various systems and their applications. *Development of educational methods and techniques adapted to the specific conditions of the developing countries.* Paris: UNESCO, 1975.

Cloward, R. D., Studies in tutoring. *Journal of Experimental Education, 1967, 36,* 14–25.

Cloward, R.D. Teenagers as tutors of academically low-achieving children: Impact on tutors and tutees. In V. L. Allen (Ed.), *Children as teachers.* New York: Academic Press, 1976.

Collins, J.F., & Calevro, M.J. *Mainstreaming special education using a peer tutoring system and minimum objective curriculum for nine eighth-grade students.* Barre Town, Vt.: Orange Washington Supervisory Union, 1974.

Conrad, E.E. *The effects of tutor achievement level, reinforcement training, and expectancy on peer tutoring.* Washington, D.C.: DHEW/OE, 1975.

Damico, S.B., & Watson, K.J. *Peer helping relationships: A study of student interactions in an elementary classroom.* Research Monograph No. 18, Florida University, 1976.

Devin-Sheehan, L., & Allen, V.L. *Peer tutoring in one-room schools.* Paper presented at annual meeting of the American Educational Research Association, Washington, D.C., March 30–April 3, 1975.

Devin-Sheehan, L., Feldman, R.S., & Allen, V.L. Research on children tutoring children: A critical review. *Review of Educational Research, 1976, 46,* 355–385.

De Vries, D., & Slavin, R. Teams-games-tournaments (TGT): Review of ten classroom experiments. *Journal of Research and Development in Education, 1978, 12,* 28–38.

Dineen, J.P., Clark, H.B., & Risley, T.R. Peer tutoring among elementary students: Educational benefits to the tutor. *Journal of Applied Behavior Analysis, 1977, 10,* 231–238.

Duff, R.E., & Swick, K. Primary level tutors as an instructional resource. *Reading Improvement, 1974, 11,* 39–44.

Ehly, S. W. *Peer tutorial models.* Paper presented at 55th Council for Exceptional Children, Atlanta, April 1977.

Ehly, S. W., & Larsen, S. C. Sex, status, and liking of tutor and learner as predictors of tutorial outcomes. *Perceptual and Motor Skills,* 1977, *45,* 335–336.

Epstein, L. The effects of intraclass peer tutoring on the vocabulary development of learning disabled children. *Journal of Learning Disabilities,* 1978, *11,* 518–521.

Evans, C.M., & Potter, R.E. The effectiveness of the S-pack when administered by sixth-grade children to primary-grade children. *Language, Speech and Hearing Services in Schools,* 1974, *5,* 85–90.

Feldman, R.S., Towson, S.M., & Allen, V.L. *Two field studies on cross-age tutoring in the school.* Technical Report No. 361, University of Wisconsin Research and Development Center for Cognitive Learning, 1975.

Feldman, R.S., Devin-Sheehan, L., & Allen. V.L. Children tutoring children: A critical review of research. In V. L. Allen (Ed.), *Children as teachers.* New York: Academic Press, 1976.

Feshbach, N.D. Teaching styles in young children: Implications for peer tutoring. In V. L. Allen (Ed.), *Children as teachers.* New York: Academic Press, 1976.

Frankosky, R.J., & Sulzer-Azaroff, B. Individual and group contingencies and collateral social behaviors. *Behavior Therapy,* 1978, *9,* 313–327.

Gardiner, W.E. Compeer assistance through tutoring and group guidance activities. *Urban Review,* 1978, *10,* 45–54.

Gartner, A., Kohler, M., & Riesman, F. *Children teach children: Learning by teaching.* New York: Harper & Row, 1971.

Hamblin, R.L., Hathaway, C., & Wodarski, J. Group contingencies, peer tutoring and accelerating academic achievement. In E.A. Ramp & B.L. Hopkins (Eds.), *A new direction for education: Behavior analysis—1971.* Lawrence: University of Kansas, 1971.

Harris, V.W., & Sherman, J.A. Effects of peer tutoring and consequences on the math performance of elementary classroom students. *Journal of Applied Behavior Analysis,* 1973, *6,* 587–597.

Harris, V.W., Sherman, J.A., Henderson, D.G., & Harris, M.S. Effects of peer tutoring on the spelling performance of elementary classroom students. In G. Semb (Ed.), *A new direction for education: Behavior analysis.* Lawrence: The University of Kansas Support and Development Center for Follow Through, 1972.

Hartup, W.W. Cross-age versus same-age peer interaction: Ethological and cross-cultural perspectives. In V.L. Allen (Ed.), *Children as teachers.* New York: Academic Press, 1976.

Holliday, F.B., & Edwards, C. Building on cultural strengths: A route to academic achievement. *Educational Leadership,* 1978, *36,* 207–210.

Jenkins, J.R., Mayhall, W.F., Peschka, C.M., & Jenkins, L.M. Comparing small group and tutorial instruction in resource rooms. *Exceptional Children,* 1974, *40,* 245–250.

Johnston, J.M., & Johnston, G.T. Instructional goal structure: Cooperative, competitive, or indivudualistic. *Review of Educational Research,* 1974, *44,* 213–241.

Jorgensen, E.S. *Cross-age, multicultural peer tutoring in an elementary resource room.* Paper presented at 56th annual international convention CEC, Kansas City, Missouri, May 1978.

Kaestle, C.F. (Ed.). *Joseph Lancaster and the monitorial school movement.* New York: Teachers College Press, 1973.

Kazdin, A.E., & Pulaski, J.L. Joseph Lancaster and behavior modification in education. *Journal of the History of the Behavioral Sciences,* 1977, *13,* 261–266.

Lancaster, J. *Improvements in education as it respects the industrious classes of the community.* London: Darton & Harvey, 1803.

Lippitt, P. Learning through cross-age helping: Why and how. In V.L. Allen (Ed.), *Children as teachers.* New York: Academic Press, 1976.

Luckner, G.W., Rosenfield, D., Sikes, J., & Aronson, E. Performance in the interdependent classroom: A field study. *American Educational Research Journal*, 1976, *13*, 115–123.

McCarty, T., Griffin, S., Apolloni, T., & Shores, R.E. Increased peer-teaching with group-oriented contingencies for arithmetic performance in behavior-disordered adolescents. *Journal of Applied Behavior Analysis*, 1977, *10*, 313.

McGee, C.S., Kauffman, J.M., & Nussen, J. Children as therapeutic change agents: Reinforcement intervention paradigms. *Review of Education Research*, 1977, *47*, 451–477.

Melaragno, R.J. Beyond decoding: Systematic schoolwide tutoring in reading. *The Reading Teacher*, 1974, *27*, 157–160.

Melaragno, R.J. The tutorial community. In V.L. Allen (Ed.), *Children as teachers*. New York: Academic Press, 1976.

Melaragno, R.J. Pupil tutoring: Directions for the future. *Elementary School Journal*, 1977, *77*, 304–307.

Melaragno, R.J., & Newmark, G. A tutorial community works towards specified objectives in an elementary school. *Educational Horizons*, 1969/1970, *48*, 33–37.

Niedermeyer, F.C. A model for the development or selection of school-based tutorial systems. In V.L. Allen (Ed.), *Children as teachers*. New York: Academic Press, 1976.

Oakland, T. & Williams, F.C. An evaluation of two methods of peer tutoring. *Psychology in the Schools*, 1975, *12*, 166–171.

Patterson, R.T., Jr. *Planning and implementing a peer tutoring approach to individualized instruction to improve reading achievement*. ERIC Document ED131434, 1976.

Reigert, J.F. *The Lancasterian system of instruction in the schools of New York City*. New York: Arno Press, 1969. (Originally published, 1916.)

Rosen, S., Powell, E.R., Shubot, D.B., & Rollins, P. Competence and tutorial role as status variables affecting peer-tutoring outcomes in public school settings. *Journal of Educational Psychology*, 1978, *70*, 602–612.

Rosenbaum, P.S. *Peer-mediated instruction*. New York: Teachers College Press, 1973.

Sanders, M.R., & Glynn, T. Functional analysis of a program for training high and low preference peers to modify disruptive class behavior. *Journal of Applied Behavior Analysis*, 1977, *10*, 503.

Sherman, J.A., & Harris, V.W. Effects of peer tutoring and homework assignments on classroom performance. In T. Thompson & W. Dockens, III (Eds.), *Applications of behavior modification*. New York: Academic Press, 1975.

Slavin, R.E. A student team approach to teaching adolescents with special emotional and behavioral needs. *Psychology in the Schools*, 1977, *14*, 77–84.

Slavin, R.E., & Wodarski, J.S. *Decomposing a student team technique: Team reward and team task*. Paper presented at annual meeting of the American Psychological Association, San Francisco 1977.

Snell, M.E. Higher functioning residents as language trainers of the mentally retarded. *Education and Training of the Mentally Retarded*, 1979, *14*, 77–84.

Sowell, V., Candler, A.C., Blackburn, G.M., & Blackburn, D. *Peer tutoring as an instructional procedure for exceptional students*. Paper presented at 56th annual Council for Exceptional Children, Kansas City, Missouri, May 1978.

Stainback, W.C., & Stainback, S.B. Effects of student to student tutoring on arithmetic achievement and personal social adjustment of low achieving tutees and high achieving tutors. *Education and Training of the Mentally Retarded*, 1972, *7*, 169–172.

Stainback, W.C., Stainback, S.B., & Lichtward, F. The research evidence regarding the student to student tutoring approach to individualized instruction. *Educational Technology*, 1975, *15*, 54–56.

Strain, P., Cooke, T., & Apolloni, T. The role of peers in modifying classmates' social behavior: A review. *Journal of Special Education*, 1976, *10*, 351–356.

Strodtbeck, F.L., Ronchi, D., & Hansell, S. Tutoring and psychological growth. In V. L. Allen (Ed.), *Children as teachers*. New York: Academic Press, 1976.

Stokes, T.F., & Baer, D.M. Preschool peers as mutual generalization-facilitating agents. *Behavior Therapy*, 1976, 7, 549–556.

Ulman, J.D., & Sulzer-Azaroff, B. Multielement baseline design in educational research. In E. Ramp & G. Semb (Eds.), *Behavior Analysis: Areas of research and application*. Englewood Cliffs, N.J.: Prentice-Hall, 1975.

Vacc, N.A. Self help: Peer tutor training for the mentally retarded. *Education and Training of the Mentally Retarded*, 1978, 13, 60–63.

Wagner, P. Children tutoring children. *Mental Retardation*, 1974, 12, 52–55.

Wagner, P., & Sternlicht, M. Retarded persons as "teachers": Retarded adolescents tutoring retarded children. *American Journal of Mental Deficiency*, 1975, 79, 674–679.

Weiner, A., Goldman, R., Lev, R., Toledano, U., & Rosner, E. Applying the helper-therapy principle: A children-teacher-children project. *Child Welfare*, 1974, 53, 445–451.

7

Group-Oriented Contingencies and Peer Behavior Change

CHARLES R. GREENWOOD AND HYMAN HOPS

INTRODUCTION

The peer group is, numerically, the largest source of potential behavior-change agents for coping with problematic behavior in children, far outnumbering both parents and teachers. Yet its latent power to facilitate academic and social gains in school settings has been attended to only recently (V.L. Allen, 1976; Bronfenbrenner, 1970). Developmental psychologists have been exhaustively describing the increasing influence of a child's peers in the socialization process for years (Hartup, 1970; Piaget, 1932). With increasing age, children were shown to depend more upon peer-group pressure and affiliation than upon the family, with maximal influence occurring during adolescence (Hartup, 1970).

Recent research has not only affirmed the role of peers and their importance in the development of normal social repertoires in children but has extended this influence down to infancy and toddlerhood (Lewis & Rosenblum, 1975). Specific behavioral repertoires have been shown to be unique to child–child interactions and not dependent upon mother–

CHARLES R. GREENWOOD • Bureau of Child Research and Departments of Special Education and Human Development, University of Kansas, Lawrence, Kansas 66044. HYMAN HOPS • Oregon Research Institute, Eugene, Oregon 97401. This chapter was prepared with assistance from National Institute of Child Health and Human Development Program Project Grant, 2 PO1 HD 03144, University of Kansas, and NH Biomedical Research Support Grant RR05612, Oregon Research Institute.

child or sibling interaction (Mueller & Brenner, 1977; Mueller & Vandell, 1979). Most importantly, a dynamic technology has unfolded in the last 15 years empirically demonstrating the deliberate use of peers as behavior-change agents in the academic setting. Their influence has been directed toward facilitating academic accomplishments, reducing instances of deviant and disruptive behavior, increasing work and study skills, increasing production and efficiency, and teaching social-interaction skills. Thus, the power of the peer group is now being harnessed toward pragmatic and socially useful ends.

Peer-group involvement in school settings can be grouped into at least two broad categories in which (a) peers are trained to be tutors or cotherapists, or (b) their assistance is obtained through cooperative-reinforcement contingencies. In the first case, peers are taught to distribute points or reinforcers, record data, give instructions, impose contingencies, and so on (Greenwood, Sloane, & Baskin, 1974; Phillips, Phillips, Wolf, & Fixsen, 1973). The second case involves peers by manipulating contingency arrangements so that peers are given access to earned reinforcers and/or the reinforcement is dependent to some extent upon their behavior (Greenwood, Hops, Walker, Guild, Stokes, Young, Keleman, & Willardson, 1979; Hops, Walker, Fleischman, Nagoshi, Omura, Skindrud, & Taylor, 1978).

The purpose of this chapter will be to focus on the second case, the technology of contingency arrangements that enlist peer influence. These procedures have been commonly described as "group contingencies" or "group-oriented contingencies" (see Greenwood, Hops, Delquadri, & Guild, 1974; Hayes, 1976; Kazdin, 1977a; Litow & Pumroy, 1975; McLaughlin, 1974; Neumann, 1978; S.G. O'Leary & O'Leary, 1976). It is presently not known what proportion of behavior-change procedures involve group-oriented contingencies. It is our guess, however, that such procedures are widely represented among instances of behavioral technology. Litow and Pumroy list nearly 100 studies of this type in their review.

Since several reviews currently exist, the purpose of this chapter will not be to summarize the literature but rather to focus on procedural aspects of group-oriented contingencies. The preponderance of studies conducted in school settings have reported on uses related to classroom behavior management. Our objective will be to broaden this perspective and discuss the implications of these procedures for the treatment and study of peer social interaction, a topic not adequately addressed in previous reviews.

We will discuss, in addition, the various attempts to classify group-oriented methods in order to provide the reader with a more unified understanding of the contribution of various components. These components include (a) procedures, (b) social agents involved, (c) recipients of reinforcement, (d) responders and behavioral requirements, and (e) characteristic effects and outcomes. Finally, we will discuss implications for further research and development.

BACKGROUND EVENTS IN EARLY BEHAVIORAL RESEARCH

A short 15 years ago, Patterson (1965) described the successful behavior modification of Karl, a hyperactive boy in a public-school classroom. The behavior-change agent was a research psychologist visiting the classroom attempting to apply laboratory-derived principles of behavior to a problem in classroom management. What has evolved since has been an explosion of studies designed to directly involve parents, teachers, and peers of targeted children as behavior-change agents.

Patterson recognized early that the relationship of the person delivering the services to the target child was a critical aspect of the entire intervention procedure, affecting the impact of the procedures per se. He noted that attempts to maintain or generalize successful behavior change would rest, in large part, upon concurrent changes in the everyday social-interaction patterns of the target subject's social agents in the natural setting (Patterson, Shaw, & Ebner, 1969). This concept is now a foundation of current behavioral practice with respect to maintenance and generalization of behavior change (Stokes & Baer, 1977).

That peers, for example, might play a powerful role in maintaining deviant student behavior was widely asserted by social psychologists and more clearly documented by behavioral-observation methods. Studies showed that preschoolers provided immediate consequences for peer aggression (Patterson, Littman, & Bricker, 1967), that delinquent girls frequently reinforced socially deviant peer responses and punished "conforming" behavior (Buehler, Patterson, & Furniss, 1966), that teachers and peers socially reinforced from 15% to 55% of student "hyperactive" behavior (Ebner, 1967), and that teachers spent more time attending to deviant students for inappropriate behavior than to well-behaved students for appropriate responding (Walker & Buckley, 1973).

The "hero procedures" (Patterson et al., 1969), Patterson's early effort to reprogram social agents in the natural setting, was directed at systematically refocusing peer social acclaim upon desirable behavior and eliminating peer social attention for undesirable responding. The basis for the peer procedure at that time appeared more theoretical and anecdotal than empirical. The specific procedures involved (a) the direct reinforcement of the target subject, Karl, with M & M's on a variable-interval schedule, for improved attending and sitting still, and (b) the sharing of the earned M & M's with class members after the session. Instructions to the class were as follows:

> Karl has some trouble with sitting and that makes it hard for him to learn some things. This box sitting on his desk is a "work box."* Each time the light flashes, it tells him that he has been sitting still and working. When he sits still, he earns candy for himself *and for the rest of you. When he is finished, the counter will tell us how much candy he has earned. He can pass it out to the rest of you at the end of the class period. If you want him to earn a great deal of candy, don't pay any attention to him when he makes noise, gets out of his chair or walks around the room.* (italics added) (Patterson *et al.*, 1969, p. 20)

It is clear that these initial attempts were designed to eliminate peer social reinforcement for inappropriate behavior. Interestingly enough, Patterson *et al.* (1969) reported incidences of positive social reinforcement via spontaneous "ovations" and "applause" after the candy had been distributed.

Straughn, Potter, and Hamilton (1965) applied a similar procedure to facilitate a student's answering response.

> This is a magic box which we are going to use to help Gene. Gene has trouble answering when the teacher or someone else speaks to him. It is very important that he learns to talk in the classroom when asked. *Also, by talking, Gene can earn a party for the class. Each time he talks when asked, the light will go on. We will count up how many times he has talked each day and mark it on his chart. When the chart is full, Gene will earn a party for the class. You can help Gene earn the party for you by helping him to talk.* (italics added)

Gene's frequency of talking and responses to the instructor substantially improved. Results also indicated that as a result of the contingency, peer approaches to Gene significantly increased as well. Thus, it was demonstrated that peer-group influence could be selectively enlisted to facilitate responding in combination with the procedures applied by the teacher.

A similar application was also made to increase accuracy in academic responding (Evans & Oswalt, 1968). In three experiments, class members were reinforced if a single student was correct in spelling words, completing a math problem, or answering a question selected from the day's lesson. If the student's answer was correct, the class was either dismissed early or the teacher read to the class. If the student was wrong, the class continued with the lesson until the regular dismissal time.

These early studies represent the initial development of group-oriented classroom-management procedures as part of the evolution, over the past 15 years, of a systematic behavioral technology dealing with a wide range of human problems (see Kazdin & Bootzin, 1972; K.D. O'Leary & Drabman, 1971; S.G. O'Leary & O'Leary, 1976). The application of behavior programs and procedures frequently required their deployment in a variety of group settings in education, mental health, day care, and most recently in such areas as business, group living, rehabilita-

---

*Patterson assigned the fictitious name "Karl" to a series of subjects on whom he developed the "hero procedures" as well as what was to become the "Karl Box."

tion, and vocational training. It is not uncommon today to involve the social agents naturally inherent in these groups to assist in the modification of individuals' problematic behavior (Tharp,& Wetzel, 1969). State-of-the-art behavioral technology consists of "packaged" and "dissemination-oriented" behavioral-service programs designed and empirically tested to produce socially important behavior changes in these settings (Paine, 1979). Patterson's work has culminated in treatment procedures for the aggressive child in the home and school (see Patterson, Reid, Jones, & Conger, 1975). Other outstanding examples are the home-style treatment of predelinquent youth in the Achievement Place model (see Phillips, Phillips, Fixsen, & Wolf, 1972), the *Responsible Parenting Program* (Clark-Hall, 1977), and CORBEH's four teacher-consultant-mediated school-intervention programs: *PASS* (Greenwood, Hops, Delquadri, & Walker, 1977), for increasing academic survival skills of low-functioning children; *CLASS* (Hops, Beickel, & Walker, 1976), directed at the acting-out child in the regular classroom setting; *PEERS* (Hops, Fleischman, Guild, Paine, Street, Walker, & Greenwood, 1978), for increasing the social involvement of withdrawn children; and *RECESS* (Walker, Street, Garrett, Crossen, Hops, & Greenwood, 1978), designed to reduce negative-aggressive social behavior.

Generally, such packaged programs are the culmination of four to ten years of research and development which include (a) component analyses to identify effective procedures, (b) experimental- and control-group designs, (c) social-validation research, (d) development of training materials and procedures, (e) extensive replication, and (f) dissemination to social agents in the natural setting.

Specifically designed as behavioral alternatives to current procedures in general practice, each set of procedures must (a) be cost-effective in time required to implement, ease of implementation, and time required to train others to deliver the services; (b) involve social agents in the natural setting, for example, parents, teachers, and peers, in such roles as reinforcing agents, teaching parents, managers, and trainers; and (c) no longer involve the original developers in direct-service roles.

We predict that the next 10 to 15 years will see the wide-scale application of specific uses of behavioral technology by trained social agents in the natural setting. Moreover, specific techniques that are now emerging in the literature are very likely destined to become the common practice in the future. Group-oriented contingency procedures currently span this range of development, as will become evident throughout this chapter.

PERSPECTIVES ON GROUP-MANAGEMENT PROCEDURES

Let us now consider a number of issues surrounding the use and potential benefits of all forms of treatment, including group-management procedures. These issues include (a) effectiveness, (b) side effects, (c)

generalization and maintenance, (d) procedural efficiency, (e) social validation, and (f) ethical considerations. The following discussion will set
the stage for a comprehensive examination of the diverse group arrangements that have been employed.

Effectiveness

The power of behavior-change procedures is defined by the extent to
which they are able to produce immediate, high-magnitude effects on the
target behavior. In this chapter we shall consider the evidence for the
contributions that group procedures make to overall treatment effectiveness. Patterson's early use of the "hero procedures" was primarily based
on theory supported by anecdotal evidence. It was assumed that sharing
reinforcers with the peer group resulted in peer behavior changes that
contributed to the primary contingencies. Although peer cooperation has
been widely acclaimed, there has been little evidence presented based on
direct measurement and analysis outside laboratory settings.

Side Effects

Side effects are typically unplanned effects on target or other behaviors that arise serendipitously during the application of a procedure.
These effects can be either positive or negative. Side effects have been
frequently noted in research with group contingencies and the majority of
them have been positive. In the forefront are reports of increased social
cooperation among peer-group members. Some examples have been
spontaneous tutoring (Coyne, 1978; Hamblin, Hathaway, & Wodarski,
1971; McCarty, Griffin, Apolloni, & Shores, 1977), prompting and correct-
ing a target subject (Dineen, Clark, & Risley, 1977), reminders to make a
response (Alexander, Corbett, & Smigal, 1976; Speltz, Moore, &
McReynolds, 1979), social reinforcement for earning consequences for the
group (Axelrod, 1973; Feingold & Migler, 1972; Schmidt & Ulrich, 1969),
refraining from reinforcing competing responses (Sulzbacher & Houser,
1968), and increased social interaction (Dineet *et al.*, 1977; Frankosky &
Sulzer-Azaroff, 1978; Johnson, Goetz, Baer, & Green, 1973). Many of
these effects were noted when the primary focus of the contingencies was
the control of disruptive behaviors or increased academic production.
Although much less frequently, negative side effects have also been
in group-contingency procedures. These have ranged from threats to
criticism and harassment directed at noncontributing members of the
group (Axelrod, 1973; V.W. Harris & Sherman, 1973; Packard, 1970).

Generalization and Maintenance

"Generalization" and "maintenance" refer to the spillover of behavior change to other settings, subjects, and/or behaviors and the persistence of such changes following termination of treatment, respectively. The power of behavior-change procedures, in addition to initial effectiveness, should be considered in terms of their wide-ranging and durable effects. It was apparent years ago that procedures implemented by experimenters did not maintain after program removal. Generalization of behavior change to other settings was either not addressed or found not to occur (Walker & Buckley, 1972). In fact, generalization of treatment effects from school to home and vice versa was not only absent (Bernal, Delfini, North, & Kreutzer, 1976; Martin, Johnson, Johansson, & Wahl, 1976; Wahler, 1969), but on occasion negative contrast effects were found instead, with treated children showing more deviant behavior in the untreated setting (Walker, Hops, & Johnson, 1975).

As described by Patterson, early efforts were directed at directly involving natural social agents in treatment on the assumption that they would assist in maintaining the procedures over the long run. Thus, interest arose in the peer group as a possible source of continued social reinforcement in support of therapeutic goals (K.D. O'Leary & O'Leary, 1972; Patterson, McNeal, Hawkins, & Phelps, 1967; Solomon & Wahler, 1973). Teachers and parents were also directly trained to implement treatment procedures (Hall, Fox, Willard, Goldsmith, Emerson, Owen, Davis, & Porcia, 1971; Patterson *et al.*, 1969) or to take over their management (Hops, Fleischman, Guild, Paine, Street, Walker, & Greenwood, 1978; Patterson, Cobb, & Ray, 1972).

Research has suggested, however, that it is not simply the involvement of social agents but the maintenance of their reinforcing behavior that is related to the durability of the child's behavior. When social agents discontinue the procedures, the target behaviors tend to reverse (Brown, Montgomery, & Barclay, 1969; Cossairt, Hall, & Hopkins, 1973). More complex procedures are required that shift reinforcement schedules (Hops, Greenwood, & Ford, 1976), for example, or entrap behavior changes with reduced contingency control in the natural setting (Baer & Wolf, 1970). Teacher feedback and public posting of group performance levels have also been used to occasion group ovations and other forms of group self-reinforcement that can be continued following the initial treatment package. A well-developed technology of group-oriented procedures must incorporate effective procedures for establishing generalization and maintenance of treatment effects.

Procedural Efficiency

Patterson, Shaw, and Ebner (1969) noted that to be truly effective, behavior-change procedures must function with a minimum disruption of routine classroom activities and at a modest cost of professional time. It has been our experience that the greater the demand for behavior change placed on the teacher, the less likely the teacher is to implement the program and maintain the procedures.

From the outset, behavioral procedures have faced the costly problem of simultaneously establishing behavior-change programs for more than a single individual. Early attempts to individually apply token economies to those living in group settings (Ayllon & Azrin, 1968; Birnbrauer, Wolf, Kidder, & Tague, 1965) required much professional time to monitor and record behavior and dispense tokens and back-ups. Special contingencies for the responses of each group member were simply not practical.

Thus, Bushell, Wrobel, and Michaelis (1968) demonstrated that operant techniques could be simultaneously applied to the study and work behaviors of individuals in a group. Each subject received the same amount of reinforcement for each response. In this case, uniform behavior requirements were used classwide in the form of standardized class rules. The teacher moved about the room giving tokens to students actively working in compliance with the rules. Students not in compliance did not earn tokens. Students earning a preestablished number of tokens could buy special-event and snack tickets entitling them to a range of desirable consequences. These procedures demonstrated the practicality of uniform behavior targets for all individuals and showed a trend toward development of standard back-up consequences. Indigenous reinforcers were used in place of M & M's, money, and trinkets, which are costly to buy and obtain.

The next move toward procedural efficiency was to reduce the teacher's task of distributing tokens to individual students. The good-behavior game (Barrish, Saunders, & Wolf, 1969) similarly utilized uniform behavior requirements (rules) for the group. Recording of behavior points was accomplished by having the teacher tally rule violations for groups. Thus, tallying violations and consolidating individual tallies considerably reduced recording requirements.

The group-oriented procedures used, then, were (1) groupwide behavioral criteria (rules), (2) teacher recording of consolidated responses, and (3) group-oriented, naturally available consequences. The major advantage of these procedures appears to be in reducing teacher time and energy to dispense tokens or record behavior and operate the program on a daily basis. Other procedures have also been developed (Greenwood,

Hops, Delquadri, & Guild, 1974) which eliminate tokens and complex reinforcement menus and use uniform group consequences.

The trend in cost efficiency of group-management procedures has been one of (1) refinement of effective procedures, (2) use of uniform behavior requirements for all students rather than individuals, (3) use of central and consolidated recording and point-dispensing mechanisms (standard contingencies) to save teacher time and effort, and (4) standardization of indigenous consequences for group consumption rather than individually tailored reinforcers or menu listing.

Social Validation

The purposes and dimensions of social validation have been described in detail by Kazdin (1977a) and Wolf (1978). In one sense, social validation is the use of subjective measurement to establish the importance of behavior change brought about through behavioral intervention. Those individuals providing subjective judgment may vary. Thus, preferences for intervention procedures may be established by polling participants or by recording their choices over time (McMichael & Corey, 1969). Target behaviors may be selected by polling experts or the client group that will be served by the procedures (Fawcett & Miller, 1975; Maloney, Harper, Braukmann, Fixsen, Phillips, & Wolf, 1976).

Another form of social validation, with the purpose of establishing the importance of treatment effects, can be made by means of intersubject comparison. The level of behavior change can be compared with (a) a set of normative data established on the normal peer group (Walker & Hops, 1976), (b) behavioral levels of untreated control groups, or (c) subjects under alternative treatment conditions.

Assessing client satisfaction with the procedures and the consequent behavior change is a third means of establishing social validity. Clients' feedback may also provide information on the more subtle aspects of the program that were not objectively measured (Wolf, 1978). Social-validation measures can provide data on the clinical, social, or applied importance of the behavioral changes obtained (Kazdin, 1977).

Ethical Considerations

The inclusion of peer influence in group-contingency arrangements poses a number of distinctive ethical issues that are just beginning to emerge and that will play a greater role in the eventual acceptance of these procedures by social agents on a large-scale basis. First, group procedures may be at odds with conventional values and ways of thinking in American society that are strongly oriented toward the individual. Thus, a potential hesitancy to employ group procedures has been noted (Axelrod, 1973; Hamblin; et al., 1971). Similarly, clients may initially not wish to participate in systems in which others' behavior will to some extent determine the consequences.

Because of the complexity inherent in group procedures, the possibility of unpredictable side effects is high. However, a pretreatment discussion of such events with the group membership may have a detrimental effect on the procedures. Side effects may have to be eliminated before a set of procedures can be useful without biasing the group.

The question of how much explanation to the consumer is necessary also bears consideration. Arguments need to be developed that will assess the risk–benefit potential for both participants and social agents involved. Further alternative procedures and their outcomes must be compared. It is possible that investigations into the possible side effects of group contingencies offer the most promising new directions for research.

Even though American values are individually oriented and emphasize competition for excellence and achievement, strong precedent also exists for cooperation, response sharing, and response exchange. The latter form the basis for social-skills development, specific behaviors whose absence is related to low levels of social competence (Hersen & Bellack, 1977).

Satisfactory resolution of these issues, in many respects, will determine the future impact of group-oriented behavior-change procedures. Our attention will now turn to understanding the various types of group-oriented procedures.

UNDERSTANDING GROUP-CONTINGENCY ARRANGEMENTS

The basis of operant strengthening is the contingency arrangement relating an organism's response to a suitable reinforcer (Millenson, 1967). In token systems, for instance, points are dispensed contingent upon an individual emitting a specific response or response class; criteria for back-up reinforcement are set based upon the individual's performance; and back-up reinforcers are selected from a list specifically designed with the subject's history and preferences in mind. Individual-behavior contracts are examples of individual-contingency systems (DeRisi & Butz, 1975; Homme, Csanyi, Gonzales, & Rechs, 1969). The advantage of the individual system is that it maximizes the probability of an effective behavior change occurring for that individual.

However, as previously discussed, efficiency factors have spawned procedures involving groups which have added several dimensions to these elementary procedures. The degree of interest in group procedures is demonstrated in the literature; no less than six different classification schemes were found in our review. Table 1 contains brief summaries of these six taxonomies for thinking about group-oriented procedures.

Hake and Vukelich (1972) classify procedures designed to elicit cooperation with reference to animal studies and nonapplied laboratory studies of humans. Greenwood, Hops, Delquadri, and Guild (1974), Litow and Pumroy (1975), S.G. O'Leary and O'Leary (1976), Kazdin (1977a), and Neumann (1978) review and organize applied studies. The range of these classification schemes and their bases will now be discussed.

Paradoxically, the greatest area of agreement among the authors of these different classification systems is their general dislike and criticism of the frequently used term "group contingency." Specifically, this term has been criticized for a lack of clarity great enough to pose problems in replication and communication among researchers (Greenwood, Hops, Delquadri, & Guild, 1974). Litow and Pumroy (1975) argue that the term "group contingency" is erroneous as it implies that a group performs, whereas it is the behavior of the individual members that is actually being measured. No matter what the contingency statement, reinforcement always follows the response of an individual. Borrowing from Bandura (1969), they suggest that "group-oriented contingency" be substituted as a more meaningful term for these procedures. But Neuman (1978) finds this term misleading, preferring to focus on more precise social conditions of reinforcement. In his view, a contingency system is not group-oriented simply because behavioral criteria are used by all members.

Kazdin (1977a) used the term "standardized contingencies" to cover those situations wherein individual contingencies are applied to a group on a memberwide basis. Thus, he defines group contingencies based upon the performance of the group as a whole. However, in the view of S.G. O'Leary and O'Leary (1976), only those systems in which consolidated records of group behavior are used, for example, classroom noise (Schmidt & Ulrich, 1969), can truly be called "group contingency"; the authors note, however, that very few behaviors actually meet this criterion. Whereupon Neumann (1978) argues that even when group-contingency procedures are used, the analyses should be nonconsolidated so that the effect on individual members can be studied.

At this point one may ask, "Why the confusion and disagreement? And why have so many systems emerged to describe group procedures? Will the real group contingency please step forward!" In the remainder of this section, we will present each of these classificatory schemes and attempt to integrate them with a full account of group-contingency procedures.

TABLE 1.

Summary of Current Classification Schemes for Understanding Group-Oriented Behavior-Change Procedures

Authors	Settings	Classification scheme	Classification based upon	Levels or dimensions
Hake & Vukelich, 1972	Experimental	Cooperation procedures	Procedural dimensions	1. Interdependent vs. dependent response requirements 2. Response sharing vs. response exchange 3. Social responding vs. non-social responding 4. Forced cooperation vs. alternative response procedures

Greenwood, Hops, Delquadri, & Guild, 1974	Applied	Token-procedures	Procedural components required to carry out token economies	1. Behavioral criterion established
				  a. for individuals
				  b. for groups
				2. Point dispensing and/or recording completed
				  a. for individuals
				  b. for groups
				3. Backup consequences
				  a. for individuals
				  b. for groups

Litow & Pumroy, 1975	Applied	Group-oriented contingencies in classroom management	Reinforcement dependencies of participants	1. Dependent group-oriented contingencies 2. Independent group-oriented contingencies 3. Interdependent group-oriented contingencies

Kazdin, 1977a	Applied	Contingencies in token programs	1. Individualized 2. Standardized 3. Group All may include group or individual back-up consequences
S. G. O'Leary & O'Leary, 1976	Applied	Individual-to-group-contingency continuum	1. Type 1: An individual earns reinforcement for the group 2. Type 2: Contingencies for individua but the performance of all is consider in awarding the consequences 3. Type 3: The individual is indirectly involved in the group contingency

Neumann, 1978	Applied	Social conditions of reinforcement	1. Reinforcing agent
			  a. designated
			  b. nondesignated
			2. Recipients of reinforcement
			  a. contingently delivered
			  b. noncontingently delivered
			3. Group response requirement
			  a. no requirement
			  b. for designated participants
			  c. for nondesignated participants

COOPERATION PROCEDURES

An early review of cooperation procedures in laboratory research was provided by Hake and Vukelich (1972). They describe cooperation procedures as situations wherein reinforcers for two subjects are to some extent dependent upon responses of the other individual. Under these conditions, cooperative responding will result in an *equitable* division of reinforcers and responses. Thus, a cooperation effect is simply an increase in cooperative responding.

Hake and Vukelich indicate several procedural dimensions upon which cooperation procedures can be classified. The first dimension is the continuum along which the behavior of the partner determines the probability of reinforcement for the other member of the dyad. Thus, reinforcement can be totally or partially dependent upon the behavior of others. The latter condition is called *interdependent*. The extreme *dependent* condition is exemplified by the procedures used by Patterson and his colleagues (Patterson *et al.*, 1969; Patterson *et al.*, 1972). In their procedures, reinforcement for the group members is completely dependent upon the behavior of the target subject. In contrast, procedures used by McCarty, Griffin, Apolloni, and Shores (1977) demonstrate individual reinforcement dependent upon the behavior of each subject and only partially dependent upon the group. Students earned money based on the number of correctly solved math problems, but no reinforcement became available unless each had successfully completed three problems.

A second dimension deals with the balance in the distribution of responses and reinforcers earned by group members. Response sharing is said to occur when equal effort and subsequent reinforcement are required and are attainable. Each student having to complete a fixed assignment—for example, three problems—to earn a fixed number of points—for example, 5—is an example in which responding and reinforcement are equitably shared. Obviously, response sharing can occur only in an interdependent system. Response-exchange procedures describe an inequitable response–reinforcement relationship among participants. This situation occurs frequently when individuals of unequal skill levels are assigned to work on a common project. An inequitable work load can result, however, in equal reinforcement for all members of the group—for example, a common grade. Thus, effort is exchanged rather than shared.

A third dimension is related to knowledge of peer involvement. In nonsocial procedures, the subjects did not know that reinforcement was dependent upon another's performance. This was done primarily to study the laws of conditioning directly by controlling social stimuli. Social procedures involved full awareness of participants' response requirements and interdependencies.

Alternatives to cooperation represent the fourth dimension. Forced-cooperation procedures are created when the only alternative behavior results in nonreinforcement. Alternative response procedures allow cooperative or noncooperative responding to lead to reinforcement. Many life situations appear to operate in either or both modes. Reinforcers can be obtained by cooperation or through other routes, each with varying probabilities of success and cost. The amount of effort required to obtain reinforcement appears to be one determinant of choice of cooperative or alternative modes.

Three of the four dimensions identified by Hake and Vukelich (1972) have a direct bearing on group-contingency arrangements. Although these procedures have not been extensively used or studied in applied settings, they provide an interesting perspective on social-behavior effects during group-oriented contingencies and may explain side effects that are frequently noted. The dependent-independent dimension is a clear way of classifying much of the literature, although the problem of how to quantify the procedures along the continuum still exists. The focus on response sharing and response exchange also appears to be a useful means of conceptualizing the activity of group participants in some systems. How are the responses and reinforcers distributed in most group-oriented arrangements? Is it a factor that is considered in designing the contingency? Are side effects a function of the potential inequalities produced by a system? Indeed, in the applied uses of group procedures, researchers have not dealt with the processes occurring under these conditions but have focused monadically on the major outcome measure, for example, reduced disruptive behavior or increased academic performance.

The dimension of forced vs. alternative responding also provides a useful conceptual framework for dealing with group contingencies. Most of the procedures presented in the literature are forced. Reinforcement is not available without the completion of some dependent response requirement.

The varying combinations and possible interactions of these three dimensions may do much to explain many of the side effects noted by researchers. For example, one might speculate that forced cooperation may produce instances of peer tutoring when required in response-exchange contingency (McCarty et al., 1977) or instances of criticism and harassment when required in a response-sharing contingency (Packard, 1970). Such combinations may also explain to some extent efforts to subvert or beat the system (V.W. Harris & Sherman, 1973). We will return to these issues in a later section.

TOKEN-PROCEDURE COMPONENTS

The scheme developed by Greenwood, Hops, Delquadri, and Guild (1974) highlights some of the essential procedural characteristics that are used in token systems. Token procedures were described as generally composed of three essential components: (1) behavioral criteria (terminal performances), (2) point dispensing and/or recording procedures, and (3) back-up consequences. Each of these variables can be established in a program for individual members or the group. The eight cells in Table 2 describe the logical combinations of these components to form group-oriented systems.

Within this framework, the study by Bushell, Wrobel, and Michaelis (1968) corresponds to Cell 5, and describes a program wherein (1) behavioral criteria are applied groupwide, but (2) tokens are dispensed to individual students, and (3) back-up consequences are purchased by individuals who chose which back-ups they wished to buy. The conditions in Cell 8 are met in studies using the "good-behavior game" (Barrish *et al.*, 1969; V.W. Harris & Sherman, 1973; Medland & Stachnik, 1972). Here, (a) rules are established groupwide, (b) infractions are recorded on the blackboard as a consolidated group total, and (c) consequences are made available to the entire group if specific point levels are not exceeded.

TABLE 2.
Possible Combinations of Token Procedural Components

		Behavioral criteria established for		
		Individuals Dispensing and/or recording for		Group Dispensing and/or recording for	
		Individual	Group	Individual	Group
Back-up consequences for	Individual	1	3	5	7
	Group	2	4	6	8

Reprinted from Greenwood, C. R., Hops, H. Delquadri, J., & Guild, J. Group contingencies for group consequences in classroom management: A further analysis. *Journal of Applied Behavior Analysis*, 1974, 7, 413–425.

Generally, procedures including decibel meters, clocklights, or other group-performance recording meet the same criteria (Hops & Cobb, 1973; Packard, 1970; Schmidt & Ulrich, 1969).

Multiple procedures are also possible. Hamblin (1971) describes procedures that combine Cell 1 and Cell 7. Response requirements were set for both individuals and the group on mathematics materials; individual and group recording procedures (nonconsolidated) were employed; and individuals were free to purchase back-up consequences.

The system used by Greenwood, Hops, Delquadri, and Guild (1974) appears to eliminate considerable confusion contained in the group labels and provides a systematic procedure for describing the features which make up the contingencies—namely, behavior criteria, point dispensing and/or recording, and back-up consequences.

<small>GROUP-ORIENTED CONTINGENCIES</small>

Litow and Pumroy (1975) organized group-oriented procedures into three general classes based on Bandura's (1969) conceptualization of group-reinforcement contingencies. These are (1) independent, (2) dependent, and (3) interdependent group-oriented systems.

Independent Systems

In the independent system, behavioral requirements are uniform and apply groupwide. However, reinforcement of group members depends entirely upon their own performance. The Bushell *et al.* (1968) study cited previously is an example of this system. Here, behaviors reinforced by teachers were established to compete with disruptive behavior and included instances of "work" and "appropriate behavior," for example, tending to instructions, working independently, cooperating with others, and so on. The teacher passed out tokens to individuals contingent on these behaviors. Students could then buy reinforcement tickets from their individual token earnings. Each person's consequences were totally independent of the performance of any other individual.

Dependent Systems

When the consequence for the group is not made available until the successful completion of response requirements by one or more of the group members, that system is a dependent one. The Patterson "hero procedures" is a good example (Patterson *et al.*, 1969). Karl alone earned the reinforcement he shared with the class after the session. Of the studies reviewed by Litow and Pumroy (1975), the least number utilized this procedure.

Interdependent Systems

In the interdependent systems, behavioral requirements are applied groupwide to all members. Reinforcement, however, is dependent upon an aggregate, collective, or consolidated measure of the group's performance. Various methods have been used to monitor collective group responding. Electronic devices like decibel meters (Schmidt & Ulrich, 1969), timerlights, and clocklights (Hops & Cobb, 1973, 1974; Greenwood, Hops, Delquadri, & Guild, 1974; Greenwood, Hops, & Walker, 1977a,b; Packard, 1970) have been used to monitor group noise levels and appropriate-class-behavior time, respectively. Frequency counts of disruptive behaviors have been recorded using electronic counters, hand counters, data-sheet tallies, and chalkboard tallies. These can be recorded separately for individuals and then (a) summed or averaged, or (b) simply tallied regardless of specific contributing individuals with the total frequency or rate used as the criterion measure.

Neumann (1977) has recently described these measures as either consolidated, wherein individual performance is not retrievable (Greenwood, Hops, Delquadri, & Guild, 1974; Packard, 1970; Schmidt & Ulrich, 1969) or nonconsolidated, wherein both individual and group measures may be retrieved (V.W. Harris & Sherman, 1973). Each of the measurement procedures has particular advantages and disadvantages which will be reviewed later.

Of the 32 studies using interdependent procedures reviewed by Litow and Pumroy (1975), 21 focused on the class as the unit using electronic recording or averaged individual recordings. Eleven others divided the class into teams or small, competing groups.

A number of studies used a combination of independent systems with interdependent procedures. Several investigations compared the relative effectiveness of interdependent with independent systems; the relative power of dependent systems was not tested. Of the 14 comparative studies, seven found no differences, and six of the remaining seven found in favor of the interdependent, group-oriented contingencies.

Litow and Pumroy (1975) acknowledge that their classification system is simply a first step in providing order in the behavior-analytic research involving group arrangements. As such, it does provide us with some broad categories along a single dimension for grouping and conceptualizing research in this area.

CONTINGENCIES IN TOKEN PROGRAMS

Kazdin (1977a) proposes three categories of contingencies in token procedures that organize the behavioral-response criterion which is the basis for reinforcement. They are (a) individualized, (b) standardized, and (c) group contingencies. In the individual case, behavior requirements and specific consequences are tailored for a specific target. In the standardized category, the same contingencies, that is, behaviors, criteria, and consequences, would be applied groupwide. The only "group" feature would be the response requirement, that is, the same rules would apply to all. Points, however, are awarded individually to each student on the same basis, and with consequences equally available to all individuals who have the points to purchase them. In group contingencies, the criterion for reinforcement is based upon the performance of the entire group as a single unit. The individual behaviors of all group members are considered collectively.

In contrasting the group and standardized contingencies, we can see that the standardized system simply sets "groupwide" requirements for individual members. Reinforcement, however, is not dependent upon the performance of other group members. In the group system, the same standardized requirements exist; however, the availability of the backups is dependent upon the behavior of other group members meeting the established groupwide criterion for reinforcement.

A common procedure for establishing the criterion for reinforcement in group procedures is averaging the behavior of individual members. Other variations include the use of a total single score without recording individual performance (Barrish et al., 1969; V.W. Harris & Sherman, 1973; Medland & Stachnik, 1972). Subgroup performance—for example, high or low performers—may also be used to determine the reinforcement for the entire group (Drabman, Spitalnik, & Spitalnik, 1974; Hamblin et al., 1971).

Kazdin's organization makes clear the differences between those programs that are strictly individualized and programs with groupwide standardized contingencies for individual members. However, little distinction is made among all of the different dependent and interdependent relationships existing in the group-contingency system.

The Individual-to-Group-Contingency Continuum

S.G. O'Leary and O'Leary (1976) point out that it is the group "consequence" and not the contingency that is the primary common feature existing among the variety of group arrangements. The contingency dimension is conceptualized as a continuum from strictly individualized to one that is based upon the performance of the group as a single unit. Three types representing the two extremes and the middle are defined. Type I procedures are those in which consequences shared by the entire group are based on the performance of single target subjects. The work of Patterson (1965) provides the primary example of this end of the continuum. Type II procedures are cases in which contingencies are still individualized but the behavior of the entire group is considered in awarding the consequence. This situation can be illustrated by the McCarty *et al.* (1977) study in which individual consequences were not provided unless each student in the group had met a specific criterion. The Type III procedure uses the consolidated performance of the group as the basis for awarding consequences to group members, the only true "group-consequence" arrangement. Illustrations of this end of the continuum include using the level of classroom noise (Schmidt & Ulrich, 1969) or the amount of on-task time accumulated by the group as a whole (Greenwood, Hops, Delquadri, & Guild, 1974).

The O'Leary and O'Leary taxonomy, like Kazdin's (1977a) is general and focuses along a single dimension of the complex array of group arrangements which have been presented in the literature. Consequently, its usefulness for understanding group-oriented contingencies is limited.

SOCIAL CONDITIONS OF REINFORCEMENT

A sixth framework for thinking about group-oriented procedures has been offered by Neumann (1978) based on the social conditions of reinforcement. His system focuses on the arrangement of people and their response requirements in group-oriented systems. Three major dimensions are described: (a) the reinforcing agent, (b) the recipient response requirement, and (c) the group response requirement.

The reinforcing agent in a group procedure may be designated or nondesignated. For instance, the classroom teacher in the "good-behavior game" would be formally designated and trained to provide reinforcers. However, peers who provide social reinforcement to each other as the result of a group-contingency arrangement (Straughn *et al.*, 1965) would be described as nondesignated. In this manner the distinction between trained roles and enlisted roles is distinguished.

The recipients are the group members who actually receive consequences. As previously discussed, in group-oriented contingencies this may be as few as one or as many as there are group members. Recipients may receive consequences contingently or noncontingently. In the Karl study (Patterson *et al.*, 1969), the subject received reinforcement contingent upon increases in attending and work. His peer group received reinforcement on a noncontingent basis. They met no recorded response requirement and unless they actually interfered with Karl's point earning, no specific contingent requirements were established. In the Packard (1970), Hops and Cobb (1973, 1974), and Greenwood, Hops, Delquadri, and Guild (1974) studies, all recipients received contingent reinforcement.

The final dimension in this scheme is the group-response criteria to be met before any member may receive reinforcement. Systems may (1) have no group criterion level, or (2) have criteria for designated or non-designated group members. The Patterson "hero-procedures" design had no group standard to meet. Only Karl, the target, was designated to have a criterion for reinforcement. Bushell *et al.* (1968) had no group criterion; all children were designated and each had to meet a "standardized" groupwide criterion. In the Greenwood, Hops, Delquadri, and Guild (1974) study, groups were designated, and a group criterion was in effect.

The Neumann (1978) scheme contributes a clear view of the requirements and lack of requirements placed on the persons involved in group-oriented procedures. The notion that social agents are trained to apply procedures or are simply enlisted in the contingency provides information on a dimension of group arrangements not attended to in other taxonomies. In contrast to Litow and Pumroy (1975) and Greenwood, Hops, Delquadri, and Guild (1974), however, strictly individualized procedures are not included in the scheme.

SUMMARY

In an attempt to clarify group-contingency procedures, six major classification systems have been reviewed. They ranged from categories derived in laboratory studies of cooperation (Hake & Vukelich, 1972) to systems based entirely on procedures used in token-economy systems for classroom management.

Some of the classification schemes focused on a single dimension of group arrangements (Kazdin, 1977a; Litow & Pumroy, 1975; S.G. O'Leary & O'Leary, 1976), whereas others conceptualized more complex taxonomies involving the interaction of at least three independent dimensions (Greenwood, Hops, Delquadri, & Guild, 1974; Hake & Vukelich, 1972; Neumann, 1978). For example, the Greenwood, Hops, Delquadri, and Guild (1974) classification system focused on three procedural components of the token economy, and its three-way interaction provides an all-inclusive conceptualization of individual and group procedures. The single category attended to by all was the continuum along which the contingent relationship between behavior and consequence varied from strictly individualized at one extreme to the treatment of the group as a single unit at the other. The notion of dependence vs. interdependence used by both Hake and Vukelich as well as Litow and Pumroy to identify those relationships in which the group consequence is totally or partially dependent on the behavior of one or more group members is particularly relevant to the appreciation of group-oriented arrangements and the occurrence of positive and negative side effects emanating from them. Neumann (1978) described the role of the social agents involved in the procedures. A major contribution is the distinction of the reinforcing agent as either trained or simply enlisted in the contingency in a nonspecific manner. Hake and Vukelich's dimensions include the level of reciprocity and the degree of alternative responding allowed in the systems. Both offered more complex conceptualizations of group arrangements with the potential for producing powerful behavior changes and side effects.

It is clear from the previous discussion that the frequently used term "group contingency" is imprecise and at best represents one point along a single dimension within the complex array of group antecedent and consequent conditions. The term "group-oriented contingencies," suggested by Litow and Pumroy (1975), appears more aptly suited as a summary term to include all possible group arrangements. Additionally, it is clear that there are three different classes of group-oriented contingent relationships which are meaningful and functionally different from one another. These are (a) standardized (Kazdin, 1977a), in which individual contingencies are established with groupwide criteria, (b) dependent, in which group reinforcement is dependent upon the individual behavior of one or more group members, and (c) interdependent, in which group reinforcement is dependent upon the behavior of the group as an aggregate or consolidated unit (Litow & Pumroy, 1975). In the succeeding sections of this chapter, we shall continue to use the term "group-oriented contingencies" to refer to the variety of group arrangements. Additionally, we shall classify studies into standardized, dependent, and interdependent categories. This classification scheme appears to most clearly describe the important dimensions of group-oriented contingencies and should facilitate organization and discussion.

REVIEW: APPLICATIONS OF GROUP-ORIENTED MANAGEMENT

The purpose of this section is to review the application of group-oriented procedures to a variety of behaviors targeted for intervention in school settings. We will examine the settings and procedures designed for the management of three major response classes: (a) academic-related behavior, (b) academic responding, and (c) peer social interaction.

CONTROL OF ACADEMIC-RELATED BEHAVIOR

The studies to be reviewed here focus on classroom behaviors that are not academic per se, but are assumed and/or demonstrated to be related to academic achievement or responding. Most of the literature can be subsumed under two broad classes. These involve efforts to (a) decrease disruptive and/or counterproductive behavior, or (b) increase academic survival skills. Disruptive targeted behaviors include talk-outs (Hall *et al.*, 1971), obscene gestures (Sulzbacher & Houser, 1968), and classroom noise levels (Schmidt & Ulrich, 1969). Academic survival skills, behaviors positively related to academic achievement, include attending to task, following directions, and talking to peers about relevant academic matters (Cobb & Hops, 1973; Greenwood, Hops, Delquadri, & Walker, 1977; Hops & Cobb, 1973, 1974).

Standardized Contingencies

The single group feature in this contingency, as previously described, is the establishment of similar response requirements for all individuals. Perhaps the most widely used system of this type utilizes teacher approval contingent upon individuals' appropriate classroom behavior (e.g., Thomas, Becker, & Armstrong, 1968). Standardized token systems have also been established (Hops, 1971); some include both groupwide positive reinforcement and response cost contingencies for appropriate and disruptive behaviors, respectively (Walker, Hops, & Feigenbaum, 1976).

Contingencies established for the entire group can also be complex. Greenwood (1975) reported a token system in a special classroom in which the tokens changed over time from chips to points to credit cards, as students were faded to more natural contingencies.

The advantage of standardized, groupwide contingencies lies primarily in the uniformity of behaviors that occasion reinforcement. Thus, staff or paraprofessional staff can be easily trained to identify and consequate a single list of relevant behaviors. The major disadvantages are in the staff cost of dispensing points and operating token- or point-purchasing systems that individualize back-up reinforcers.

Dependent Contingencies

The best example of this system is Patterson's (1969) "hero procedures," designed to modify the behavior of a single child. Using Greenwood, Hops, Delquadri, and Guild's (1974) classification scheme (see Table 2), the behavioral requirements, the recording, and the point dispensing are all individualized; the consequence is applied to the entire group. The group back-up is used for two purposes: (a) to provide a more powerful consequence in the form of increased peer approval for appropriate classroom responding, and (b) to eliminate peer attention for disruptive, nonproductive behavior. While group behavioral requirements are stated, they are not recorded and consequently their contingent relationship to the child's behavior and to the group consequence is nonspecific and noncontingent (Neumann, 1978). Other studies have used similar procedures (Rosenbaum, O'Leary, & Jacob, 1975).

A highly developed, school-based program using the "hero procedures" as the primary contingency is the CLASS program (Hops, Beickel, & Walker, 1976). This program incorporates both an individualized token-reinforcement system for appropriate on-task behavior and a response-cost procedure for off-task disruptive behavior. Additional contingencies applied to the individual child include a systematic expulsion procedure for stealing, fighting, and continued noncompliance. The major consequence is provided at school to the entire group, although the child also receives an individual back-up at home dependent upon school performance. The program's effectiveness has been demonstrated over the short and long term (Hops, Walker, Fleischman, Nagashi, Omura, Skindrud, & Taylor, 1978).

The advantages of the "hero procedures" rest primarily on the power of peer influence to augment directly or indirectly the reinforcement effectiveness of token reinforcers (Kazdin & Geesy, 1977; Wolf & Risley, 1970). These procedures also appear relatively easy to implement, requiring the classroom teacher to record a single child's behavior on a point card which can be carried around (Hops, Beickel, & Walker, 1976). The system is also much more "efficient" and less intrusive than the electronic "workbox" operated by an experimenter or other apparatus foreign to the classroom environment (Patterson, 1965; Ray, Shaw, & Cobb, 1970; Walker & Buckley, 1972).

Its disadvantages lie primarily in the nonspecific monitoring of peer-group response requirements. The peer group may not always provide the social reinforcement for on-task behavior or the ignoring of inappropriate behavior required to support the primary contingency.

Drabman, Spitalnik, and Spitalnik (1974) compared three other forms of dependent systems to a completely individualized one. Each system required individual monitoring of all group members. Each member of the group was awarded points individually for appropriate behavior; the consequence was minutes of free time based on the members' points. System 1 awarded the group consequence based upon the member with the *lowest* number of points; System 2 used the *highest* number earned by a member; System 3 used the number of points earned by a *randomly* drawn member. No differences were noted in the effects produced among these three systems and between these and the completely individualized one. In contrasting Drabman's systems with the "hero procedures," the effect of the former was to reduce the disruptive behavior of the entire group at the additional cost of monitoring all members individually.

Interdependent and Mixed Contingencies

In this section we will review two sets of procedures that have been researched extensively with considerable replication. Both the good-behavior game (Barrish *et al.*, 1969) and PASS, the Program for Academic Survival (Greenwood, Hops, Delquadri, & Walker, 1977) are excellent illustrations of the procedures and implications of interdependent systems.

The Good-Behavior Game. This set of procedures was originally designed to reduce disruptive classroom behavior (Barrish *et al.*, 1969). The students are divided into two teams and compete for reinforcers available within the classroom setting. Disruptive behavior by any team member results in the possible loss of reinforcement to the team. The game involved the following procedures: (a) The teacher presents a list of rules or behaviors that apply to all group members. These rules state the disruptive behaviors members are not to perform—for example, talk without permission, talk while raising hand, make vocal noises, sit on top of desks, and so on. The original study included 11 such specific rules. (b) If the teacher observed a member breaking a rule, a tally mark was made on the chalkboard for the team. (c) By the end of the session, the team with the *fewest* marks won and received reinforcement; the losing team did not and continued with the lesson. If work was not completed, some students stayed after school.

Both teams won if the point total for each team was less than five. The winning team(s) had their names recorded on a posted "star chart," lined up for lunch first, and received a 30-min special-project period prior to the day's end. If a team had not received more than 20 marks in a week, it would get the extra weekly privilege of going to recess four min early. The game was effective in reducing out-of-seat and talk-out behaviors monitored by independent observers.

Subsequent studies have replicated the game in grades 4–6 and in multiple instructional periods (for example, English, reading, math, science, and spelling), and have found it dramatically effective in reducing disruptive-behavior targets (V.W. Harris & Sherman, 1973; Medland & Stachnik, 1972).

A problem noted in all three reports is the refusal of some students to participate. In the first two studies, a time-out contingency was individually arranged for the offending student(s). The tallies awarded to these students were also removed from the group's total. Thus the group was not exceedingly punished by offending members. In the third study, refusers were assigned to a third team and the losing team required to spend time after school. Consequently the original group was not punished.

Dietz and Repp (1973) reported a variant of the good-behavior game in the application of differential-reinforcement-of-low-rate (DRL) procedures. Groups earned reinforcement for not exceeding predetermined low levels of inappropriate responding. The behavior of the group members was recorded as a single unit. The procedure was found to be effective in a TMR classroom. Furthermore, successively decreasing DRL limits reduced disruptions to zero levels in a regular high-school business class.

The amount of teacher effort to implement the game seems not unreasonable. Further, the V.W. Harris and Sherman (1973) study used early dismissal and time after school as back-up reinforcers, which proved less costly and more natural to the setting than the star charts, victory tags, and "special activities" used by Barrish et al. (1969) earlier.

The Program for Academic Survival Skills (PASS). The PASS program is a spin-off of the Packard (1970) and Willis and Crowder (1972) studies using a timer and light to record group time engaged in appropriate behavior pinpoints. The procedure was further developed in studies by Hops & Cobb (1973, 1974) and Cobb & Hops (1973), followed by additional work developing the procedure into a dissemination-oriented package for teacher-consultants and classroom teachers (Greenwood, Hops, Delquadri, & Guild, 1974; Greenwood et al., 1977b; Greenwood, Todd, Hops, & Walker, 1979).

The program proceeds as follows: (a) The teacher presents rules for behavior (classroom survival skills) as in the "good-behavior game," but these are positively stated. The rules include elements of attending to task, work (e.g., writing, coloring, volunteering), talking to peers about academic work, and following teacher's directions. (b) The teacher uses a clock with remote switch to record the amount of time all members are engaged in "survival skills." While teaching and observing the class, the teacher turns off the clock when at least one student is not appropriate. Attached to the clock is a light providing feedback. The light is on when the class is following the rules. (c) Group consequences are made available for exceeding previous performances in the early stages and for meeting or exceeding an 80% maximum criterion in later portions of the program. Next, a schedule is used to program reward-frequency decrease and increase delay as students are required to maintain more consecutive days at 80% level for reward. Procedures are designed to finally remove the program from the classroom with maintenance checks made by the teacher (Greenwood et al., 1977a). Four clocklight units similar to that employed in PASS have been described in the literature (Greenwood, Hops, Delquadri, & Guild, 1974; Kubany, Weiss, & Sloggett, 1971; Packard, 1970; Willis & Crowder, 1972).

There are several advantages to the PASS system. The teacher uses a single measure of group survival skills, thus reducing the bookkeeping involved in monitoring individual students. Further, teachers have informed us that in having to scan the group constantly they actually learn a great deal about the behavior of their individual students and their own curriculum programming. Higher-functioning students require increased amounts of curriculum materials. Because insufficient materials are prepared, these students spend a good deal of time playing (Cobb, 1970). The PASS program has additional advantages in its packaged format and efficient training time for teachers (12 hr) and consultants (18 hr).

The major disadvantage of the PASS program is the clocklight unit. Because they are not widely available, these lights must be custom-built. Remote-control units, although easier to handle, are more expensive. Some teachers and principals are also not impressed with the mechanical nature of the program. However, such problems are usually reduced or eliminated once the power of the program to increase survival skills becomes evident.

Other Systems. Greenwood, Sloane, and Baskin (1974) reported on a group-oriented, interdependent procedure for increasing the social-approval, point-dispensing, and point-removal behavior of peer managers to the level demonstrated by the classroom teacher. This contingency made the behavior of the manager dependent upon the study behavior of the group, while the group's study behavior was being reinforced by contingent manager praise and point dispensing. The peer manager received points from the teacher based upon the group's behavior; three of four students had to be engaged in study behavior for points to be earned. However, the results suggested that manager dispensing was best maintained under an individual, independent contingency in which reinforcement for point dispensing was not dependent upon group behavior. Had an additional contingency been added in which the group's behavior was made contingent upon peer-manager behavior, then a more reciprocal exchange may have been created (Neumann, 1978).

A variety of other interdependent contingencies have also been used for controlling disruptive behavior. The back-up reinforcement and its criterion are not always predetermined. Long and Williams (1973) used an adjusting system so that the amount of reinforcement received (in minutes) was inversely proportional to the amount of disruptive behavior displayed during the period. In a collective cost contingency, the prospect of gradually diminishing reinforcement opportunity appears to control disruptive behavior effectively (Axelrod, 1973; Gallagher, Sulzbacher, & Shores, 1967; Sulzbacher & Houser, 1968).

Other systems have simply used absolute criteria. Alexander (1976) required group members to attend 100% of their school classes during the week to earn lunch money for next week. If only one student failed, the group missed lunch money that week. In fact, in this study the group procedure was found to be dramatically better than a similar individual procedure.

Interdependent systems have been reported using teacher social consequences alone as back-up events. McAllister, Stachowiak, Baer, and Conderman (1969) taught a teacher to frequently provide group-praise statements for instances when all members were observed on-task and for work improvement. Concurrent individually specific (i.e., name and behavior) reprimands were applied to instances of class rule violations. They noted that the reduction in disruptive behavior levels may have been due to (1) the reinforcing properties of group praise, and (2) peer-group pressure to avoid name-specific disapproval.

Summary

We have reviewed a number of group-oriented procedures for decreasing disruptions or increasing academic survival skills. Behavior requirements were most frequently noted in terms of posted behavior rules specifying disruptive responses or academic survival skills. Strategies generally focused on either outcome, and rarely were both targets included in the contingencies. Recording of behaviors occurred primarily as a result of either (1) consolidated or nonconsolidated tallies of individual disruptive-behavior occurrences, or (2) consolidated records of behavior using electronic recording devices. Consequences were either (1) earned, (2) earned and lost, or (3) lost. Group-oriented contingencies are clearly capable of implementing response-cost strategies for occurrences of disruptive behavior. In the good-behavior game, team competition between groups appeared as an additional force within a group-oriented framework. Behavior changes were facilitated in some cases by the use of shifting criteria for shaping either high or low levels of behavior, and in some cases mixed contingency systems were concurrently in operation. Side effects were noted in the cases of dependent and interdependent procedures.

CONTROL OF ACADEMIC RESPONDING

In contrast to the preponderance of research focusing upon control of disruptive behavior or survival skills in applied settings, applications to academic production and achievement are relatively infrequent. The literature using group-oriented procedures can be classified as follows: (1) studies of disruptive behavior change in which academic achievement was monitored, (2) studies in which academic response targets were treated, and (3) studies in which both behavior and achievement targets were treated.

Standardized Contingencies

Several reports of standardized contingencies to increase academic responding have been noted. Low-achieving sixth-grade students received points for correctly completing classroom work assignments (Wolf, Giles, & Hall, 1968). The points were redeemable for candy, clothing, money, and so on. Similarly, Clark, Lachowicz, and Wolf (1968) increased the work-assignment completion of school dropouts using points with money back-ups. Other variations have been reported by Hopkins, Schutte, and Garton (1971).

Dependent and Mixed Contingencies

Evans and Oswalt (1969) used a dependent, group-oriented system in three experiments to accelerate the academic performance of underachievers. The procedure involved asking a low-achieving student to spell a word aloud at the end of the day's lesson. If correct, the group was reinforced with early dismissal; if wrong, the lesson continued. In spelling (Study I), two subjects increased to above 90% on weekly 10-word spelling tests when the procedure was in effect. In math (Study II), subjects increased to above 70% accuracy on tests. In social science (Study III), a gain of 15 percentage points was made by the experimental subjects.

Based on an above-mentioned procedure established by Drabman *et al.* (1974), Hamblin, Hathaway, and Wodarski (1971) compared the effects of group reinforcement dependent upon (a) the lowest performer, (b) the highest performer, and (c) the average group performance. The results indicated the lowest-performer group contingency produced higher achievement overall with the least amount of variability in student gains. Observational data showed that to a great extent these results were produced by spontaneous peer tutoring. The high-performer contingency, in contrast, benefited high achievers and produced wide variability in achievement with particularly detrimental effects on low-performers.

Brooks and Snow (1972) reported a dependent system for a single target subject including both disruptive- (leaving seat or area) and academic-performance requirements (completion of portions of assigned work). This procedure was established both to control the target's behavior and to refocus peer-group attention on socially and educationally worthy behavior. Anecdotal reports indicated he received a great deal of peer attention for leaving class and for trading stolen objects. The system involved (a) points traded for a group activity for the class, (b) point-based monetary rewards for the subject only, and (c) a one-min loss in group activity for each inappropriate behavior he emitted. Unfortunately, the results were only narratively reported. However, group-leaving and out-of-seat behaviors dropped to zero and all academic assignments thereafter were completed. The program was terminated in the second week, and post checks six weeks later indicated no reoccurrence of inappropriate behavior.

Dineen et al. (1977) applied a dependent procedure to spelling with third-grade students. In addition to extensive training of peer tutors, a contingency was established in which the tutor and the tutee received point reinforcement dependent upon the latter's performance. Results indicated dramatically improved spelling performance for both students. The tutees' gains seemed to result directly from the increased practice. The improvement in the tutors' spelling may have been attributable to the particular interactive behaviors involved in tutoring—for example, reading and spelling the words aloud to the tutee since they never took tests covering the words they had tutored.

Interdependent and Mixed Contingencies

The greatest number of studies were found to involve interdependent systems. Lovitt, Guppy, and Blattner (1969) report a mixed independent-interdependent system for increasing spelling accuracy in a group of 32 fourth-graders. The independent contingency allowed group members, once they had demonstrated 100% accuracy on daily tests, to forgo further tests that week. The interdependent contingency specified that on days on which all group members managed 100% accuracy, the total class was allowed to listen to the radio for 15 min. The effect of the first system was to dramatically increase the number of 100% papers compared to baseline. The two procedures concurrently in operation continued this upward trend. A clear comparison of the two procedures was not possible.

Graubard (1969) reported a similar mixed system in which reinforcers were purchasable with points but only after each group member had earned a minimum number. Points were earned for (a) following school rules, and (b) academic output. An interesting aspect in this study was that all back-up reinforcers were consensually agreed upon previously by class members. These included kites, goldfish, shirts, and money. Results indicated that the program both increased the rate of progress through

SRA reading materials and substantially reduced disruptive behavior. Peer influence was noted to occur as group members would remind transgressors that inappropriate behavior affected them all. These reminders were noted to come most frequently from students highest in sociometric status and acknowledged as group leaders.

S.H. Wilson & Williams (1973) also included behavior and academic-performance requirements by blending two concurrent interdependent contingencies. Each of several groups of nine to 12 members in an open-spaced classroom setting operated by four teachers participated. Each group could earn a total of 10 min of free time in two five-min periods if (a) all group members completed writing assignments with no more than six errors in 20 min, and (b) none of the students misbehaved during the 20-min period. Instances of individual misbehavior reduced the group free time by one min each. Results indicated that (a) work completed dramatically increased, (b) disruptive behavior decreased, and (c) appropriate behavior increased. Off-task behavior was shown to decline in only one phase of the ABAB design when the procedures were in effect. Only one negative incidence of peer pressure was reported, and following the study teachers reorganized the procedure to include their entire day.

In contrast, Winett, Buttersby, and Edwards (1975) reported an interdependent procedure applied directly to academic production only with collateral effects on social behavior and teacher interaction with students. These procedures, applied in a class of 27 sixth graders, required that 80% of the group members in the class hand in a completed paper. The teacher scanned each paper for neatness and accuracy but corrected them later. If the 90% level was reached, the work period was followed by outdoor recess; if not, group members remained at their desks for the same time period. The procedure produced a strong effect on work completed, to over 70% in math and language. Gains were also noted in social behavior, including attentiveness. Interestingly, however, a marked decrease was noted in working as a class vs. working independently, suggesting spontaneous peer tutoring was not facilitated in this system in contrast to the Hamblin *et al.* (1971) study. An increase was also noted in positive teacher social behavior.

McLaughlin (1979) used an interdependent system based upon group average accuracy in Sullivan programmed reading materials. Points were given based upon the group average as follows: 90–100% = 60 points; 80–89% = 40 points; 70–79% = 20 points; 0–69% = 10 points. Substantial increases in accuracy were noted. Peer comments were also noted not to occur frequently in the classroom setting. Furthermore, the students generally preferred the group system to a completely individualized system.

A version of the good-behavior game applied to compositional variables in creative-writing instruction was reported by Maloney and Hopkins (1973). A recording system was developed for scoring the sentence-structure elements in writing samples of 14 fourth, fifth, and sixth graders during a remedial, six-week summer-school session. Two teams were created. Members received points for using different adjectives, different action verbs, and different sentence beginnings. Members of the winning team went to recess five min early and received a small piece of chocolate. Both teams won if their total team points were greater than 80% of the total possible team maximum set by the experimenter. If both teams were below the criterion with no marked differences between them, the reinforcement was made available to all. Both objective measures of usage and subjective measures of story quality improved substantially. Peer pressure in response to the game was not reported.

McCarty et al. (1977) mixed independent and interdependent systems in a class of four behavior-disordered adolescents in a psychiatric hospital. Students earned monetary rewards for correct multiplication problems. However, a minimum criterion of three correct problems for each student was established before any could obtain money. Rates of antecedent peer-teaching verbalizations covaried with the introduction of the contingent increases in computational behavior. The majority of verbalizations involved answers to number-fact questions or redirecting peers to engage in task activities. Coyne (1978) found peer tutoring to occur in college students participating in an introductory educational-psychology course. High-performance peers were paired with low-functioning peers in an interdependent contingency established on the performance of the team pair. Both subjects were required to score 90% or better on a unit-mastery test to receive five bonus points for each exam. This procedure was more effective than individual study assignments. Half to two-thirds of the students reported liking the procedure and indicated it was effective in improving academic performance. Proportionately fewer students assigned to an independent-study group found it effective or viewed it favorably. The author concluded that "pairing" students with others who do better on tests and rewarding them for their combined performance results in considerable improvement for the lower-level student.

A reduction in weekly spelling test errors was reported with elements of team competition and cooperative peer tutoring (Delquadri, 1979). The interdependent procedure involved dividing the class into two teams that competed for the highest point total. Winning with associated social praise, posting of the key winners, and ovation constituted the back-up reinforcement. Teams were reconstituted each week. On each team, peers were paired randomly. Each tutored the other by reading a word for the tutee to write down in a notebook. Each tutee earned points, three for each correctly spelled word, and one point for correctly rewriting the word three times. The tutor earned points from the teacher for "good tutoring." Halfway through the 20-min period the peers switched roles. Results in a reversal design indicated classwide reductions in spelling errors. Anecdotal notes indicated the procedure dramatically increased social interaction among students and that the teacher spontaneously applied the technique to math in a later period.

Summary

Group-oriented procedures were reviewed demonstrating the modification of academic-behavior targets, specifically task completion, rate, and aspects of accuracy. As in areas reviewed previously, interdependent and mixed studies were in the majority. In some cases, correct academic responding was modeled and "perfect papers" posted, similar to posted rules for disruptive or academic-survival-skill behaviors. Recording of behaviors was based entirely upon consolidated or nonconsolidated counts of individual performances. These included correct papers, correct problems, or team points. The measure of group performance and criterion was applied to determine success or failure to achieve group reinforcement. All three categories of procedures were noted to be effective in modifying academic response targets. A number of mixed, group-oriented procedures were also used as well as cost contingencies. In some instance, procedures were simultaneously applied to both academic performance and either (a) reduced disruptive behaviors or (b) compliance with classroom rules. Positive and negative side effects were noted specific to uses of dependent or interdependent group-oriented procedures and peer tutoring.

CONTROL OF PEER SOCIAL INTERACTION

In the previous sections, social interaction among peers within group-oriented contingency systems was seen primarily as a by-product of efforts to modify other target behaviors. In this section, we will focus directly on methods designed to change peer-group social behavior. It is impossible to conceptualize these methods as occurring within a non-group-oriented system, since the target behavior by its very nature is group- or other-oriented. Consequently, we will include in our discussion studies involving independent, individualized contingencies in which the group is not involved in the contingencies and is simply the object of the target behaviors.

Most of the studies included here have been designed to (a) accelerate positive social interaction in withdrawn, socially unresponsive children, (b) decrease negative interaction in socially negative and abusive children, and (c) accelerate cooperative interactions in social-play and -activity settings.

Independent Contingencies

Early studies of social interaction demonstrated the power of teacher praise and attention (K.E. Allen, Hart, Buell, Harris, & Wolf, 1964; Hart, Reynolds, Baer, Brawley, & Harris, 1968; Milby, 1970) and social and material reinforcers (Reynolds & Risley, 1968) for modifying the problematic social behavior of young children. Obviously, the procedures were implemented in group settings, but the peers were not directly involved. Increases in proximity and cooperation (Hart et al., 1968), conversation and parts of speech (Reynolds & Risley, 1968), and general increases in peer interaction (K.E. Allen et al., 1964) were achieved.

Other studies attempted to change the stimulus value of the target child for the peer group. Given the reciprocal nature of social interaction, Baer and Wolf (1970) hypothesized that reinforcing social behaviors in a low-interacting child will provide the child with a set of entry behaviors into the natural community of peer reinforcement. Using an ABAB reversal design, they demonstrated the maintenance of social behavior without reinforcement after the fourth treatment phase was terminated. In a similar vein, Kirby and Toler (1970) instructed a five-year-old noninteractive preschooler to pass out candy to his classmates. The procedure required the child to ask the peers which of two types of candy they preferred. The target child was reinforced by the teacher for passing out the candy and the peers were reinforced with candy for responding to the child's social initiations.

Social behavior may be influenced by teacher attention directed at collateral nonsocial behaviors. Teacher's reinforcement of on-feet behavior in a 3½-year-old who spent much of the time crawling on the ground had the additional effect of increased interaction with the peer group (F.R. Harris, Johnston, Kelley, & Wolf, 1964). Apparently, in an upright position, the child was a more powerful S^D for peer-group social responsiveness. Similarly, Buell, Stoddard, Harris, and Baer (1968) increased a child's use of playground equipment using teacher prompts and contingent social praise. With increased use of the swings on the playground, the child also increased touching others, verbalizing, and cooperative play with reduced levels of baby talk. Thus, individualized procedures can result in increased peer-group involvement by direct manipulation or by changing related nonsocial behaviors.

Standardized Contingencies

Several instances of systems standardized across the entire group designed to increase social interaction were reported. These studies involve groups of socially withdrawn children in special classrooms or psychotherapy settings with procedures established groupwide. Clement and Milne (1967) used token reinforcement within a psychotherapy setting to increase the social behavior of third-grade shy, withdrawn boys. The boys were seen weekly for 14 weeks in typical 50-min sessions. Token reinforcement by the therapist exchangeable for toy back-ups appeared to increase social behavior in the group. Therapist verbal reinforcement alone seemed to have the opposite effect, depressing social interaction. In a replication of this study with second- and fourth-grade boys, the application of social and token reinforcement increased the frequency of social play and proximity to one another (Clement, Roberts, & Lantz, 1970), as noted in the first study.

Two studies conducted in an experimental classroom setting used social and token reinforcement to increase the social behavior of withdrawn, low-interacting children. Walker, Hops, Greenwood, & Todd (1975) differentially reinforced six withdrawn children for (a) starting an interaction, (b) responding to a peer's positive initiation, and (c) continuing a positive interaction. Increases were noted in rate of interaction and percentage of time interacting under social-praise-plus-token conditions. Social-interaction levels for most children were maintained during reversal phases. Furthermore, follow-up checks at three and six months after the children had been returned to the regular classroom showed continued improvement relative to each child's respective peer group. In a second study, Walker, Greenwood, Hops, & Todd (1979) provided token and social reinforcement for the same three topographic components singly and in combination. Increases in the first two response classes produced no concomitant increase in percentage of time spent in social behavior. Only reinforcing continuing interactions or reinforcing all three components simultaneously produced dramatic social behavior changes.

Dependent Contingencies

Dependent, group-oriented contingencies in social-interaction research are not as simple as those conducted to modify academic responding or other forms of classroom behavior. The complexities are inherent in the social-interactive nature of the target behavior. For example, in one of a series of studies, Walker and Hops (1973) made a low-interacting student's token reinforcement contingent upon the peer group's initiations to her. In another case, the peer group's reinforcement was dependent upon the target child's initiations to them. In both instances there was no knowledge of peer involvement (Hake & Vukelich, 1972). The peer group in the first study and the target child in the second were not aware of the contingent arrangements. Yet it was their behavior that determined the availability of reinforcement for their peer(s). Consequently, the knowledgeable individuals had to prime the uninformed so as to produce increased initiating behavior as well as reinforcement. Both of these arrangements were successful. However, in the second case, the child was initially overwhelmed by the sudden increase in peer initiations, temporarily suppressing her social initiations.

In another study, subjects' reinforcement was made dependent upon their responses following peers' initiations to them (Hops, Walker, & Greenwood, 1979; Walker et al., 1979) While the established contingency was standardized and independent, each individual's reinforcement was contingent upon his or her own behavior. The functional contingency, however, was a dependent one since others' initiations were required before a subject could emit a reinforceable response. As it later turned out, an interdependent system developed. Subjects made contractual agreements through gestures or verbally before the session to exchange initiations with one another so as to maximize the likelihood of being reinforced. This contingency did not produce clear effects and was extremely awkward to implement.

Patterson et al. (1969) established a dependent system by making peer-group reinforcement (extra recess) contingent upon improvement in the target child's ball-catching ability. To facilitate the contingency, a peer tutor was trained to hand-shape the required behavior in the target while being monitored throughout the training sessions. The contingency also produced increases in the target's interaction with the entire peer group.

The PEERS program (Hops et al., 1978a, Hops et al., 1979) is a packaged dissemination-oriented program for increasing the social behavior of low-interacting, withdrawn children. A major component of the program is a dependent, group-oriented contingency. In this system, the reinforcement of the subject and group members is dependent upon measured increase in the target subject's percentage of playground social behavior. Both subjects and peers are informed about the program, its response requirements and back-up rewards for the class. Peers are instructed that initiating interaction and play with the subject will facilitate the availability of the group reward. In order to moderate the rush of peer initiations to the target, two to four peer helpers are selected each day to be primarily responsible for helping the target talk and play at recess. Points are recorded by a teacher-consultant on the playground. Elements of shaping, by increasing the interaction criterion, and program fadeout are designed to increase and maintain the subject's interactive changes (Hops et al., 1978a).

Similar procedures applied to four preschool children in separate classrooms during free-play time (Greenwood *et al.*, 1979; Todd, 1977) indicated that in addition to changes in rate and duration of interaction, subjects made more initiations, were initiated to more by peers, were more reciprocal by completing more interactive opportunities, and spent less time alone, observing peers, and alone at task.

A packaged program has been developed for treatment of negative/ aggressive peer interaction in school settings. The RECESS program (Walker, Street, Garrett, Crossen, Hops, & Greenwood, 1978) uses a dependent, group-oriented response-cost system. The target subject is awarded one point for each five min of recess prior to each session, and loses points contingently for each occurrence. Given that 80% of the points remain by the end of the session, an activity is made available to the class as a group. As in the CLASS program (Hops, Beickel, & Walker, 1976), individual contingencies with home consequences based upon social behavior at school are also included.

Interdependent Contingencies

Dyadic, interdependent systems have been established to increase social interaction in one or both members. Johnson *et al.* (1973) paired a low-interacting girl with various classmates in game conditions outside the classroom. The procedures required motor and verbal reciprocated responding with reinforcement contingent on the dyad's performance. The instructions were as follows:

> This is a game for both of you to play. Here's how it works. Jill, a light will come on in one of these windows in front of you. (The teacher pointed to each of them.) When the light comes on, you should tell Lynn what color it is. Tell her, "Lynn, press red." Then, Jill, you push the red window. Now Lynn, when Jill tells you what color to push, you find it and push it. If both of you press the right window, BOZO here, will tell you "That was right!" by blinking his nose and putting a marble here for both of you to share. If you earn enough marbles, you may trade them for two red tokens. (p. 7)

During the 50 days of treatment and pairing with three classmates, generalization to other children in the regular class setting was noted. Similar interdependent response requirements have been used to establish ball rolling or block passing in retarded children (Whitman, Mercurio, & Caponigri, 1970).

More subtle and complex interdependent contingencies may be used to establish long mutual-interaction sequences. Walker and colleagues (1979) reinforced low-interacting children for maintaining a dyadic interaction. Given the initiation of Child A to Child B, the response of B to A and the continued responding of A to B and then B to A, the teacher reinforced all subsequent social responses occurring within the same interaction, that is, without a five-sec pause. Both subjects received the same number of points. The contingency proved powerful in increasing the overall percentage of time spent interacting.

Minimum standards for social responding were set for all members of a group of socially withdrawn students (Walker, Hops, Greenwood, & Todd, 1975). The criterion was based on the level of behavior recorded during a previous individualized token phase. When all members reached or exceeded the criterion, the total number of points earned was equally divided among the students present. A second contingency ensured that the group continued interacting after meeting minimum levels. The total number of points earned by the group had to exceed the average number earned during the previous five-day phase before any points could be spent on that day. The effects of the group arrangement were not greater than the previous individualized system. Further, negative side effects were noted in the frequent pressure applied to the lowest responders to interact more. It is possible that group-oriented procedures will be less effective when all members of the group are low social responders. In this case, the lowest-interacting child who received most of the group pressure was the least responsive subject to be involved in a two-year period. Perhaps, as suggested by Kazdin and Bootzin (1972), those characterized as more withdrawn respond less well to token-based treatments, and in this case to group-oriented contingencies.

An interdependent procedure involving two socially aversive students and their peer group was designed to decrease the rate of negative-aggressive peer interactions (Walker, McKibben, & Todd, 1975). Each subject was designated the target in one of two alternating sessions each day. In each session, one point was earned for every three-min period in which negative responses were absent. If the subjects earned 16 of 20 possible points between them after both sessions each day, the entire class received a previously selected high-interest activity. A bonus back-up was also made available if the criterion was met for four of five days each week.

The procedure was effective in controlling socially negative-aggressive behavior for the designated target child during each session. Little evidence of consistent generalization was noted for the nondesignated child for whom the contingencies were not in effect. The authors suggested the inclusion of response-cost procedures may have made the contingencies more powerful.

Summary

Group-oriented procedures for modifying various forms of peer social interaction have been discussed. Independent, individualized contingencies were included because it was impossible to conceive of non-group methods that do not involve at least one other member of the peer group. The major objectives of these studies were to increase the positive interaction of socially withdrawn children and to decrease the antisocial behavior of socially negative/aggressive children. The social value of children as S^D's for their peers was manipulated by reinforcing (a) proximity to others, (b) the use of common play equipment, (c) standing upright vs. crawling, and (d) having the child pass out candy to the peer group. Standardized contingencies involving social plus token reinforcement were shown to be effective in both psychotherapy and experimental class settings. However, reinforcement of individual topographic components of social interaction were less effective and more disruptive than the reinforcement of all social responding.

Dependent contingencies were more complex. In some, the target(s) had no knowledge of the contingencies and had to be primed by their peers to respond appropriately. Potentially negative side effects occurred when uninformed, withdrawn subjects were overwhelmed by the sudden increase in peer-group attention. Generally, positive reinforcement procedures are used with the socially withdrawn, and response-cost contingencies with the socially negative/aggressive child. On occasion, response cost may become necessary for a withdrawn child after interaction increase results in socially inappropriate behavior because of the absence of social skills.

Interdependent contingency arrangements showed that long-term dyadic interaction with representatives of the larger peer group outside the classroom may generalize to social interaction with all classmates in the regular class setting. Similar contingencies were also used to increase the duration of interactions among a group of withdrawn children. Setting minimum requirements for all members of a group of socially withdrawn children did not produce rates of social interaction higher than that produced by a standardized contingency arrangement. This outcome may have been attributable to the nonresponsivity of a low-interacting child even under group pressure. Overall, the studies reviewed have shown that there is considerable evidence that group-oriented procedures can be effective for modifying social behavior among problematic children.

SECTION SUMMARY

In this section we have reviewed types of group-oriented procedures applied to four major areas of problematic behavior. Examples of independent, dependent, and interdependent group contingencies were presented along with studies demonstrating their application to (a) the classroom management of appropriate and inappropriate behavior, (b) academic responding, (c) production and administration of services, and (d) peer relations and social interaction. The preponderance of reported applications was noted to be in the area of disruption and academic survival skills. Relatively fewer studies were noted in each of the remaining three areas and each offers considerable promise for research and development. Overwhelming consistencies across areas were found in (a) the applicability of procedures, and (b) reports of positive and negative side effects as a result of dependent and interdependent systems. Similar side effects were not nearly as frequently reported for the independent systems, with most occurring in the area of social interactions. These side effects offer both interesting benefits and problems that will be considered in the next section. Our attention will now turn to an analysis of the effectiveness of group-oriented procedures.

EFFECTIVENESS OF GROUP-ORIENTED PROCEDURES

In any discussion of the power of treatment procedures applied to the alleviation of specific problems, at least three primary issues deserve consideration. First, we must ask whether the specific procedures are effective in modifying the behavior(s) of those subjects to whom they are applied. Effectiveness here implies that change in behavior is relatively immediate, of sufficient magnitude to solve the problem, and is durable over time and generalizable to other settings, peers, and behaviors. Second, we should examine the relative effectiveness of different procedures applied to the same problem in the same population. Litow and Pumroy (1975), for example, confound the issue of relative effectiveness with the primary purpose of each procedure by not specifying the identity of the target population in each case. The third issue concerns the relative difference in cost-efficiency between these procedures. Cost-efficiency matters include not only dollar amounts, but the degree of effort required to implement the procedure, its likelihood of being used again, its attractiveness to implementation personnel, and potential positive and negative side effects. In selecting a specific set of treatment procedures, it is wise to consider each of these important issues.

PEER REINFORCEMENT EFFECTIVENESS

Early studies in laboratory settings demonstrated that peer social reinforcement was indeed effective in increasing a number of child behaviors (Hartup, 1964; Patterson & Anderson, 1964). Wahler (1967) and, more recently, Strain, Shores, and Timm (1977) provided evidence for functional relationships between selective uses of peer attention and social initiations to behavior change in targeted peers. Other studies have gone on to show that peers can administer social or token reinforcement within a token economy as behavior-change agents or peer managers (Greenwood, Hops, Delquadri, & Guild, 1974; Phillips *et al.*, 1973; Surratt, Ulrich, & Hawkins, 1969).

The preceding discussion has also shown that the involvement of peers in a variety of group-oriented contingencies across four major areas of children's problematic behavior can have powerful results (see Hayes, 1976; Litow & Pumroy, 1975; McLaughlin, 1974; Neumann, 1978). However, as these procedures increase in complexity beyond the demonstrations of the effects of peer social approval, the processes by which these contingencies operate become less clear. Considerable evidence is available to show that working toward group as opposed to individual goals produces more cooperative behavior in children (Bryan, 1975; Combs & Slaby, 1977; Sherif, Harvey, White, Hood, & Sherif, 1961, cited in Bryan, 1975). Working toward a common goal also increases children's liking for one another (Heber & Heber, 1957, cited in Combs & Slaby, 1977). Extrapolating from these studies, one may conclude that the application of group-oriented procedures may act to change the stimulus value of target children for their peers and vice versa. Such effects have yet to be demonstrated.

Several studies have shown that earning reinforcers for the peer group may be a powerful motivating procedure. Wolf & Risley (1967, cited in Bandura, 1969) and Wolf, Hanley, King, Lachowicz, and Giles (1970) reported results indicating that the disruptive behavior of a female student was maintained at lower levels when she earned points to be shared with the group rather than just for herself. This occurred even when her individual earnings were larger than under peer conditions by a 5:1 ratio. More recently, Kazdin and Geesey (1977) demonstrated in a simultaneous-treatment design that this same procedure was also more effective for accelerating child attentive behavior in a classroom setting. The questions of what factors affect the stimulus value of children for one another and why some children respond more favorably to group contingencies than others (Hayes, 1976) have not received much examination. Even partial answers to these questions would facilitate the application of these procedures to a diverse set of children's problem behaviors.

COMPARISONS AMONG PROCEDURES

Comparisons between independent (individualized and standardized) and interdependent contingencies have been most frequently reported. Of the three possible outcomes, some studies indicate that the two systems are equally effective, others that the interdependent system is more powerful. In very few instances were independent systems shown to be superior (Drabman, 1976; Hayes, 1976; Kazdin, 1977a; Litow & Pumroy, 1975; S.G. O'Leary & O'Leary, 1976; Walker, 1979).

Hayes (1976) notes that many of these comparisons were methodologically weak, confounded by differences in subject characteristics, group size, density of reinforcement, and so on. As an illustration of this point, a standardized contingency was found to be superior to an interdependent system in a study conducted in a group home for the treatment of delinquents (Phillips et al., 1973). This outcome prompted the authors to note that their older, more deviant subjects (relative to those used in most other studies) may have been less likely to respond to group pressure and consequences and may require more individual reinforcement. Others have noted that some subjects (particularly adolescents) are more responsive to group (peer) reinforcement than to adult social praise or feedback (Hayes, 1976).

Even within similar systems, subtle variations in procedures may affect the outcome. Two slightly different forms of an interdependent contingency were compared for their effect on college students in an introductory psychology course. In a rather well-designed study (Speltz et al., 1979), students were asked to produce four test questions prior to each lecture. If two-thirds of the students in each group met the criterion, extra credit was provided in one of two ways: (a) to the entire group (All-Member), or (b) only to those who submitted the questions (Responders). Both interdependent systems proved to be superior to a standardized and a noncontingent arrangement; however, the Responder condition produced more test questions overall than did the All-Member condition. The authors note that more research is required in evaluating the effects of more stringent and/or lenient contingency arrangements. The minimum criterion for each student and/or the minimum number of students required to meet the criterion could have been shifted up or down in varying combinations with potentially different results.

These and other studies suggest that differences in outcome may be related to subject characteristics, reinforcement density, and subtle variations in procedures. More research is certainly required before any definitive conclusions can be reached.

At the same time, we should consider possible implications of the evidence accumulated thus far. If these findings (i.e., that independent standardized and interdependent contingencies are equally effective) continue to hold even under more stringent methodological conditions, then selection of the appropriate group-oriented procedure in each case may have to be determined by other relevant variables. These may include the extent of positive or negative side effects, the effort or ease required to implement the procedures, and the satisfaction ratings of the consumer as well as those implementing the procedures. It is clear that making procedural comparisons is not a simple task. These issues will be discussed in subsequent sections.

SIDE EFFECTS

Both positive and negative side effects have been consistently reported for group-oriented contingencies that make the negative qualitatively different from the positive and from independent arrangements. And, as noted above, the type of side effect may have a critical bearing on whether a specific procedure is considered appropriate for remediating a specific problem in a given setting.

Positive Side Effects

In the authors' experience with school personnel, most seem to expect negative side effects in the form of harassment or physical punishment to be the predicted outcome of group-oriented contingencies. In fact, there is considerable evidence, although much of it is anecdotal, to suggest that positive side effects occur more often. Social praise, encouragement, and approval have been noted as natural social consequences (Alexander et al., 1976; Patterson et al., 1969).

Some researchers have collected objective data on the positive side effects of group procedures. In a version of the "hero procedures," peers made increased numbers of social initiations to a noncommunicative target (Straughn et al., 1965). Peer tutoring has been noted in several studies. Hamblin et al. (1971) found increases in tutoring with increases in group-contingent involvement. When group-oriented contingencies operated during math periods, McCarty et al. (1977) noted that "The majority of verbalizations involved answers to number fact questions or redirecting peers to engage in on-task activities" (p. 313).

Frankosky and Sulzer-Azaroff (1978) reported a concomitant increase in positive peer interaction and decreases in negative interaction among retarded adults during a group-contingency program wherein individual tokens were a function of group productivity. Positive social behaviors included (1) discussion or comments directed and not directed at peers, (2) cheering or verbalized excitement, (3) requests for assistance or instruction, and (4) verbalizations of friendship. Positive nonverbal behaviors included (1) helping a peer, (2) gestures of friendship (e.g., handshaking, hugging, back patting, etc.), and (3) gestures apparently for assistance (e.g., pointing at objects, etc.).

Introducing a group-oriented cost contingency in a classroom setting made peer social reinforcement of inappropriate behavior incompatible with the contingency. Thus, peer approval of disruptive behavior was dramatically reduced for a single acting-out subject with increased time on task noted for the group (Sulzbacher & Houser, 1968).

Side effects may change the interactive relationship between students and staff. Increased school attendance and reduced curfew violations produced by a group-oriented procedure also made the violations an issue between the violater and her peers but not with the staff who implemented the procedures (Speltz et al., 1979). The authors also noted the absence of physical harm even though peers were firm in expressing their future expectations. Similar results were reported by Pierce and Risley (1974). In both cases, single violations affected the consequences of all members.

Negative Side Effects

While negative side effects have been frequently reported in dependent and interdependent systems, none of the studies we reviewed reported actual physical harm or violence to anyone involved. Rather, milder forms of peer pressure have been commonly noted. These have included verbal harassment (Barrish et al., 1969; V.W. Harris & Sherman, 1973), threatening gestures and facial grimaces (Schmidt & Ulrich, 1969), and scolding (Packard, 1970). Axelrod (1973) recorded 14 threats in an interdependent response-cost system vs. none in an independent procedure. Wilson & Williams (1973) recorded on threat in their study; others have not reported any (McLaughlin, 1979; Switzer, Deal, & Bailey, 1977). Such negative effects were also observed directed at adults (Schmidt & Ulrich, 1969).

Some researchers have speculated that in some cases behavior-change effects can be attributed to the avoidance of peer consequences, rather than their positive influence (McAllister et al., 1969). It has also been noted that some children—for example, high achievers—who are accustomed to individualized systems may become frustrated when their best efforts alone are not enough to maintain the reinforcement (see Chapter 10, this volume).

Summary

The side effects in dependent and interdependent systems appear to be the spontaneous result of peers attempting to maximize their reinforcement under the terms of the contingency. In only four of the studies reviewed were side effects objectively measured. These studies documented tutoring, social initiations to peers, or other incidences of peer assistance. The majority of side effects are anecdotal reports, and more definitive research is needed with respect to specific causal factors and their contributions to the primary treatment effect. Research should also address the correlation between negative side effects and the use of cost contingencies, negatively stated behavior rules, and instructions that might mediate the occurrence of such undesirable effects. Since side effects are inadequately reported, it was not possible to ascertain from our review of literature that negative side effects might not be more frequently noted under these versions of group-oriented procedures.

We would also expect that research of this type would find that both positive and negative side effects contribute substantially to the primary behavior change. Thus, negative effects may be an essential component of the total behavior-change procedure.

In Combination with Other Treatment Components

Rarely have group-oriented procedures been used in isolation in applied research. In the laboratory setting, it is possible to keep target subjects naive as to the social nature of a contingency (Hake & Vukelich, 1972). Very few studies have reported similar procedures in an applied setting (Walker & Hops, 1973, Wilson & Hopkins, 1973). Generally, target subjects and peers are given, at the very minimum, instructions and training about the operation of the contingencies and their respective behavior requirements for reinforcement. In this section, we will discuss the effects that may be attributed to the diverse set of treatment components that have been used in combination with group-oriented contingencies.

Instructions

Instructions about behavioral requirements, the type of contingency, tokens, and back-up reinforcers are nearly always used. Component-analysis studies with group-oriented (Medland & Stachnik, 1972; Packard, 1970) and individualized contingencies (Madsen, Becker, & Thomas, 1968; K.D. O'Leary, Becker, Evans, & Saudargas, 1969) have shown that instructions to improve behavior are not sufficient for behavior change. When feedback in light-form is added to classroom rules, more variable effects have been noted (Greenwood, Hops, & Delquadri, & Guild, 1974; Packard, 1970). However, overall, the data convincingly demonstrate that although instructions and rules may facilitate the speed of change, group members will not substantially change behavior without contingent consequences.

Grouping and Criterion Performance Levels

The grouping of individual class members within interdependent, group-oriented contingencies appears related to their performance directly and as a consequence of side effects produced by each arrangement. In a component analysis of the good-behavior game, V.W. Harris and Sherman (1973) found that dividing the class into teams who compete with one another was more effective in reducing disruptive behavior than a simple group contingency for the entire class. The difference was partly attributable to differing procedures used under team conditions. A team which had emitted more than the maximum number of disruptive behaviors allowed for reinforcement in any one session could still win if the other team accumulated more marks before the end of the period. Consequently, the possibility of "winning" remained constant throughout the period. Anecdotal data indicate that part of the reinforcement for winning was the opportunity to verbally harass the losing team after the session.

In another study, the pairing of low- and middle- with high-performing college students and the establishing of a 90% criterion for each member of the dyad resulted in higher performances overall (Coyne, 1978). This arrangement produced higher scores for every student paired with a high performer and was superior to individual arrangements. The data suggest that the gains were produced by peer tutoring alone and in combination with the group contingency.

Peer tutoring was a side effect produced in another study as a by-product of the dependent-contingency arrangement. Hamblin *et al.* (1971) found that establishing class reinforcement contingent upon the academic progress of the three lowest-performing students was most facilitative of academic gain groupwide compared to a similar contingency obtained using high performers. The low group's contingency also increased the amount of tutoring offered to them by the higher-performing students whose reinforcement was dependent upon the lows. Others have suggested that a group response requirement of average difficulty may produce the most favorable response across the entire group (Speltz *et al.*, 1979).

Thus, academic and behavioral gains can be facilitated by group-oriented contingencies dependent upon low or average performers and by dividing the class into competing teams or cooperative pairs also motivated by interdependent systems. Although effects are noted across the entire class, major effects are produced for low performers with no evidence of losses to high performers who act as tutors. As demonstrated by Dineen (1977), tutors may also show gains in academic performance as a function of increased practice during tutoring.

Shaping and Criterion Performance Levels

On occasion, shaping of target behaviors to higher performance levels may be necessary. The contingent behavior requirements may simply produce performance levels at the lowest possible level. For example, V.W. Harris and Sherman (1973) found that in their version of the good-behavior game students generally scored as many disruptive behaviors as allowed by the criteria. Further, once the team had lost the game, continued levels of disruption occurred. Some students were more clearly the culprits and special procedures (a third team) were instituted to control their behavior. Greenwood, Hops, Delquadri, and Guild (1974) report using a moving three-day average system for shaping the group survival-skill level upward session by session. The criterion is established at 1% more than the average level over the previous three days. To receive reinforcement, the average must be exceeded. The maximum criterion is established at 80%. Thus, each class improves at its own rate.

Back-up Consequences

The availability of back-up consequences is a critical component of any program designed to produce maximum effective behavior change in disruptive, appropriate, or social behaviors (V.W. Harris & Sherman, 1973; Greenwood, 1974; Medland & Stachnik, 1972; Packard, 1970; Walker *et al.*, 1979). When contingent consequences are removed, there is a dramatic reversal in target behaviors. In contrast, Delquadri (1979) found in a version of the good-behavior game that feedback, public posting, and team winning by total points alone were sufficient to dramatically reduce spelling errors. However, the subjects in Delquadri's study were not behaviorally problematic. Thus, for some subjects and with academic targets, a combination of team competition, feedback, and public posting may be effective without the addition of back-up consequences.

With Mixed Individual Contingencies

Combinations of group-oriented dependent and individualized contingencies have been reported, although few have isolated their independent effects. The CLASS program for acting-out students (Hops, Beickel, & Walker, 1976) and the RECESS program for socially negative/ aggressive children (Walker, Hops, & Greenwood, 1978), for example, provide an individual home reward system for points earned in addition to a group consequence at school. These procedures are attempts to refocus parental reinforcement to desirable school performance and to extend reinforcement control from school to home.

Behavioral Rehearsal

As part of many instructional procedures, behavioral rehearsal or role play has been included to teach students system rules and contingencies (Greenwood, *et al.*, 1977a,b; Hops, Walker, Fleischman, Nagashi, Omura, Skindrad, & Taylor, 1978; Walker, Hops, & Greenwood, 1978; Walker, Street, Garrett, Crossen, Hops, & Greenwood, 1978). During the process, the roles of the student and the adult will be exchanged to demonstrate the behaviors that earn and lose points in the system. No attempts have been made to isolate the effects that result from this procedure, but as with other instructional elements, the procedure is not likely to produce any lasting behavior change unless back-ups are made available.

Response Cost

A number of group-oriented procedures use response cost or contingent point loss as the consequence system to control disruptive and/or aggressive behavior. Students are awarded points at the beginning of the session which are lost in varying proportions or numbers contingent upon specific, targeted responses. The remaining points are traded for back-up consequences at the end of the session (Axelrod, 1973) or may also be accumulated for later exchange if too few are retained to purchase available activities (Walker, Hops, & Greenwood, 1978; Walker, Street, Garrett, Crossen, Hops, & Greenwood, 1978).

Point loss has also been used in combination with point earning (Hops, Beickel, & Walker, 1976) as a means of accelerating appropriate behaviors and decelerating disruptive ones. This combination has been found to be highly effective (Kazdin, 1977a; Walker, 1979). Replicated studies have shown that appropriate and inappropriate social behaviors may be under independent control (Walker, Hops, Greenwood, Todd, Street, & Garrett, 1979).

Individual and Group Praise

Many procedures include contingent teacher praise for individual and/or group performance. McAllister (1969) used individual reprimands with names and group praise to control attending to task in a junior-high class. Praise is often included as a secondary tactic increasing the teacher's reinforcement control and as a maintenance procedure after the group-oriented contingency system has been removed (Greenwood,

Hops, Delquadri, & Guild, 1974; Greenwood *et al.*, 1977b; Greenwood, Hops, Walker, Guild, Stokes, Young, Keleman, & Willardson, 1979).

Many other components have been investigated in combination with group-oriented contingencies, including symbolic modeling (Walker & Hops, 1973), social-skills tutoring (Hops *et al.*, 1979), correspondence training and verbal reporting (Risley & Hart, 1968; Rogers-Warren & Baer, 1976), and peer-pairing games (Hops, Fleischman, Guild, Paine, Street, Walker, & Greenwood, 1978; *et al.*, 1979). It is clear that few of these effects have been isolated and much more research is required to assess their individual and combined contributions.

Maintenance and Generalization Effects

The majority of studies using group-oriented contingencies have not reported outcome data beyond immediate and primary effects. The major advances in behavioral research in the last 15 years have been in moving treatments into the hands of natural social agents in natural settings. Even so, the available data in group-oriented research continue to show that maintenance and generalization remain contingency-specific and that changes generalize to and persist in settings which, in some sense, continue the treatment procedures (Walker & Buckley, 1972).

Maintenance

The primary variables studied which are designed to foster persistence of treatment effects have been (a) the fading of reinforcement schedules once criterion has been met, and (b) the fading of program stimuli (e.g., graphs, charts, rules, etc.). Greenwood, Hops, Delquadri, and Guild (1974), and Greenwood *et al.* (1977b) demonstrated fading group-reinforcement occasions by increasing the number of 80% periods required from two per day to one per five days. Depending upon the group's successful performance under the leaner-reinforcement schedules, program stimuli (PASS clocklight, posted rules, and graph) were also faded. Maintenance of treatment effects was noted three weeks later at follow-up. In a subsequent study (Greenwood *et al.*, 1977a) these procedures were compared to two 15-day enhancement procedures. The latter consisted of (a) a prolonged removal of visible program materials including posted rules and graph, and (b) continuation of the full program. In contrast to a control group, the results indicated all three sets of procedures were effective in maintaining appropriate behavior six and nine weeks later. Further, there was no difference among the regular PASS procedures and the two longer enhancement conditions.

Generalization Effects

Like maintenance, generalization of effects has not been widely studied. Treatment applied in one setting to establish social cooperation had some temporary effects in activity and free-play settings (Walker, Street, Garrett, Crossen, Hops, & Greenwood, 1978).

Greenwood and Hops (1976) found minimal across-setting generalization when teachers were trained to use the PASS program in only one instructional setting. A later study replicated this finding and noted that the minimum components of the full PASS program required to generalize effects to student behavior change in a second setting were the introduction of behavior rules and contingent teacher approval (Hops, Greenwood, & Guild, 1980).

It is clear that very little has been done to evaluate the generalizability and durability of group-oriented systems. The complexity of these procedures, as seen in the diverse number of treatment components included in such systems, opens the door to a variety of interesting research problems with potentially productive implications for generalization and maintenance of treatment effects.

SOCIAL VALIDATION

Earlier we described social validation as a means of assessing the clinical, social, and applied importance of behavioral treatments and effects (Kazdin, 1977b). Assessment may be (a) subjective and based on clients' or expert judges' ratings of the importance of treatment procedures or target behaviors and of their satisfaction with the results, or (b) more objective by comparison with relevant treatment and/or non-treatment control groups. Few studies using group-oriented contingencies have incorporated social-validation measures. Those that have (a) examined client satisfaction with various aspects of the treatment procedures and outcome, and (b) assessed the importance of behavior changes in contrast to equivalent control groups not receiving treatment and to normative data bases on large pools of appropriate comparison subjects.

Client Satisfaction

The majority of reporting on clients or other social agents to date has been anecdotal. Subjects have been informally questioned or interviewed at the end of studies. Hamblin (1971) reported some hesitancy of students to enter contingency systems in which one individual had to depend on another. Teachers generally preferred group-oriented to individual systems (Barrish *et al.*, 1969; Drabman *et al.*, 1974).

More systematic data collection has also been conducted. At Achievement Place, a treatment program for delinquent (Phillips *et al.*, 1972) boys' preferences for particular managerial systems involving elements of group vs. individual task assignments and group vs. individual performance contingencies were studied (Phillips *et al.*, 1973). The boys used a secret-ballot system to vote for the system they preferred. An individual-assignment and individual-consequence system without point-loss contingencies was most preferred. In subsequent research, an elected peer manager who gave and took away points on the basis of individual performance represented the preferred procedure and proved most effective according to objective data.

Greenwood and Guild (1977) and Greenwood, Hops, Walker, Guild, Stokes, Young, Keleman, & Willardson (1979) reported an extensive poll of over 500 students at two different sites who participated in the PASS program. Questions were organized in four areas: (1) peer pressure, (2) satisfaction, (3) behavior and achievement, and (4) continuance of the program. With respect to pressure, 58% and 74%, respectively, indicated peers got angry at them when they were keeping the clocklight off. When asked if the program made anyone (peers or the teacher) nervous, the majority (75%, 89%) said no, but 10% and 25% answered affirmatively.

Satisfaction with the program was evident (93%, 94%) when asked if they liked the clocklight; 99% and 98% like earning group rewards; and 95% and 92% liked working with the whole class for rewards.

Behavior and achievement questions indicated that most (85%, 85%) thought they got more work done; that the rules established helped them work better (98%, 95%); that they spent more time working and less time goofing off (71%, 74%); and reported more (77%, 67%) right answers because of the program.

Questions on continuance of the program indicated 76% and 84% would like the system used next year, 17% and 11% wanted to quit using the program, and 28% amd 34% would prefer to work for rewards on their own.

A close analysis of these responses showed that no differences in satisfaction were reported by children who had made large behavior changes (i.e., who were low at baseline). One might expect, if change were difficult, that large-change subjects would have disliked the system to a greater extent.

A further comment regarding the interpretation of the data in the two studies is required. In the Greenwood and Guild survey, opinions were asked about alternate conditions for which the subjects had no immediate experience. For example, the question "Would you rather earn rewards by yourself?" assumed that they had had a previous opportunity to do so. The balloting in the Phillips (1973) studies was conducted with regard to experienced alternatives. Preference baselines are probably different in these conditions and should be taken into account.

In a study of independent vs. interdependent contingency systems, McLaughlin (1979) had students rate their preference for each system on a seven-point scale. Results indicated mean ratings of 6.5 vs. 7.0 for the individual vs. group systems. Although equally preferred, the group procedure was from 2% to 25% more effective for increasing accuracy in programmed reading. Coyne (1978) reported that two-thirds of the students favored interdependent tutoring contingencies, and the same number also reported the procedure to be effective for increasing their academic performance. Thus, future selection of procedures might consider both client preference and the power of the procedure to effect change in the targeted behavior(s).

Judgments of those personnel implementing the procedures should also be considered in the total evaluation. Greenwood (1979) had teachers and the teacher-consultants who trained them rate their satisfaction using a five-point Likert scale. Mean satisfaction ratings were 4.1 and 5.0, respectively. They also rated highly the behavior-change and achievement gains produced by the program. High ratings were obtained on the techniques they learned and the process of interaction between teachers and teacher-consultants required to implement the program. Regardless of how effective a program may be, if implementation personnel are dissatisfied or find the effort beyond their capability, the net result is likely to be abandoning the program or ineffectual implementation should it be tried again.

Control-Group Comparison

Few studies have reported comparisons of group-oriented procedures to equivalent nontreated control groups. Such comparisons study intersubject change under experimental procedures vs. those ongoing natural-service procedures in similar settings—comparisons which are not made in single-subject designs. In addition, experimental control-group studies assess the generality of effects over large numbers of subjects and school settings.

Hops, Walker, Fleischman, Nicholes, and Greenwood (1976) and Hops, Walker, Fleischman, Nagoshi, Omura, Skindrud, & Taylor (1978) reported such an evaluation using the CLASS program, a dependent contingency system with earning and cost procedures. Within two independent school sites (27 experimental, 27 control), the procedures increased participants' levels of appropriate classroom behavior significantly above that maintained for the control group. The effects were repeated in a subsequent study (Hops, Walker, Fleischman, Nicholes, & Greenwood, 1976).

Similar studies and results have been reported for the PASS program (Cobb & Hops, 1973; Hops & Cobb, 1973, 1974; Greenwood *et al.*, 1977a,b; Greenwood, Hops, Walker, Guild, Stokes, Young, Keleman, & Willardson, 1979). These studies are generally conducted after single-subject designs have been used to assess the effects of the individual components that make up the final package.

Normative Data

The use of normative data has been increasing as a means to select or identify children with below-"typical" levels of behavior, and as a way of evaluating the power of treatments to remediate deficits (Patterson, 1974; Walker & Hops, 1976).

The three group-oriented procedures used to modify social interaction of socially withdrawn children in the Walker and Hops (1973) studies, for example, used average peer-interaction rates as normative estimates by which to evaluate the magnitude of change produced by these procedures. All the treatments were effective by these criteria. Similarly, the PEERS and RECESS programs provide peer norms for percentage of social behavior and negative peer-interaction rates, respectively (Hops & Greenwood, 1981; Walker, Hops, & Greenwood, 1978). These can be used by teacher-consultants to assess the effect of implementing the program on targeted children.

Secondary Objective Measures

Social validity can also be assessed using secondary measures to ascertain process effects related to the primary outcome measures. In studies of changes in disruptive and appropriate behavior in school settings, measures of achievement (Hops & Cobb, 1973; Greenwood *et al.*, 1977b; Greenwood *et al.*, 1979), sociometrics (Drabman *et al.*, 1974), and teacher ratings of student behavior change (Greenwood *et al.*, 1979) may provide additional measures for judging the value of the primary behavior change.

Observational measures of spontaneous peer tutoring (McCarty *et al.*, 1977) or of groupwide social processes (McLaughlin, 1979) provide information concerning the operation of important variables so anecdotally ascribed to group-oriented procedures.

COST EFFICIENCY

Perhaps the most agreed-upon point is that interdependent systems are the most cost-efficient per pupil involved (Litow & Pomroy, 1975). Uniform group-behavior requirements are often easier to construct and monitor than individualized behavioral requirements. Similarly, recording and points are more efficiently handled, and it is much easier to arrange several reinforcers for the entire group than to develop a reinforcement menu for each subject (Hermann & Tramontana, 1971).

Some researchers have provided data on monetary costs and time required to train for and implement the procedures. The PASS program implementation required about $15–$20 per student per classroom for consultant and teacher stipends during the training period in addition to approximately $120 per class ($N = 25$) for the packaged materials and clocklight (Greenwood et al., 1979). Consultants were trained in full two-day workshops and implemented the program via six two-hour teacher-training meetings and approximately 17 15-min classroom visits. The program was implemented over a period of 30 to 45 days.

Other investigators have been concerned for some time with person-hour costs of implementing behavior-change programs in school and home settings (Patterson, 1976; Patterson et al., 1972). Patterson (1974) indicated that approximately 20 to 30 hr of intervention time were required for aggressive, acting-out students in the regular classroom. Other investigators have not provided similar costs, so comparisons are difficult. It is clear that much more data should be made available about the cost efficiency of group-oriented procedures to facilitate their total evaluation—especially at the dissemination stage.

SUMMARY

How effective are group-oriented procedures? The answer depends upon the specific question being posed. There is considerable evidence that the three group-oriented procedures; standardized, dependent, and interdependent, are all effective in producing immediate and substantial primary behavior changes. The evidence with respect to the relative effectiveness of these systems is best documented between independent and interdependent systems. The data have shown these to be equally effective, or the interdependent system to be superior. Few studies have demonstrated that dependent systems are as effective as independent systems in producing change in individual target subjects. Those studies available suggest that the dependent system may be more powerful because of the effects of peer influence added to the primary contingency. Social-validation research, while not extensive, has shown that teachers overwhelmingly tend to prefer interdependent systems since they report (anecdotally) handling more students with less effort. Students have also indicated preferences for interdependent systems. Although peer pressure has been evident, the majority have not wished to discontinue using the program. Issues concerning maintenance and generalization of effects are not well documented and require major research attention. The often-noted side effects of group procedures appear confined to dependent and interdependent systems and support the power of behavior change through both positive and negative peer behaviors.

AREAS FOR RESEARCH AND DEVELOPMENT

In this chapter we have discussed the need for research and development in several important areas related to group-oriented contingencies. Here we will deal with three areas that we think have the greatest implications for applying these contingencies in modifying social and academic problematic behavior. Our focus will be on: (a) the facilitating patterns of peer social cooperation, (b) generalization and maintenance of treatment effects, and (c) package development and dissemination.

THE FACILITATING PATTERNS OF PEER SOCIAL COOPERATION

To a greater or lesser extent, group-oriented contingencies facilitate various forms of social cooperation among group members. This is so whether the effects have been measured in the laboratory or in natural settings (Bryan, 1975). Unfortunately, research has not taken us much beyond this point, with many questions about the processes involved in facilitating cooperation among peers left to be answered. For example, what characteristics of these contingencies produce differential forms of social cooperative behavior? Are some more suited to specific target behaviors and others successfully applied across many behavior-change situations? The majority of studies reviewed here have largely ignored in-depth analyses of aspects of social cooperation and exchange and have instead focused primarily on primary measures of outcome. Now we must focus our attention beyond the point of asking "What works?"—to the question "Why does it work?" The absence of such research demonstrates our present ignorance about the total impact that these procedures can have on the social-interactive behaviors that are by-products of these contingencies.

Let us look at some potential consequences of reinforcement sharing in both dependent and interdependent contingencies: (a) The sociometric status of the child and his potentially reinforcing value to the group may increase; (b) controlling the availability of peers' reinforcers may act to reinforce the target behaviors of others that earned the privilege; (c) increases in spontaneous initiations are made to target children; (d) peer social reinforcement (praise and applause) may strengthen the target behaviors; and (e) peers monitor, prompt appropriate, and punish inappropriate responding.

It appears that when systems are established in which group reinforcement is dependent upon one or more classmates or the collective group performance, the members of the group develop strategies for maximizing the probability of a reinforcer being made available. These strategic behaviors are the side effects of group-oriented contingencies about which little research has been done. We know that the group closely monitors the performance of those target students whose behavior determines the availability of reinforcement, and try to influence their performance. The group's "assistance" is as likely to be positive (praise, encouragement, tutoring) as negative (threats, harassment, criticism).

There are several factors which appear to influence the peer group's behavior. For example, the performance level of the target children whose behavior determines reinforcement affects the behavior of the entire group. When the criterion is based (a) completely on the academic behavior of low performers in the group as in a dependent model, or (b) partially on their behavior as in a high-low peer-pairing interdependent model, higher-functioning peers are motivated to teach, monitor, and otherwise help the lower performers accelerate their academic functioning to achieve the necessary goals. No research has examined the best method of selecting low-functioning target students. Several studies have used the lowest three performers in the class. But why three? And are there other subject characteristics that can be included in the selection process?

What of the effect of group size on peer-group responsiveness? Is a low performer whose behavior determines reinforcement more likely to be forgotten or supported in a larger group? In one dependent study using the CLASS program, one target child earned reinforcers for a team-teaching group numbering 120 students. The applause at the end of each session was overwhelming. Further analogous systems have not been applied to disruptive or social-interaction targets and may provide interesting new approaches.

Strategy development can also be directed at escaping or avoiding the contingent primary-performance requirements. Such behaviors include direct refusal to continue (Barrish et al., 1969; V.W. Harris & Sherman, 1973) and having other students complete the response requirements for targets (Speltz et al., 1979). Under some conditions of interdependent contingencies, higher-performing students may substitute their work for low-performing subjects. How can this problem be averted? Research is needed in this area.

Maximizing Peer Influence

So far, the majority of studies have recorded the beneficial side effects of group-oriented procedures, such as spontaneous peer tutoring, verbal praise, and so on. But very few have attempted to instruct the children in the specific behaviors that would facilitate and maximize the effects attributable to the contingency arrangements. For example, in two studies (Delquadri, 1979; Hamblin et al., 1971), students were instructed that they could provide tutoring to peers to help them reach the criterion for reinforcement. In other studies, instructions are usually provided about the contingencies and the behavioral requirements with little attention paid to how best to meet these criteria. Peers in dependent systems are instructed that they can help the target student by encouraging certain behaviors or by ignoring others. However, the extent to which instructions are effective or essential is not known. Instructions about the indirect effect of specific peer behaviors could speed up the process with more precise forms of responding. Moreover, accurate instructions and peer training could possibly eliminate negative or counterproductive behaviors. For example, in the PEERS program (Hops, Fleischman, Guild, Paine, Street, Walker, & Greenwood, 1978; Hops et al., 1979), the peer group is instructed in how to help the target earn points for social behaviors. Prior to each daily session, a brief setup session is held in which the specific target behaviors that earn points and the specific peer behaviors that can provide assistance are listed and discussed. Peers are called upon and asked how they can help. Unfortunately, no data are available on whether these instructions actually affect the group's behavior during the following recess period.

Variations in levels of interdependency and mixed systems should also be studied. So far, we have no objective scoring system for measuring the different levels of interdependent systems. An interlocking system was used in one study reported by Walker and Hops (1973) wherein peers were reinforced for the target's social initiations and she was reinforced for the group's initiations to her. But the specific arrangement produced an inequitable peer–target initiation ratio. The authors speculated that a more balanced interlocking system would prevent the target from being overwhelmed by the peer group. This problem has also been reported by Greenwood, Todd, Hops, & Walker (1979). In this case, the addition of shaping or fading through shifting criterion could be used to effectively establish peer initiations at some optimum levels and then to program maintenance by lowering the requirements to approximate reciprocity levels in the natural setting.

Interdependent systems can be arranged to promote social interaction and cooperative responding. In a laboratory study (Mithaug & Burgess, 1968), peers in dyads developed particular strategies involving cooperative responding to maximize group points earned. In a later study, adding a verbal contingency increased the number of verbalizations to resource peers (those controlling materials necessary to complete the task). Further, when the size of the group was doubled and the number of resource peers increased, verbalizations were more wide-spread, involving all of the available peers (Mithaug & Wolfe, 1976). Thus, by arranging the antecedent conditions in specific ways, Mithaug and colleagues were able to increase the frequency of verbalizations and the number of peers interacted with. In most studies such effects are usually not programmed or measured precisely. More attention must be given to arranging antecedent events such as instructions to the peer group, and to programming the availability of tutors and resource people in order to obtain maximum effects from group-oriented contingencies.

Documenting Facilitative and Peer-Pressure Events

Primary considerations must be given to more objective measures of peer social effects arising in group-oriented systems. McCarty *et al.* (1977), for example, measured peer-tutoring by-products with an observation system in addition to the primary effects of the contingency on academic production. These processes are some of the next-most pressing questions to be answered. The majority of studies report such process effects anecdotally. Observatiaon systems, peer reports and ratings, and teacher observations all seem to be needed to document the processes.

Social-Skills Practice

Dependent and interdependent contingencies not only provide consequences for behaviors but also provide opportunities and antecedents for children to respond. In academic settings, for example, Delquadri (1979) used an interdependent system of peer tutoring in spelling which dramatically decreased errors on Friday spelling tests. While no inter-action data were reported, the use of half the class to tutor the other half in pairs greatly increased reciprocal interaction, word-writing opportunities, and feedback on these responses. Thus, a cost-effective approach to individualizing response opportunities was developed. Similar applications to social behavior were documented by Todd (1977) and Greenwood, Todd, Hops, & Walker (in press) wherein a dependent procedure was used to increase opportunities for withdrawn children to complete interactions. A number of researchers have argued that skill-acquisition failure, retardation, (Bijou, 1966), deficiencies in reading (Becker, 1977), in academic skills in general (Hall, Delquadri, & Greenwood, 1980), and in social interaction (Greenwood *et al.*, 1979) have been a result of insufficient opportunity to practice and be reinforced for making responses.

Furthermore, the development of social-skills curriculum—for example, social-skills tutoring (Hops, Fleischman, Guild, Paine, Street,

Walker, & Greenwood, 1978) around tasks involving known inter-dependencies and reciprocities among peers—appears to be a productive research area (Mithaug & Wolfe, 1976).

MAINTENANCE AND GENERALIZATION RESEARCH

As previously reviewed, little research has been conducted on these effects within group-oriented contingencies. On primary target behaviors, studies could be designed to assess and compare maintenance—for example, under conditions of peer involvement vs. limited involvement, or independent vs. interdependent. One might find greater maintenance of academic performance in interdependent systems because of continued tutoring or social interaction established under these conditions. In this respect the dependent and interdependent systems to a greater extent reprogram social contingencies. Although preliminary studies suggest some generalization effects for social interactions are a function of interdependency training, many questions remain. Can generalization be noted over several settings and maintenance of generalized effects programmed? Hops and colleagues (Hops et al., 1979; Hops et al., 1980) found that lesser procedures were required to extent program effects to second settings.

Understanding the Entrapment Hypothesis

Do behaviors become maintained by natural communities of reinforcement as described by Baer and Wolf (1970)? They hypothesized that the social behavior of children, when increased to a frequency and quality equivalent to that of normative interactive levels, would be maintained strictly by the peer social system. Satisfactory research has not been forthcoming in this area to confirm or deny this intriguing notion. Studies have suggested that specific skill development such as playground-apparatus skills (Buell et al., 1968), reinforcement-sharing skills (McCarty et al., 1977), or athletic skills (Broekhoff, 1977) are related to and may increase social interaction and/or sociometric status. Hops (1979) reported that two measures of social behaviors—total social and verbal behavior, treated with the PEERS program in one recess period—generalized to a second period in which the total procedure was not in effect. Others have reported instances of failure of social interaction rates to return to baseline or to drop at all following reinforcement procedures increasing rates to high levels (Walker et al., 1975). Might these be instances of trapping? Unfortunately, the processes by which interaction might be "caught" and maintained by the peer social system remains to be described. These studies will require observational measures of social interaction to document the reciprocal-entrapment process. The importance of this research to our understanding of social-behavior interventions is essential.

PACKAGE DEVELOPMENT AND DISSEMINATION

The last important step must be the development of intervention packages in the form of training materials and procedures for the social agents who are in positions to use them. This process is exemplified by the CLASS, PASS, PEERS, and RECESS programs (Hops *et al.*, 1979; Walker, Hops, & Greenwood, 1978), in which research and development have been targeted at the production of behavior-change packages for use by classroom teachers and teacher-consultants. Our review has demonstrated that several group-oriented procedures have had sufficient replication. The good-behavior game, for example, has had applications to disruptive behavior, academic production, and production in a rehabilitation setting. The development of materials and procedures beyond the research reports in the literature would have a more dramatic impact on the use of these procedures in human-service settings. Other procedures reviewed have not had sufficient research and replication to move to this last aspect of development.

At this level of implementation, research questions become, "What are the most effective means of training social agents to use the procedures?" (Hops, Walker, Fleischman, Nicholes, & Greenwood, 1976) and "When used in the natural setting, how do these procedures compare with respect to other procedures currently available in this setting?" (Greenwood , Hops, Walker, Guild, Stokes, Young, Keleman, & Willardson, 1979; Hops, Walker, Fleischman, Nagoshi, Omura, Skindrud, & Taylor, 1978).

Finally, questions concerning the training of trainers are also important. Some behavioral programs have established mastery criteria for trainers with certification procedures, and have developed jobs and position descriptions for trainers.

As group-oriented procedures become more widely practiced in human-service settings and packaged for use, the issues dealing with package development and dissemination will take on greater significance.

IMPLICATIONS AND CONCLUSIONS

The objective of this chapter has been to present a discussion of group-oriented contingency procedures with an emphasis on peers as behavior-change agents. We have described peer-group interaction processes that can affect development of an effective behavior-change technology. Sections of the chapter have discussed (a) background and perspectives in behavior change, (b) means of categorizing and understanding group-oriented contingencies, (c) review of applications used to control individual behavior in groups, in the management of disruptive, academic, and social behavior in classroom settings and peer interactions in more social settings, (d) the effectiveness of group-oriented contingencies, and (e) suggested areas of research and development.

When we consider the historical perspective of the "hero procedures" used in 1965 vs. the widely researched "good-behavior game" and the dissemination-oriented treatment package—for example, CLASS, PASS, PEER & RECESS—we see that in 1980 the development of group-oriented intervention procedures ranges over a wide spectrum of technology development and sophistication. As is true in the field in general, the next steps for use and application can be specified. Experiments to establish that dependent and independent group contingencies work are needed only in applied settings where limited applications have been made—business, rehabilitation, and so on. In contrast, studies of generalization and maintenance of behavior changes are most obviously lacking, even in classroom settings. For example, the good-behavior game, an extensively replicated procedure, has not, to our knowledge, included procedures for program maintenance; nor have follow-up data been presented, or generalization effects assessed. Furthermore, only in limited cases have dependent or interdependent procedures been applied extensively to large numbers of subjects, as for example, in the case of CLASS and PASS programs.

The cooperative social aspects of these procedures need extensive attention in future research. The mostly anecdotal reports of these spontaneous side effects need further "process" documentation to see how they contribute to total intervention effects and to the teaching and learning of social behaviors.

Most promising appears to be the possibility of developing social-behavior training and intervention techniques that directly capitalize on positive and negative peer influence. We can explore further the opportunities these procedures create for targets to make responses.

K. D. O'Leary and Drabman (1971) noted that the problems in group-oriented procedures appeared to be (a) the possibility that one or more children might not be able to perform the behavior required, (b) undue pressure on a particular individual, and (c) the possibility that one or more subjects may "beat the system." Procedures described in the literature reviewed here appear available to prevent these outcomes. In the first case, group- or individual-performance requirements can be established and shifted upward in a shaping procedure to ensure success for low-skilled children. In the second case, the use of previously evaluated procedures, including data on client preference and satisfaction, can prevent "undue" negative pressure. In the third case, "beating the system" has been handled by providing individualized contingencies to augment offenders, and requiring all responses to be made in the presence of the change agent to prevent cheating, for example. Thus, although these issues, presented in 1971, are still relevant in group applications, efforts have been made to limit these pitfalls and negative side effects.

The efficiency of group-oriented procedures appears to be a major benefit of their use. As we have seen, they seem to be as effective as strictly individualized procedures. This point is dramatically documented in comments made by a teacher-consultant using the PASS program.

> In my situation as a learning specialist at Knott School, I had been involved with many of the students individually in the classroom and would have proceeded with them one by one—a time consuming process. This particular classroom (31 third graders) had about 10–15 difficult students. Due to this particular intervention, the need to write, design, monitor, evaluate, conference, etc., has been all but eliminated.
>
> 1. The program suddenly made changes that would have taken a long time to accomplish.
> 2. The program gave both myself and the teacher new and/or different applications of classroom technique.
> 3. The incidence of these children requiring my direct assistance has dropped dramatically, also these children are not in the office for disciplinary reasons.
>
> The program entirely turned around the attitude of both teachers and classrooms. It has been well worth the time and has freed me to work with other students for whom I would not have had time.
>
> Learning Specialist

Thus, group-oriented procedures have provided and will continue to provide an important dimension to applied-behavior-change methods.

ACKNOWLEDGMENT

The authors wish to acknowledge the assistance of Carmen Root, Kate Ketcham, Susan Brewster, and Linda Rangus in the typing and preparation of this manuscript.

REFERENCES

Alexander, R. N., Corbett, T. F., & Smigel, J. The effects of individual and group consequences on school attendance and curfew violations. *Journal of Applied Behavior Analysis*, 1976, *9*, 221–226.

Allen, K. E., Hart, B., Buell, J.S., Harris, F. R., & Wolf, M. M. Effects of social reinforcement on isolate behavior of a nursery school child. *Child Development*, 1964, *35*, 511–518.

Allen, V. L. (Ed.). *Children as teachers*. New York: Academic Press, 1976.

Axelrod, S. Comparison of individual and group contingencies in two special classes. *Behavior Therapy*, 1973, *4*, 83–90.

Ayllon, T., & Azrin, N. H. *The token economy: A motivational system for therapy and rehabilitation*. New York: Appleton-Century-Crofts, 1968.

Baer, D. M., & Wolf, M. M. The entry into natural communities of reinforcement. In R. Ulrich, T. Stachnik, & J. Mabry (Eds.), *Control of human behavior*. Glenview, Ill.: Scott Foresman, 1970.

Bandura, A. *Principles of behavior modification*. New York: Holt, Rinehart & Winston, 1969.

Barrish, H. H., Saunders, M., & Wolf, M. M. Good behavior game: Effects of individual contingencies for group consequences on disruptive behavior in a classroom. *Journal of Applied Behavior Analysis*, 1969, *2*, 119–124.

Becker, W.C. Teaching reading and language to the disadvantaged: What we have learned from field research. *Harvard Education Review*, 1977, *47*, 518–543.

Bernal, M. E., Delfini, L. F., North, J. A., & Kreutzer, S. L. Comparison of boys' behaviors in homes and classrooms. In E. J. Mash, L. A. Hamerlynck, and L. C. Handy, *Behavior modification and families*. New York: Brunner/Mazel, 1976.

Bijou, S.W. A functional analysis of retarded development. In N. Ellis (Ed.), *International review of research in mental retardation*. Vol. 1. New York: Academic Press, 1966.

Bijou, S. W., Birnbrauer, J. S., Kidder, J. D., & Tague, C. E. Programmed instruction as an approach to the teaching of reading, writing, and arithmetic to retarded children. *Psychological Record*, 1966, *16*, 505–522.

Birnbrauer, J. S., Wolf, M. M., Kidder, J. D., & Tague, C. E. Classroom behavior of retarded pupils with token reinforcement. *Journal of Experimental Child Psychology*, 1965, *2*, 219–235.

Broekhoff, J. A search for relationships: Sociological and social-psychological considerations. *The Academy Papers*, 1977, *11*, 45–55.

Bronfenbrenner, V. *Two worlds of childhood*. New York: Simon & Schuster, 1970.

Brooks, R. B., & Snow, D. L. Two case illustrations of the use of behavior-modification techniques in the school setting. *Behavior Therapy*, 1972, *3*, 100–103.

Brown, J. C., Montgomery, R., & Barclay, J. R. An example of psychologist management of teacher reinforcement procedures in the elementary classroom. *Psychology in the Schools*, 1969, *4*, 336–340.

Bryan, J. H. Children's cooperation and helping behaviors. In E. M. Hetherington (Ed.), *Review of child development research* (Vol. 5). Chicago: University of Chicago Press, 1975.

Buehler, R. E., Patterson, G. R., & Furniss, J. M. The reinforcement of behavior in institutional settings. *Behavior Research and Therapy*, 1966, *4*, 157–167.

Buell, J., Stoddard, P. Harris, F. R., & Baer, D. M. Collateral social development accompanying reinforcement of outdoor play in a preschool child. *Journal of Applied Behavior Analysis*, 1968, *1*, 167–173.

Bushell, D., Wrobel, P. A., & Michaelis, M. L. Applying "group" contingencies to the classroom study behavior of preschool children. *Journal of Applied Behavior Analysis*, 1968, *1*, 55–61.

Clark, M., Lachowicz, J., & Wolf, M. M. A pilot basic education program for school dropouts incorporating a token reinforcement system. *Behavior Research and Therapy*, 1968, *6*, 183–188.

Clark-Hall, M. *Responsive parenting program*. Lawrence, Kansas: H & H Enterprise, 1977.

Clement, P. W., & Milne, D. C. Group play therapy and tangible reinforcers used to modify the behavior of 8-year-old boys. *Behavior Research and Therapy*, 1967, *5*, 301–312.

Clement, P. W., Roberts, P. V., & Lantz, C. E. Social models and token reinforcement in the treatment of shy, withdrawn boys. *Proceedings of the 78th Annual Convention of the American Psychological Association*, 1970, *5*, 515–516.

Cobb, J. A. *Survival skills and first grade achievement* (Report No. 1). Center at Oregon for Research in the Behavioral Education of the Handicapped, University of Oregon, 1970.

Cobb, J. A., & Hops, H. Effects of academic survival skills training on low achieving first graders. *Journal of Educational Research*, 1973, *67*, 108–113.

Combs, M. L., & Slaby, D. A. Social skills training with children. In B. Lahey & A. Kazdin (Eds.), *Advances in clinical child psychology* (Vol. 1). New York: Plenum Press, 1977.

Cossairt, A., Hall, R. V., & Hopkins, B. L. The effects of experimenter's instructions, feedback, and praise on teacher praise and student attending behavior. *Journal of Applied Behavior Analysis*, 1973, *6*, 89–100.

Coyne, P. D. The effects of peer tutoring with group contingencies on the academic performance of college students. *Journal of Applied Behavior Analysis*, 1978, *11*, 305–307.

Delquadri, J. C. *Experimental development of procedures to increase opportunities for academic responses in the classroom.* Paper presented at 5th Annual meeting of the Association for Behavior Analysis, Dearborn, Michigan, June 1979.

DeRisi, W. R., & Butz, G. *Writing behavioral contracts: A case simulation practice manual.* Champaign, Ill.: Research Press, 1975.

Dietz, S. M., & Repp, A. C. Decreasing classroom misbehavior through the use of DRL schedules of reinforcement. *Journal of Applied Behavior Analysis*, 1973, *6*, 457–463.

Dineen, J. P., Clark, H. B., & Risley, T. R. Peer tutoring among elementary students: Educational benefits to the tutor. *Journal of Applied Behavior Analysis*, 1977, *10*, 231–238.

Drabman, R. S. Behavior modification in the classroom. In W. E. Craighead, A. E. Kazdin, & M. J. Mahoney (Eds.), *Behavior modification: Principles, issues, and applications.* Boston: Houghton Mifflin, 1976.

Drabman, R. S., Spitalnik, R., & Spitalnik, K. Sociometric and disruptive behavior as a function of four types of token reinforcement programs. *Journal of Applied Behavior Analysis*, 1974, *7*, 93–101.

Ebner, M. J. *An investigation of the role of the social environment in the generalization and persistence of the effect of a behavior modification program.* Unpublished doctoral dissertation, University of Oregon, 1967.

Evans, G. W., & Oswalt, G. L. Acceleration of academic progress through the manipulation of peer influence. *Behavior Research and Therapy*, 1968, *5*, 1–7.

Fawcett, S. B., & Miller, L. K. Training public-speaking behavior: An experimental analysis. and social validation. *Journal of Applied Behavior Analysis*, 1975, *8*, 125–136.

Feingold, L., & Migler, B. The use of experimentation dependency relationships as a motivating procedure on a token economy ward. In R. D. Rubin, H. Fensterheim, J. D. Henderson, & L. P. Ullmann (Eds.), *Advances in behavior therapy.* New York: Academic Press, 1972.

Frankosky, R. J., & Sulzer-Azaroff, B. Individual and group contingencies and collateral social behavior. *Behavior Therapy*, 1978, *9*, 313–327.

Gallagher, P., Sulzbacher, S. I., & Shores ,R. L. *A group contingency for classroom management of emotionally disturbed children.* Paper presented at meeting of the Council for Exceptional Children, Wichita, Kansas, March 1967.

Graubard, P. S. Utilizing the group in teaching disturbed delinquents to learn. *Exceptional Children*, 1969, *36*, 267–272.

Greenwood, C. R. *Shifting requirements in the classroom token economy: Steps toward social control.* Paper presented at the annual meeting of the Western Psychological Association, San Francisco, April 1975.

Greenwood, C. R., & Guild, J. J. *Student consumer satisfaction: Variation as a function of actual behavior change?* Poster presentation at the 11th annual meeting of the Association for the Advancement of Behavior Therapy, AABT Atlanta, December 1977.

Greenwood, C. R., & Hops, H. Generalization of teacher praising skills over time and setting: What you teach is what you get! Paper presented at the 45th annual convention of the Council for Exceptional Children, Chicago, April, 1976. (ERIC Document Reproduction Service, No. ED 127 762).

Greenwood, C. R., Hops, H., Delquadri, J., & Guild, J. Group contingencies for group consequences in classroom management: A further analysis. *Journal of Applied Behavior Analysis*, 1974, *7*, 413–425.

Greenwood, C. R., Sloane, H. N., Jr., & Baskin, A. Training elementary age peer-behavior managers to control small group programmed mathematics. *Journal of Applied Behavior Analysis*, 1974, *7*, 103–114.

Greenwood, C. R., Hops, H., Delquadri, J., & Walker, H. M. *The Program for Academic Survival Skills (PASS): Consultant's manual*. Center at Oregon for Research in the Behavioral Education of the Handicapped, University of Oregon, 1977.

Greenwood, C. R., Hops, H. & Walker, H. M. The program for academic survival skills (PASS): Effects on student behavior and achievement. *Journal of School Psychology*, 1977, *15*, 25–35.(a)

Greenwood, C. R., Hops, H. & Walker, H. M. The durability of student behavior change. A comparative analysis at follow-up. *Behavior Therapy*, 1977, *8*, 631–638.(b)

Greenwood, C. R., Hops, H., Walker, H., Guild, J., Stokes, J., Young, K. R., Keleman, K., & Willardson, M. Standardized classroom management program: Social validation and replication studies in Utah and Oregon. *Journal of Applied Behavior Analysis*, 1979, *12*, 235–253.

Greenwood, C. R., Todd, N. M., Hops, H., & Walker, H. M. *Global and specific behavior change targets in the assessment and behavior modification of socially withdrawn preschool children*. Paper presented at meeting of the Association for Advancement of Behavior Therapy, San Francisco, December 1979.

Greenwood, C. R., Todd, N. M., Hops, H., & Walker, H. M. Behavior change targets in the assessment and behavior modification of socially withdrawn preschool children. *Behavioral Assessment*, 1981, in press.

Hake, D. F., & Vukelich, R. A classification and review of cooperation procedures. *Journal of the Experimental Analyais of Behavior*, 1972, *18*, 333–343.

Hall, R. V., Fox, R., Willard, D., Goldsmith, L., Emerson, M., Owen, M., Davis, F., & Porcia, E. The teacher as observer and experimenter in the modification of disputing and talking-out behaviors. *Journal of Applied Behavior Analysis*, 1971, *4*, 141–149.

Hall, R. V., Delquadri, J., & Greenwood, C. R. *The importance of opportunity to respond to children's academic success*. Paper presented at the Symposium on Serving Young Handicapped Children—Issues and Research, University of Washington, Seattle, February 1980.

Hamblin, R. L., Hathaway, C., & Wodarski, J. Group contingencies, peer tutoring, and accelerating academic achievement. In E. A. Ramp & B. L. Hopkins (Eds.), *A new direction for education: Behavior analysis–1971* (Vol. 1). Lawrence: University of Kansas, 1971.

Harris, F. R., Johnson, M. D., Kelley, S., & Wolf, M. M. Effects of positive social reinforcement on regressed crawling of a nursery school child. *Journal of Educational Psychology*, 1964, *55*, 35–41.

Harris, V. W., & Sherman, J. A. Use and analysis of the "good behavior game" to reduce disruptive classroom behavior. *Journal of Applied Behavior Analysis*, 1973, *6*, 405–417.

Hart, B. M., Reynolds, N. J., Baer, D. M., Brawley, E. R., & Harris, F. R. Effect of contingent and non-contingent social reinforcement on the cooperative play of a preschool child. *Journal of Applied Behavior Analysis*, 1968, *1*, 73–76.

Hartup, W. W. Friendship status and the effectiveness of peers as reinforcing agents. *Journal of Experimental Child Psychology*, 1964, *1*, 73–76.

Hartup, W. W. Peer interaction and social organization. In P. H. Mussen (Ed.), *Carmichael's manual of child psychology* (Vol. 2) (3rd ed.). New York: Wiley, 1970.

Hayes, L. A. The use of group contingencies for behavioral control: A review. *Psychological Bulletin*, 1976, *83*, 628–648.

Heber, R. F., & Heber, M. E. The effects of group failure and success on social status. *Journal of Educational Psychology*, 1957, *48*, 129–134.

Herman, S. H., & Tramontana, J. Instructions and group versus individual reinforcement in modifying disruptive group behavior. *Journal of Applied Behavior Analysis*, 1971, *4*, 113–120.

Hersen, M., & Bellack, A. S. Assessment of social skills. In A. R. Ciminero, K. R. Clahoun, & H. E. Adams (Eds.), *Handbook of behavioral assessment*, New York: Wiley, 1977.

Homme, L., Csanyi, A., Gonzales, M. A., & Rechs, J. R. *How to use contingency contracting in the classroom*. Champaign, Ill.: Research Press, 1969.

Hopkins, B. L., Schutte, R. C., & Garton, K. L. The effects of access to a playroom on the rate and quality of printing and writing of first- and second-grade students. *Journal of Applied Behavior Analysis*, 1971, 77–88.

Hops, H. The school psychologist as a behavior management consultant in a special class setting. *Journal of School Psychology*, 1971, *9*, 473–483.

Hops, H., & Cobb, J. A. Survival behaviors in the educational setting: Their implications for research and intervention. In L. A. Hamerlynck, L. C. Handy, & E. J. Mash (Eds.), *Behavior change: Methodology, concepts, and practice*. Champaign, Ill.: Research Press, 1973.

Hops, H., & Cobb, J. A. Initial investigations into academic survival skills training, direct instruction, and first-grade achievement. *Journal of Educational Psychology*, 1974, *66*, 548–553.

Hops, H., & Greenwood, C. R. Social skill deficits. In E. J. Mash & L. G. Terdal (Eds.), *Behavioral assessment of childhood disorders*. New York: Guilford Press, 1981, in press.

Hops, H., Beickel, S. L., & Walker, H. M. *Contingencies for learning academic and social skills (CLASS): Manual for consultants*. Center at Oregon for Research in the Behavioral Education of the Handicapped, University of Oregon, 1976.(a)

Hops, H., Greenwood, C. R., & Ford, L. H. *Manipulating group reinforcement schedules: Problems in long term maintenance of treatment effects* (Report No. 23). Center at Oregon for Research in the Behavioral Education of the Handicapped, University of Oregon, 1976.(b)

Hops, H., Walker, H. M., Fleischman, D., Nicholes, J. S., & Greenwood, C. R. *Inter-state generality of a packaged training and intervention program for acting-out children in the regular classroom*. Paper presented at annual meeting of the Association for Advancement of Behavior Therapy, New York, December 1976.(c)

Hops, H., Fleischman, D., Guild, J., Paine, S., Street, A., Walker, H., & Greenwood, C. *Procedures for establishing effective relationship skills (PEERS)*. Center at Oregon for Research in the Behavioral Education of the Handicapped, University of Oregon, 1978.(a)

Hops, H., Walker, H. M., Fleischman, D. H., Nagoshi, J. T., Omura, R. T., Skindrud, K., & Taylor, J. CLASS: A standardized in-class program for acting-out children. II. Field test evaluations. *Journal of Educational Psychology*, 1978, *70*, 636–644.(b)

Hops, H., Walker, H. M., & Greenwood, C. R. PEERS: A program for remediating social withdrawal in school. In L. A. Hamerlynck (Ed.), *Behavioral systems for the developmentally disabled. I. School and family environments*. New York: Brunner/Mazel, 1979.

Hops, H., Greenwood, C. R., & Guild, J. J. *Programming generalization of teacher-student behavior change across classroom instructional settings.* Center at Oregon for Research in the Behavioral Education of the Handicapped, University of Oregon, 1980.

Johnson, T. L., Goetz, E. M., Baer, D. M., & Green, D. R. *The effects of an experimental game on the classroom cooperative play of a preschool child.* Paper presented at the 5th annual Southern California Conference on Behavior Modification, Los Angeles, October 1973.

Kazdin, A. E. *The token economy: A review and evaluation.* New York: Plenum Press, 1977.(a)

Kazdin, A. E. Assessing the clinical or applied importance of behavior change through social validation. *Behavior Modification,* 1977, *4,* 427–452.(b)

Kazdin, A. E., & Bootzin, R. R. The token economy: An evaluative review. *Journal of Applied Behavior Analysis,* 1972, *5,* 343–372.

Kazdin, A. E., & Geesy, S. Simultaneous-treatment design comparisons of the effects of earning reinforcers for one's peers versus for oneself. *Behavior Therapy,* 1977, *8,* 682–693.

Kirby, F. D., & Toler, H. C. Jr. Modification of preschool isolate behavior: A case study. *Journal of Applied Behavior Analysis,* 1970, *3,* 309–312.

Kubany, E. S., Weiss, L. E., & Sloggett, B. B. The good behavior clock: A reinforcement/time out procedure for reducing disruptive classroom behavior. *Journal of Behavior Therapy and Experimental Psychiatry,* 1971, *2,* 173–179.

Lewis, M., & Rosenblum, L. A. (Eds.). *Friendship and peer relations.* New York: Wiley, 1975.

Litow, L., & Pumroy, D. K. A review of classroom group-oriented contingencies. *Journal of Applied Behavior Analysis,* 1975, *8,* 341–347.

Long, J. D., & Williams, R. L. The comparative effectiveness of group and individually contingent free time with inner city junior high school students. *Journal of Applied Behavior Analysis,* 1973, *6,* 465–474.

Lovitt, T. C., Guppy, T. E., & Blattner, J. E. The use of a free-time contingency with fourth graders to increase spelling accuracy. *Behavior Research & Therapy,* 1969, *7,* 151–156.

Madsen, C. H., Jr., Becker, W. C., & Thomas, D. R. Rules, praise, and ignoring: Elements of elementary classroom control. *Journal of Applied Behavior Analysis,* 1968, 139–150.

Maloney, K. B., & Hopkins, B. L. The modification of sentence structure and its relationship to subjective judgments of creativity in writing. *Journal of Applied Behavior Analysis,* 1973, *6,* 425–433.

Maloney, D. M., Harper, T. M., Braukmann, C. J., Fixsen, D. L., Phillips, E. L., & Wolf, M. M. Teaching conversation-related skills to predelinquent girls. *Journal of Applied Behavior Analysis,* 1976, *9,* 371.

Martin, S., Johnson, S. M., Johansson, S., & Wahl, G. The comparability of behavioral data in laboratory and natural settings. In E. J. Mash, L. A. Hamerlynck, & L. C. Handy (Eds.), *Behavior modification and families.* New York: Brunner/Mazel, 1976.

McAllister, L. W., Stachowiak, J. G., Baer, D. M., & Conderman, L. The application of operant conditioning techniques in a secondary school classroom. *Journal of Applied Behavior Analysis,* 1969, *2,* 277–285.

McCarty, T., Griffin, S., Apolloni, T., & Shores, R. E. Increased peer-teaching with group-oriented contingencies for arithmetic performance in behavior-disordered adolescents. *Journal of Applied Behavior Analysis,* 1977, *10,* 313.

McLaughlin, T. F. A review of applications of group-contingency procedures used in behavior modification in the regular classroom: Some recommendations for school personnel. *Psychological Reports,* 1974, *35,* 1299–1303.

McLaughlin, T. F. *The effects of individual and group contingencies on reading performance of special education students.* Paper presented at the 5th annual convention of the Association for Behavior Analysis, Dearborn, Michigan, June 1979.

McMichael, J. S., & Corey, J. R. Contingency management in an introductory psychology course produces better learning. *Journal of Applied Behavior Analysis,* 1969, *2,* 79–84.

Medland, M. B., & Stachnik, T. J. Good-behavior game: A replication and systematic analysis. *Journal of Applied Behavior Analysis*, 1972, *5*, 45–51.

Milby, J. B., Jr. Modification of extreme social isolation by contingent social reinforcement. *Journal of Applied Behavior Analysis*, 1970, 149–152.

Millenson, J. R. *Principles of behavioral analysis*. New York: Macmillan, 1967.

Mithaug, D. E., & Burgess, R. L. The effects of different reinforcement contingencies in the development of social cooperation. *Journal of Experimental Child Psychology*, 1968, *6*, 402–420.

Mithaug, D. E., & Wolfe, M. S. Employing task arrangements and verbal contingencies to promote verbalizations between retarded children. *Journal of Applied Behavior Analysis*, 1976, *9*, 301–314.

Mueller, E. The maintenance of verbal exchanges between young children. *Child Development*, 1972, *43*, 930–938.

Mueller, E., & Brenner, J. The origins of social skills and interaction among play group toddlers. *Child Development*, 1977, *48*, 854–861.

Mueller, E., & Vandell, O. Infant-infant interaction. In J. D. Osofsky (Ed.), *Handbook of infant development*. New York: Wiley, 1979.

Neumann, J. K. The analysis of group contingency data. *Journal of Applied Behavior Analysis*, 1977, *10*, 755–758.

Neumann, J. K. A classification scheme of social conditions of reinforcement within group operant systems. *Journal of Applied Behavior Analysis*, 1978, *11*, 435.

O'Leary, K. D., & Drabman, R. Token reinforcement programs in the classroom. *Psychological Bulletin*, 1971, *75*, 379–398.

O'Leary, K. D., & O'Leary, S. G. *Classroom management: The successful use of behavior modification*. New York: Pergamon Press, 1972.

O'Leary, K. D., Becker, W. C., Evans, M. B., & Saudargas, R. A. A token reinforcement program in a public school: A replication and systematic analysis. *Journal of Applied Behavior Analysis*, 1969, *2*, 3–14.

O'Leary, S. G., & O'Leary, K. D. Behavior modification in the school. In H. Leitenberg (Ed.), *Handbook of behavior modification and behavior therapy*. Englewood Cliffs, N.J.: Prentice-Hall, 1976.

Packard, R. G. The control of "classroom attention": A group contingency for complex behavior. *Journal of Applied Behavior Analysis*, 1970, *3*, 13–28.

Paine, S. *Issues in the dissemination of standardized behavioral programs*. Symposium presented at the 5th annual convention of the Association for Behavior Analysis, Dearborn, Michigan, June 1979.

Patterson, G. R. An application of conditioning techniques to the control of a hyperactive child. In L. Ullman & L. Krasner (Eds.), *Case studies in behavior modification*. New York: Holt, Rinehart & Winston, 1965, pp. 370–375.

Patterson, G. R. Interventions for boys with conduct problems: Multiple settings, treatments, and criteria. *Journal of Consulting and Clinical Psychology*, 1974, *42*, 471–481.

Patterson, G. R. Parents and teachers as change agents: A social learning approach. In D. Olson (Ed.), *Treating relationships*. Lake Mills. Graphic Press, 1976.

Patterson, G. R., & Anderson, D. Peers as social reinforcers. *Child Development*, 1964, *35*, 951–960.

Patterson, G. R., & Ebner, M. J. *Applications of learning principles to the treatment of deviant children*. Paper presented at the APA Convention, Chicago, 1965.

Patterson, G. R., Littman, R. A., & Bricker, W. Assertive behavior in children: A step toward a theory of aggression. *Monographs of the Society for Research in Child Development*, 1967, *32*(5), Serial No. 113.

Patterson, G. R., McNeal, S., Hawkins, N., & Phelps, R. Reprogramming the social environment. *Journal of Child Psychology and Psychiatry*, 1967, *8*, 181–195.

Patterson, G. R., Shaw, D. A., & Ebner, M. J. Teachers, peers, and parents as agents of change in the classroom. In F. A. M. Benson (Ed.), *Modifying deviant social behaviors in various classroom settings*. Monograph No. 1, Department of Special Education, University of Oregon, 1969.

Patterson, G. R., Cobb, J. A., & Ray, R. S. Direct intervention in the classroom: A set of procedures for the aggressive child. In F. W. Clark, D. R. Evans, & L. A. Hamerlynck (Eds.), *Implementing behavioral programs for schools and clinics*. Champaign, Ill.: Research Press, 1972.

Patterson, G. R., Reid, J. B., Jones, R. R., & Conger, R. E. *A social learning approach to family intervention. I. Families with aggressive children*. Eugene, Oregon: Castalia, 1975.

Phillips, E. L., Phillips, E. A., Fixsen, D. L., & Wolf, M. M. Achievement Place: Modification of the behaviors of predelinquent boys within a token economy. *Journal of Applied Behavior Analysis*, 1971, 4, 45–59.

Phillips, E. L., Phillips, E. A., Fixsen, D. L., & Wolf, M. M. *The teaching family handbook*. Lawrence: University of Kansas Printing Service, 1972.

Phillips, E. L., Phillips, E. A., Wolf, M. M., & Fixsen, D. L. Achievement Place: Development of the elected manager system. *Journal of Applied Behavior Analysis*, 1973, 6, 541–561.

Piaget, J. *The moral judgment of the child*. Glencoe, Ill.: Free Press, 1932.

Pierce, C. H., & Risley, T. R. Recreation as a reinforcer: Increasing membership and decreasing disruptions in an urban recreation group. *Journal of Applied Behavior Analysis*, 1974, 7, 403–412.

Ray, R. S., Shaw, D. A., & Cobb, J. A. The work box: An innovation in teaching attentional behavior. *The School Counselor*, 1970, 18, 15–35.

Reynolds, N. J., & Risley, T. R. The role of social and material reinforcers in increasing talking of a disadvantaged preschool child. *Journal of Applied Behavior Analysis*, 1968, 1, 253–262.

Risley, T. R., & Hart, B. Developing correspondence between the non-verbal and verbal behavior of preschool children. *Journal of Applied Behavior Analysis*, 1968, 1, 267–282.

Rogers-Warren, A., & Baer, D. M. Correspondence between saying and doing: Teaching children to share and praise. *Journal of Applied Behavior Analysis*, 1976, 9, 335–354.

Rosenbaum, A., O'Leary, D., & Jacob, R. G. Behavioral intervention with hyperactive children: Group consequences as a supplement to individual contingencies. *Behavior Therapy*, 1975, 6, 315–323.

Schmidt, G. W., & Ulrich, R. E. Effects of group contingent events upon classroom noise. *Journal of Applied Behavior Analysis*, 1969, 2, 171–179.

Sherif, M., Harvey, O. J., White, B. J., Hood, W. R., & Sherif, C. W. *Inter-group conflict and cooperation: The robbers' cave experiment*. Norman: Institute of Group Relations, University of Oklahoma, 1961.

Solomon, R. W., & Wahler, R. G. Peer reinforcement control of classroom problem behavior. *Journal of Applied Behavior Analysis*, 1973, 6, 49–56.

Speltz, M. L., Moore, J. E., & McReynolds, W. T. A comparison of standardized and group contingencies. *Behavior Therapy*, 1979, 10, 219–226.

Stokes, T. F., & Baer, D. M. An implicit technology of generalization. *Journal of Applied Behavior Analysis*, 1977, 10, 349–367.

Strain, P. S., Shores, R. E., & Timm, M. A. Effects of peer social initiations on the behavior of withdrawn preschool children. *Journal of Applied Behavior Analysis*, 1977, 10, 289–298.

Straughn, J. H., Potter, W. K., Jr., & Hamilton, S. H., Jr. The behavioral treatment of an elective mute. *Journal of Child Psychology and Psychiatry*, 1965, 6, 125–130.

Sulzbacher, S. I., & Houser, J. E. A tactic to eliminate disruptive behaviors in the classroom: Group contingent consequences. *American Journal of Mental Deficiency*, 1968, 73, 88–90.

Surratt, P. R., Ulrich, R. E., & Hawkins, R. P. An elementary student as a behavioral engineer. *Journal of Applied Behavior Analysis*, 1969, 2, 85–92.

Switzer, E. B., Deal, T. E., & Bailey, J. S. The reduction of stealing in second graders using a group contingency. *Journal of Applied Behavior Analysis*, 1977, *10*, 267–272.

Tharp, R. G., & Wetzel, R. J. *Behavior modification in the natural environment*. New York: Academic Press, 1969.

Thomas, D. R., Becker, W. C., & Armstrong, M. Production and elimination of disruptive classroom behavior by systematically varying teacher's behavior. *Journal of Applied Behavior Analysis*, 1968, *1*, 35–45.

Todd, N. M. *The effects of verbal reporting and group reinforcement in increasing the interaction frequency of preschool socially withdrawn children*. Unpublished thesis, University of Oregon, 1977.

Wahler, R. G. Child-child interactions in free field settings: Some experimental analysis. *Journal of Experimental Child Psychology*, 1967, *5*, 278–293.

Wahler, R. G. Oppositional children: A quest for parental reinforcement control. *Journal of Applied Behavior Analysis*, 1969, *2*, 159–170.

Walker, H. M. *The acting-out child: Coping with classroom disruption*. Boston: Allyn & Bacon, 1979.

Walker, H. M., & Buckley, N. K. Programming generalization and maintenance of treatment effects across time and across settings. *Journal of Applied Behavior Analysis*, 1972, *5*, 209–224.

Walker, H. M., & Buckley, N. K. Teacher attention to appropriate and inappropriate classroom behavior: An individual case study. *Focus on Exceptional Children*, 1973, *5*, 5–11.

Walker, H. M., & Hops, H. The use of group and individual reinforcement contingencies in the modification of social withdrawal. In L. A. Hamerlynck, L. C. Handy, & E. J. Mash (Eds.), *Behavior change: Methodology, concepts, and practice*. Champaign, Ill.: Research Press, 1973, pp. 269–307.

Walker, H. M., & Hops, H. Use of normative peer data as a standard for evaluating classroom treatment effects. *Journal of Applied Behavior Analysis*, 1976, *9*, 159–168.

Walker, H. M., Hops, H., Greenwood, C. R., & Todd, N. M. *Social interaction: effects of symbolic modeling and individual and group reinforcement contingencies on the behavior of withdrawn children* (Report No. 15). Center at Oregon for Research in the Behavioral Education of the Handicapped, University of Oregon, 1975.

Walker, H. M., Hops, H., & Johnson, S. M. Generalization and maintenance of classroom treatment effects. *Behavior Therapy*, 1975, *6*, 188–200.

Walker, H. M., McKibben, T., & Todd, N. M. *The use of a cooperative group contingency in reducing negative peer interactions* (Report No. 21). Center at Oregon for Research in the Behavioral Education of the Handicapped, University of Oregon, 1975.

Walker, H. M., Hops, H., & Feigenbaum, E. Deviant classroom behavior as a function of combinations of social and token reinforcement and cost contingency. *Behavior Therapy*, 1976, *7*, 76–88.

Walker, H. M., Hops, H., & Greenwood, C. R. *Issues, procedures, and perspectives in the identification and remediation of interactive child behavior disorders within the school setting*. Paper presented at a Society for Research in Child Development study group, "The Development of Friendship," Champaign, Illinois, November 1978.

Walker, H. M., Street, A., Garrett, B., Crossen, J., Hops, H., & Greenwood, C. R. *Reprogramming environmental contingencies for effective social skills (RECESS): Consultant's manual*. Center at Oregon for Research in the Behavioral Education of the Handicapped, University of Oregon, 1978.

Walker, H. M., Greenwood, C. R., Hops, H., & Todd, N. M. Differential effects of reinforcing topographic components of social interaction: Analysis and direct replication. *Behavior Modification*, 1979, 3, 291–321.

Walker, H. M., Hops, H., Greenwood, C. R., Todd, N. M., Street, A., & Garrett, B. *The comparative effects of teacher praise, token reinforcement, and response cost in reducing negative peer interactions* (Report No. 25). Center at Oregon for Research in the Behavioral Education of the Handicapped, University of Oregon, 1979, in preparation.

Whitman, T. L., Mercurio, J. R., & Caponigri, V. Development of social responses in two severely retarded children. *Journal of Applied Behavior Analysis*, 1970, 3, 133–138.

Willis, J., & Crowder, J. A portable device for group modification of classroom attending behavior. *Journal of Applied Behavior Analysis*, 1972, 5, 199–202.

Wilson, C. W., & Hopkins, B. L. The effects of contingent music on the intensity of noise in junior high home economics classes. *Journal of Applied Behavior Analysis*, 1973, 6, 269–276.

Wilson, S. H., & Williams, R. L. The effects of group contingencies on first graders' academic and social behavior. *Journal of School Psychology*, 1973, 11, 110–117.

Wolf, M. M. Social validity: The case for subjective measurement or how applied behavior analysis is finding its heart. *Journal of Applied Behavior Analysis*, 1978, 11, 203–214.

Wolf, M. M., & Risley, T. Analysis and modification of deviant child behavior. In A. Bandura (Ed.), *Principles of behavior modification*. New York: Holt, Rinehart & Winston, 1970.

Wolf, M. M., Giles, D. K., & Hall, R. V. Experiments with token reinforcement in a remedial classroom. *Behavior Research and Therapy*, 1968, 6, 51–64.

Wolf, M. M., Hanley, E. L., King, L., Lachowicz, J., & Giles, D. K. The timer-game: A variable interval contingency for the management of out-of-seat behavior. *Exceptional Children*, 1970, 37, 113–117.

8

RECESS: Research and Development of a Behavior Management Package for Remediating Social Aggression in the School Setting

HILL M. WALKER, HYMAN HOPS, AND
CHARLES R. GREENWOOD

INTRODUCTION

The RECESS program is a comprehensive behavior-management package for use with socially negative/aggressive children in grades K–3. "RECESS" is an acronym for "Reprogramming Environmental Contingencies for Effective Social Skills."

The RECESS program is one of four comprehensive behavior-management packages developed, tested, and validated by CORBEH (Center at Oregon for Research in the Behavioral Education of the Handicapped), a research-and-development center funded by the Bureau of the Handicapped, U.S. Office of Education, from 1971–1979. During this period, a separate package was developed and tested for each of the following behavior disorders: (1) *acting-out behavior*, (2) *low academic-survival skills*, (3) *social withdrawal*, and (4) *socially negative-aggressive be-*

HILL M. WALKER ● Division of Special Education, College of Education, University of Oregon, Eugene, Oregon 97403.   HYMAN HOPS ● Oregon Research Institute, Eugene, Oregon 97401. CHARLES R. GREENWOOD ● Bureau of Child Education and Departments of Special Education and Human Development; University of Kansas, Kansas City, Kansas 66044.

havior. The packages designed for each of these behavior disorders are, respectively: CLASS, PASS, PEERS, and RECESS.*

The goal of the RECESS program is to reduce the frequency of socially negative and/or aggressive child behavior to within normal limits in playground and classroom settings, and to simultaneously teach a constructive, cooperative pattern of interactive behavior. If this outcome is achieved, it is anticipated that the social development and, in some cases, academic achievement of socially negative/aggressive children will be substantially improved (Patterson, Reid, Jones, & Conger, 1975).

This chapter describes the RECESS program and the research-and-development procedures used to develop and test it within school settings. The following major topics are addressed in this chapter: (1) behavioral characteristics of the socially negative/aggressive child; (2) a review of research on techniques for reducing socially negative/aggressive child behavior; (3) description and overview of the RECESS program; (4) development and testing of the RECESS program; (5) implementation issues and guidelines; and (6) conclusions and implications.

BEHAVIORAL CHARACTERISTICS OF THE SOCIALLY NEGATIVE/AGGRESSIVE CHILD

Children whose behavior is characterized as socially negative and/or aggressive are of great concern to parents, educators, and mental-health professionals, primarily because of: (a) the aversive properties of this behavior pattern, and (b) its potential to significantly impair social adjustment and development. Substantial attention by researchers and therapists has been increasingly focused upon the tasks of (1) investigating the backgrounds of such children, (2) analyzing their interactive behavior, and (3) developing viable strategies for teaching them cooperative, adaptive patterns of behavior. A considerable knowledge base on child aggression is emerging as a result of these efforts. For example, Patterson *et al.* (1975) suggests that aggressive children are likely to come from families in which all family members demonstrate relatively high rates of aggression toward each other. If such is the case, it seems likely that many children would acquire this behavior pattern prior to entering school. Certainly, if aggression is a characteristic behavior pattern within a family, siblings would be expected to learn and exhibit aggressive responses early in their developmental histories. In cases where an ag-

*Information on CORBEH, the packages and supporting research reports, as well as copies of the packages themselves can be obtained by writing to CORBEH, Clinical Services Building, Center on Human Development, University of Oregon, Eugene, Oregon 97403.

gressive pattern of behavior has been acquired early and is learned within the family context, one can expect that it will be extremely difficult to change and that very powerful intervention procedures will be required to accomplish the task.

It is possible but unlikely that aggressive behavior patterns are at times learned exclusively in the school setting. However, it should be noted that in spite of the extensive research carried out on social behavior in children (Achenbach, 1978; Strain, Cooke, & Apolloni, 1976; van Hasselt, Hersen, Whitehill, & Bellack, 1979), relatively little is known about the *true* dynamics of peer groups as vehicles for teaching either constructive or destructive patterns of behavior. It is possible that peer groups, such as those encountered at school, are very efficient at teaching *either* appropriate or inappropriate behavior patterns to their members. It is difficult to predict in advance whether a child will acquire a positive or a negative behavior pattern under such circumstances. The factors determining which behavior pattern will be acquired are extremely complex and at present not adequately understood. It would seem that regardless of the antecedent conditions for aggressive behavior in children, very powerful procedures must be implemented in whatever settings it occurs in order to effectively teach a new pattern of constructive, cooperative behavior.

There is a very high probability that children identified in school settings as socially negative/aggressive will be males. In the process of developing the RECESS program, the authors accepted referrals for the problem of socially negative/aggressive child behavior from local elementary schools over a three-year period. The great majority of children referred were boys. Of the 32 children who met eligibility criteria for the program, only two were female. Patterson and his associates (1975) have reported similar findings.

This outcome probably reflects genuine sex-role differences attributable to the differential training and behavioral expectations to which boys and girls are exposed in the socialization process. It may also be a reflection of the general cultural bias that aggressive behavior is more acceptable in boys than girls. Child-rearing practices appear to be in a state of flux at present on this question. It remains to be seen how these changes will affect child behavior in general and, in turn, our perception of it.

Patterson *et al.* (1975) notes that the socialization process appears to be severely impeded for many aggressive children. Their behavioral adjustments are often immature and they do not seem to have learned the key social skills necessary for initiating and maintaining positive social relationships with others. Peer groups often reject, avoid, and/or punish aggressive children, thereby excluding them from positive learning experiences with peers. Socially negative/aggressive children often have

academic difficulties and may achieve at lower levels than their classmates. Further, there is some evidence that such children often have
behavioral-adjustment problems as adults (Robins, 1966). Thus, early
acquisition of a negative/aggressive pattern of behavior may have profound implications for a child's development and perhaps adulthood
status as well.

Patterson and his associates have studied very carefully the proc-
cesses by which aggressive behavior is acquired and maintained within
family units. They have concluded that aggressive behavior is acquired
primarily through the mechanisms of *modeling* and *reinforcement*. That is, a
child observes parents, peers, and/or siblings displaying aggressive behavior, proceeds to imitate it, albeit often crudely, and is then instrumen-
tally reinforced for engaging in the behavior.

Patterson and Reid (1970) have described a *reciprocity–coercion
hypothesis* to account for the process by which an aggressive behavior
pattern is gradually built into a child's repertoire. The hypothesis holds
that a child learns to apply highly aversive demands to a parent, sibling,
or peer (called *coercive mands)* in order to produce a desired result such as
getting one's way. Coercive mands consist of such things as temper
tantrums, hitting, yelling, whining, pouting, threatening others, and so
on. They are applied with the goal of forcing the submission of the
interacting partner(s). Such behaviors are highly unpleasant and most
adults and children will quickly give in rather than endure a prolonged
period of time in which they are exposed to them at a high intensity level
and/or rate of occurrence. Consequently, a mutually reinforcing interaction pattern can develop wherein the aggressive child's coercive mands
are positively reinforced by the submission of the parent, sibling, or peer.
Simultaneously, the submissive or avoidant responses of the target (victim) of the aggressive child's coercive mands (parent, sibling, or peer) are
powerfully strengthened by termination of the coercive mands as soon as
the aggressive child has succeeded. Consequently, the aggressive child
and the target of the aggression are both reinforced in their characteristic
responses to each other. Aggressive behavior is thus powerfully maintained by the natural social environment. It is not surprising that aggressive behavior is one of the most difficult behavior patterns to permanently
change.

The characteristic behavior patterns of aggressive children have been
described in numerous research studies reported in the literature. Patterson *et al.* (1975) described 14 categories of "noxious" behaviors characteristic of socially negative/aggressive children. The list consists of such
behavior categories as *yelling, whining, destructiveness, humiliation, noncompliance, negativism, physical negative,* and *command negative.* As is obvi-

ous, engaging in any of these response categories would tend to impede the development of positive social interactions with others.

Additional descriptions of aggressive behavior in children have been reported by such researchers as Pinkston, Reese, LeBlanc, and Baer (1973). Their description includes the following categories: *choking, head pushing, biting or threatening to do so, pinching, pushing, poking, hitting, kicking, motor attacks on peers' materials,* and *verbal aggression*. Verbal aggression is defined as verbalizations that threaten, forbid an activity, or indicate a negative judgment about a person or the person's possessions. Examples include such statements as "I don't like you!" "You're dumb!" or "This is our house; you can't play here!" Examples of motor attacks on materials include knocking down, kicking, or pushing over structures built or being built by peers. P. Brown and Elliott (1965) also distinguish between verbal and physical aggression in their description of aggressive child behavior. Physical aggression consists of pushing, pulling, holding, hitting, striking, annoying, teasing, and interfering. Examples of verbal aggression include disparaging remarks and threats. Bostow and Bailey (1969) describe a seven-year-old child who was so aggressive that he could not be allowed to interact with other children in playground situations. At home, he would physically attack other persons and break furniture. His aggressive behavior included biting, hitting, kicking, scratching, and head butting.

The above descriptions of socially negative/aggressive behavior in children bear a remarkable degree of similarity across different research studies and settings. Although there are probably *qualitative* (intensity) as well as *quantitative* (frequency) differences in the behavioral responses of normal and socially negative/aggressive children, it is usually the frequency at which such children engage in aggressive behaviors that separates them from normal or nonaggressive children. The goal of most intervention procedures for social aggression in children, including the RECESS program, is to reduce their frequency of aggressive behavior to within normal limits.

In developing the RECESS program, the authors have identified a set of behavioral responses that powerfully discriminate between socially negative/aggressive children and normal children. These responses also provide a characteristic behavioral profile of children for whom the RECESS program was designed (see Table 1).

This behavioral profile was developed by having samples of both normal and socially negative/aggressive children rated by their teachers on a large number of items descriptive of social behavior in playground and classroom settings. Of the items dealing with socially negative/ aggressive behavior, the seven items listed in Table 1 proved to be most

TABLE 1.
Behavioral Responses Discriminating between
Socially Negative/Aggressive and Normal Children

---

1. Disturbs other children: teases, provokes fights, interrupts others.
2. Openly strikes back with angry behavior to teasing of other children.
3. Argues and must have the last word in verbal exchanges.
4. Displays physical aggression toward objects or persons.
5. Uses coercive tactics to force the submission of peers: manipulates, threatens.
6. Speaks to others in an impatient or cranky tone of voice.
7. Says uncomplimentary or unpleasant things to other children: engages in name calling, ridicule, verbal derogation.

---

sensitive in discriminating between the two samples. Items 3, 4, and 5 are especially sensitive in this regard.

The seven behavioral responses listed in Table 1 are one of the primary criteria used in identifying appropriate candidates for the RE-CESS program. Children to whom the RECESS program was applied in its development have all received higher than normal ratings by their teachers on these items.

In summary, socially negative/aggressive children appear to have learned a behavior pattern that is based primarily upon the aversive control of the behavior of others. As noted earlier, the social environment supports such a behavior pattern naturally through the processes of submission and avoidance. As also noted, it is very difficult to change a behavior pattern of this type, partly because aggressive behavior has such powerful instrumental value.

RESEARCH ON TECHNIQUES FOR REDUCING SOCIALLY NEGATIVE/AGGRESSIVE CHILD BEHAVIOR

In a review of the research literature on cooperative behavior in children, Cook and Stingle (1974) conclude that (1) cooperative behavior in children is associated with positive social interactions, and (2) children are significantly more cooperative when they are interacting with someone with whom they have previously had positive interactions. However, they note that disagreement among investigators over what constitutes cooperative behavior has led to a series of idiosyncratic studies in this area with no cohesive knowledge base relating to how cooperative behavior is developed and maintained in children.

Children who are socially negative and/or aggressive are almost invariably deficient in cooperative behavior. As Cook and Stingle note, the ability to be cooperative with others in social situations appears to be a key skill in maintaining positive interactions. In addition to decelerating rates of socially negative and aggressive responses, it is essential that intervention procedures for aggressive children also teach the skills involved in being cooperative with others. Unfortunately, many intervention studies of aggressive behavior reported in the literature have not systematically attended to the task of teaching cooperative behavior. It is possible that *durable* changes in a negative/aggressive behavior pattern are difficult to achieve unless cooperative responses are systematically developed as part of the intervention program.

As a rule, intervention procedures for aggressive behavior reported in the literature consist of a combination of treatment variables. Sewell, McCoy, and Sewell (1973), for example, reported a study in which they used a combination of positive reinforcement, omission training, and time-out to control the severe aggressive and disruptive behavior of four adolescent retardates in a hospital setting. This combination of variables proved to be highly effective in reducing the subjects' levels of antagonistic social behavior.

The omission training (positive reinforcement delivered for the *absence* of aggressive responses) was effective in controlling less severe forms of antagonistic social behavior without the necessity of using aversive control procedures. This contingency was very easy to administer since it required ward attendants only to deliver reinforcers for periods of time in which aggressive responses were absent.

Additional studies have been reported by Brown and Elliott (1965) and by Pinkston *et al.* (1973) in which positive procedures only have been used to control aggressive behavior in children. Brown and Elliott carried out a study in a nursery-school class in which they successfully manipulated the aggressive responses of 27 three- and four-year-old boys using a combination of attending to acts imcompatible with aggression and ignoring aggressive behavior. The intervention procedures were implemented via the classroom teachers, who responded to instructions and cues from the experimenters. The procedures were only moderately successful in reducing the subjects' verbal and physical aggression. In a follow-up period, there was substantial recovery of the original preintervention levels of both verbal and physical aggression. A second intervention period produced a further reduction in aggressive behavior. However, no follow-up data were reported beyond the second intervention period, so it is impossible to judge the power of this procedure in producing *durable* changes in children's aggressive behavior.

Pinkston *et al.* (1973) reported a study in which an interesting technique was used to control the aggressive behavior of a three-year-old preschooler. The technique consisted of ignoring the subject's aggressive behavior, whenever possible, and attending instead to whatever child he

268   HILL M. WALKER *ET AL.*

was attacking. The authors developed this technique as an alternative to
the usual methods of coping with aggression, namely, either ignoring or
punishing it. The technique proved to be effective in controlling the
subject's aggressive behavior as teacher attention was a powerful
stimulus for him. As part of the study, the authors showed that the
subject's aggressive behavior was, to a large extent, maintained by the
attention it generated from the teacher. When this attention was redi-
rected to the victim of his aggression and his aggressive behavior was
simultaneously ignored, the target subject greatly reduced his frequency
of aggression toward others. However, as the authors note, the results
might have been very different if the technique had been applied during
periods of high-rate aggression. A major difficulty with this procedure is
the amount of direct monitoring of child behavior it requires and the
problems that are involved in getting to each aggressive episode in time to
intervene effectively.

In addition to the problems mentioned above, there are some additional considerations in the use of positive only or neutral procedures,
such as extinction, to control aggressive behavior in children. For example, some episodes of aggressive behavior cannot be ignored because of
the possibility of physical and/or psychological harm to the victim. Thus,
a direct restraining response to aggression may often be required when
using ignoring procedures to control aggression even though it is not
provided for in the therapeutic program. In such cases, the aggressive
child may learn that restraining responses and accompanying adult attention can be produced simply by escalating the intensity or magnitude of
the aggressive behavior.

If intervention procedures for aggression are used which do not
directly consequate aggressive behavior but instead either ignore it or
reinforce incompatible social behavior such as cooperation or positive
social interactions, the aggressive responses may be either unaffected
or merely temporarily suppressed in the presence of such contingencies. The relative cost effectiveness of such indirect procedures may
be low, considering the time and energy that must be invested in their
delivery.

Walker, Hops, Greenwood, Todd, Street, and Garrett (in preparation) conducted a study in which the outcome described above occurred.
A combination of teacher praise, token reinforcement, and cost contingency (subtraction of earned points) was used to consequate the behavior of a group of socially negative/aggressive children within an experimental class setting. The authors found that a combination of teacher
praise and token reinforcement produced only moderate and temporary
increases in rates of positive social interaction. These procedures had no
impact whatsoever on the subjects' rates of negative/aggressive behavior.
Only when a cost contingency was applied directly to negative/aggressive

responses were their rates affected. Further, Kazdin (1972), in a review of cost contingency procedures, notes that behavioral responses to which cost has been applied tend to stay suppressed after cost contingency has been terminated.

Taken together, this evidence suggests that, at least in some cases, negative/aggressive responses must be consequated directly in order to provide cost-effective behavioral changes that will show evidence of durability over time. There seems to be some question as to whether the use of positive/neutral intervention procedures by themselves are sufficiently powerful to produce pragmatically significant and enduring changes in aggressive behavior, especially in high-rate aggression. As noted, a combination of positive social reinforcement and ignoring procedures was only minimally to moderately effective in controlling the verbal and physical aggression of a class of 27 preschool boys (Brown & Elliott, 1965). The procedure used by Pinkston *et al.* (1973) was effective in suppressing a preschool boy's aggressive behavior in the classroom. However, the feasibility and effectiveness of this procedure in controlling higher-rate and more intense aggressive episodes remains untested. It is possible that as the social-behavior repertoires of aggressive children increase in complexity with age and as the children become more skilled and invested in this behavior pattern, both more powerful and more complex intervention procedures would be required to effectively change their behavior.

Intervention procedures of this type would no doubt consist of positive reinforcement techniques for cooperative, positive social behavior and mild punishment procedures (response cost, time-out) for negative and/or aggressive social behavior. Walker, Hops, and Fiegenbaum (1976) conducted a study in which they found that a combination of positive reinforcement for appropriate behavior and mild punishment for inappropriate behavior was substantially more effective than positive procedures alone in controlling child deviance in a sample of acting-out children. Some studies that have used intervention procedures of this type in coping with aggressive child behavior are reviewed below.

Brown, Reschly, and Sabers (1974) used a combination of positive reinforcement, time-out, and response-cost procedures to control aggressive behavior (kicking, hitting, biting, or pushing) in a Head-Start classroom. Rewards were dispensed on an hourly basis. A child was placed in a three-min time-out if aggressive behavior was exhibited during this period. At the end of the hour, all children who had not been placed in time-out were given rewards; those who had one or more time-outs received no rewards—that is, response cost. This procedure was highly effective in reducing the overall rate of aggressive behavior in the classroom. The addition of group contingencies to the intervention procedure increased its effectiveness even further. A postintervention probe session showed that behavior changes maintained at intervention levels after the procedures were terminated.

Bostow and Bailey (1969) used a combination of brief time-out and reinforcement procedures to control severe disruptive and aggressive behavior for two retarded patients in a hospital-ward setting. The authors were dealing with *severe* aggressive behavior in both cases. Whenever aggressive behavior occurred, time-out was immediately applied. The subjects were also systematically reinforced for the absence of aggressive behavior during social interactions with others. The procedures proved to be extremely effective in controlling the subjects' aggressive behavior. Within a week after intervention began, the frequency of both disruptive and aggressive behavior was reduced to near zero levels.

As previously noted, Walker *et al.* (in preparation) investigated the effects of teacher praise, token reinforcement, and response cost (loss of earned points) upon the interactive behavior of aggressive children. The study was carried out within an experimental classroom setting during free-play periods. The study involved two experiments with a different group of six aggressive children, grades K–3, participating in each experiment.

In Experiment 1, the variables of teacher praise, token reinforcement and response cost were introduced sequentially and evaluated accordingly, that is, teacher praise alone, then teacher praise plus token reinforcement, and finally teacher praise plus token reinforcement plus response cost. Teacher praise and token reinforcement were applied to instances of positive, cooperative interactive behavior. Results showed that teacher praise alone *decreased* the proportion of positive interactions for the subjects in this study. That is, initially teacher praise served as a punishing stimulus for the subjects' positive interactive behavior by suppressing it. This result suggests that positive adult attention and praise do not automatically serve as reinforcing stimuli for all children, especially aggressive children. Similar results for problem children have been reported in the professional literature by Herbert, Pinkston, Hayden, Sajwaj, Pinkston, Cordua, and Jackson (1973), Thomas, Becker, and Armstrong (1968), O'Leary, Becker, Evans, and Saudargas (1969), Wahler, Winkel, Peterson, and Morrison (1965), and Wahler (1969).

The addition of positive token reinforcement in Experiment 1 of the above study produced an initial increase in the subjects' positive interactive behavior. However, after approximately four days of intervention, the subjects' levels of positive social interaction returned to their appproximate baseline averages. Thus, token-reinforcement procedures proved to be initially effective in increasing positive social interactions but not in maintaining them over time.

However, the combination of teacher praise, token reinforcement, and response cost (for negative/aggressive responses) proved extremely effective in both producing and maintaining positive interactive behavior over time. This treatment combination reduced the subjects' negative and aggressive behavior to near zero levels.

After this initial group of subjects was returned to their respective regular classrooms, a second group of aggressive children was selected and assigned to the experimental classroom. Instead of introducing the treatment variables (i.e., teacher praise, token reinforcement, and response cost) in sequential fashion during Experiment 2, all three were applied in combination from the first day of intervention to judge their global impact in changing negative/aggressive child behavior and in maintaining such changes over time. The results closely replicated those observed in Experiment 1 when these three variables were in effect. The subjects' negative/aggressive behavior was virtually eliminated during the entire intervention period, which lasted approximately two months.

Patterson and colleagues (1975) have reported procedures for remediating aggressive child behavior in both home and school settings. Their intervention "package" contains such components as (a) adult praise, (b) point systems, (c) powerful back-up rewards, (d) response cost, (e) time-out, (f) group contingencies, and (g) extensive training and monitoring of both parents and teachers. These procedures have proven, in combination, to be highly effective in reducing aggressive child behavior in both settings. Their impact appears to be greatest when they are implemented simultaneously in both home and school settings.

Though the above review is by no means exhaustive, the available evidence on techniques for remediating child aggression seems to indicate that (1) cooperative behavior may be a *key* ingredient in developing a pattern of positive social interaction among socially negative/aggressive children, and (2) a combination of positive reinforcement procedures for positive interactive behavior and mild punishment procedures for socially negative/aggressive interactive behavior may be necessary to effectively change the overall behavior patterns of aggressive primary-grade-level children, whose social-behavior repertoires may be substantially more complex than those of preschool children. Both of these issues were systematically considered in developing the RECESS program.

DESCRIPTION AND OVERVIEW OF THE RECESS PROGRAM

The RECESS program represents a cost-effective set of procedures for assisting playground supervisors and classroom teachers in the task of managing the behavior of socially negative/aggressive children. The playground, and sometimes classroom, behavior of such children can be extremely difficult for adults to manage effectively. The RECESS-program procedures are delivered via a resource consultant who serves playground supervisors and teachers in a consultative capacity, for example, as a counselor, school psychologist, resource teacher, social worker, and so forth. The consultant assumes responsibility for setting the program up, gaining control of the child's playground and/or classroom behavior, and training playground supervisors and teachers to operate the program effectively on their own.

Though the RECESS program is intended for use primarily in regular, K–3 playground and classroom settings, the program should work effectively, with minor adjustments, in special settings for handicapped children or in the upper-elementary grades. However, RECESS has not as yet been tested in such settings, and its effectiveness in applications of this type has not been established.

As noted, the RECESS program focuses upon the negative/aggressive child's social interactions with peers and attempts to (1) decrease socially negative/aggressive responses to within normal limits, and simultaneously to (2) teach a positive, constructive pattern of relating to others. Because the program is primarily concerned with interactive behavior occurring between the socially negative/aggressive child and his or her peers, the primary intervention setting is the playground, where social interactions are free to occur in an unconstrained fashion. However, the program can be extended to the classroom setting if either the child's social or academically related behavior is problematic in this setting.

The RECESS program consists of four sequential phases. They are: (1) recess only, (2) classroom extension, or program continuation, (3) fading, and (4) maintenance. During the *recess-only* phase, the program operates only during the child's recess. This phase is divided into two parts: (a) consultant-operated (days 1–7), and (b) recess-supervisor-operated under consultant supervision (days 8–10). During the *classroom-extension* (program-continuation) phase, the program is extended to the classroom, if necessary. If not, the program is continued as in Phase 1. This phase lasts approximately 15 days. During the *fading* phase, the major program components are eliminated with the goals of making the program easier to manage and reducing the aggressive child's dependence upon external procedures for behavioral control. This phase also lasts approximately 15 days. Thus, the first three phases together last a total of 40 school days. The *maintenance* phase is designed to continue indefinitely and consists of a low-cost variation of the intervention procedures. The goal of this phase is to provide an occasional special reward for the child's maintenance of a positive interactive behavior pattern and to ensure continued adult praising of specific instances of positive social behavior.

The RECESS program consists of the following program components: (1) systematic training via prepared scripts and role playing for the target child and other class members in cooperative, positive interactive behavior; (2) a response-cost point system in which points are subtracted for inappropriate social and/or classroom behavior, for example, rule breaking; (3) adult praise (consultant, teacher, playground supervisor) for positive, cooperative interactive behavior; and (4) concurrent group and individual reinforcement contingencies with the group reward available at school and the individual reward available at home. These components are described below.

TRAINING IN SOCIALLY APPROPRIATE BEHAVIOR

Socially negative/aggressive children are not always aware that their behavior is negative, aggressive, or otherwise inappropriate. In a program such as RECESS, children *must* be able to discriminate the positive and negative aspects of their behavior. Consequently, the target child and the other class members are systematically taught how to be cooperative and polite in social interactions.

Discriminations among four separate response classes are taught in the social-skills training procedure. These are: (1) positive social, verbal behavior, (2) negative social, verbal behavior, (3) positive social, nonverbal behavior, and (4) negative social, nonverbal behavior. Each response class is carefully defined for the target child with examples given and modeled by the program consultant. The consultant first meets with the target child and goes through the training procedures individually. After mastery has been demonstrated, the consultant goes through the same training procedures with the child's peers and is assisted in this process by the target child. The child and peers are expected to demonstrate correct discrimination over several examples of each response class before mastery is assumed. These training procedures are built into the RECESS program as a first step in the intervention process.

RESPONSE-COST POINT SYSTEM

During Phase 1, the target child is awarded one point on a card for each five min of recess at the beginning of the recess period. The child's task is to retain the points during the recess period by (a) interacting positively and cooperatively with others, and (b) following playground rules. One point is subtracted for each instance of negative/aggressive social behavior or playground-rule violations. If all points are lost during a given recess period, the child "sits out" the remainder of the recess period.

If the program is extended to the classroom, the target child must earn access to each recess period by following classroom rules and interacting positively in the academic period immediately preceding it. As on the playground, the child is awarded points on a card and retains them by behaving appropriately in the classroom. If all points are lost for a given classroom period, access to the next recess is denied and the child is unable to earn playground points for that period.

PRAISE

During Phase 1, praise is delivered to the target child for positive interactive behavior during recess periods. Initially, all praise is delivered by the program consultant on a fairly dense schedule of reinforcement. Later in the phase, the playground supervisors are trained and supervised in the correct application and timing of praise. If the classroom extension is implemented, the teacher praises the child on a regular basis during class periods.

The correct use of praise is seen as a very important component of the RECESS program. If applied correctly, praise can be a powerful natural stimulus for increasing positive social behavior. It also has an important role to play in the maintenance of behavior changes over the long term. Therefore, it is *extremely important* that the major social agents in the RECESS program (teachers, recess supervisors, and parents) master correct praising techniques and apply them appropriately.

GROUP AND INDIVIDUAL CONTINGENCIES

If the target child meets specific behavioral criteria during recess periods throughout the day, a group-activity reward is made available for the entire class near the end of the school day. In addition to this, the target child can take the points retained during the day and exchange them for an individual reward arranged at home. Points can be exchanged daily or accumulated toward purchase of more expensive items. The program consultant assists the parents in constructing a reward menu and monitors its implementation during the program's operation.

Because the locus of an aggressive child's interactive difficulties usually involves peers, a systematic effort is made to involve peers in the intervention procedures and in the sharing of rewards earned by the target child at school. Consequently, peers are motivated to assist the target child in acquiring and maintaining a new, more constructive pattern of behavior. Involving the target child's peers increases the RECESS program's complexity somewhat; however, the gains achieved appear to more than offset whatever minor logistical difficulties are created by this increased complexity.

In developing the RECESS program, an attempt was made to construct an intervention package which incurs the lowest possible cost (in terms of time spent) to classroom teachers, playground supervisors, counselors, and parents during implementation while simultaneously producing powerful treatment effects for most of the children to whom it is applied. The results obtained to date on the RECESS program suggest that this goal has been largely achieved.

As described earlier, the RECESS program is set up and initially operated by a program consultant. However, within a short time the intervention procedures involve all significant social agents with whom the child has daily contact. These agents include the classroom teacher, the playground supervisors, the child's parents, and the child's peers. The reasons for their involvement are threefold. First, by involving all these social agents in the behavior-change program, the impact of the intervention procedures is increased and may contribute to a more powerful overall treatment effect. Second, research on program-maintenance effects suggests that if significant changes in the target child's behavior are to be maintained over the long term, social agents in the child's immediate environment, for example, parents, teachers, peers, and so on, must reinforce and actively support such changed behavior (Patterson, McNeal, Hawkins, & Phelps, 1967; Patterson, Cobb, & Ray, 1973). The most direct way to achieve this outcome is to teach such individuals to alter their social responses to the target child so as to support the positive changes in his or her behavior. Third, the available evidence suggests that human behavior tends to be a function of the situation in which it occurs (Johnson, Bolstad, & Lobitz, 1976; Mischel, 1968, 1969). Given that this is the case, one would not expect behavior changes produced in one setting to automatically generalize to nontreatment settings where the intervention procedures had not been implemented. This is precisely what the research literature on this topic is showing (Herman & Tramontana, 1971; Johnson et al., 1976; O'Leary et al., 1969; Walker, Mattson, & Buckley, 1971). Consequently, by involving social agents in the intervention procedures from multiple settings—classroom, playground, home—the chances are maximized that behavior changes will be achieved in the majority of settings in which the child interacts.

The roles of all individuals involved in implementing the RECESS program are carefully defined and structured. These roles are briefly described below.

PROGRAM CONSULTANT'S ROLE

As noted earlier, the consultant assumes responsibility for setting the program up, initially operating it, training classroom teachers and playground supervisors to run it, and ensuring that it operates effectively. The consultant is the key social agent in the delivery of the RECESS program and in determining whether its goals are achieved. The consultant's conscientiousness, attentiveness to detail, and motivation are critical factors in this process.

Given the nature of the RECESS program and the existing pressures for delivery of child services within mainstream educational settings, the authors feel that the teacher-consultant model is an ideal vehicle for delivering the RECESS-program procedures within the school setting (Berry, 1972). This model has proven extremely effective as a service-delivery vehicle for the three behavior-management packages already developed by CORBEH, namely, CLASS, PASS, and PEERS. It is anticipated that the provision of teacher-consultants will be an increasingly popular staffing pattern and service-delivery vehicle in school settings, particularly as Public Law 94-142 becomes operational.

CLASSROOM TEACHER'S ROLE

The classroom teacher plays a critical role in the following program areas and tasks: (1) referral and initial identification of appropriate candidates for the RECESS program, (2) assisting the program consultant in making the program operational, (3) praising the child's behavior and arranging for daily group-activity rewards at school, and (4) managing the extension of the program to the classroom if required. The teacher also completes rating scales on the child's behavior at certain points and maintains a daily-record form which summarizes the program's results.

A manual of procedures (the *Teacher Manual*) has been prepared for the classroom teacher and is required reading for each participating teacher. The manual details implementation tasks for which the teacher is responsible. Guidelines for carrying out such tasks are included. By way of preparation, the teacher meets with the consultant for discussion of the material presented in the *Teacher Manual*. Modeling and role-playing techniques are used by the consultant to teach critical program skills. Once the consultant withdraws from an active role in the program, the teacher assumes a coordinative responsibility for ensuring that the program operates as it should on a daily basis.

RECESS SUPERVISOR'S ROLE

Since the RECESS program is primarily concerned with social interactive behavior in playground settings, the recess supervisor plays a key role in implementing the program. As with the classroom teacher, a procedural manual (the *Recess Supervisor Manual*) has been prepared for each recess supervisor to assist in correct implementation of the procedures. The procedures used by the consultant for training recess supervisors are similar to those used for training the classroom teacher(s).

The consultant operates the program on the playground for the first seven program days, thereby modeling correct application procedures for the recess supervisors and simultaneously demonstrating the program's effectiveness in teaching the child a new pattern of interactive behavior. From days 8 to 10, the recess supervisor runs the program under the consultant's supervision and receives cuing, prompting, and postsession feedback relating to details of implementation. From day 11 on, the recess supervisor has complete responsibility for operating the program on the playground. The supervisor's major program responsibilities include (a) carefully observing the target child's interactive behavior on the playground, (b) marking off points on the child's point card for either negative/aggressive social behavior or violation of playground rules, and (c) praising instances of the child's positive interactive behavior.

PARENTS' ROLE

Parents have several levels of involvement in the RECESS program. Initially, they are asked to give consent for their child to be screened as a candidate for the program. If the child qualifies, the RECESS-program procedures are explained to them in detail and they are asked to grant their informed consent for the child's participation. Once the program becomes operational, the consultant works with the parents in arranging for the delivery of individual program rewards at home. The parents are also asked to actively praise the child's progress in the program. By Phase 3, the frequency of the home-reward delivery is faded. Each week or two during the program, the parents are informed of the child's progress, the home-reward system is monitored, and parents are apprised of program-phase changes occurring at school.

THE ROLE OF PEERS

The target child's peers play a crucial role in the RECESS program. As noted earlier, the locus of the target child's problem(s) is in social interactions with peers. Thus, in order to change the target child's social behavior, it is essential that peers be directly involved in the intervention procedures.

Prior to implementation of the program procedures, the RECESS program and how it operates are explained in detail to the child's peers. Their role in facilitating the target child's positive interactive behavior is discussed and specific techniques are suggested for achieving this goal.

Peers are taught to discriminate between positive and negative social behavior in exactly the same way as is the target child. Finally, peers are motivated to assist the target child in acquiring a new pattern of inter-active behavior via a reinforcement contingency wherein school-activity rewards earned by the target subject are shared equally with peers.

If the RECESS-program procedures are implemented effectively by all personnel involved, there is a high probability that the following program goals will be achieved: (1) The target child will be taught to clearly discriminate between positive and negative social behavior and between appropriate and inappropriate classroom behavior; (2) the target child will be exposed to a powerful set of behavior-change procedures resulting in immediate and substantial changes in playground and/or classroom behavior; (3) playground supervisors and classroom teachers will be taught to operate the program under the supervision of a trained resource consultant; (4) as a result of their involvement in the program, supervisors and teachers may acquire some behavior-management skills that can contribute to more effective child management in general and lead to the prevention of behavior problems in some instances; and finally (5) parents will learn to reinforce and support the child's changed school behavior at home—an important feature in producing enduring changes in child behavior. The achievement of these program goals will likely have a significant impact upon the socially negative/aggressive child's overall development and school adjustment.

The RECESS-program procedures require a fairly substantial in-vestment of time, energy, and effort on the part of school personnel and the children's parents. However, the program is only as complex as is necessary in order to produce reliable and desirable changes across the range of socially negative/aggressive children normally encountered in school settings. If the program's procedures are implemented correctly and conscientiously, the results will generally be well worth the invest-ment of those involved.

DEVELOPMENT AND TESTING OF THE RECESS PROGRAM

As a rule, four to five years of research-and-development work are invested in the development and testing of each of the behavior-management packages produced by CORBEH. The RECESS program is the last of a series of four such packages under development by CORBEH. Four years of work, to date, have been invested in its development.

CORBEH uses a three-stage process, consisting of three separate but interrelated research programs, to develop and test each package. The final goal of this process is the production of a thoroughly tested, workable, and cost-effective package that will be of value to school professionals in managing children with behavior disorders. Each research stage has a different set of goals in relation to development of the overall package. The three stages occur sequentially, with the program building upon the results obtained in each preceding stage.

In Research Stage 1, which occurs within a tightly controlled, experimental classroom setting, the goal is to develop a set of intervention procedures that will be effective in remediating the behavior of children representative of the behavior disorder in question, for example, socially negative/aggressive behavior. The emphasis is upon developing the most economical, yet effective, set of procedures possible for changing the behavior of such children. In this type of research setting, it is possible to carefully analyze the effectiveness of specific intervention techniques both in isolation and in combination with each other. Once an effective set of procedures is identified, they can be applied and evaluated within the mainstream settings of the playground and regular classroom. One or two years of research activity are invested in the Stage 1 program.

The goal of Research Stage 2 is to adapt the identified procedures for effective use within the settings in which the final package will be used, that is, the regular classroom and the playground. Two years of research are usually carried out at this level. During the first year, a series of studies is conducted to identify effective methods and formats for delivering the intervention procedures in an optimal fashion, within classroom and playground settings. During this time, procedures for training classroom teachers and playground supervisors to correctly use the procedures are evaluated. During the second year of Stage 2, a standardized intervention package is developed and evaluated on a sample of children representative of the behavior disorder in question. The package is applied in exactly the same fashion to all children in the sample in order to test its effectiveness and to identify problem areas of a procedural nature.

Research Stage 3 is devoted to field testing and to demonstrating that the intervention package can work, both feasibly and effectively, when applied by school professionals employed in local school districts. The research focus at this level is upon school personnel who will actually use the package in managing child behavior and upon the development of training procedures for teaching such individuals how to correctly implement the procedures. In field testing, the progress of target children is judged against that of children who are not exposed to the package but who do receive the treatment services normally available for such behavior problems.

The nature and outcomes of Research Stage 1 of the RECESS program were described earlier in this chapter. In a review of Stage-1 research, results with two groups of six socially negative/aggressive children indicated that a combination of teacher praise, token reinforcement, and response cost was extremely effective in reducing negative/ aggressive behavior. Although the target children's changed behavior showed some deterioration upon reintegration into their respective regular classrooms, their levels of socially negative/aggressive behavior were well below preintervention levels.

During the first year of Research Stage 2 (1975–1976 academic year), seven experiments involving nine target children were carried out in regular classroom and playground settings. Four of the experiments were classroom interventions, two were recess interventions, and one was a classroom plus recess intervention. These studies were designed to investigate the following variables: (1) the concurrent use of group and individual contingencies to deliver rewards for appropriate behavior, (2) alternative procedures for delivering response cost for inappropriate behavior, (3) procedures for fading both the frequency of reinforcement and major program components such as teacher praise and point systems, (4) procedures for extending the program to additional classroom and/or playground periods beyond the primary intervention period, and (5) the extent to which the procedures produce generalization and/or maintenance of intervention effects within and across treatment settings. The results and outcomes of this research are described below.

1. The concurrent use of group-activity rewards at school and individual rewards at home proved to be both feasible and effective. Some children appeared to respond to both reward systems equally well whereas others responded primarily to one or the other.

2. There was no difference in effectiveness in the two forms of response-cost delivery investigated. In one form, points were awarded noncontingently at the start of the period and then subtracted for inappropriate behavior as it occurred. In a second form, points were earned for appropriate behavior during the period and then a portion of the earned points were subtracted whenever inappropriate behavior occurred. The first variation proved significantly easier for recess supervisors and classroom teachers to use.

3. It was possible to drastically reduce the number of times children were awarded points with only minimal effects upon child behavior. After the intervention procedures had been in effect for a period of time (usually two to three months), it was possible to gradually withdraw major program components without disrupting achieved intervention effects.

4. Procedures were developed, using a point card, for extending the intervention procedures to classroom and playground periods throughout the school day (Hops, Beickel, & Walker, 1976). If specified behavioral

criteria were achieved across these periods, a group-activity reward was made available at the end of the school day.

5. Clear evidence of generalization of intervention effects to nonintervention playground periods was apparent in some of the experiments. Generalization was also achieved from intervention classroom periods to nonintervention classroom periods. However, these effects were not constant or predictable across target children. Thus, it was not possible to expect the occurrence of such effects as an automatic result of exposure to the RECESS program.

6. Maintenance of intervention effects after program termination showed the same pattern of outcomes. Some target children's behavior maintained well, and others' did not. However, it was not possible to identify causal factors that would account for the failure to achieve satisfactory maintenance effects. The great majority of studies on program-maintenance effects reported in the literature have produced similar findings (Kazdin & Bootzin, 1972; O'Leary & Drabman, 1971; Walker & Buckley, 1972).

During the 1976–1977 school year, the second year of Stage 2, a standardized intervention package was applied to the behavior of a sample of 10 socially negative/aggressive children in grades K–3. The findings from the experiments described above were incorporated into this final package. The procedures were first implemented in each child's respective playground periods and later extended to the classroom. This final version of the RECESS program contained the program elements described earlier: training in socially appropriate interactive behavior, teacher praise, a response-cost system, and group and individual contingencies.

Table 2 presents data on the impact of the program's application upon the target children's rates of negative responses during social interactions. Inspection of Table 2 indicates that, as a group, the 10 children averaged .69 negative and/or aggressive responses per min prior to participating in the RECESS program. This is a much higher rate than for normal children under similar circumstances. Normative data collected on the interactive behavior of 30 normal children revealed that they averaged .11 negative/aggressive responses per min during social interactions with peers.

When the program was applied to the target children's interactive behavior in recess periods, their negative-response rate dropped from .69 to .04 per min. The rate averaged .05 when the playground supervisor operated the program under the consultant's direct supervision. When the supervisor assumed complete control of the program in Phase 2, the rate increased to .14 per min. During Phase 3, when the major program

TABLE 2.
Negative-Response Rate during Pre-intervention and Intervention Phases
for 10 Socially Negative/Aggressive Children during Recess and Classroom Periods

Phases	Subjects										Total group	
Recess	1	2	3	4	5	6	7	8	9	10	$\bar{X}$	S.D.
Baseline	.91	.99	.85	.97	1.06	.34	.55	.22	.47	.11	.69	.35
Ia (Consultant-operated)	.01	.07	.06	.02	.01	.11	.01	.04	.03	.03	.04	.03
Ib (Recess-supervisor-operated—consultant present)	.17	.04	.03	.05	.06	.02	.02	.02	.01	.00	.05	.04
II (Recess-supervisor-operated—extended to classroom)	.02	.05	.11	.24	.32	.09	.07	.01	.18	.14	.14	.09
III (Fading)	.08	.12	.13	—	.38	.13	.10	.02	—	—	.12	.11
Classroom												
B1 (Pre-recess program)	.00	—	.28	.11	.22	.25	.00	.46	.41	.10	.26	.16
B2 (Post-recess program)	.02	.19	.15	.25	.07	.28	.00	.15	.26	.07	.15	.10
II (Class extension)	.00	.06	.04	.18	.09	.08	.00	.05	.06	.05	.07	.05
III (Fading)	.01	.00	.01	—	.04	.13	.00	.12	—	—	.05	.05

components were gradually withdrawn, the rate was slightly lower at .12. Inspection of the data for each individual subject indicated there was a substantial treatment effect achieved for all target children.

As mentioned above, the program was extended to the classroom during Phase 2. Two samples of baseline data were recorded in each target child's regular classroom—one prior to the Phase 1 intervention and one immediately after. The negative-response rate during the first baseline period was .26, and in the second .15. When the program was implemented in the classroom, the rate dropped to .07. During fading, the rate dropped slightly further to .05.

Data are not available for the final maintenance phase for this sample of children, since few of them actually progressed to this point in the program during the limited time available for implementation. However, the data show that the procedures were highly effective in reducing the subjects' negative-response rate to within normal limits. Further, the rate remained within normal limits during the classroom and fading phases, a period of five to seven weeks. The negative-response rate in the classroom showed a similar but less dramatic effect when the program was extended to this setting. The second classroom baseline was substantially lower than the first. This reduction may reflect some generalization of intervention effects from the playground to classroom during Phase 1.

Table 3 presents data for the 10 children on the rate of rule breaking in recess and classroom settings during the program phases. The RECESS program is applied to instances of rule breaking in recess and classroom settings as well as to socially negative/aggressive behavior. The table shows that the RECESS program produced a substantial reduction in the playground-rule-breaking rate. The rate remained at low levels through the remaining program phases. Because the rate was initially so low in the classroom, it was not possible to show a treatment effect.

Table 4 shows the effect of the program upon the subjects' positive-interaction rate. The data in Table 4 show that the RECESS program had little impact in either direction upon the target children's positive-interaction rate. This is a desirable result, as the children's preprogram rate of positive interaction was already at a normal level. The major impact of the program appears to be upon (1) negative-response rate, and (2) rule-breaking rate in playground settings.

These data are impressive in demonstrating the power of the RECESS program in reducing socially negative/aggressive behavior. The data further show that the target child's negative/aggressive behavior remains within normal limits in most cases after playground supervisors assume control of it. The importance of this finding for the long-term maintenance of program gains is critical.

During the 1977–1978 school year, the RECESS program was field

TABLE 3.
Rule-breaking Rate in Recess and Classroom Settings

Phases	Subjects										Total group	
	1	2	3	4	5	6	7	8	9	10	$\bar{X}$	S.D.
Recess												
Baseline												
Ia (Consultant-operated)	.20	.88	.52	.66	.21	.06	.07	.17	.19	.31	.30	.27
Ib (Recess-supervisor-operated—consultant present)	.02	.04	.02	.01	.01	.05	.02	.09	.02	.02	.03	.02
	.05	.03	.02	.10	.03	.02	.00	.17	.00	.05	.04	.05
II (Recess-supervisor-operated—extended to classroom)	.08	.04	.16	.16	.07	.03	.01	.01	.02	.06	.07	.05
III (Fading)	.02	.04	.04	—	.19	.01	.01	.04	—	—	.04	.06
Classroom												
B1 (Pre-recess program)	.00	—	.03	.05	.01	.00	.00	.10	.05	.00	.03	.03
B2 (Post-recess program)	.19	.08	.00	.13	.09	.01	.00	.15	.00	.00	.06	.07
II (Class extension)	.00	.02	.04	.03	.12	.03	.00	.02	.00	.01	.03	.03
III (Fading)	.00	.00	.01	—	.46	.02	.00	.01	—	—	.04	.17

TABLE 4.
Positive-Response Rate across Program Phases for 10 Socially Negative/Aggressive Children

Phases	Subjects										Total group	
	1	2	3	4	5	6	7	8	9	10	$\bar{X}$	S.D.
Recess												
Baseline	3.07	3.91	5.30	5.23	3.18	4.08	1.56	1.91	5.00	3.50	3.92	1.30
Ia (Consultant-operated)	2.37	5.70	5.98	5.31	2.53	4.47	1.90	1.60	5.10	2.89	3.88	1.69
Ib (Recess-supervisor-operated—consultant present)	2.91	5.73	6.15	6.12	3.65	3.95	2.32	1.22	4.65	2.43[a]	4.12	1.72
II (Recess-supervisor-operated—program extended to classroom)	3.03	3.79	5.64	4.63	2.44	4.54	1.80	1.88	5.13	3.88	3.83	1.34
III (Fading)	3.17	3.81	5.61	—	2.90	3.77	2.00	2.01	—	—	3.26	1.24
Classroom												
B1 (Pre-recess program)	.29	—	3.04	3.14	1.30	2.98	.18	2.98	3.51	1.82	2.46	1.28
B2 (Post-recess program)	1.86	1.31	2.85	2.02	1.42	2.40	.43	1.98	3.67	1.80	2.09	.88
II (Class extension)	.57	1.27	2.66	2.13	2.18	1.77	.18	1.68	1.96	.74	1.75	.79
III (Fading)	.75	1.10	1.10	—	2.36	2.49	.55	2.48	—	—	2.35	.86

[a] One data point only.

tested in the Portland, Oregon public schools. Field testing represents the final developmental stage of the RECESS program. The purpose of this stage was to determine whether school personnel, employed in school districts as teacher-consultants, would be able to implement the RECESS program effectively following an intensive three-day training workshop. In field testing, the primary determinant of effectiveness was the extent to which target-child behavior changed as a result of exposure to the RECESS program.

A total of 12 teacher-consultants participated in a three-day RECESS training workshop conducted in February 1978. Because of scheduling difficulties, role conflicts, and time constraints, only five of these consultants actually implemented the program for a socially negative/aggressive child who qualified for the program. Implementation occurred over a three-month period from March to June 1978. All target children were enrolled in regular classrooms during the course of the field testing.

The training workshop was conducted by CORBEH staff involved in the development of the RECESS program. The focus of training activities was upon building in (1) *conceptual mastery* of the RECESS program, for example, knowledge of selection criteria and procedures, program materials, implementation guidelines, and so on, and (2) *behavioral mastery* of key program components directly affecting the quality of implementation. A combination of reading, lecture, discussion, and testing procedures was used to ensure conceptual mastery of the material. Modeling, observation of videotaped sequences of critical program components, role-playing and performance-feedback techniques were used to build in behavioral mastery of program components. Acceptable levels of both types of mastery were achieved during the workshop training activities.

Following the workshop, consultants were instructed to identify *two* socially negative/aggressive children enrolled in K–3 regular classrooms prior to initiating program implementation activities. When a consultant had identified two candidates who met eligibility criteria, a randomization procedure was used to designate one of the children as experimental and the other as control. The experimental subject was exposed to the RECESS program over a three-month implementation period. Control children were not exposed to the RECESS program but were free to receive whatever treatment services were made available by the school district.

Because of the closing of school in June, none of the experimental subjects progressed beyond Program Phase 3 (fading). Results of the field test are presented in summary form by baseline and program phases below. All data reported were recorded on the subjects' interactive behavior during regularly scheduled recess periods.

Table 5 presents the average per min rate of negative/aggressive

TABLE 5.
Summary Table of Field-Test Results
for Experimental and Control Subjects

		Experimental subjects	Control subjects
Referral/baseline	$\bar{X}$ =	1.06	.62
	S.D. =	.82	.27
	Range =	17-2.38	.27-.91
Recess only	$\bar{X}$ =	.03	.69
(Program Phase 1)	S.D. =	.04	.34
	Range =	.00-.10	.22-1.01
Classroom extension or	$\bar{X}$ =	.10	.33
program continuation	S.D. =	.10	.39
(Program Phase 2)	Range =	.01-.24	.00-.89
Fading	$\bar{X}$ =	.06	.44
(Program Phase 3)	S.D. =	.10	.39
	Range =	.00-.18	00-.62

responses for experimental and control subjects across baseline and program phases during field testing. Phase means, standard deviations, and ranges are presented in the table for experimental and control subjects during each phase.

All baseline and program-phase means are based upon a *minimum* of two days of observation data recorded for each subject during regularly scheduled recess periods. However, larger amounts of data (up to five days per subject) were collected during baseline and Phase 2 because of the greater length of these phases. Two to three days of data were recorded for each subject in the shorter Program Phases 1 and 3. Equivalent amounts of data were recorded for experimental and control subjects in each phase.

Significance tests were conducted between experimental- and control-group means for each phase. A significant difference $(p < .01)$ was obtained between experimental- and control-group means in Program Phase 1 (recess only). All other mean differences (baseline, Phases 2 and 3) were not significant.

Inspection of Table 5 shows a powerful reduction in the negative/ aggressive response rate for experimental subjects from baseline to Program Phase 1. There was an increase in this rate for control subjects during the same phases. The rate for experimental subjects remained well below that of control subjects during the remainder of the field-testing period (Phases 2 and 3). However, the mean differences for experimental and control subjects during these phases were not statistically significant because of subject mortality. One experimental and two control subjects were lost during Phase 2. An additional experimental subject was lost during Phase 3. Although mean differences were substantial in these phases, the small N's prevented the attainment of statistical significance.

Given the constraints operating during field testing of the RECESS program—initially small N's, subject mortality—the overall results are most gratifying. The results show that (1) teacher-consultants can be trained effectively to operate the program within an intensive three-day training workshop, and (2) trained consultants can apply the program procedures with a degree of precision which results in a treatment effect superior to that *normally* available for socially negative/aggressive child behavior in grades K–3. Questions not answered in the field test were: (1) Can teacher-consultants train recess supervisors to assume control of the program (Phase 2) in a way that maintains a superior treatment effect for experimental subjects? (2) Can major components of the RECESS program be faded out or eliminated in a way that maintains this effect? (3) Does the initial treatment effect achieved for experimental subjects maintain or persist over the long term, for example, across multiple school years? Unfortunately, it was not possible to answer these and related questions during the current field test of the RECESS program. However, there seems to be little question regarding the program's effectiveness in reducing the rate of negative/aggesssive social responses for children enrolled in mainstream K–3 settings.

IMPLEMENTATION ISSUES AND GUIDELINES

In developing the RECESS program, it has become apparent that the perspectives or attitudes of primary intervention agents (playground supervisors, classroom teachers, and program consultants) toward the program can powerfully mediate their responses to it. Similar effects have been noted with the other behavior-management packages developed by CORBEH (CLASS, PASS, and PEERS). This issue is of critical importance in the overall implementation process.

The authors have found that if social agents such as teachers, playground supervisors, and program consultants are philosophically opposed to an intervention program or do not see it as cost-effective (i.e., do not feel that the amount of work required in the implementation process justifies expected outcomes), their application of its procedures will likely be affected in a negative way. Such individuals often hold assumptions about intervention programs that are highly unrealistic. For example, it is sometimes expected that programs like RECESS should produce instant and enduring changes in child behavior with a minimum of effort required by those involved in implementation. It is also sometimes ex-

pected that behavior changes will automatically generalize to nonintervention settings and will endure indefinitely once the intervention procedures are terminated. Perhaps the sensational medical cures of recent
years, with their instant and powerful effects, have influenced our expectations concerning behavioral-intervention procedures. Unfortunately,
behavioral-intervention programs which do not produce such effects are
often judged to be failures and rejected by those in a position to benefit
from their application. This is indeed unfortunate, for both the children
and school personnel involved.

At present, there are no instant cures for complex behavior disorders
analogous to those which exist for many physical diseases. Furthermore,
there are not likely to be any such cures in the foreseeable future given the
nature of human behavior and current technologies for changing it.
Complex behavior disorders are usually acquired over a number of years,
become ingrained into a person's overall behavior pattern, and are usually very difficult to change. To effectively change a complex behavior
disorder, the following elements are usually minimal requirements: (1)
the application of powerful intervention procedures in *all* settings where
behavior is problematic and change is desired; (2) consistent and identical
application of the procedures across all intervention settings; (3) exposure
to the intervention procedures for a sufficient period of time for them to
impact, in a therapeutically significant way, upon the behavior disorder
(usually three months to a year depending upon the child's responsiveness); and (4) implementation of a low-cost variation of the intervention
procedures over the long term in order to build in permanent behavior
change(s). In other words, contingencies in the target settings need to be
permanently changed in order to facilitate and support the changed
behavior. If the contingencies in the target settings resume their preprogram nature, the child's behavior can be *expected* to resume its preprogram status.

The research literature is increasingly showing that the above elements are required in order to produce significant and enduring changes
in human behavior. In this context, there are a number of critical implementation issues that must be addressed in relation to (1) the RECESS
program in general, (2) the response of both target children and social
agents to various program procedures, and (3) the expectations of social
agents concerning the program and its outcomes. These include (a) the
philosophical orientation and behavioral standards of social agents who
implement the program, (b) the generalization of intervention effects
across settings, (c) the maintenance of intervention effects after termination of formal intervention procedures, (d) the response of socially
negative/aggressive children to the RECESS-program procedures, (e) the
decay of intervention effects when playground supervisors assume con-

trol of the program, and (f) the quality of implementation efforts by social agents involved.

Each of these issues is discussed briefly below. Procedures for responding in a systematic fashion to logistical problems and procedural barriers represented by such issues are contained in Section V of the RECESS consultant manual ("Common Objections to the RECESS Program"). It is strongly recommended that this section of the manual be studied carefully prior to program implementation.

PHILOSOPHICAL ORIENTATION AND BEHAVIORAL STANDARDS OF IMPLEMENTATION SOCIAL AGENTS

The authors have experienced a substantial amount of difficulty in achieving optimally effective program application among playground supervisors and teachers (a) who were philosophically opposed to the RECESS-program procedures, (b) who believed only in the use of positive procedures to change behavior, or (c) whose standards concerning appropriate vs. inappropriate child behavior were lax and/or inconsistent from situation to situation. The attitudes of such individuals can powerfully affect the way in which they implement the RECESS-program procedures. There are no easy solutions to the implementation problems that may arise in such situations.

If a particular playground supervisor or teacher is extremely hostile to the use of behavioral procedures, it is usually a good idea to try and talk through the reasons behind the hostile feelings about them. It is possible that the objections do not apply to the RECESS program or apply in only a limited way. If so, it may be possible to resolve them via discussion and question- and-answer sessions.

If the reluctant social agent agrees to "give it a try" but seems unlikely to follow the program guidelines in a conscientious manner, or if the social agent is so hostile that trial implementation of the program will not even be considered, it may be best not to implement the program in that setting or period. However, the program procedures can be implemented in all other settings or periods where the target child's behavior is a problem and cooperation of social agents can be obtained. It is rare to find an individual so hostile that consideration of the program is precluded; however, when it does occur, it is best to avoid program application rather than coerce the individual's participation. Under coercion, a reluctant social agent is unlikely to operate the program properly and the possibility of program failure would be greatly increased.

If the social agent has no major objections to the program but believes only in the use of positive procedures to change child behavior, the response-cost program component may be difficult for the individual to implement. Response cost is perhaps *the* most essential and powerful component of the RECESS program in teaching a new pattern of interactive behavior. Failure to apply response cost in a strict and consistent fashion can have a devastating effect upon the program's effectiveness. In such situations, the target child can be taught that sometimes rule violations and/or socially negative/aggressive interactive behavior will be consequated and sometimes they will not. As a result, the child may try to "get away with" whatever level of inappropriate behavior the situation will bear. Nothing could be more counterproductive to achieving the goals of the RECESS program than this.

If a social agent has problems with the use of mild punishment procedures, the basis for these objections should be explored thoroughly prior to program implementation. Both the necessity of and reasons for the use of positive and mild punishment procedures in combination should be explained by the consultant. Substantive objections of this nature should be resolved, if possible, on a logical-conceptual basis (research findings presented earlier in this chapter should be helpful in this process). In addition, the social agent's use of response cost should be supervised very carefully until it is determined that this program component is being implemented correctly and as needed.

An equally serious problem affecting program implementation has to do with lax and/or inconsistent behavioral standards on the part of school personnel charged with implementing the program. This can become an acute problem when the target child has a number of different playground supervisors and teachers throughout the day. If these individuals have very different behavioral standards or are internally inconsistent with respect to such standards, very serious implementation problems can arise. Children in general and especially deviant children are very sensitive to the behavioral expectations and standards that different social agents hold. They are also sensitive to the consequences that are applied to enforce or back up such expectations or standards. Deviant children are quick to take advantage of inconsistencies either among or within social agents in school settings.

The RECESS program provides a very clear and precisely defined set of standards governing (a) positive social behavior, and (b) basic school-rule violations on the playground and in the classroom. In order for the RECESS program to work effectively, these standards must be carefully and consistently maintained via program-application processes. Ineffective program application as a result of social agents' inconsistency with respect to behavioral standards is one of the most potentially serious problems facing the consultant in applying the RECESS program.

It is the consultant's responsibility to ensure that such standards are consistently maintained. Extensive monitoring of the implementation efforts of all social agents connected with the program is required. When inconsistencies are noted, a number of strategies can be tried by the consultant such as discussion, direct observation and feedback, modeling, and/or role playing. Under no circumstances should the consultant compromise the program's behavioral standards to accommodate a given social agent's inconsistency of application.

THE GENERALIZATION OF INTERVENTION EFFECTS ACROSS SETTINGS

As noted earlier, the research literature is consistently showing that intervention effects with respect to child behavior are specific to the settings in which the intervention procedures are directly applied. Generalization of intervention effects to nonintervention settings is the exception rather than the rule (O'Leary & Drabman, 1971). Occasionally, such generalization effects *are* achieved (Kazdin, 1973; Walker *et al.*, 1971), but it is difficult to identify either the features of the intervention procedures or the conditions that account for such effects. Furthermore, such effects cannot be reliably produced by currently available intervention procedures.

Although there was some evidence in the research-and-development work on the RECESS program to indicate that the procedures occasionally produced generalization effects, they were not of sufficient strength or predictability to be incorporated into the program as an expected outcome for every child. Therefore, it is best to assume that changes in the target child's behavior will *only* be achieved in those periods in which the program procedures are directly implemented. If the program procedures are implemented on the playground, one should expect changes in the target child's behavior *only* on the playground. Behavioral improvement *may* occur in the classroom following the introduction of the program during recess periods, but it should not be *expected* until the program is actually extended to that setting.

It would, of course, be gratifying if predictable and reliable generalization effects to nonintervention settings could be achieved via the RECESS program. However, the program does not reliably produce them nor does any other program currently available. In short, if behavioral improvement is desired in a given setting, intervention procedures should be extended to that setting to achieve them.

THE MAINTENANCE OF INTERVENTION EFFECTS AFTER TERMINATION OF FORMAL INTERVENTION PROCEDURES

Literally hundreds of studies reported in the literature show that when intervention procedures are in effect, child behavior is responsive and usually changes. Similarly, when the procedures are abruptly withdrawn or terminated, child behavior usually returns to preintervention levels. This method of introducing and withdrawing intervention procedures has been used successfully to establish the causal role of intervention procedures in producing behavior change(s). However, it also demonstrates convincingly the reversibility of behavioral-intervention procedures: after intervention procedures are withdrawn, the maintenance of changes in child behavior should not be expected (Kazdin & Bootzin, 1972; O'Leary & Drabman, 1971; Walker et al., 1971). Unless systematic efforts are made to build in maintenance of treatment gains (Greenwood, Hops, & Walker, 1977; Walker & Buckley, 1972), it is extremely unlikely that changed child behavior will persist over the long term.

Given the findings of the above studies, a maintenance phase has been built into the RECESS program. This phase consists of an easy-to-manage, low-cost variation of the intervention procedures which remains in effect indefinitely. During maintenance, teacher praise for appropriate behavior is continued and a surprise group-activity reward is occasionally made available to the entire class if the target child responds appropriately for a reasonable period of time. This phase was incorporated into the RECESS program because it was assumed that without it the RECESS program *would not* automatically produce maintenance effects. Only when the postintervention environment is actively programmed to support changed child behavior are such effects likely to be achieved.

THE RESPONSE(S) OF SOCIALLY NEGATIVE/AGGRESSIVE CHILDREN TO THE RECESS/PROGRAM PROCEDURES

As a general rule, socially negative/aggressive children and their classmates respond quite positively to the RECESS-program procedures. Usually the child and his or her classmates are excited about the program rewards and look forward to the intervention periods. Frequently, however, there is a period in which the child tests the program procedures to see if they will be implemented as stated. If testing does occur, it is vitally important that the RECESS-program procedures not be relaxed, diluted, or compromised in any way in order to accommodate such a reaction. Perhaps the best response to this problem is to make sure that the RECESS-program procedures are applied as precisely and effectively as possible. Extra adult attention in the form of positive prompts and feedback on an ongoing basis and special coaching-and-discussion sessions with the consultant may also be implemented to assist the target child in meeting the program requirements.

Many socially negative/aggressive children are extremely powerful individuals. Through the use of such tactics as coercive mands, physical and psychological intimidation, and verbal or physical aggression, they are able to dominate situations and to control the behavior of those with whom they interact. This sense of power and control can be extremely reinforcing to socially negative/aggressive children. In rare cases, this power can be more reinforcing than the rewards contained in the RECESS program. When such is the case, the RECESS program by itself is not sufficiently powerful to teach the socially negative/aggressive child a totally new pattern of interactive behavior. Instead, a massive home and school intervention program would probably be required to produce significant behavioral changes. Patterson and colleagues (1975) have designed such a program. The program requires the extensive involvement of both parents and school personnel and is more comprehensive than the RECESS program. However, it should be noted that it is rare to find socially negative/aggressive children in grades K–3 for whom the RECESS program will not be at least moderately effective.

THE DECAY OF INTERVENTION EFFECTS WHEN PLAYGROUND SUPERVISORS ASSUME CONTROL OF THE PROGRAM

As the data presented earlier indicate, there is sometimes a considerable decay in the achieved treatment effects when the consultant turns operation of the program over to the playground supervisor. This is to be expected, since the consultant operates the program on a one-to-one basis while the playground supervisor must operate the program (a simplified version) while attending to his or her normal playground duties. Because of extremely heavy supervisory pressures, most playground supervisors are not in a position (and are not expected) to monitor the target child's interactive behavior as closely as the consultant does. Consequently, subtle instances of negative and/or aggressive behavior can slip by unnoticed by the supervisor.

Many target children are sensitive to this program change and become aware of the supervisor's reduced ability to monitor their interactive behavior. However, the program is still quite effective in controlling the more overt forms of socially negative/aggressive behavior once the playground supervisor assumes control of it.

The extent of decay in treatment effects depends upon a number of factors including (1) the severity of the target child's behavior problems, (2) the initial impact of the program upon the target child's interactive behavior, (3) the conscientiousness of the playground supervisor in applying the program, and (4) the number of children the supervisor is responsible for on the playground. Careful monitoring and support of the playground supervisor's implementation efforts can also be an important factor in this regard.

The quality and precision of implementation efforts by all social agents participating in the RECESS program are the most important factors in determining the program's overall effectiveness. As a general rule, if the program is applied correctly, the results will reflect it—it is the consultant's responsibility to see that this happens. As previously stated, the consultant's primary functions in the RECESS program are (1) to set the program up, (2) to operate it initially in an exemplary fashion, (3) to train others in how to use it, and (4) to monitor and support their implementation efforts. The skill and conscientiousness with which the consultant carries out these tasks bear a direct relationship to how effective the RECESS program is in changing child behavior.

CONCLUSIONS AND IMPLICATIONS

The research-and-development process involved in the production of the RECESS program raises a number of *efficacy, research,* and *service-delivery* questions that merit some brief dicussion.

EFFICACY

Judging the efficacy of any intervention program is rapidly becoming a complex and difficult process as researchers and program developers broaden the number of dependent variables used to assess treatment effects. Frequently, changes occur on some of these dependent measures and not on others. In the absence of an a priori designation of primary and secondary dependent measures, the overall effectiveness of a given intervention might be questioned depending upon the value or relative importance assigned to individual measures. Occasionally, the program developer's assignment of value or importance differs from that of the larger research community. In the authors' estimation, this situation is likely to become more rather than less complicated in the future. It is possible that at some future point the research community focusing on interactive- or interpersonal-behavior disorders in children may have to develop a consensus relating to appropriate criteria and measures for judging the treatment efficacy of intervention programs.

A somewhat rarely used standard of efficacy involves the appropriateness of the match between program complexity and severity or deviance level of the behavior disorder being dealt with. This is an especially appropriate standard for the RECESS program and for similar programs which deal with well-developed repertoires of aggressive or deviant child behavior.

Children who qualify for the RECESS program are easily the most deviant of the four populations of children for whom CORBEH developed behavior-management packages. As noted earlier in the chapter, the use of positive-only techniques (praise, point systems with back-up reinforcers) produced only minimal and transitory effects in the interactive repertoires of the aggressive children involved. Only when their negative/aggressive social responses were directly exposed to a deceleration contingency (response cost) was a therapeutically significant change achieved in their behavioral repertoires.

This relative unresponsiveness to conventional and commonly used treatment procedures combined with the instrumental value frequently associated with aggressive behavior makes behavior disorders of this nature extremely difficult to permanently change. Usually, complex intervention programs are necessary to achieve this goal. The RECESS program is designed to focus maximum power, precision, and resources on the task of reducing aggressive child behavior to within normal limits in the school setting. Unfortunately, this power is not achieved without considerable program complexity. However, the authors tried to achieve a workable balance between these two factors in the initial construction, testing, and revision of the RECESS program. If implemented correctly, there is a high probability that the RECESS program will induce a moderate-to-strong treatment effect in the behavioral repertoires of most aggressive children in grades K–3.

The question of treatment outcome and success in applied settings is one that deserves attention—especially in relation to behavioral programs. Baer, Wolf, and Risley (1968) and Walker and Hops (1976) have described some standards for judging the effectiveness of behavioral programs. However, neither addressed the question of at what point a given treatment is judged to be a success or failure. Implicitly, an intervention procedure or program is usually judged to be a failure unless it produces, at a minimum, acceptable, short-term follow-up effects and in some cases long-term effects. The absence of generalization of treatment changes to nonintervention settings is sometimes, although less frequently, used to judge an intervention to be a failure. Usually, the magnitude of treatment effect achieved *during* the intervention program is not a consideration in offsetting a judgment of failure when maintenance and/or generalization effects fail to occur.

The authors suggest that, at least in some cases, this may be a less than appropriate temporal standard for judging treatment success. Producing behavior change(s) can be viewed as a two-stage process. In the first stage, a set of procedures is required to initially produce therapeutically significant changes in the target behavior(s). A second set of procedures, sometimes varying substantially from the original ones in content, structure, and delivery, may be required to achieve acceptable levels of maintenance and generalization. A powerful technology exists for producing initial behavior changes during and sometimes immediately after an intervention procedure is in effect. However, the available technology for producing maintenance and generalization effects is currently in its infancy. There have been numerous failures of maintenance and/or generalization in the past, and there will likely be many more in the future until a high-level technology is developed in this area.

If an intervention program or procedure produces an acceptable treatment effect during its application, then it should be judged a success. If acceptable maintenance or generalization effects are not achieved, it is a failure of maintenance or generalization and not of the intervention program per se. Even if it were possible to hold specific interventions accountable for reliably producing maintenance or generalization effects, it would be extremely difficult to identify those specific attributes or features of the intervention that accounted for such effects. In those relatively rare instances when maintenance or generalization effects attributable to interventions are encountered, the authors have yet to see a study where such effects were casually related to specific characteristics or components of the intervention program.

A more fruitful approach to this task may be to focus on a careful analysis of the posttreatment environment with the goal of reprogramming it to actively support the changed behavior and to prepare the child for entry into and survival within it. Similarly, specific procedures can be developed and implemented that will greatly facilitate the transfer and generalization of behavior change(s) to previously untreated settings (Hops, Walker, & Greenwood, 1979; Stokes & Baer, 1977).

Over the long term, this general strategy may prove to be much more productive than to continue searching for intervention programs and strategies that automatically yield unprogrammed maintenance and generalization effects. If Mischel (1968, 1969) is correct in his arguments regarding the situational specificity of human behavior, then maintenance and generalization effects should *not* be expected when dealing with social behavior in children. The knowledge base accumulated to date on this question seems to bear Mischel out (Walker, 1979).

This is not to suggest that different variations of the same treatment procedure or differing amounts of exposure to the same treatment would not produce differential maintenance and possibly generalization effects. However, the amount of precision, control, and fidelity necessary to conduct such comparative studies would be difficult to marshal within applied settings. Further, obtaining funding for studies of this nature would likley be difficult even though they have the potential to identify interventions that may reliably produce maintenance and possibly generalization effects. Given a continuing trend of shrinking resources, a more cost-effective strategy may be to focus our efforts on whatever settings maintenance and generalization are expected in.

A final efficacy issue concerns the general cost effectiveness of behavioral-intervention programs. There are perhaps no precise measures of this variable. The authors define it as a ratio between the effort or energy involved in implementing a program and the amount and value of the gain produced in child behavior.

Aggressive behavior in the school setting is an aversive phenomenon for all school personnel, including peers. Intensive aggressive responses place severe pressures upon the behavior-management skills of teachers and playground supervisors and are likely to prompt an immediate referral to whatever specialized services exist for remediation of this problem. Given these facts, it is possible that the time investment required in the RECESS program's application may prove to be acceptable to educators.

RESEARCH

The optimal treatment strategy for the remediation of aggressive behavior in children would probably involve a combination of the following elements: (a) social-skills training using role-playing, coaching, and/or modeling techniques, and (b) the arrangement of natural interactive settings or situations where target children can apply their newly acquired skills in social exchanges with normal peers and receive positive feedback and reinforcement for appropriate interactive behavior. The RECESS program includes both of these components in addition to a cost contingency for negative/aggressive responses. An analysis of each separate components has not been carried out to determine the relative contributions of each of these variables to the global treatment effect produced by the RECESS program. It is probable that all three elements are necessary to reliably produce socially significant behavior changes in the repertoires of the majority of aggressive children encountered in the school setting.

However, van Hasselt *et al.* (1979), in a recent review of social-skills research with children, cites evidence that social-skills training alone can effectively reduce aggressive behavior in at least some children. It may be that with certain types or severity levels of aggressive behavior, external reinforcement systems and/or deceleration contingencies (e.g., response cost) would not be required to produce acceptable treatment effects.

Research on this question could be extremely valuable in developing optimally cost-effective interventions.

There is some very tentative evidence in the literature (Bornstein, Bellack, & Hersen, 1977; Gottman, Gonso, & Schuler, 1976) that social-skills training using coaching, modeling, and role-playing techniques will show evidence of maintenance and generalization. However, other evidence cited by van Hasselt, Hersen, Whitehill, & Bellack (for example, Beck, Forehand, Wells, & Quante, 1978) did not support this effect. A clear knowledge base on this question would also be of great value to researchers and practitioners in this area.

If social-skills training does reliably produce maintenance and/or generalization effects, it would clearly be a superior strategy to either (a) reinforcing the occurrence of positive interactive responses in natural settings, or (b) punishing the occurrence of negative/aggressive responses or reinforcing their absence (omission training). In fact, van Hasselt *et al.*, 1979 questions the appropriateness of simply reinforcing an increased frequency of interpersonal interactions when a target child lacks the specific social skills required for competent performance within social situations. However, it is not clear to what extent aggressive children are actually deficient in the social-skills repertoire commonly described in the literature. Aggressive children may have quite acceptable mastery of such skills but simply choose not to use them. In such cases social-skills training would probably have little impact upon the quality of their interactive behavior. Research on the social-skills repertoires of samples of normal and aggressive children would document the existence of such deficits and provide useful information for planning effective interventions.

The question of appropriate dependent measures for use in evaluating intervention programs for aggressive behavior in children is assuming increasing importance, and is one on which there appears to be little consensus. It would seem that information on the following variables would be most valuable in the future evaluation of such programs: (a) sociometric status, (b) quality of interactive behavior in natural settings as determined by direct-observational data, (c) appropriate measures of social competence, and (d) academic achievement. Effective programs for the remediation of child aggression could conceivably impact upon all of these variables. Of these four variables, general social competence would probably be the most difficult to measure accurately. However, if a systematic data base on intervention programs were available which included all these measures, a basis would exist for comparatively evaluating such programs.

The research questions described above by no means exhaust the relevant possibilities in this area. However, they appear to be logical and necessary next steps in the continuing development of a cost-effective technology for the treatment of aggressive behavior in children.

The RECESS program is primarily a deceleration-intervention procedure. Even though all children who qualify for it are exposed to a positive reinforcement system and a social-skills training procedure using direct-instruction techniques, the program focuses upon negative/aggressive social responses which prove disruptive of positive interactive behavior. There are several reasons for this focus.

For example, analysis of the interactive behavior of aggressive children who qualified for the RECESS program consistently showed their rates of positive social responses and interactions to be well within the normal range. However, their negative/aggressive response rates were consistently seven to eight times higher than those of normal children. Consequently, it makes little sense to focus primarily on the positive interactive behavior of such children since (a) it is already within the normal range, and (b) research carried out in the RECESS program's development shows that reinforcement of positive-interaction rate has essentially no impact on negative-interaction rate.

Furthermore, the authors have found deceleration procedures to be substantially easier for school personnel to implement (e.g., teachers and playground supervisors) while producing acceptable treatment effects. Initially, in the program's development, target children earned praise and points for positive interactive behavior and lost earned points for negative or aggressive interactive behavior. However, points were later simply awarded (on a point card) at the start of the period and a portion of them subtracted for each instance of negative/aggressive behavior. This delivery option was much easier to administer, produced equivalent treatment effects, and did not suppress the target children's interactive behavior. However, it should be noted that adult praise (e.g., playground supervisors, consultant, teacher(s), and parents) was consistently applied to the child's appropriate interactive behavior.

There are numerous delivery options for RECESS and its components. For those aggressive children who meet its eligibility criteria, the authors recommend that it be applied according to guidelines specified in the program-consultant manual. However, for children who do not meet all the criteria, a number of delivery options exist wherein various program components (rather than the full program) can be used effectively. For example, an aggressive child with social-skills deficits would benefit from the social-skills training procedure either in isolation or in combination with the program's feedback and reinforcement components applied to interactive behavior. In contrast, an aggressive child without such deficits but with a strongly developed repertoire of negative/aggressive responses would perhaps benefit most from the response-cost point system, back-up rewards, and suspension procedures. The practitioner is urged to consider other program variations of this nature which respond to the specific behavioral deficits or excesses of children who do not meet RECESS eligibility criteria.

Variations in service-delivery options are also possible with RE-CESS. Because the program is designed primarily for use on the playground, the classroom teacher can assume the consultant's program responsibilities. However, in such instances, it would be most helpful if a teacher aide were available to assist with program implementation and share teaching responsibilities.

Finally, CORBEH research on the minimum amount of in-service training necessary for consultants to successfully coordinate program implementation suggests that successful application can be accomplished with no external training. However, if program implementation is attempted in the absence of such training, a thorough *conceptual* mastery of the program and its components is considered absolutely essential.

ACKNOWLEDGMENTS

The authors wish to recognize the creative roles of the following individuals in developing the RECESS program: Annabelle Street, Barbara Garrett, and Jack Crossen.

Thanks are also due Ms. Darlene George for typing this manuscript.

REFERENCES

Achenbach, T. M. Psychopathology of childhood: Research problems and issues. *Journal of Consulting and Clinical Psychology,* 1978, 46 (4), 759–776.

Baer, D. M., Wolf, M. M., & Risley, T. R. Some current dimensions of applied behavior analysis. *Journal of Applied Behavior Analysis,* 1968, 1, 91–97.

Beck, S., Forehand, R., Wells, K., & Quante, A. *Social skills training with children: An examination of generalization from analogue to natural settings.* Unpublished manuscript, University of Georgia, 1978.

Berry, K. *Models for mainstreaming.* San Rafael, Calif.: Dimensions, 1972.

Bornstein, M., Bellack, A., & Hersen, M. Social skills training for unassertive children: A multiple baseline analysis. *Journal of Applied Behavior Analysis,* 1977, 10, 183–195.

Bostow, D. E., & Bailey, J. B. Modification of severe disruptive and aggressive behavior using brief timeout and reinforcement procedures. *Journal of Applied Behavior Analysis,* 1969, 2, 31–37.

Brown, D., Reschly, D., & Sabers, D. Using group contingencies with punishment and positive reinforcement to modify aggressive behaviors in a Head Start classroom. *The Psychological Record*, 1974, *24*, 491–496.

Brown, P., & Elliott, R. Control of aggression in nursery school class. *Journal of Experimental Child Psychology*, 1965, *2*, 103–107.

Cook, H., & Stingle, S. Cooperative behavior in children. *Psychological Bulletin*, 1974, *81*, 918–933.

Gottman, J., Gonso, J., & Schuler, P. Teaching social skills to isolated children. *Child Development*, 1976, *4*, 179–197.

Greenwood, C. R., Hops, H., & Walker, H. M. The durability of student behavior change: A comparative analysis at follow-up. *Behavior Therapy*, 1977, *8*, 631–638.

Herbert, E. W., Pinkston, E. M., Hayden, M. L., Sajwaj, T. E., Pinkston, S., Cordua, G., & Jackson, C. Adverse effects of differential parent attention. *Journal of Applied Behavior Analysis*, 1973, *6*, 15–30.

Herman, S. H., & Tramontana, J. Instructions and group versus individual reinforcement in modifying disruptive group behavior. *Journal of Applied Behavior Analysis*, 1971, *4*, 113–119.

Hops, H., Beickel, S. L., & Walker, H. M. *Contingencies for learning academic and social skills (CLASS): Consultants' Manual.* Center at Oregon for Research in the Behavioral Education of the Handicapped, University of Oregon, 1976.

Hops, H., Walker, H. M., & Greenwood, C. R. PEERS: A program for remediating social withdrawal in school. In L. A. Hamerlynck (Ed.), *Behavioral systems for the developmentally disabled. I. School and family environments.* New York: Brunner/Mazel, 1979.

Johnson, S. M., Bolstad, O. D., & Lobitz, G. K. Generalization and contrast phenomena in behavior modification with children. In E. J. Mash, L. A. Hamerlynck, & L. C. Handy (Eds.), *Behavior modification and families.* New York: Brunner/Mazel, 1976.

Kazdin, A. E. Response cost: The removal of conditioned reinforcers for therapeutic change. *Behavior Therapy*, 1972, *3*, 533–546.

Kazdin, A. E. Role of instructions and reinforcement in behavior changes in token reinforcement programs. *Journal of Educational Research*, 1973, *64*, 63–71.

Kazdin, A. E., & Bootzin, R. R. The token economy: An evaluative review. *Journal of Applied Behavior Analysis*, 1972, *5*, 343–372.

Mischel, W. *Personality and assessment.* New York: Wiley, 1968.

Mischel, W. *Towards a reconceptualization of personality.* Paper presented at the Western Psychological Association Meeting, Vancouver, B.C., 1969.

O'Leary, K. D., & Drabman, R. Token reinforcement programs in the classroom. *Psychological Bulletin*, 1971, *75*, 379–398.

O'Leary, K. D., Becker, W. C., Evans, M. B., & Saudargas, R. A. A token reinforcement program in a public school: A replication and systematic analysis. *Journal of Applied Behavior Analysis*, 1969, *2*, 3–13.

Patterson, G. R., & Reid, J. B. Reciprocity and coercion: Two facets of social systems. In C. Neuringer & J. Michael (Eds.), *Behavior modification in clinical psychology.* New York: Appleton-Century-Crofts, 1970.

Patterson, G. R., McNeal, S., Hawkins, N., & Phelps, R. Reprogramming the social environment. *Journal of Child Psychology and Psychiatry*, 1967, *8*, 181–195.

Patterson, G. R., Cobb, J. A., & Ray, R. S. A social engineering technology for retraining the families of aggressive boys. In H. Adams & L. Unikel (Eds.), *Georgia symposium in experimental clinical psychology* (Vol 2). Springfield, Ill.: Charles C. Thomas, 1973.

Patterson, G. R., Reid, J. B., Jones, R. R., & Conger, R. E. *A social learning approach to family intervention. I. Families with aggressive children.* Eugene, Ore.: Castalia, 1975.

Pinkston, E. M., Reese, N. M., LeBlanc, J. M., & Baer, D. M. Independent control of a preschool child's aggression and peer interaction by contingent teacher attention. *Journal of Applied Behavior Analysis*, 1973, *6*, 115–125.

Robins, L. N. *Deviant children grown up*. Baltimore: Williams & Wilkins, 1966.

Sewell, E., McCoy, J. F., & Sewell, W. R. Modification of an antagonistic social behavior using positive reinforcement for other behavior. *The Psychological Record*, 1973, *23*, 499–504.

Stokes, T., & Baer, D. M. An implicit technology of generalization. *Journal of Applied Behavior Analysis*, 1977, *10*, 349–367.

Strain, P. S., Cooke, T. P., & Apolloni, T. *Teaching exceptional children: Assessing and modifying social behavior*. New York: Academic Press, 1976.

Thomas, D. R., Becker, W. C., & Armstrong, M. Production and elimination of disruptive classroom behavior by systematically varying teacher's behavior. *Journal of Applied Behavior Analysis*, 1968, *1*, 35–45.

van Hasselt, V. B., Hersen, M., Whitehall, M., & Bellack, A. Social skill assessment and training for children: An evaluative review. *Behaviour Research and Therapy*, 1979, *17*, 413–437.

Wahler, R. G. Oppositional children: A quest for parental reinforcement control. *Journal of Applied Behavior Analysis*, 1969, *2*, 159–170.

Wahler, R. G., Winkel, G. H., Peterson, R. S., & Morrison, D. C. Mothers as behavior therapists for their own children. *Behaviour Research and Therapy*, 1965, *3*, 113–124.

Walker, H. M. *The acting out child: Coping with classroom disruption*. Boston: Allyn & Bacon, 1979.

Walker, H. M., & Buckley, N. K. Programming generalization and maintenance of treatment effects across time and across settings. *Journal of Applied Behavior Analysis*, 1972, *5*, 209–224.

Walker, H. M., & Hops, H. Use of normative peer data as a standard for evaluating classroom treatment effects. *Journal of Applied Behavior Analysis*, 1976, *9*, 159–168.

Walker, H. M., Mattson, R. H., & Buckley, N. K. The functional analysis of behavior within an experimental classroom. In W. C. Becker (Ed.), *An empirical basis for change in education*. Chicago: Science Research Associates, 1971.

Walker, H. M., Hops, H., & Fiegenbaum, E. Deviant classroom behavior as a function of combinations of social and token reinforcement and cost contingency. *Behavior Therapy*, 1976, *7*, 76–88.

Walker, H. M., Hops, H., Greenwood, C. R., Todd, N. M., Street, A., & Garrett, B. *The comparative effects of teacher praise, token reinforcement, and response cost in reducing negative peer interactions* (Report No. 25). Center at Oregon for Research in the Behavioral Education of the Handicapped, University of Oregon, in preparation.

9

Children as Instructional Agents for Handicapped Peers

A Review and Analysis

CLIFFORD C. YOUNG

INTRODUCTION

The purpose of this chapter is to examine the developing body of literature on the use of pupils as effective and efficient instructional resources to influence behavior change in handicapped pupils. Included in this chapter are: (1) a discussion of conclusions drawn from programs in which general-education pupils taught their peers, and the implications those conclusions may have for special-education programs involving handicapped learners; (2) an analysis of the paradigms employed to train the pupil-instructors; and (3) an examination of paradigms in which adult intervention was shifted from direct to limited involvement, especially where the adult was allowed to spend instructional time giving specialized one-to-one instruction to pupils who were in need of such intensive assistance.

It is generally accepted that handicapped children benefit most from one-to-one or small-group instruction (Apolloni, Cooke, Shores, & Simberg, 1978). One-to-one instruction is highly beneficial to the learner because the material being taught can be tailored to the learner's needs. Unfortunately, one-to-one instruction is very expensive in terms of teacher utilization of his or her time (Brown, Nietupski, & Hamre-

---

CLIFFORD C. YOUNG • George Peabody College for Teachers, Vanderbilt University, Nashville, Tennessee 37203.

Nietupski, 1976). Additionally, the teacher must provide some constructive activity for the other children in the class while he or she is teaching a single learner.

Small-group instruction may be a desirable alternative to one-to-one instruction when more than one child can be taught at one time. Small-group instructional formats are predicated on the assumption that children in the group are functioning at a fairly homogeneous level on the skills being taught (Wagner & Sternlicht, 1975). However, even carefully grouped children tend to progress at different rates through material to be learned (Jenkins, Mayhall, Peschka, & Jenkins, 1974). Wagner and Sternlicht have noted that the heterogeneity of performance in level or in rate of acquisition by handicapped children often necessitates individualized, one-to-one instruction. This necessity carries with it several logistical problems, the main one being that one teacher cannot possibly provide extensive, one-to-one instruction to an average-size class of learners without assistance.

One-to-one instruction can still be a viable means of teaching when teacher aides, paraprofessionals, or pupils are employed as instructional assistants. Ellson (1976) has mentioned that each teacher aide costs school systems about one-third of a teacher's salary. While paraprofessionals such as parents or volunteers do not require additional school-system expenditures, the use of those resources poses problems relating to their availability, reliability, and the range of use in the classroom.

An educational resource that may cost the school district no additional money and is readily available in all classrooms is the pupil when used as an instructional agent. Nonhandicapped children have been used to teach other nonhandicapped children in general-education classrooms with varying degrees of success for many years (Allen, 1976). The evidence concerning the efficacy and efficiency of the technology of utilizing pupils as instructional agents with handicapped learners, although appealing, is still in its infancy.

Although Wagner (1974) has implied that pupils can be used as instructional agents, and has reviewed a few studies that show promise for pupil-mediated interventions or programming with handicapped learners, no systematic examination of pupil-mediated interventions across academic and social targets with handicapped learners has been published as yet.

This chapter critically examines the available published literature on pupils serving as instructional agents for handicapped children. In order to lay the groundwork for the specific directions taken in reviewing this literature, an overview of general-education, pupil-mediated instruction is included. One parameter defining the studies to be included in the latter sections of this chapter is that the handicapped learners who were involved in the pupil-mediated programming were in attendance at a facility or service-delivery system that served children or youth diagnosed as mentally retarded, socially withdrawn, behavior-disordered, multiply handicapped, or exhibiting deficiencies in at least two major skill areas.

A second parameter of this chapter is that literature included has described specific pupil responses emitted to effect behavior change in other pupils. At a minimal level of involvement, the pupil may simply dispense rewards for appropriate behavior on the part of the learner. At a more sophisticated level, a model presented by Crowder (1959) serves as an illustration. Crowder has defined pupil intervention based on three features: (1) The pupil provides the antecedent events to which the learner should respond, (2) the learner is required to make some response, and (3) the pupil provides feedback to the learner about the appropriateness of his or her response. Perhaps the essential feature of this model is that it implies that there is active and direct pupil–learner interaction. In any case, whether the pupil is a reinforcing agent, or conducting a complete teaching session, he or she should be a primary agent for stimulating learner responding. If the teacher remains in the role of primary agent of instruction, then the possible reutilization of instructional time may be limited.

For purposes of clarity and consistency, five terms will be defined at the outset. First, the term "pupil-assistant" is used to refer to the child or adolescent who has been selected to be trained as the mediator of instruction. Second, the term "learner" is used to identify the recipient of pupil-assistant instruction or intervention. Third, "training" is used to denote activities where the pupil-assistant is being taught the behaviors he or she will employ when instructing the learner. Fourth, "teaching" is used to refer to teaching sessions involving the pupil-assistant and the learner. Fifth, "generative approach" refers to programs that employed adult-trained pupil-assistants who later functioned as trainers of new generations of pupil-assistants.

This chapter will focus on four major issues: (1) general-education, pupil-mediated instruction and the extent to which research findings with normally functioning pupil-assistants and learners can be applied to pupil-mediated programming with handicapped populations, (2) adult involvement in training a pupil to function in the role of an instructional agent for handicapped learners, (3) the extent of adult involvement in implementing and monitoring pupil–learner instructional sessions; and (4) the extent to which the adult can decrease his or her direct involvement during pupil–learner instructional sessions. The last issue is one of efficiency from a time-expenditure perspective. Given that an adult will have to utilize his or her time to train pupil assistants and monitor instructional sessions, does the use of a pupil-mediated instruction procedure result in reutilization of his or her time for planning or specialized one-to-one instruction?

GENERAL-EDUCATION PUPIL-MEDIATED INSTRUCTION

Pupils have been used as instructional resources for centuries (Bell, 1832). An abundance of anecdotal reports (Bean & Luke, 1972; M. M. Harris, 1971; Landrum & Martin, 1970; Lane, Pollack, & Sher, 1972; Rime & Ham, 1968) and carefully controlled research investigations (Allen & Feldman, 1974; Erickson & Cromack, 1972; Robertson, 1972; Snapp, Oakland, & Williams, 1972) have explored the implications of using pupils as teachers of normally functioning children.

Most of the research to date has been designed only to determine if the existing pupil-assisted programs are efficacious (Devin-Sheehan, Feldman, & Allen, 1976). Several longitudinal, pupil-assisted programs cited by Devin-Sheehan (1976), such as the Ontario-Montclair Program (R. Lippitt & Lippitt, 1968), the Pacoima Tutorial Community Project (Melaragno, 1973), the Homework Helpers Program (Cloward, 1967), and Youth Tutoring Youth (Cairns, 1972) have shown superior learner gains in reading, math, and language for low-achieving children and teenagers when compared to control groups. The efficacy of using pupils as instructional resources has also been shown with short-term studies on reading tasks (Hamblin & Hamblin, 1972; Harrison, 1976; Hassinger & Via, 1969), mathematics (Harrison, 1976; Stainback & Stainback, 1972), and affective behavior and self-concept (Balmer, 1972; Pfeil, 1969).

After examining the relative influence of demographic factors on the successful outcomes of pupil-mediated instruction, Devin-Sheehan and colleagues (1976) draw few substantive conclusions. They report inconclusive evidence to support hypotheses concerning outcome predictability and sex, race, and socioeconomic status. They do indicate that age differential between tutors and learners seems to result in better learner performance when the tutor or pupil-assistant is older. However, Devin-Sheehan and colleagues are quick to point out that it may be that older children are simply more skilled at teaching than younger children. Thus, demographic factors alone do not allow one to predict successful outcomes with pupil-mediated instruction.

One consistently documented finding is that structured versions of pupil-assistant training and teaching appear to be more successful when compared to both less structured procedures that may be based on the pupil's experience or ingenuity, or to no pupil-assistant training at all (G. V. Harrison, 1976; P. Lippitt, 1976; Melaragno, 1977; Neidermeyer, 1976).

Clearly, pupil-assistant training is crucial when evaluating pupil-assistant instruction. It is unclear, however, exactly what types of training are most efficient because few studies have treated pupil-assistant training as an independent variable.

One comprehensive system that is generative in nature and offers promise as a model from an efficiency perspective is the Madras System discussed by Thiagarajan (1973). In that system, pupils serve one of three functions: learner, tutor, and tester, in succession. Instruction is modularized so that learners must seek out tutors to teach them the material. When tutor and learner feel that the material is learned, that pair finds a tester who administers a mastery test. With such a system, students take responsibility for finding learners, tutors, and testers as the need arises. As stated by Thiagarajan, "the teacher has to prime the system by teaching and testing the first student on each unit" (p. 12). From that point on, the system should be one that is self-maintaining. Also, if the system functions as designed, the teacher's role becomes one of manager and planner, rather than direct instructor.

Starlin (1971) has discussed a second example of generative pupil-assistant programming in which the classroom teacher spent a minimal amount of time (five min per day for 17 days) training one pupil to correctly identify geometric shapes. After demonstrating mastery of that skill, the trained pupil next trained other classmates, who in turn served as pupil-assistants for the rest of the class. Generative approaches such as those described above appear to be efficient from the perspective of teacher use of his or her time.

Unfortunately, the role of the teacher has often been an overlooked variable in pupil-assisted instruction (Blackman, 1972; Mayhall, Jenkins, Chestnut, Rose, Schroeder, & Jordan, 1975; Melaragno, 1976; Thiagarajan, 1973). Klaus (1975) has written that "a tutorial program should be planned as a complement to the teacher's role rather than as a replacement for it" (p. 73). He further maintains that the teacher is in the best position to provide the factors that are crucial to the success of pupil-assisted instruction, and summarizes those factors as follows:

> Two factors seem to be important if the program is to be a lasting one. First, a program is not likely to survive unless at least one dedicated individual is willing to assume ultimate responsibility for making it work well, and, second, that person must have the time needed to monitor what goes on, resolve day to day difficulties, and plan whatever changes are needed to keep the program on track. (p. 88)

In the same vein, Blackman (1972) has discussed the interactive roles of the teacher and researcher and has concluded that researchers appear to be interested more in answering their research questions and less in meeting the needs of teachers. In support of Blackman's statement, Klaus

(1975) surveyed 13 major pupil-mediated programs and identified only one program that involved the classroom teacher as the major management resource. Thus, the existing literature to date on pupil-assisted instruction appears to have ignored the primary program implementer, the classroom teacher.

In light of the above anecdotal reports and research investigations, pupil-mediated instruction appears to be a viable alternative to direct teacher instruction with general-education populations. The efficacy of pupil-assistant instruction is a demonstrated fact. Unfortunately, few conclusive statements about specific factors that may influence successful outcomes of pupil-mediated instruction can be made unequivocally. Furthermore, the issue of efficiency is one that has not been dealt with in any consistent or systematic fashion.

In summary, three critical issues relevant to pupil-mediated instruction with handicapped learners emerge from an examination of general-education programs. First, although it has been shown that structured training and teaching programs are the most viable and efficacious ways to ensure successful outcomes with pupil-involved instruction, specification of the training formats that lend themselves to positive outcomes for both nonhandicapped and handicapped learners is needed. Second, the role of the teacher has largely been ignored. If the teacher is the primary program implementer, then a major issue to be resolved is the function of the teacher in the instructional process. Finally, although the issue of efficacy has a substantial general-education empirical foundation, the related issue of efficiency clearly needs to be examined. The next section of this chapter will critically examine special-education, pupil-mediated instruction programs with specific emphasis on these three issues.

SPECIAL-EDUCATION PUPIL-MEDIATED INSTRUCTION

In light of the evidence that normal children can teach other normal children, it is reasonable to ask the question whether normal or handicapped children can teach handicapped children? The studies to be reported in this section focus on that question, as well as the utility of the reported interventions for special-education teachers. First to be discussed are investigations where the adult(s) participated in the intervention or in direct teaching throughout the course of the intervention. This section will be followed by a discussion of investigations where the researchers were able to decrease adult involvement at some point during the direct-teaching sessions.

Consistent Adult Involvement

Guralnick (1976) has mentioned that some handicapped children may not benefit from observational-learning paradigms because of insufficiently developed observational skills. With this type of child, adult prompting may be required for the child to complete tasks to be learned. The studies to be discussed in this chapter share two common factors: (1) pupil-assistants were involved in the teaching sessions, and (2) adults were always physically present and usually prompted pupil-assistants and/or learners in the completion of the target behaviors.

An adult-modeling procedure was implemented by Paloutzian, Hasazi, Streifel, & Edgar (1971) where one adult demonstrated a "social-interaction response" (e.g., passing a bean bag; walking to another child and gently stroking his or her face; pulling a peer in a wagon; pushing another child in a swing; rocking another child in a rocking chair) by performance of that response in front of one severely retarded child (the learner). A second severely retarded child (the pupil-assistant) served as an object for purposes of demonstration. Following the command "Do this!" paired with adult and pupil-assistant demonstrations of the behavior to be imitated, the learner was allowed to imitate, or be prompted physically through the desired response. A second adult then gave social praise and a spoon of ice cream upon completion of the response. To complete a trial, the roles of the two children were reversed so that the assistant became the learner, and vice versa.

Describing this training program in greater detail, Paloutzian *et al.* (1971) mentions that different children were paired with each other and different adult models were used with the intent of fostering generalization across trainers and children.

The 10 subjects (mean chronological age 78.1 months, mean developmental age 15.3 months) were given 20 trials per session, and each subject was required to respond on 95% of the trials without physical prompting for two consecutive days before the next response was introduced. The investigators report that each subject required only 10 training sessions to demonstrate performance of the five behaviors to criterion.

The procedure employed by Paloutzian (1971) required the constant involvement of two adults. Similar adult involvement occurred in a series of studies employing a peer-imitation-training (PIT) paradigm (see Peck, Cooke, & Apolloni, this volume).

Extensive adult involvement also typifies an investigation by Morris and Dolker (1974). In that study the investigators paired high- and low-socially-active retarded children (average age of eight years, and IQ score of under 30), and conducted 10 trial sessions in which one high social interactor was asked to roll a ball to a low social interactor. If the low interactor failed to return the ball to the high interactor, the experimenter prompted and guided the low interactor in returning the ball, thus completing the ball-rolling cycle. Testing sessions every second day were used to assess the frequency of completed cycles when the experimenter neither prompted nor reinforced the learner.

Results indicate that a stable level of completed ball-rolling cycles occurred after 14 teaching sessions. There is one limitation to this study when considering it as a suggested intervention to be used by teachers: the experimenter was heavily involved in prompting and reinforcing both pupil-assistant and learner behavior. Morris and Dolker's use of retarded children as both pupil-assistants and learners may have prohibited the withdrawal of direct adult involvement.

With children who exhibit a low rate of positive responding to assistant initiations, one simple procedure that has been used to increase the rate of positive interaction is to have the learner dispense reinforcers to peers. For example, Kirby and Toler (1970) induced a socially isolate, preschool-age boy to pass out candy during free-play time, which resulted in increases in cooperative-play and proximity behavior (being within three feet of other children). Kirby and Toler report that the teacher in their investigation spent less than one hr of her time to train and prompt the child to dispense candy during the 25 sessions of the study.

Another study has examined the effects of giving out candy, or, as stated by the investigators, the shaping of a "generosity response" (Wiesen, Hartley, Richardson, & Roske, 1967). After an initial three-hr training period where retarded children gave out candy to each other noncontingently, an intervention was instituted where both members of a dyad were reinforced for being within three feet of, and looking at or gently touching each other. The experimenter would give one child an M & M to give to the other child on a variable-interval schedule of 50 sec. Gradual changes in proximity and cooperative behavior were observed during the intervention phase. A return to baseline and a reinstatement of the pupil-assistant reinforcement procedure demonstrated that two of the three dyads intervened upon were under reinforcement control. The experimenters note that the third dyad consisted of two highly aggressive boys who had past experiences fighting with each other such that being within three feet of each other may have been aversive.

This procedure was not directly compared with the more traditional procedure of having an adult reinforce both members of the dyad; however, data for the two pairs that showed improvement are reasonably consistent with what might be expected employing the more standard technique. A closer examination of the procedure detailed by Wiesen *et al.* (1967) shows that the experimenter always gave candy to the pupil-assistant to give to the learner such that the procedure, although pupil-involved, also demanded one hr of the experimenter's time each day to dispense candy and to intervene upon inappropriate behavior. Thus, in terms of teacher time expended, this simple procedure appears to be very expensive in relation to the short-term gain in learner performance.

Taken as a whole, the above studies have shown that pupil-assistants classified as normally functioning (Peck, Cooke, & Apolloni this volume) as well as severely retarded and/or delayed (Morris & Dolker, 1974; Paloutzian *et al.*, 1971; Weisen *et al.*, 1967) can assist the teacher or adult in teaching a skill or set of skills to severely handicapped children. The typical target skill was a simple motor response, and with the exception of Peck's (this volume) technique, no formal pupil-assistant training occurred prior to direct teaching. In most instances, training was incorporated into the direct-teaching sessions.

An examination of the direct-teaching formats used in the consistent-teacher-involvement studies reveals that an imitation-reinforcement procedure was employed whereby the pupil-assistant demonstrated the target behavior to be performed by the learner, who was initially prompted through the response by the adult. With the exception of the two studies that were concerned with increasing proximity to peers (Kirby & Toler, 1970; Wiesen *et al.*, 1967), an imitation-training paradigm appears to be the most widely used tactic with learners functioning at a preacademic level.

During direct-teaching sessions, at least one adult was present to prompt and reinforce both pupil-assistant and learner responding. Although the approximate number of trials to criterion across most of the behaviors targeted in the above studies seems consistent with results from adult-mediated experiments, no clear data on the relative efficacy of such peer-mediated treatment are available. One point is clear, however: direct teacher involvement is required to implement and monitor the above programs. The next section examines those investigations in which teacher involvement was decreased as direct teaching progressed.

DECREASING TEACHER INVOLVEMENT

Clearly, children can be used as models for appropriate peer responding when teachers prompt and reinforce peer responding. Such a teaching tactic may necessitate that the teacher be present when teaching sessions are conducted. One recent alternative is to systematically decrease the teacher's involvement from the direct-teaching process, whereby the assistant functions independently of the teacher.

Perhaps the major advantage to decreasing teacher involvement is that the teacher may reutilize his or her time for planning or direct instruction of pupils in need of individual professional assistance. The studies to be examined in this section were designed to decrease teacher or adult involvement. The related issues of implementing and monitoring pupil-mediated tactics will also be considered in this section.

Using self-maintenance skills as the target behavior, Wagner and Sternlicht (1975) used staff recommendations as the basis for selecting 17 mentally retarded females to participate as pupil-assistants. Assistants ranged in age from 15 to 22 years (mean age of 19.1 years) and in IQ from 12 to 63 (mean IQ of 34).

A group of 14 children in need of help in self-dressing, and 12 of those children who needed to learn appropriate eating skills, were chosen randomly from a pool of children observed by the residential staff to span the lower range of self-maintenance skills. Target children had an average IQ and age of 16 and 11.7, respectively.

The 17 assistants were given 30 hr of training in how to teach dressing skills (12 days for 2½ hr per day). Two special education professionals conducted the training using verbal instruction, staff demonstrations, and role playing. No mention was made concerning the relative progress of each assistant during training, or of the specific skills each assistant should have learned. Following the completion of the dressing-skills training, pupil-assistants were next trained in the teaching of self-feeding. This second activity also took 30 hr to complete.

During teaching sessions, two professionals remained in the room with the pupil-assistants and the learners, providing instruction and support, but mainly prohibiting the pupil-assistants from inadvertently reinforcing inappropriate learner behavior. The professional gradually decreased modeling and feedback to the pupil-assistants, but how this was accomplished, by what criteria, and when it occurred, were not specified by the investigators.

Anecdotally, the investigators report that pupil-assistants who were able to function independently as teachers were assigned the job as "team leader." In this new capacity they assisted and gave support to less competent and confident assistants. Thus, Wagner and Sternlicht (1975) appear to have created a generative model in which skilled assistants take on the responsibility for assisting in the teaching of self-maintenance skills by other peers to younger retarded children.

It is difficult to evaluate this investigation because very little information is provided concerning the relative progress of each pupil-assistant and learner. Although 30 hr were allotted for pupil-assistant training, it may be assumed that some pupil-assistants progressed faster than others through the initial training. This differential progress is neither specified nor discussed. Further, with the exception of mentioning instruction, staff demonstrations, and role playing, the pupil-assistant training procedure is not specified in enough detail to allow for replication.

Also employing a generative model, which they have labeled the "therapeutic pyramid", Whalen and Henker (1969) first taught behavior-management techniques to a 22-year-old girl who had an IQ of 51 and a diagnosis of congenital cerebral defect and epilepsy. She subsequently trained a 19-year-old girl with an IQ of 49 and a diagnosis of encephalopathy due to anoxemia at birth. The second girl was responsible for training two additional pupil-assistants. One pupil-assistant was a 15-year-old boy with an IQ of 54 and retardation of unknown etiology. The other pupil-assistant was a 17-year-old hydrocephalic boy with an IQ of 48.

The training sessions began with an observation period. The pupil-assistants watched the investigator demonstrate the teaching process using another resident who was learning to follow simple commands. Following this observational period, the pupil-assistant conducted the teaching sessions with teacher feedback and suggestions for improvement. Assistant motivation was maintained by praise and tokens. After demonstrating the correct use of basic teaching techniques (e.g., modeling, contingent praise, constructive feedback), the pupil-assistant was allowed to teach other assistant-trainees.

Regarding training results, Whalen and Henker (1969) mention that the assistants learned to: (1) ignore misbehavior, (2) make fine discriminations between correct and incorrect responses, (3) prompt responses and systematically fade those prompts, and (4) prevent frustration in the learner by following difficult tasks with easy ones. However, they do not present data showing whether the skills specified above were: (1) in the pupil-assistants' repertoires prior to training, or (2) taught to them, and, if so, the number of training sessions or time required to train those skills to criterion.

Whalen and Henker (1969) provide impressive evidence of the efficacy of their model in which the first pupil-assistant (and a second pupil-assistant, after the first assistant left the institution) taught 40 imitative responses over 42 sessions to a 6½-year-old, presumed deaf, behavior-disordered, epileptic boy. Similar progress was reported for two other assistant–learner dyads who showed gains in verbal and nonverbal imitation.

This investigation is of particular interest because retarded adolescents in an institution (and not normally functioning youth, volunteers, or paraprofessionals) taught a set of skills to younger retarded children who were also institutionalized. While the experimenters trained only one assistant, this individual then trained other assistants with minimal experimenter involvement.

In a follow-up investigation, Whalen and Henker (1971) report that pupil-assistants who varied widely in maturity, academic development, dependability, cooperation, and general social competence were selected to replicate the efficiency and efficacy of the "therapeutic-pyramid" approach. The five pupil-assistants ranged in chronological age from 16 to 24 years, and in IQ from 43 to 68.

A professional therapist trained two undergraduate research assistants who, in turn, trained the five pupil-assistants in basic behavior-management techniques mentioned earlier in this review under the training results for the original investigation by Whalen and Henker (1969).

Although Whalen and Henker (1971) report positive changes in both assistant and learner behavior, they are quick to point out that they conducted a research investigation, and not a program that could be easily adapted in most applied settings. The use of elaborate data systems and the continuous monitoring of several aspects of program implementation by the investigators may prohibit the direct replication of their model to a less controlled environment. However, if detailed data analyses are curtailed and replaced with less sophisticated measures of learner progress, their model may be used in an applied setting by in-service personnel. As already shown, and to be again demonstrated, generative approaches have been used with modification across a variety of settings and with various populations of learners and pupil-assistants.

Snell (1979) conducted an investigation that parallels the studies by Whalen and Henker (1969, 1971). Her study employed six training groups (one staff attendant, two retarded trainers, and four retarded learners per group). She described her pupil-assistants as follows:

> some understandable and meaningful speech; visual and mental ability sufficient to arrange training materials corresponding to a hand-drawn picture and to imitate a brief teaching demonstration; arm control sufficient to manipulate materials and prompt students. The trainers differed widely in IQ, personality, talent for training, and speech or motor handicaps. (p. 78)

The pupil-assistants ranged in age from 19.25 to 45.42 years (mean age of 28.46 years), and in mental age from 3.56 to 12.50 years. The learners ranged in age from 6.83 to 25.33 years, with mental ages ranging from .48 to 2.48 years (mean mental age of 1.61 years). Snell described her learners as follows:

> sat for at least 30 seconds with little self-stimulatory behavior; grasped and moved objects; exhibited no extreme aggression or sensory deficits. The students were profoundly retarded and nonvocal, although a few had some receptive skills. (p. 78)

Resident attendants were selected from a group of volunteers. All were female employees who had a mean age of approximately 29 years, 5 months.

The training of the attendants to supervise the pupil-assistants who taught the learners was conducted in three phases. In the first phase, the experimenter modeled the training procedure (Active Response In-service Training Method; see Herbert, 1976), which is a systematic antecedent-response-consequence procedure. Phase 1 lasted two weeks. Phase 2 consisted of the experimenter observing the resident attendant working with the pupil-assistants during a three-week period. This phase allowed the experimenter to systematically fade her involvement from the direct-instruction sessions. A third phase, also with a duration of three weeks, resulted in almost complete experimenter non-involvement. Snell reports that over the eight weeks, each learner received a mean of 13 hr of training. She also reports that except for brief demonstrations given to pupil-assistants by resident attendants and experimental staff, all of the direct contact with learners was by the pupil-assistants.

Snell reports significant gains for learners of four of the six pupil-assistants on language acquisition. She notes that the learners who failed to show language gains were taught by pupil-assistants who were profoundly retarded and had learners who were lowest in attending skills and IQ. This recent investigation by Snell and the earlier studies by Whalen and Henker show promise for the "therapeutic-pyramid" approach

In an experimental setting, Apolloni et al. (1978) examined the relative effects of adult vs. pupil-assistant teaching, using a ball-rolling response as the dependent variable. Employing a group design, the investigators report that an adult worked with one group of severely retarded children, while a nonhandicapped, 9.4-year-old male served as the pupil-assistant to a second group of similar children to teach the ball-rolling response to their respective groups. No pretraining of the pupil-assistant was necessary. This is not surprising, given the age of the pupil-assistant and his level of functioning. A second nonretarded child helped in the intervention as the recipient of the ball rolling from the learners.

Results of this study indicate that adult and child were both successful in teaching the ball-rolling skill to their respective groups. An examination of the data reveals that both groups averaged just over 11½ ball-rolling responses per min over the three days of training. Furthermore, the pupil-assistant functioned independently from adult direction during the teaching sessions.

Also concerned with interactive behavior, Guralnick (1976) employed two triads, each composed of one preschool-age handicapped learner and two nonhandicapped pupil-assistants, to study the minimum level of training necessary to increase social responsiveness on the part of the handicapped learners. Following the first intervention, from which it was reported that merely having the handicapped children observe play by the pupil-assistants was not effective in increasing the learners' levels of cooperative play, a second intervention was implemented in which the two pupil-assistants were provided training sessions using role playing and verbal descriptions to instruct them in how to attend selectively to the handicapped child's appropriate behaviors and how to encourage interaction. During each teaching session, the pupil-assistants were instructed to play only with the toy the handicapped learner had previously preferred most. Gradual decreases in isolate behavior occurred on the part of the handicapped child. To demonstrate that pupil-assistant involvement with the toy was related to behavior change, a second toy was used as the focus of attention. For the next two sessions, solitary play with the first toy was observed, after which the handicapped child engaged in cooperative play around the second toy and the pupil-assistants. Additionally, the frequency of the children's positive verbalizations increased with the introduction of the selective-attention procedure and correlated with the increase in higher levels of cooperative play.

An explanation offered by Guralnick for the differential results between the modeling and selective-attention conditions is that the target children's observation of pupil-assistant-modeled behavior for five min a session may have been too short a time period, as well as too unsystematic to be effective in producing behavior change.

The procedure of using pupil-assistants as reinforcing agents and models to effect behavior change requires very little pupil-assistant training time, especially if the specific learner behaviors to be demonstrated are easily observable and can be rewarded when they occur. The changes in learner behavior as a function of the changes in pupil-assistant attention suggest that Guralnick's procedure is a viable one that may be used by a classroom teacher with relative ease.

A series of five studies (Ragland, Kerr, & Strain, 1978; Strain, 1977; Strain, Shores, & Timm, 1977; Strain, Kerr, & Ragland, 1979; Young & Kerr, 1979) has used an imitation-reinforcement training paradigm to teach age peers to function as therapists or as teacher confederates for the purpose of increasing the play behavior of withdrawn children. The specific assistant-training process used in each investigation was first described by Strain and colleagues (1977). Each training session lasts 20 min and consists of two phases. In Phase 1, 10 trials occur during which time phrases such as "Come play!" "Let's play,————!" or "Throw the ball!" are demonstrated by the investigator. The pupil-assistant is instructed to imitate the investigator following the demonstration of the behavior. During Phase 2, an additional motoric behavior, physically giving the toy, is included in the total behavior to be imitated. Twenty Phase-2 trials occur during each session.

During the intervention phase of these investigations, the trained pupil-assistant is instructed prior to each session to engage in play behavior with the target children, or learners. Teachers and/or investigators in the playroom merely observe the ongoing play and remain apart from the children. They do not prompt or reinforce social behavior exhibited by any of the children.

The pupil-assistants selected by Strain and colleagues have included normally functioning, three- and four-year-old, socially active preschoolers; two 11-year-old, behavior-disordered males; and a moderately retarded six-year-old male. For each of the investigations, no more than seven pupil-assistant training sessions were required to teach the pupil-assistant to reliably emit the social-approach behaviors with the investigator. Furthermore, once trained, one pupil-assistant was reemployed in a second study such that additional training for that child was unnecessary.

The pupil-assistant training paradigm employed in the above studies is a simple procedure and requires no special skill or prior training for a teacher to use. It does imply the assumption that once a pupil-assistant emits the trained behaviors in a training setting, he or she will emit those same behaviors in a free-operant setting. Young and Kerr (1979) found that they had to add a procedure not used in the earlier studies by Strain and colleagues where the pupil-assistant gave out food contingent upon the learner's responding to his initiations to play. This procedure was implemented because of the initial low rates of responding behavior on the part of the learners. Thus, the severity of social withdrawal may warrant additional tactics not specified in the program suggested by Strain and colleagues.

One disadvantage of the above studies is that training and teaching sessions occurred outside of the classroom. Although the investigations by Ragland (1978) and Strain (1979) were teacher-involved (i.e., the classroom teacher trained the pupil-assistants), the teaching sessions were conducted when pupils other than the learners were engaged in activities which freed the teacher to become involved in the pupil-assistant teaching process. Although this situation represents an approximation to teacher implementation in the classroom, the training and teaching sessions were conducted when the teacher was free from interruptions from other pupils. Thus, it remains to be seen whether a teacher can implement this type of pupil-assistant training and teaching in a naturalistic rather than experimental setting.

An investigation was conducted in the classroom by the classroom teacher in a study by Jenkins et al. (1974). This study involved the teaching of words printed on flashcards; nonhandicapped fifth graders were brought to a resource room and participated as pupil-assistants. These assistants were trained during a 1½-hr introductory session, in which the teacher demonstrated the teaching process, the use of contingent praise, taking time samples of learner progress, and a way for charting learner progress. Following the introductory session, three pupil-assistants and three retarded seven- to 10-year-old learners were paired for 10-min teaching sessions during which the pupil-assistant presented flash cards to the learner. The learner was required to recognize and pronounce a set of 10 words drawn from a commercially available reading series. Pupil-assistants were expected to present the flash cards, wait for a response, and contingently praise a correct response, or provide feedback for an incorrect response.

In the "guided-participation" model described by Jenkins *et al.* (1974), the teacher initially prompted and reinforced pupil-assistant teaching, as well as provided helpful teaching hints. At some point an "intermittent-guidance" model (i.e., limited feedback) was put into effect, but the point at which this occurred was not specified by the investigators.

Each pupil-assistant also conducted a daily proficiency test that followed the teaching session. During these one-min time samples, the pupil-assistant presented a flash card to the learner, allowed a two-sec response-lag period, and recorded the learner's response. The investigators report an interobserver agreement of better than .90 for the pupil-assistant's compliance with the two-sec-response-lag rule, and for his or her recording of correct and incorrect responses.

Jenkins and colleagues (1974) do not specify the types of teacher prompting and assistance that were systematically eliminated as the teacher's involvement changed from "guided participation" to "intermittent participation." They do indicate that "intermittent participation" was in effect by the eighth session. Perhaps cross-age formats, such as the one employed in this investigation, facilitate decreases in teacher involvement, especially when compared to intraclass programs where tasks may have to be extensively taught to the pupil-assistants prior to their becoming direct instructors of others.

An intraclass approach was used in a very thorough investigation conducted by Brown, Fenrick, and Klemme (1971) and will be discussed in detail because it is an excellent example of generative programming that successfully and systematically decreased teacher involvement. Brown *et al.* (1971) employed a modeling paradigm where two trainable mentally retarded girls, 12 and 14 years old, with IQ scores of 47 and 44, respectively, learned 10 words presented on flash cards during teacher-led, small-group sessions. Concurrently, each girl was taught her own set of 10 words that she would later teach to her classmate. Thus, prior to the actual teaching phase of this study, each girl had: (1) observed and participated in a one-to-one instructional format, (2) observed and participated in a small-group instructional format, and (3) learned 10 words chosen for her to teach to her peer, as well as 10 words learned by both girls.

A teacher aide conducted the initial training, which consisted of both the one-to-one and small-group instructional sessions. During these sessions, the aide followed a very specific antecedent-response-consequence procedure that included: (1) presenting the flash card and an opening question, "What does this say?" (2) rewarding correct answers with social praise, and (3) consequating errors by modeling the correct response, requesting the learner to imitate the word, repeating the model and request to imitate, and finally repeating, "What does this say?" Using a simple data sheet, the aide recorded correct and incorrect responses to the opening question. Following a three-day baseline period in which no feedback was given for errors or corrects, 23 sessions (about 25 min per day) were necessary to teach the two girls to correctly label their respective groups of 10 words.

The first pupil-assisted teaching phase involved teacher prompting and reinforcement while each girl taught the set of words she had learned in the one-to-one training sessions to the other girl. However, beginning with the second session, the pupil-assistants presented the flash cards without being prompted. By the end of the ninth session, the pupil-assistants recorded learners' correct and incorrect responses and dispensed contingent social reinforcement. After the thirteenth session, the aide removed herself from the teaching area. And finally, during the sixteenth session, the aide began teaching another student in another part of the room. Thus, after 17 sessions the pupil-assistants were conducting their own one-to-one instruction sessions independent of teacher assistance or feedback.

An examination of the number of words labeled correctly by each learner shows a steady upward trend with mastery of most of the 10 words occurring during the fourteenth session. Thus, Brown *et al.* (1971) demonstrated that trainable retarded adolescents could function in the role of teacher and teach a simple labeling response without direct teacher involvement.

The relevance of this procedure can be seen when teacher utilization of time is considered as a critical factor. Not only did the teacher model the systematic format the assistants would be expected to use in later pupil-assistant-learner teaching sessions, the teacher did so within the structure of ongoing classroom teaching. The skills taught to the pupil-assistants, and later to the learners, were skills that were relevant to the students' needs; thus the teacher was able to teach functional skills while concurrently training pupil-assistants.

Having demonstrated that they could use a systematic teaching procedure with each other, the two girls were next allowed to teach a set of five words to five of their peers in a small-group instructional format. These five subjects ranged in age from 12 to 14 years and had IQ scores from 33 to 44. Although the small-group instructional format was more complex than the one-to-one format (e.g., it was necessary to make sure all learners could see the word, record correct and incorrect responses for five learners, and give edible reinforcers for correct responding), by the seventh session the adult teacher and aide no longer needed to assist the pupil-assistants and merely observed the teaching sessions from a corner of the room. Besides learning a systematic way to teach peers in a one-to-one format, the two adolescent retarded girls were able to conduct more complex teaching sessions involving five learners, and to do so independently after seven teaching sessions that were adult-assisted.

In summary, an examination of the type of pupil-assistant training paradigms used by investigators who decreased adult involvement during pupil-assistant teaching sessions shows that combinations of demonstration, verbal instruction, and role playing were the most predominantly employed tactics—in contrast to the imitation training paradigm used in adult-involved studies. When normally functioning children or youth were selected as pupil-assistants (Apolloni et al., 1978; Guralnick, 1976; Jenkins et al., 1974; Strain, 1977; Strain et al., 1977), very little training time was required (an average of two hr, when reported). When retarded adolescents served as pupil-assistants (Brown et al., 1971; Wagner & Sternlicht, 1975; Whalen & Henker, 1969, 1971; Young & Kerr, 1979), up to 30 hr of training were needed.

Few studies mentioned the criterion level at which the pupil-assistant demonstrated competence on the skills he or she would need during direct instruction. Most investigations reported that the pupil-assistant received training and/or was trained to use the teaching procedures. Unfortunately, in most instances those procedures were not clearly specified.

All of the studies reported in this section succeeded in decreasing adult involvement to a level at which the pupil-assistant was independently conducting teaching sessions. However, procedures and criteria used to systematically decrease adult involvement are conspicuously absent. It appears that monitoring occurred only from the perspective of learner performance. If measurement of pupil-assistant and adult behavior was taken, it was not documented in the reports.

Finally, from a cost-effectiveness standpoint, it appears that the most advantageous procedure is one in which a generative model was used. Clearly, training one student to teach a response to other students without reutilizing the skills of the pupil-assistant may take valuable teacher time for pupil-assistant training that could have been better utilized in direct teacher instruction in a small-group format.

IMPLICATIONS FOR FUTURE RESEARCH

The technology of utilizing pupils as instructional resources is still in its infancy. Children and youth have been teaching each other for years, both in formal classroom situations as well as informally among siblings and friends. Only recently has there been an effort to examine the effects of pupil-mediated instruction with handicapped learners. From those initial studies, several research questions have emerged.

One area of weakness with most of the pupil-assistant, peer-mediated, or confederate-involved programming and research to date is that the studies were predominantly clinical ones that did not examine the possibility of reutilizing the trained pupil-assistants. With the exception of the "therapeutic-pyramid" model, little has been done to demonstrate the generative effect of training a pupil to perform as a teacher, or as a trainer of additional potential pupil-assistants. Clearly, research is needed that will examine the possibility of establishing reciprocal instruction among pupil-assistants.

A second question of interest deals with the role of in-service personnel in assistant-mediated instruction. Less than half of the studies reviewed involved in-service personnel in the training and management of the pupil-assistant. From the prevailing research, one cannot conclude that tightly controlled, experimenter-implemented programs are directly usable by in-service personnel. There is a need to transform experimental research into a form that is pragmatic and usable by in-service personnel. When this is done, the functional utility of pupil-assistant instruction can be better assessed.

A third area of neglect that needs to be addressed is the expenditure of teacher time relative to assistant and learner performance. This research area is complex because of the interactive nature of: (1) the functioning levels of the assistants and learners, (2) the skill(s) being taught to the assistants and learners, and (3) the type of pupil-assistant involvement relative to the involvement of the teacher. An attempt to examine the published literature dealt with in this chapter using the above factors as focal points has resulted in great covariation among the demographic and other variables not treated as discussion points. This covariation has limited the summary statements that may have been made had fewer variables been critical to the implementation of pupil-assistant teaching programs. The implication is that research is needed in which factors are systematically varied, which may result in more definitive statements. Perhaps the major conclusion that can be drawn from this chapter is that more research is needed to clarify the ambiguities that currently exist with regard to factors that effect successful outcomes when using pupils as instructional resources.

In summary, it has been shown that handicapped pupils can benefit from instruction by children and youth who were either handicapped or nonhandicapped. Depending on such factors as the handicapping condition of the learner and pupil-assistant, teacher involvement can be shifted from direct to limited participation. Instructional activities have ranged from ball rolling to self-help skill training. And, in a few instances, there appears to be the potential for training a cadre of pupil-assistants within a generative-programming approach. Although there appears to be evidence that pupils can be effectively and efficiently used as instructional agents, our knowledge about the use of pupils in that capacity is still at an elementary level.

ACKNOWLEDGMENTS

The author acknowledges Dr. Joseph Stowitschek, who provided encouragement and guidance on earlier drafts of this chapter.

REFERENCES

Allen, V. L. (Ed.). *Children as teachers.* New York: Academic Press, 1976.

Allen, V. L., & Feldman, R. S. Learning through tutoring: Low-achieving children as tutors. *Journal of Experimental Education,* 1974, *42,* 1–5.

Apolloni, T., Cooke, T. P., Shores, R. E., & Simberg, S. Adult and child directed social behavior training: Trained and generalized outcomes. *Journal of Special Education Technology,* 1978, *1,* 12–20.

Balmer, J. Project tutor: Look. I can do something good. *Teaching Exceptional Children,* 1972, *4*(4), 166–175.

Bean, R., & Luke, C. As a teacher I've been learning. *Journal of Reading,* 1972, *16,* 128–132.

Bell, A. *Bell's mutual tuition and moral discipline.* London: C. G. F. Livingstone, 1832.

Blackman, L. S. Research and the classroom: Mahomet and the mountain revisited. *Exceptional Children,* 1972, *39,* 181–191.

Brown, L., Fenrick, N., & Klemme, H. Trainable pupils learn to teach each other. *Teaching Exceptional Children,* 1971, *4,* 18–24.

Brown, L., Nietupski, J., & Hamre-Nietupski, S. *Hey, don't forget about me: New directions for serving the severely handicapped.* Reston, Va.: Council for Exceptional Children, 1976, pp. 2–15.

Cairns, G. F., Jr. *Evaluation of the Youth Tutoring Youth project, summer, 1971.* Research and development report 5, No. 9. Atlanta: Atlanta Public Schools, 1972 (ERIC Document Reproduction Service No. ED 064-455).

Cloward, R. D. Studies in tutoring. *Journal of Experimental Education*, 1967, *36*, 14–25.

Crowder, N. A. Automatic tutoring by means of intrinsic programming. In E. H. Galanter (Ed.), *Automatic teaching: The state of the art*. New York: Wiley, 1959.

Devin-Sheehan, L., Feldman, R. S., & Allen, V. L. Research on children tutoring children: A critical review. *Review of Educational Research*, 1976, *46*, 355–385.

Ellson, D. G. Tutoring. In N. L. Gage (Ed.), *The psychology of teaching methods*. Chicago: The National Society for the Study of Education, 1976.

Erickson, M. R., & Cromack, T. Evaluating a tutoring program. *Journal of Experimental Education*, 1972, *41*, 27–31.

Guralnick, M. J. The value of integrating handicapped and nonhandicapped preschool children. *American Journal of Orthopsychiatry*, 1976, *46*, 236–245.

Hamblin, J. A., & Hamblin, R. L. On teaching disadvantaged preschoolers to read: A successful experiment. *American Educational Research Journal*, 1972, *9*, 209–216.

Harris, M. M. Learning by tutoring others. *Today's Education*, 1971, *60*, 48–49.

Harrison, G. V. Structured tutoring: Antidote for low achievement. In V. L. Allen (Ed.), *Children as teachers*. New York: Academic Press, 1976.

Hassinger, J., & Via, M. How much does a tutor learn through teaching reading. *Journal of Secondary Education*, 1969, *44*, 42–44.

Herbert, B. The Active Response In-service Training Method as a method for use with teachers and aides in public school programs for moderate to severely retarded students. (Doctoral dissertation, Michigan State University, 1975.) *Dissertation Abstracts International*, 1976, *36*, 599A (University Microfilms, No. 76-5568).

Jenkins, J. R., Mayhall, W. F., Peschka, C. M., & Jenkins, L. M. Comparing small group and tutorial instruction in resource rooms. *Exceptional Children*, 1974, *40*, 245–251.

Kirby, F. D., & Toler, H. C. Modification of preschool isolate behavior: A case study. *Journal of Applied Behavior Analysis*, 1970, *3*, 309–314.

Klaus, D. J. *Patterns of peer tutoring: Final report*. Washington, D.C.: National Institute of Education, Report No. AIR-47000-2-75-FR, 1975.

Landrum, J. W., & Martin, M. D. When students teach others. *Educational Leadership*, 1970, *27*, 446–448.

Lane, C., Pollack, C., & Sher, N. Remotivation of disruptive adolescents. *Journal of Reading*, 1972, *15*, 351–354.

Lippitt, P. Learning through cross-age helping: Why and how. In V. L. Allen (Ed.), *Children as teachers*. New York: Academic Press, 1976.

Lippitt, R., & Lippitt, P. Cross-age helpers. *Today's Education*, 1968, *57*, 24–26.

Mayhall, W. F., Jenkins, J. R., Chestnut, N. J., Rose, M. A., Schroeder, K. L., & Jordan, B. Supervision and site of instruction as factors in tutorial programs. *Exceptional Children*, 1975, *42*, 151–154.

Melaragno, R. J. *Influence of the tutorial community project on reading achievement at Pacoima Elementary School, with addendum report on the Pacoima Tutorial Community Project*. Unpublished manuscript, Pacoima, California School District, January 1973.

Melaragno, R. J. The tutorial community. In V. L. Allen (Ed.), *Children as teachers*. New York: Academic Press, 1976.

Melaragno, R. J. Pupil tutoring: Directions for the future. *Elementary School Journal*, 1977, *77*, 384–387.

Morris, R. J., & Dolker, M. Developing cooperative play in socially withdrawn children. *Mental Retardation*, 1974, *12*, 24–27.

Niedermeyer, F. C. A model for the development or selection of school-based tutorial systems. In V. L. Allen (Ed.), *Children as teachers*. New York: Academic Press, 1976.

Paloutzian, R. F., Hasazi, J., Streifel, J., & Edgar, C. L. Promotion of positive social interaction in severely retarded young children. *American Journal of Mental Deficiency*, 1971, *75*, 519–524.

Pfeil, M. They got the feeling that everybody's somebody. *Journal of American Education*, 1969, *5*, 21–24.

Ragland, E. U., Kerr, M. M., & Strain, P. S. Effects of peer social initiations on the behavior of withdrawn autistic children. *Behavior Modification*, 1978, *2*, 565–578.

Raver, S. A., Cooke, T. P., & Apolloni, T. Developing nonretarded toddlers as verbal models for retarded classmates. *Child Study Journal*, 1978, *8*, 1–8.

Rime, L., & Ham, J. Sixth-grade tutors. *Instructor*, 1968, *77*, 104.

Robertson, D. J. Intergrade teaching: Children learn from children. In S. L. Sebasta & C. J. Wallen (Eds.), *The first R: Readings on teaching reading.* Chicago: Scientific Research Association, 1972.

Snapp, M., Oakland, T., & Williams, F. C. A study of individualizing instruction by using elementary school children as tutors. *Journal of School Psychology*, 1972, *10*, 1–8.

Snell, M. E. Higher functioning residents as language trainers of the mentally retarded. *Education and Training of the Mentally Retarded*, 1979, *14*, 77–84.

Stainback, W. C., & Stainback, S. B. Effects on student to student tutoring on arithmetic achievement and personal social adjustment of low achieving tutees and high achieving tutors. *Education and Training of the Mentally Retarded*, 1972, *7*, 169–170.

Starlin, C. Peers and precision. *Teaching Exceptional Children*, 1971, *3*, 129–132, 137–140.

Strain, P. S. Effects of peer social initiations on withdrawn preschool children: Some training and generalization effects. *Journal of Abnormal Child Psychology*, 1977, *5*, 445–455.

Strain, P. S., Shores, R. E., & Timm, M. A. Effects of peer social initiations on the behavior of withdrawn preschool children. *Journal of Applied Behavior Analysis*, 1977, *10*, 289–298.

Strain, P. S., Kerr, M. M., & Ragland, E. U. Effects of peer-mediated social initiations and prompting/reinforcement procedures on the social behavior of autistic children. *Journal of Autism and Developmental Disabilities*, 1979, *9*, 41–54.

Thiagarajan, S. Madras system revisited: A new structure for peer tutoring. *Educational Technology*, 1973, *13*, 10–13.

Wagner, P. Children tutoring children. *Mental Retardation*, 1974, *12*, 52–55.

Wagner, P., & Sternlicht, M. Retarded persons as "teachers": Retarded adolescents tutoring retarded children. *American Journal of Mental Deficiency*, 1975, *79*, 674–679.

Whalen, C. K., & Henker, B. A. Creating therapeutic pyramids using mentally retarded patients. *American Journal of Mental Deficiency*, 1969, *74*, 331–337.

Whalen, C. K., & Henker, B. A. Pyramid therapy in a hospital for the retarded: Methods, program evaluation, and long-term effects. *American Journal of Mental Deficiency*, 1971, *75*, 414–434.

Wiesen, A. E., Hartley, G., Richardson, C., & Roske, A. The child as a reinforcing agent. *Journal of Experimental Child Psychology*, 1967, *5*, 109–113.

Young, C. C., & Kerr, M. M. The effects of a retarded child's social initiations on the behavior of severely retarded school-aged peers. *Education and Training of the Mentally Retarded*, 1979, *14*, 185–190.

10

Peer-Oriented Behavioral Technology and Ethical Issues

CHARLES R. GREENWOOD

The ethical and philosophical implications of behavioral technology applied to human affairs has been a controversial topic from its earliest formulation as a deterministic psychology (Watson, 1963, pp. 164–165), and recently as a result of Skinner's writings (1948, 1966a, 1966b, 1971). Adding to this over the last 10 years, undercurrents in American society have created the impetus for methods guaranteeing against misuse of behavioral control. Perhaps the foremost contributing factor has been the proliferation of behaviorally based programs and methodology to nearly every facet of society (Goodall, 1972). For example, behaviorally trained psychologists are using the techniques in schools, homes, businesses, prisons, mental-health settings, vocational settings, rehabilitation settings, medical settings, and so on, touching the lives of literally thousands of individuals. This proliferation undoubtedly is related to the effectiveness of the technology for solving relevant social and behavioral problems. Thus, it seems that legal, legislative, and professional-group policies to control and monitor the quality of behavioral treatments are increasingly being forced upon practitioners as society reexamines the nature of its institutions.

Other factors also contribute to this trend. The collection and use of information about persons in conjunction with high-speed computers has enabled public and private agencies to control individuals in a manner in which they have little knowledge and no control. The public has lately become sensitized to and looked for abuses in large-scale social and medical experimentation (Gray, 1975; Katz, 1972; Stolz, 1977). In addition,

CHARLES R. GREENWOOD • Bureau of Child Research and Departments of Special Education and Human Development, University of Kansas, Lawrence, Kansas 06044. This chapter was prepared with the assistance of NICHHD Program Project Grant, 2 P01 HD 03144, to the Bureau of Child Research, University of Kansas.

there has been a general loss of confidence in the "professionals" in American society. The professions were previously left responsible for the ethical and competent conduct of members within their own ranks. But the skyrocketing malpractice cases in medicine, the adverse publicity accruing to the legal profession during the Watergate affair, the controversy over termination of federally funded behavior-modification research projects of the LEAA (Begelman, 1975), and the scrutiny of technology and professional behavior in the popular literature (Hilts, 1974) are suggestive of the scope of the problem. The cumulative effect for behavioral research has been development of formalized assurances—for example, HEW Guidelines for Research with Human Subjects *Institutional Guide*, (1971), court cases defining issues related to treatment and research (Gray, 1975; Katz, 1972; Martin, 1975), and, by far the most severe, actual termination of projects—for example, LEAA. Additional measures of this impact on the psychological professions in particular, represented by the Association for the Advancement of Behavior Therapy (AABT) and the American Psychological Association (APA), have been (1) the formulation of committees to draft procedures for ethical and professional conduct; (2) a flurry of specialized conferences convened to discuss both ethical and professional issues—for example, the Drake Conference on Professional Issues in Behavior Analysis (Wood, 1974); and (3) the number of recent articles on ethical practice of psychology and behavioral research (Begelman, 1975; Martin, 1975; Robinson, 1974; Sajway, 1977; Stolz, 1977; Stolz, Wienckowski, & Broom, 1975). Clearly this response has been an effort to retain professional control by formulating procedures, advocating professional responsibilities, and educating members and the public.

The purpose of this chapter will be to reflect upon current issues related (1) to behavior-change technology, and (2) to the specific application of the technology with children or peer groups in the role of behavior-change agents. Emphasis will be upon current ethical, legal, and media views of behavioral technology and their practical implications to practitioners interested in using peer change strategies. Of necessity, the scope of the chapter will be limited to these current practical issues. For more in-depth consideration of these issues, the reader is referred to the suggested reading list at the end of the chapter.

This chapter is organized into seven major sections and a summary. The first section is designed to provide a brief overview of current aspects of applied behavioral technology and features often incorrectly attributed to it. The objective will be to establish a framework for discriminating the correct and responsible application of behavioral procedures from other similar procedures and practices. The next five sections are devoted to a discussion of central issues relevant to the use of peers as behavior change agents, ranging from issues of control to issues of peer competence and accountability when in the behavior change role. In the seventh section, a proposed set of guidelines for the ethical use of peers as change agents is established, covering procedures, the behavior change subject, and peer managers. The chapter concludes with a summary of major points.

Aspects of Behavioral Technology Defined

"Behavioral technology" is a general term referring to the collection of behavior-change techniques, mostly derived from experimental-psychology learning research with animals. Included are the techniques derived from both operant- (Sidman, 1960; Skinner, 1938, 1953) and classical- (Millenson, 1967) conditioning research disciplines. This collection of procedures and techniques is designed to influence the behavior of organisms, including humans, in predictable, reliable ways, by means of manipulation of environmental stimuli. The technological nature of these procedures results from the experimental work done for each particular procedure to define its parameters and effects. In other words, the principles of behavior technology are defined to the point where they are usable across a range of change agents and clients or behavior-change problems.

Behavior Modification

"Behavior modification" is perhaps the most widely used referent to behavior-change technology and most commonly known by the layman. Unfortunately, the term in some respects has been attributed meanings that were not originally assigned to it by psychologists, such that its usage is no longer clear (Hopkins, 1975). As originally coined (Krasner & Ullmann, 1965), the term referred to the application of operant learning principles developed in experimental psychology to human populations in applied settings, for example, hospitals, clinics, schools, and so on. Such commonly used procedures as positive reinforcement, extinction, or time-out from positive reinforcement are procedures frequently referred to within the context of the term "behavior modification." These procedures have been widely used in the last 10 to 15 years to teach more effective behavior to human populations demonstrating extremely difficult behavior problems such as retardation, autism, aggression, or delinquency. The techniques have also been applied more recently to more normal human affairs in home, business, and school settings.

Behavioral Engineering

"Behavioral engineering" is another term related to planned behavior-change technology. This term refers directly to the planning aspects of behavior change—that is, to the question, "What arrangements of environmental stimuli are required to produce the change desired?" (Homme, Baca, Cottingham, & Homme, 1970). The elements of behavioral engineering center around the use of contingency management and stimulus control.

Contingency management deals directly with the relationships between the desired behavior and its environmental consequences. These relationships are typically planned and arranged by the engineer or change agent to affect the behavior by either increasing or decreasing the frequency of its occurrence.

Stimulus control, on the other hand, involves the consideration of the specific stimulus conditions or context in which the desired response is to occur. For example, a child taught to respond correctly to the sound of *a* only in the presence of a teacher-presented card containing *a* and not in the presence of *t* or *p* is an example of stimulus control. By managing contingencies in such a way as to increase the frequency of responding in the presence or context of *a*, behavioral engineering is accomplished. Through such a process, the right response is taught to occur at the right time and place.

BEHAVIOR ANALYSIS

"Behavior analysis" refers to the experimental demonstration that specific environmental procedures are in fact causally related to a specific response. As described by Baer, Wolf, and Risley (1968):

> Analytic behavior application is the process of applying sometimes tentative principles of behavior to the improvement of specific behaviors, and simultaneously evaluating whether or not any changes noted are indeed attributable to the process of application—and if so, to what parts of that process. In short, analytic behavioral application is a self-examining, self-evaluating, discovery-oriented research procedure for studying behavior.

Behavior analysis is the major research thrust of behavior technology in applied human settings such as schools, homes, businesses, or hospitals. The intent of behavior-analytic research is the discovery of new, scientifically validated techniques which may be applied to human behavior to improve functioning and alleviate suffering.

BEHAVIOR THERAPY

"Behavior therapy" is distinguished from behavior modification, engineering, and analysis, as it typically refers to the clinical application of behavior technology. This application traditionally originated in one-to-one, therapist–client relationships, but has expanded to include groups of clients. While behavior therapy is typically initiated within a clinical setting, treatment using behavioral procedures may in fact occur in other settings in which behavior-change goals have been established. To a large extent, the practice of behavior therapy includes the participation of the client in establishment of behavior-change goals in the form of a behavioral contract between the therapist and client (Davison & Stuart, 1975; Hare-Mustin, Marecek, Kaplan, & Liss-Levinson, 1979). The treatment procedures are then applied until evaluation data planned in the client's program indicate that changes have been satisfactorily achieved. This use of performance data is a distinctive factor, differentiating behavior therapy from other psychotherapeutic points of view.

What Behavior Technology Is Not

Mind Control—Brainwashing?

As mentioned previously, the terms "behavior modification" and "behavioral engineering," both through professional misuse and usage in the mass media, have come to mean something among the lay public that professionally was never intended. The overzealousness of some professionals in their advocacy of behavior applications to basic societal institutions such as the family, education, and government has turned many potential supporters against behavior technology.

> I am amazed at the disservice some behaviorists do to each other in explaining themselves to novice students and to the lay public. Questions of control, of responsibility, and of freedom have been poorly handled in most cases. Skinner's latest book, *Beyond Freedom and Dignity*, has been misinterpreted because it fails to present the issues in a way that deals adequately with current belief and expectations. (Becker, 1972, p. 12)

Also referring to *Beyond Freedom and Dignity*, Krasner notes;

> People have reacted to the title in many instances without having read the book and have cited the title as an illustration of the anti-humanism of behavior modifiers, particularly those influenced by Skinner. (Krasner, 1976, p. 640)

As a result, behavioral procedures are often viewed as mechanistic forms of control designed to thwart the right of individuals and virtually erase individual differences among people. Many of the futuristic novels (Orwell's *1984*, Wilson's *A Clockwork Orange*, Huxley's *Brave New World*) have portrayed societies where control of mind, human eugenics, and basic societal values have been removed from the hands of individuals. While the potential exists for any technology to be abused, Skinner (1971), for example, comments that behavior technology is ethically neutral. Behavior technology for the most part has been used to maximize human behavior potential and establish self-control in cases where it was conspicuously absent. A case in point is the behavioral literature dealing with difficult populations, for example, chronic mental patients (Ayllon & Azrin, 1968); autism and childhood schizophrenia (Lovaas, Freitas, Nelson, & Whalen, 1977); sociopathic children (Patterson, 1971, 1975); and retardation in children (Guess, 1969; Zimmerman, Zimmerman, & Russell, 1969). Perhaps the most overlooked fact about behavior modification is that the procedures of behavior modification are public information and clients of behavior change can easily learn the techniques on their own for application to their behavior and to that of others. Moreover, since behavior change is an interactive process, it is highly possible for individuals not wishing to change their behavior to arrange consequences for those attempting to produce change in it. Countercontrol is certainly available, granted people are educated in its systematic use.

Chemotherapy

Few behaviorists would agree that chemotherapy is a major aspect of behavioral technology. For example, a review of the last 10 volumes (published since 1968) of the *Journal of Applied Behavior Analysis*, the major professional journal for behavioral application with humans, indicated only three articles dealing with drug treatment used as a behavior-change technique. In fact, many behaviorists and law persons are adamantly opposed to drug treatment with children and advocate behavioral procedures as a major alternative to drug treatment (Bendix, 1973; Hentoff, 1970; Ladd, 1970; S. Walker, 1974). Yet it is estimated that about 200,000 children in United States schools are administered amphetamines for purposes of hyperactivity control (Krippner, Silverman, Cavallo, & Healy, 1973). Several studies suggest drug effectiveness in controlling hyperactive behavior in children. Summarizing several of these, Keogh (1971) concludes, "it appears likely that medication may effect change in level of motor activity and in attention, but that the direct effect of medication on learning is unclear." In a study designed to compare the effects of drugs vs. a behavioral-educational motivation system using positive reinforcement (Ayllon, Layman, & Kandel, 1975), it was demonstrated that although drug treatment controlled hyperactive behavior, no effect was indicated for academic-performance measures. It is important to note that the behavioral-motivation system was found to be equally effective in controlling hyperactivity, with dramatically improved academic responding in comparison to the drug-treatment condition. The authors conclude by cautioning, "the control of hyperactivity by medication, while effective, may be too costly to the child, in that it may retard his academic and social growth, a human cost that school and society can ill afford."

In guidelines produced for the administration of behavioral programs by the National Association for Retarded Citizens (NARC), "physical and chemical procedures were unequivocally disavowed as 'behavioral' procedures, a distinction unfortunately often not made by other guidelines and the public" (Sajwaj, 1977, p. 532; see also May, Risley, Twardosz, Friedman, Bijou, & Wexler, 1975).

The major focus of behavior technology is with learning produced through manipulations of available, naturalistic, environmental stimuli. Although drugs may be used in behavior therapy or be evaluated using behavior-analysis research designs, the domain of behavior technology must be viewed as much broader and more inclusive. Although one occasionally sees the term "behavior-modification drug" used in the media, this is really a misnomer and a lay usage of the term "behavior modification." Simple administration of drugs to suppress or enhance the responding of an individual is not part of behavior technology in terms of its goals, its techniques, or its original conception.

Common Sense

Although many of the techniques used in behavior technology appear to be derived from common-sense experiences, the techniques have a cumulative experimental and clinical history substantiating their effectiveness. For instance, the Premack Principle (Premack, 1959) or Grandma's Law (Becker, Engelmann, & Thomas, 1971) states essentially that behaviors that occur at a high rate will tend to reinforce behaviors that occur at a lower rate, if performance of the high-rate behavior depends first upon the performance of the low-rate behavior. Restated as "Grandma's Law," the principle takes the form, "Make your bed, then you may go outside," which many persons can relate to immediately from everyday experience.

The precise definition and the effects of a behavioral principle have typically been experimentally substantiated, making the principle a scientific finding in addition to any relation it may have to common sense. In fact, many behavior principles would seem to run counter to common-sense experience: for example, teacher reprimands designed to discourage out-of-seat behavior in students have been shown to actually increase time out-of-seat (Becker *et al.*, 1971).

BEHAVIOR-CHANGE AGENTS: WHO ARE THEY?

Who are the potential users of behavior technology? Twenty years ago the users of behavioral procedures were highly trained, doctoral-level clinicians and researchers. Today, the potential users range from parents, to teachers, to business executives, to paraprofessional aides, to peers, to individuals interested in self-improvement. The flight of service delivery from the hands of the "experts" can be attributed to several factors and trends. As previously mentioned, the communicability of behavioral procedures is a major factor. Communicability has been enhanced by books on behavioral procedures directed at the lay public. Books on such subjects as toilet training (Azrin & Foxx, 1974), parenting (Becker, 1971; Patterson, 1971), and weight loss (Stuart & Davis, 1972) have facilitated wide application. Training materials and packaged programs have also been used in human-service settings to effectively train professional teachers (Greenwood, Hops, Walker, Guild, Stokes, Keleman, & Willardson, 1979) and nurses (Liberman, Teigen, Patterson, & Baker, 1973; Renne & Creer, 1976) to effectively apply behavioral procedures. Similar programs have also been developed to train paraprofessional staff in these settings. These have included aides (Mathews & Fawcett, 1977; Pierce & Risley, 1974), community mental-health workers (Fawcett & Fletcher, 1977), and peers (Greenwood, Sloane, & Baskin, 1974; Surratt, Ulrich, & Hawkins, 1969).

The use of behavioral technology has also been facilitated by economics and the demand for services. The increasing use of paraprofessionals has been a trend in mental-health and educational fields independent of the development of behavioral procedures; it has helped legitimize the use of specific procedures by a lay staff (Cowen, 1976).

A third impetus for the diffusion of procedures to paraprofessional users has been a result of behavioral research. It was early recognized that for effective and long-lasting behavior change to occur, the social agents in the clients' environments needed to be enlisted, in part to reprogram the social contingencies (Patterson, Ebner, & Shaw, 1969). Thus, the design of behavioral programs has been directed at users in the natural setting. As a result the range of potential users of behavioral procedures has expanded geometrically, in comparison to traditional service-delivery systems which rely largely upon the highly trained expert.

As demonstrated in the chapters of this book, a behavioral technology is developing which is designed for peers and peer groups. As a result, a number of common and unique ethical issues emerge that must be considered. Since in many cases peers are children, special consideration is in order. In contrast to adult paraprofessionals, their actions may be even more open to issues of responsibility, judgment, and liability. In some cases the use of peers as social-change agents is in fact problematic, and the reasons for using them may be more related to opportunities to help the tutor than the tutee. For example, Cowen (1976) described a program for "tuned-out youth" as cross-age tutors for otherwise normal children. Thus, in several areas unique risks and benefits to peers and targets of behavior change must be considered. Our discussion will now turn to a consideration of the common and unique issues concerning peers in the role of behavior-change agents.

ISSUES OF CONTROL

Perhaps in some future time, students of human rights will commonly agree that children as a minority population were the last to obtain some degree of determinism over the societal forces that control them. Even though Haley vs. Ohio* stated that the rights guaranteed to adults also apply to children, by nature of their physical and cultural dependency on adults, children formally remain a disenfranchised group. Since they are under voting age, they do not have the political means to secure their own rights (Shore, 1979). Adult control has been virtually complete, and has been widely recognized to reside within the adult family unit. Legally, children fall within the rubric of uncomprehending subjects as do adults who are intellectually or psychologically problematic with respect to their ability to make enlightened decisions about their own welfare (Katz, 1972, p. 956).

The potential for abuse of child rights under such a model is of course great and has only been recognized in recent times. N. J. Crowder and Malenfant (1975) quote Hyman and Schreiber (1975): "Until very recently, and only through the diligent and persistent hard work done by many of the newly-formed child advocacy groups . . . children had virtually no rights" (p. 14). They go on to comment that children were frequently treated as "things" in custody fights, and that though both divorcing parents have legal counsel, there is no attorney for the child. In many states now, children are represented in such cases. Also,

> a child may not have surgery or medical care unless the parents want it, and if they want it, he has it, without being asked . . . a child has no rights as to what may enter his mind—only what his parents and the state permit . . . a child must attend school until a certain specified age . . . a child may be committed to a mental institution without due process.

In 1969, the Joint Commission on the Mental Health of Children reported a number of rights of children, including (1) the right to be wanted, (2) to be born healthy, (3) to live in a healthy environment, (4) to obtain satisfaction of basic needs, (5) to receive continuous loving care, (6) to acquire the intellectual and emotional skills necessary to achieve individual aspirations, (7) to cope effectively in our society, and (8) to receive care and treatment through facilities that are appropriate to children's

*Haley vs. Ohio, 332, U.S. 596 (1948).

needs, and (9) to be reared as closely as possible within the normal social setting (reported by Shore, 1979). In addition, recent legislation for the handicapped, Public Law 94-142 (The Education of All Handicapped Children Act of 1975), has guaranteed the educational and due-process rights of handicapped children placed into special-education settings (Yohalem & Dinsmore, 1978). Prior to 1975, public education was not the birthright of all children, as handicapped children were routinely denied service in the public schools.

As might be expected from this state of affairs, even the most basic of rights under the constitution are inconsistently applied to children, and inequities are created. For example, the case of Gerald Gault (Robinson, 1974) portrays a situation where a boy under the age of 18 was sentenced to six years in an industrial school on noncriminal charges. Had he been 18, under criminal statute he would have received two months in jail and a fine not exceeding $50.

RECIPROCITY AND INFORMAL CONTROL

While it is apparent that children enjoy control of few legal rights, research indicates that they do in fact control a large proportion of their parent's and teacher's behavior because of the reciprocity of social interaction and the natural interplay of behavioral principles. Few would dispute that parents' actions are also controlled by their children. Patterson's reciprocity hypothesis (Patterson, 1975) elaborates a model of parent–child social interactions in which many of a child's behaviors—hitting, crying, and so on—are in fact prompts or reinforcers for parental responsiveness. The typical resolution of manding interactions occurs as the child's coercive behavior escalates to a point resulting in parental compliance. Compliance terminates the child's manding behavior and negatively reinforces parental compliance to aversive child requests. This outcome is a situation in which the child has mastered effective control over an area of parental responding. The unfortunate result of such dynamics is that the child learns the use of aversive behavioral tactics as opposed to more direct and valued strategies for dealing with the same circumstances. This model has been also documented with child–teacher interactions in classroom settings. Becker and colleagues (1971) noted that occurrence of out-of-seat behavior was observed to occasion a teacher reprimand for the children to sit down. Although the children did immediately comply with the command, immediately reinforcing the teacher's response, the data indicated that the total out-of-seat time in fact increased over baseline during this condition. Clearly, the balance of control in informal social-interaction processes can and does shift to children, much to the consternation of the adults responsible for managing them.

Other studies investigating the controlling properties of peer groups over group members have indicated an alarming trend for peer groups to provide social consequences for behaviors mostly at odds with those desired by adult managers. For example, Buehler, Patterson, and Furniss (1966) found in an observational study of delinquent peers that 70–80% of verbalizations of a delinquent nature were consequated positively by peers. The authors (1966) concluded that "the institution could be seen as a 'teaching machine' programmed for maintenance and acquisition of deviant behavior rather than for retraining the child to more socially adaptive behavior." A more recent study in a sixth-grade classroom (Solomon & Wahler, 1973) found that "the peers were almost exclusively attentive to deviant actions produced by problem children; prosocial behavior produced by these children was completely ignored." Through later experimental manipulations in this study, the same peer group was taught to provide reinforcing consequences to appropriate classroom behavior, resulting in improved student performance. These findings suggest the use of peer-group consequences as a means for achieving many desired behavior goals.

Peers as Control Agents: Who Benefits?

Only recently have children been taught to successfully use behavioral techniques to influence the behavior of their peers (Evans & Oswalt, 1968; Packard, 1970; Patterson et al., 1969; Surratt et al., 1969; Wahler, 1967) and their teachers (Graubard, Rosenberg, & Miller, 1971). The benefits of children learning behavior-change skills have been described as wide ranging by many researchers.

Benefits for Adults

Benefits are clearly available to adult social agents in the form of release from the managerial or instructional tasks that child peers can learn to control (Greenwood et al., 1974; Johnson & Bailey, 1974; Surratt et al., 1969). Others have noted that dependent or interdependent contingency arrangements facilitate spontaneous tutoring and peer monitoring that increase a teacher's capability of individualizing instruction to low-performing students (Hamblin, Hathaway, & Wodarski, 1971; McCarty, Griffin, Apolloni, & Shores, 1977). Used wisely, this resource can provide general therapeutic benefit to those served in peer-instructed environments. Studies have also noted that peer tutors frequently benefit directly, for example, through improved academic skills as a result of tutoring peers (Dineen, Clark, & Risley, 1977). From an equally important perspective, adult control can be maximized in the peer group where adult reinforcement control, for whatever reasons, is initially at low strength (Lovitt, Lovitt, Eaton, & Kirkwood, 1973; Nelson, Worell, & Polsgrove, 1973; Solomon & Wahler, 1973). Solomon and Wahler envision "the development of 'peer therapists' programs designed specifically to deal with deviant child behavior typically supported by the peer group."

Benefits for Children

At one level, benefits for children are in the realm of learning effective counter- and self-control required for effective survival in society. It would logically seem that such skills could be taught as effectively as reading or mathematics. "If children are to be more than recipients of someone's benevolence, they must learn how to operate on society as well as to accept being operated on" (Graubard *et al.*, 1971). Some authors have suggested teaching behavior-change methodology to children as part of normal child-rearing practices (Canton & Gelfand, 1975; N. J. Crowder & Malenfant, 1975; Graubard *et al.*, 1971; Lovitt *et al.*, 1973) and have actually developed a behavior-change curriculum for elementary- and high-school-age children (N. J. Crowder, 1974; Malenfant, Crowder, Faison, & Hall, 1975). Using these procedures, effective control of peer behavior could be fostered at the interpersonal level between and among peers. For instance, dealing with the class bully or increasing one's acceptance among a particular peer group could entail learning specific applications of behavior procedures. Not only do skills in behavior-change techniques appear beneficial; there is some evidence that the roles of social control are in fact reinforcing:

> The boys often paid more points to purchase the manager position than they could earn by being manager and seemed to indicate that other variables (e.g., the opportunity to exercise some authority over one's peers) could have maintained much of the manager's behavior. (Phillips, Phillips, Wolf, & Fixsen, 1973)

From another perspective the use of peers provides occasions for positive social behavior to occur among peers that might otherwise occur between clients and adult caretakers. The peer behavior manager learns practical skills in giving instructions, reviewing progress, giving social praise, dispensing punishment, and facilitating prosocial peer behavior. In cases wherein peers are allowed to set rules and levy consequences on a manager basis (Greenwood *et al.*, 1974; Surratt *et al.*, 1969) or within a peer-government arrangement (Fixsen, Phillips, & Wolf, 1973), essential social skills are taught.

In situations were interdependent, group-oriented contingencies are in effect, peer groups are provided opportunities to work together as a team to achieve common goals and common reinforcers. As noted in the chapter by Greenwood and Hops, this volume, strategies of cooperation among peers frequently develop that teach planning, coordination of responding, and group organization in response sharing or response exchange. In addition, individual and group instances of positive reinforcement for prosocial responding are learned and occur as either planned or positive side effects of these systems.

PEERS AS CONTROL AGENTS: WHO IS AT RISK?

An analysis of potential risks suggests pitfalls for adult supervisors, peer behavior managers/tutors, and peers as clients and/or group members.

Risks for Adult Supervisors

In most peer procedures, adults establish the peer as manager through designation, training, and/or dependent-interdependent, group-oriented contingencies. Thus the major risk to the adult supervisor stems from misapplication of procedures by peer managers or their failure to apply. The responsible use of peers will proceed as a result of approval from higher supervisory staff, adequate planning and research, and with sufficient monitoring of effects and side effects.

Monitoring of primary outcomes and side effects of peer applications is required, using applied-behavior-analysis methodology to ensure positive outcomes and to help modify substantive negative side effects should they arise. Thus, the use of direct observation, permanent product records, and social-validation measures including peer–client input aptly apply.

Risks to Peer Managers/Tutors

A primary risk is that managers will be put into positions of responsibility without the repertoire to handle specific duties. In most applications, peer managers/tutors have been required to give instructions, record and evaluate peers' performances, give and/or take away point reinforcers, operate token-reinforcement stores, and tutor using educational materials. In some cases, failure of the manager to perform these functions, whether the result of inadequate training or motivation, can result in negative peer-group consequences directed at the manager and even adult supervisors.

The use of punishment procedures by peer managers that potentially result in client "emotional" responding may also be a source of discomfort to the manager. Such procedures as token response cost, without careful preparation of the peer group, consideration of the exact procedures, and the potential group consequences, will likely create situations in which the manager will be unable to perform in the best interests of his clients.

Risks to Clients and/or Peer-Group Members

In some instances peer managers are selected because of their problematic behavior and because of the therapeutic benefits to them resulting from the peer-manager experience. Cowen (1976) reports such a system as a means of maintaining "tuned-out adolescents" in the school setting. In other settings—for example, homes for delinquent youth, classrooms for the emotionally disturbed—peer managers to some extent have particular behavior problems. The obvious risk to clients and peer-group members is that they may in some way learn inappropriate behavior or be coerced or abused by the tutor, in spite of any potential benefits that they might otherwise derive from such an arrangement. This problem, however likely, has not been widely reported in the peer literature.

Warner, Miller, and Cohen (1977) reported concern about the abuse of peer pressure, a side effect of dependent and interdependent group-oriented contingency systems. Specifically, it has been noted that competing teams or groups failing to reach criterion tend to criticize or threaten uncooperative members or losing teams. Greenwood and Hops have noted in this volume that threats, scoldings, and milder forms of peer pressure do occur and probably contribute substantially to the overall effectiveness of these procedures. The major risks appear to be the (1) severity and (2) frequency of peer-pressure events. In Chapter 7 (this volume), we noted that in none of the studies reviewed had peers been physically abused; instead, milder forms of peer pressure appeared to occur, specifically around failure to reach criterion for group reinforcement. Further research and monitoring of peer group-oriented systems must be pursued and the negative side effects minimized.

A third risk area in these systems appears to be the opportunity for cheating and/or collusion between manager and peers or within the peer group. In either case subversion of the contingencies results in antisocial, competing behavior. Without sufficient monitoring, managers may knowingly give points or simply falsify performance records. In interdependent, group-oriented contingencies, strategies may arise wherein the best performers in the group supply low achievers with academic work in order for the group to receive reinforcement. These problems are avoidable by ensuring that responses to fill requirements of the contingency are made within the framework of a monitoring system. In the case of homework and assignment preparation, it may be difficult to verify that clients actually made all of their responses without appropriate procedures, e.g., parent verification.

ESTABLISHING BEHAVIOR-CHANGE GOALS/ WHOSE VALUES?

A major concern with much of behavior technology is with the goals established for change. Who sets the goals? Are the goals established by and with the participation of the client/student or are they established in order to force compliance with the status quo or managerial aspects of the change institution itself? A recent article criticized some frequently selected behavior targets for change—appropriate and inappropriate classroom behavior. These behavioral definitions consistently tended to describe the model child as

> one who stays glued to his seat and desk all day, continually looks at his teacher or test/workbook, does not talk to or in fact, look at other children, does not talk unless asked to by the teacher, hopefully does not laugh or sing (at the wrong time), and assuredly passes silently in halls. (Winett & Winkler, 1972)

Taken as a general summation of behavioral-technology applications in the schools, Winnett and Winkler paint a bleak picture. However, it is clear that teachers and other institutional agents have in many cases pointed specifically to such goals. This fact certainly does not divorce the behavior engineer from responsibility for the changes produced (O'Leary, 1972). As to the value of these kinds of skills, within the context of academic instruction, such responses as attending to tasks or teacher, in-seat, and so on may be related to achievement in the immediate future (Greenwood, Hops, & Walker, 1977; Walker & Hops, 1976a) and functionally related to success in later college or career years. What other responses within other contexts and settings are being pinpointed for change in the school environment? Responding to the Winett and Winkler criticism, O'Leary points to innovative behavioral applications ranging from language training to social interaction in settings ranging from playground to structured tutoring.

Davison and Stuart (1975), describing the application of behavior therapy, point to the characteristic involvement of the client of behavior change in the goal-setting process. "The general goals accepted by most behavior therapists place primary emphasis on the achievement of positive behavioral changes; that is, the acquisition of skills that are positively valued by the society and the client." A second example of client participation in the establishment of change goals is reflected in a recent report from Achievement Place, a behavioral-treatment model for young delinquents. A recent review of 99 rules at Achievement Place indicated that in the boys' opinion they had developed about 50% of them (Fixsen *et al.*, 1973). The focus on *publicly specified behavior-change goals and objectives* is a hallmark of the entire discipline.

Current trends in the selection of behavior targets for change have used social-validation procedures to assess the consensus of clients or community members on the importance of specific behaviors (Kazdin, 1977; Wolf, 1978). Other social-validation procedures have established the importance of behaviors via correlation to other criterion measures. For example, Cobb (1972) demonstrated a correlational relationship between survival skills observed in the classroom setting and standardized achievement-test measures. Greenwood, Walker, Todd, and Hops (1979) established a positive correlation between interaction rates in preschool settings and teachers' rankings of verbal frequency and ratings of social skills and deficiencies. These methods validate behaviors for change.

However, the actual goals established through social validation in any particular application must reflect the values of society, the institutional setting, the persons working in the institutions, the behavior engineer, and the client. Such a process, of course, will remain a changing one as society and institutions change over time. The behavior engineer, however, would seem ethically bound to ensuring that the processes establishing behavior-change goals and values are public and that the participation of the public through social validation is assured.

RIGHTS OF BEHAVIOR-CHANGE CLIENTS

Within the last six years, much activity has occurred in the legal arena in order to determine (1) rights of individuals incarcerated in either penal or mental institutions, and (2) due-process rights of students in the public-education system. For example, the courts have ruled that incarcerated individuals have a constitutionally protected set of civil rights no different from citizens. One major impact of these rulings has been upon the distinction of absolute vs. contingent rights (Davison & Stuart, 1975). In early behavior-modification studies, inmates or patients often were required to "earn" aspects of better living conditions, such as improved sleeping facilities, privacy, and so on, that would be ordinarily provided. Court rulings (Wyatt vs. Stickney)* have required that the basic privileges be offered patients without contingent requirements in order that human dignity be maintained. Although the definition of basic privileges is open to interpretation, the intent of the ruling is clear and requires behavior engineers to become more innovative in the creation and selection of reinforcing events.

*Wyatt vs. Stickney, 344 F. Supp. 373 (m.D. Ala. 1972) (Bryce and Searcy Hospitals).

Similar activity in education has recently ensured students' rights to due process with regard to dismissal and suspension from school. Goss vs. Lopez* affirmed the right of students to due process regarding decisions primarily influencing the individuals's rights to education. The Buckley Amendment† has assured the rights of students to information in personal files maintained by educational institutions and affecting the future affairs of its students. These individual files have traditionally been off-limits to students and families. The concern in this area has been with the inability of the individual to challenge and correct information regarding the individual's behavior while in school. Public Law 94-142 has guaranteed public education to handicapped children and due process to placement decisions in special education.

Increased legal and legislative activities in the area of rights will likely continue to reflect a trend of continued definition of individuals' rights in relationship to the institutions that serve them. Although there is much concern and controversy over these rulings, effects of these decisions will only be apparent over time.

ISSUES OF CONSENT

The right to offer or withhold informed consent to participate in a treatment program or in a research study, although not a new concept, has become an established fact of life in behavioral research (*Ethical Principles*, 1974; *Ethical Standards*, 1972; *Institutional Guide*, 1971). The tenet of informed consent is to allow potential participants to make an "informed" decision concerning participation based upon the "relevant facts" pertaining to risks and benefits of such participation. This process involves the consideration of both physical and psychological risks to a person as a result of participation. Here, as in other aspects of a child's life, the parent is frequently the final arbiter of such a decision.

Protection of human subjects in experimental research reflects the question: Do the benefits to be expected in terms of knowledge and improvement of conditions to be gained by the larger society outweigh the effects of individual exposure to experimental procedures—some perhaps potentially more beneficial than others (Gray, 1975)? Most universities and institutions have formed research-review committees charged with the responsibility of insuring informed consent and protection of subjects' rights in medical and behavioral research. Their activities

*Goss vs. Lopez, 95 S. Ct. 729 (1975).
†Family Education Rights and Privacy Act, Federal Register, January 6, 1975.

have been in response to DHEW guidelines for the protection of human subjects drafted in 1971 (Gray, 1975, p. 13; *Institutional Guide,* 1971).

Evaluative research surely must be carried out if the best possible treatment programs are to be determined and are to be available to persons requiring them. Yet in order to scientifically determine the valid treatment procedure, experimentation may require subjects to delay or even forgo receipt of treatment—for instance, in the case of placebo control groups (O'Leary & Borkovic, 1978).

CONSENT AND BEHAVIORAL CONTRACTS

Behavior-analysis procedures in some aspects have been in the forefront of informed consent, as behavioral-contracting procedures have typically specified the participation requirements, change goals, consequences, and so on to the clients of behavior change. In this manner, persons entering behavioral-change programs have done so in a manner approaching the principle of informed consent required in behavioral research. An example of this approach actually involving children in the school setting, called CLASS (Hops, Beickel & Walker, 1975), required the child to sign a contract in conjunction with the teacher, a program consultant, and the child's parents after the major aspects of the program had been reviewed by all parties.

INFORMED CONSENT FOR RESEARCH

The use of informed consent in peer change programs and research becomes somewhat complex, as it may be difficult to pinpoint whom the targets of change may be. In some cases, the adult therapist or teacher may be teaching a peer manager to deliver specific instructions, rewards, and so on to student groups who are working with academic materials during a reading-instructional period. In a second situation, one child may be directly involved in a program to increase his social interaction with other siblings in a foster-home setting. The siblings are involved, as they have been told (1) that positive social interactions with the target child earns him tokens, and (2) that when he has earned 25 tokens, an activity will be made available to all of the children. In both examples, peers are involved as change agents; however, in the first case, specific skills and roles are being taught to the peer teacher whereas in the second case, simple involvement in the reward potentially increases the frequency of peer interaction with the target subject. The question becomes, "From whom is informed consent required?" Clearly, in the first case, students are subjects of treatment in the traditional sense, but applied by the peer manager. However, what of the peer-change agent? An analogous question might be, "When adults take on therapeutic roles directing change to children, is informed consent required of the adult?" If research is clearly the objective of arranging these procedures, then informed consent should be required at all levels—peer, teacher, and students. If therapeutic or educational benefit is the initiating reason, the behavioral-contracting approach would be strongly recommended to ensure clear communication of purposes, responsibilities, and consequences among the peer teacher, the adult supervisor, and the students.

The problem with establishing informed-consent procedures, of course, is the communication of the essential facts about the project which allows the participant and their parent to make an informed decision. Researchers are typically prone to provide the least amount of information possible for such a decision so as not to limit participation or interfere with the behavior under study (Gray, 1975, p. 4).

Researchers are ultimately required to have their work reviewed and approved by committees for the protection of human subjects. These committees are typically comprised of university, local, and community personnel who review procedures to determine risks and benefits and to ensure that participants are provided the opportunity to make informed decisions about participation.

Several kinds of consent procedures have been suggested to which the reader is referred (N. J. Crowder & Malenfant, 1975; Davison & Stuart, 1975). These procedures require more disclosure about research procedure as the risks to human subjects are demonstrated to increase. For instance, a subject considering participation in an observational study of supermarket traffic patterns might be required to sign a consent form with only minimal explanation. In contrast, a subject participating in a study involving physical discomfort (e.g., food deprivation) may be required to sign a consent letter in the presence of a witness not involved in the research, following full disclosure of the experimental procedures to be used (Davison & Stuart, 1975).

Issues of Competency

The issue of competency is related to the ability of peer change agents to in fact produce *effective* and *desirable* changes. However, prior to considering the competency of peer change agents, an examination of adult-competency issues must be made.

As previously mentioned, there is a clear awareness among behavioral practitioners that consumers are demanding a higher level of professionalism for behavior-change agents. Within the profession, practitioners are concerned with protecting themselves and the public from malpractice and even fraudulent activities carried out in the name of "behavior modification." Furthermore, behavioral practitioners are very much aware that traditional certification in psychology (e.g., clinical psychology) does not reliably discriminate among persons trained in the use of behavioral technology. The response to these concerns has been the consideration of alternatives ranging from certification of individuals (Sajwaj, 1977, p. 534), to certification of training programs at the university level, to certification of behavior-modification procedures (Michael, 1972). This is an effort to establish criteria for decisions concerned with (1) hiring personnel, (2) selection of the right change agent for personal therapy, and (3) cases of alleged malpractice abuse and/or professional misconduct. It is no longer possible for practitioners to be recognized as competent simply through the reputation of the person with whom they took their training.

COMPETENCIES OF BEHAVIOR ANALYSTS

Active consideration of these issues is currently taking place in the major associations of behavioral practice—AABT, APA, and so on. In addition, some innovative work (Sulzer-Azaroff, Thaw, & Thomas, 1974) is being done in task-analyzing competencies for behavior modifiers. Perhaps most relevant in this effort has been the concept of various competency levels conceivably related to job position (Sajwaj, 1977), as opposed to the common years-of-experience criterion so frequently used. For example, this division of labor ranges from the behavior analyst at the highest level, to the behavior cotechnician at the lowest level. The behavior analyst is seen as the conceptualizer, supervisor, and evaluator, whereas the behavior cotechnician carries out day-to-day operations of projects and programs. At the highest level many specific competencies were listed, whereas at the lowest level only one major area was noted. At the cotechnician level, skills related primarily to behavior observation and measurement are required. Areas that were specifically rejected for the cotechnicians were skills in administration, research design, training, consulting, and communications. Other work involving training of behavior modifiers at what might be viewed as the intermediate and low levels of the Sulzer-Azaroff competency scheme has included, for example, competency-based teacher-education programs. In a recent article (Walker, Hops, & Greenwood, 1976), two behavior-change programs were discussed in terms of the competencies required by teachers and program consultants to implement programs in classroom settings. The program consultants trained the teachers in specific skills—use of reinforcers, instructions, behavior recording, and so on; the teachers then implement the program with their children. Change in child behavior is used as the final validation criterion for the teacher and consultant competencies. These last two efforts appear most promising in developing competent professionals at the adult level. Most interesting is that both efforts reflect the application of behavior technology to the behavior of its professionals.

Other approaches in developed behavioral programs have been to create specific job descriptions with competencies and certification requirements. Achievement Place, for example, certifies teaching parents following their training and practical experience in operating a home (Baron, Maloney, & Phillips, 1979). Similarly, the Responsive Parenting Program certifies parent-workshop leaders after completion of training requirements and successful implementation of behavior-change projects in the home (Clark-Hall, 1977).

These procedures have been developed primarily in response to pressures for dissemination and replication of programs and as an attempt to ensure quality control of new programs. Paine (1979) has discussed the concept of program or procedure drift occurring in standardized behavioral programs. *Drift* is a variable describing innovation and/or deviance from proscribed application, depending upon one's point of view. This variable may explain program failure as social agents deviate from standardized, validated procedures for operating programs. The importance of monitoring program drift and agent competency appears important to both development of behavioral programs and support of ethical issues of competency.

COMPETENCIES AND PEER APPLICATIONS

Given the controversial and amorphous state of affairs of adult-competency requirements, is it possible to develop a case for competency of peer change agents? A reasonable point of departure would be to consider (1) the roles in which peers may be expected to function, and (2) the literature in which attempts have been made to train peers to use behavioral procedures. In relation to the latter consideration, the range of applications present in the literature with regard to peer characteristics (e.g., age, IQ, behavioral abnormalities, etc.) would be of interest. Similarly, the behavior-change roles that peers have been demonstrated to be capable of acquiring and the degree of training needed for them to acquire effective skills should be reviewed. These aspects of the peer-change literature appear useful in establishing what peers can effectively be taught to do and under what select conditions.

Peer Change Roles

Most of the jobs which peer change agents will be doing, though perhaps very complex in nature, will require competencies in behavior analysis probably no more involved than those of the "cotechnician" as described by Sulzer-Azaroff et al. (1974). Specifically, these skills will include elements of behavioral observation/record keeping/graphing, contingently, dispensing and removing token reinforcers, and presenting academic materials and issuing instructions of various kinds related to the task at hand. At the minimum level, peers may simply be involved in sharing of a group consequence earned by a classmate or simply be asked to play a game with or talk to a fellow classmate. Most peer interventions can be conceptualized as requiring a supervisory and training component as an essential ingredient handled by at least an adult cotechnician or a higher-skilled adult. As previously discussed, this adult will design the tasks to be performed by the peer, train the responses, monitor responding, and provide consequences to establish the responding at a proficient and competent level. The majority of training of peer managers to date has involved specific performance tasks as opposed to the teaching of behavioral principles, as would occur in the case of the adult behavior analyst. As a rule, peer managers are only taught skills sufficient to meet the specific task at hand. Only in a few instances have peers been taught behavioral principles in a general cognitive sense (N. J. Crowder, 1974; Malenfant et al., 1975).

A secondary characteristic of peer management is that it is usually a part-time job. In a classroom setting, tutoring is performed during an instructional session—for instance, reading for 35 min. Similarly, on a token-economy ward, a patient store clerk will only operate the store for trade-ins during two 20-min sessions a day, one in the morning and the second in the afternoon.

Peer Change Roles Reviewed

As reviewed in earlier chapters, the productive use of peers as educational tutors is a growing area of application. For example, Surratt (1969) trained a fifth-grade boy to record and monitor the academic work sessions of first-grade students. Dineen et al. (1977) also studied peer-tutoring effects. Similarly, Greenwood et al. (1974) taught four initially unmanageable students in a special school for emotionally disturbed children, nine to 12 years old, to give and take away points contingent upon the correct study behavior of student peers over a four-month period without detriment to student mathematics achievement. Starlin (1971), Csapo (1972), and Fixsen, Phillips, and Wolf (1972) have reported use of child peers to report, record, and graph specific behaviors. These peer recorders ranged in age from first-grade students (Starlin, 1971) to predelinquents, ages 12–16 (Fixsen et al., 1972). Wahler (1967) taught members of a preschool peer group, aged five to six, to selectively ignore specific behaviors of peers with whom they were playing a game using instructions and role-playing techniques. Wiesen, Hartley, Richardson, and Roske (1967) demonstrated that even severely retarded students (five to nine years) could learn to dispense candy reinforcers to peers following training procedures. Although these studies have demonstrated rather complex peer performance in which active training of the peer managers was required in addition to monitoring of performance over time, other studies have reported successful use of peer tutors and peer consequences with only simple instructions and involvement in group-oriented contingency arrangements. For example, in a study by Harris, Sherman, Henderson, and Harris (1972), "the teacher simply asked the students to help each other learn the words." Tutoring in this fashion was found to produce increased spelling performance compared to a free-study period of the same length. The classic study by Evans and Oswalt (1968) enlisted the reinforcing potential of the peer group by establishing a performance contingency via instructions to the class. If a specific student reached criterion, a reinforcer was earned but shared by the entire class.

These examples and those in preceding chapters are suggestive of the wide range of effective peer-group behavior-change applications across client populations, ages, and types of peer-change skills required. The skepticism of many concerning peer behavior change hinges on arguments that even if they are competent in the use of behavior procedures, peer change agents are simply not adults and subject to adult consequences in the form of legal or professional sanctions. As such, they simply cannot be trusted to use behavioral procedures. From this point of view, the potential for harm, irresponsibility, and misuse is clearly apparent. Will peers not use the techniques for their own ends? The control of competence and/or abuse, as previously discussed, can only be achieved through procedures designed to ensure accountability.

Issues of Accountability

Accountability in behavior technology, with or without peers as interventionists, is characterized by (1) pinpointing specific behavioral target behaviors of a socially or educationally relevant nature, (2) collecting data to ascertain the effects of the procedures used to achieve these goals, and (3) using experimental design to demonstrate a causal relationship between the procedures used and the changes that occurred (Baer et al., 1968). As previously pointed out, the clients of behavior change may actually participate in the determination of behavioral goals to be obtained (Davison & Stuart, 1975; Fixsen et al., 1973).

Procedures for reviewing the work of peer change agents and monitoring their application *must be employed* to ensure that the desired changes are in fact being produced.

> One feature of the project that was crucial to the success of the program contributing to the improved quality of the tutor's performance was the monitoring of the tutoring sessions. Tutoring behaviors were monitored daily, and the tutors were provided with regular feedback concerning the adequacy of their teaching responses. A less frequent schedule or some daily sampling procedure might be adequate to obtain the quality of teaching responses necessary to maintain quality student performance; however, these possibilities do need to be explored if the tutoring program is to be adapted to more general use. (Davis, 1972)

The manipulation of consequences for correct peer change behaviors in many cases is also required (Greenwood *et al.*, 1974). This is particularly important when the change agents are in fact learning these roles as a part of an overall therapeutic program in which they are participating. Subversion of the best program by delinquent or mental-patient populations is a simple matter unless the appropriate checks and consequences have been designed into the system to control them. Kale, Zlutnick, and Hopkins (1975) reported that, in a mental-ward token economy with patients serving as paymasters, store clerks, data collectors, and so on, (1) an objective determination of the extent helpers carry out responsibilities to prevent cheating and stealing, as well as (2) the use of contingent rewards and punishments in order to improve their responsibilities was required to maintain desired behavior in both peer change agents and ward patients. Systems for ensuring accountable use of peer change agents must be considered as a major element for successful application.

Issues Related to Adult Employment Contracts

In many cases, peer change agents will be taught to assume functions for which the adult teacher or therapist may in fact, by contract, be paid to provide. By means of behavioral procedures, patients and students have learned to assume these new role functions as tutors, store clerks, data collectors, work-group managers, supervisors, and so on. Although these kinds of changes approach the ideal in terms of therapeutic benefit and normalization of behavior repertoires for many patients, persons considering peer behavior-change programs should be aware of the potential for conflict in this area. Questions to be asked in such cases may be, "Who is to be payed for these services?" or "Now that the patients are handling these grounds-maintenance chores, should they be paid?" or "What are you as a behavior engineer now doing?" Care must be taken to discriminate among therapeutic gains, maintenance of the institution, and the job description of the adult cotechnician and professional behavior engineer.

GUIDELINES FOR THE RESPONSIBLE AND ETHICAL USE OF BEHAVIORAL TECHNOLOGY

A number of authors have suggested or opposed guidelines for governing ethical practice of behavior technology (N. J. Crowder & Malenfant, 1975; Davison & Stuart, 1975; Sajwaj, 1977; Stolz, 1977) regarding the various issues discussed within this chapter. The reader is referred to these sources for additional information. In this chapter, for the purpose of organizing these issues with respect to peer applications, guidelines will be organized into three major areas of consideration: (1) guidelines for procedures, (2) guidelines for subjects, and (3) guidelines for peer change agents.

GUIDELINES FOR PROCEDURES

In this author's opinion, the idea of "certification" of procedures in behavioral technology allows the institution to best manage the application of behavior technology in a highly responsible manner. Although it is discussed in the context of national professional certification, such a process certainly has applications within the local institution—the school, treatment center, or family unit. Establishment of *procedure approval* would require the creation of a committee of professionals and subject-population advocates (e.g., parents) that could consider the benefits and risks of new procedures when applied to the population under consideration. Second, the committee would consider the procedural aspects of each particular technique as it would be applied in a particular setting. Third, the consideration of data in the professional literature, data collected in the setting, and the current public attitudes toward a given procedure could be used to protect against misuse and abuse. Procedures regarded as "severe treatment procedures" (Sajwaj, 1977) could be more readily identified and their use carefully controlled.

The following questions could be considered as representing the scope of such a committee:

(1) What evidence is available supporting the procedure as effective or beneficial?
(2) How is it used?
(3) What is known about generalization and maintenance of effects produced?

(4) What staff training is required?
(5) Is it cost-effective?
(6) What has been the professional and public reaction to the procedure?
(7) Is it likely that parental permission would be freely given for such a procedure?
(8) In what form would parental permission be obtained?
(9) Would community support be available for such a procedure?
(10) How intrusive is the procedure on the life space of other subjects within the same environment?
(11) How will it fit into the overall therapeutic program for the subject?
(12) Are there side effects resulting from use of the procedure?
(13) How would the procedure be evaluated when used in our institution?
(14) Is the procedure "experimental," "standard practice," or "severe"?
(15) Under what conditions should it not be used?

Perhaps the basic issue in this procedure-review process would be consideration of the risk–benefit ratio. For example, in the case of head-banging behavior in a young child, mild electric shock could be administered contingently as part of a treatment to eliminate this behavior. Although this is obviously an undesirable aversive procedure when contrasted with other possible procedures (e.g., extinction, restraint, etc.), it becomes clear reviewing the literature that such a procedure could likely be beneficial. In fact, it could be argued that the committee was ethically amiss if it failed to recommend such a procedure in light of present attitudes and established practices.

The same electric-shock procedure applied to, say, out-of-seat behavior in a classroom setting, when reviewed within the same context, would undoubtedly be seen as extreme and inappropriate in light of alternative, more widely used and accepted procedures—for example, positive reinforcement of in-seat and ignoring out-of-seat behavior.

The next consideration would be application of the procedure in the treatment process itself. For example, when is it to be applied, to what behavior, for how long, how is it to be evaluated, and when is it to be discontinued? These considerations, although critically related to the effectiveness of the program, are also related to responsible usage by adult change agents. Certification of a procedure should entail not only approval of essential ingredients but also the salient features of its application and removal during the treatment process.

A word of caution is in order. It should be clearly established that such a committee should be responsive to "data." The goal of the committee should be to establish an understanding of a given procedure in light of standard practice as reflected in the research and clinical literature, and in the form of evaluation data within the institution itself. The role of such a committee should be the examination of procedures from a "knowledgeable" position. The committee should not exist to suppress creative or experimental procedures, but rather to ensure that they are responsibly planned and evaluated and that the potential for benefit outweighs the risks involved.

GUIDELINES FOR SUBJECTS

Guidelines for subjects of behavioral technology focus upon the subject's rights to secure the best possible treatment presently available. The following guidelines should help establish a case for the reasonable and ethical use of behavior technology in most settings from the subject's or parent's point of view. These guidelines, although suggestive, are in no way exhaustive.

(1) A written program detailing the behavior-change goals, the procedures to be used, and the evaluation method to determine progress should be prepared for each individual client.

(2) A behavioral program should have clearly stated behavior-change goals established with the participation of the client, the client's parents, and the consensual agreement of those immediately responsible for the care and education of the client.

(3) Evaluation procedures should be designed to yield an accountable record of the participant's performance under the program.

(4) Procedures are designed to generalize the changes to other appropriate settings, and/or procedures for removal are designed to generalize the change to "normal" environmental conditions of behavioral control.

(5) Procedures involving "severe" methods, for example, physical discomfort or deprivation, have been institutionally reviewed indicating that the risks appear to be outweighed by the potential benefits to the client. The principle of minimum intervention to produce the desired effect should be the guideline.

(6) Subject and parental permission and participation in development of the treatment plan are obtained.

(7) Termination or change of procedures should immediately follow when evaluation data have indicated that procedures have not been effective with the client. Procedures should not simply persist indefinitely.

GUIDELINES FOR PEER CHANGE AGENTS

The guidelines for peer change agents are designed to ensure that the peer has been "informed" regarding the nature of his or her role and the foreseeable consequences, both positive and negative, that would necessarily result from participation. These items, depending on specifics, can be handled in the form of instructions to a peer group, for example, or in a behavioral contract with a particular peer who will assume a major role.

(1) The peer(s) have been informed about their role and its relationship to the goals of the adult or institution.
(2) The peer(s) have been informed of the responses required of them, when they are to occur, and when they are to terminate.
(3) The peer(s) have had an opportunity to accept or reject participation before and during the procedure.
(4) The planned and unplanned consequences of peer participation have been presented.
(5) The peer(s) are aware of how they will be evaluated or monitored during performance of their responsibilities.
(6) Promotion opportunities to other roles, consequences, and so on for quality performance of responsibilities have been clarified.
(7) Parental permission has been secured.

GUIDELINES RECONSIDERED

It has been the author's intent to represent, in the guidelines, the institutional burden for initiating ethical considerations in the form of a committee to review behavioral procedure and the subject's right to secure the best behavioral program possible. Tightly interwoven are the additional considerations required to inform a subject in the role of peer change agent. It can be seen that the two perspectives are highly interrelated and tend to ensure that (1) procedures have been determined to be both responsible and effective, and (2) the subject is receiving the best possible treatment available within the institutional setting.

SUMMARY

The purpose of this chapter has been to examine some of the current issues related to the ethical application of behavior technology. These issues were examined in relation to children or peer groups in the role of the behavior-change agent. To establish clarification of general issues related to behavior technology, commonly used terminology was defined to allow accurate discrimination among the various areas of professional practice and popular aspects—mind control, chemotherapy, common sense, and so on—that are frequently and incorrectly associated with behavior technology. Next, the major issues related to ethical practice were reviewed. Issues of informed consent were discussed and related to the involvement of children for purposes of research and/or treatment interventions for planned behavior change. The issue of peer-manager competency was reviewed by sampling the literature to define the range of peer involvement, peer-manager populations, ages, and the scope of training required to establish peer change programs in various settings. The problem of peer behavior-change accountability was considered to result in the clear need for monitoring systems and the use of contingencies to establish and maintain effective peer responding. The final topic in this section considered the possible conflict of established roles and pay resulting from the assumption of teaching or therapeutic duties by peers. The chapter concluded with a proposed set of guidelines intended to assist persons interested in establishing peer change-agent programs in such a manner as to be ethically and responsibly based.

ACKNOWLEDGMENTS

The author acknowledges the assistance of Carmen Root in the typing and preparation of this manuscript.

SUGGESTED READING LIST

Begelman, D. A. Ethical and legal issues of behavior modification. In M. Hersen, R. M. Eisler, & P. M. Miller (Eds.), *Progress in Behavior Modification.* New York: Academic Press, 1975, pp. 159–186.

Bendix, S. Drug modification of behavior: A formal chemical violence against children? *Journal of Clinical Child Psychology,* 1973, 2 (3), 17–19.

Davison, G. C., & Stuart, R. B. Behavior therapy and civil liberties. *American Psychologist,* 1975, 30(7), 755–763.

Ethical principles in the conduct of research with human participants. Washington: American Psychological Association, 1974.

Ethical Standards of Psychologists. Washington: American Psychological Association, 1972.

Martin, R. *Legal challenges to behavior modification.* Champaign, Ill.: Research Press, 1975.

Michael, J. Panel discussion: Training behavior modifiers. In G. Semb (Ed.), *Behavior analysis and education—1972..* Lawrence: University of Kansas, Department of Human Development, 1972, pp. 26–34.

Robinson, D. N. Harm, offense and nuisance: Some first steps in the establishment of an ethics of treatment. *American Psychologist,* 1974, 29, 233–238.

Skinner, B. F. *Science and human behavior.* New York: Macmillan, 1953.

Skinner, B. F. *Beyond freedom and dignity.* New York: Knopf, 1971.

Wood, W. S. *Issues in evaluating behavior modifications: Proceedings of the first Drake conference on professional issues in behavior analysis.* Champaign, Ill.: Research Press, 1974.

Reference Notes

Crowder, N. J., & Malenfant, L. *The child as behavior analyst: Clinical, research and ethical considerations.* Paper presented at the 9th annual meeting of the Association for the Advancement of Behavior Therapy, San Francisco, December 1975.

Patterson, G. R., Ebner, M., & Shaw, D. *Efficient intervention in the school setting for the severely disruptive child.* Monograph 1. *Modifying deviant social behaviors in various classroom settings.* Eugene: Department of Special Education, University of Oregon, 1969.

Canton, N. L., & Gelfand, D. M. *Effects of responsiveness and sex of children on adults' behavior.* Paper presented at the Western Psychological Association Convention, Sacramento, April 1975.

Crowder, N. J. *Training elementary school children in the application of principles and techniques of behavior modification.* Unpublished doctoral dissertation, University of Kansas, 1974.

Malenfant, L., Crowder, J., Faison, D., & Hall, R. V. *Teaching applied behavior analysis to high school students.* Paper presented at the 9th annual convention of the Association for the Advancement of Behavior Therapy, San Francisco, December 1975.

Hops, H., Beickel, S. L., & Walker, H. M. *Contingencies for learning academic and social skills (CLASS): Manual for consultants.* Center at Oregon for Research in the Behavioral Education of the Handicapped, University of Oregon, 1975.

Baron, R., Maloney, K., & Phillips, E. Dissemination of the teaching–family group home model. In S. Paine (Chair), *Issues in the dissemination of standardized behavioral programs.* Symposium presented at the 5th annual convention of the Association for Behavior Analysis, Dearborn, Michigan, June 1979.

Paine, S. *Issues in the dissemination of standardized behavioral programs.* Symposium presented at the 5th annual convention of the Association for Behavior Analysis, Dearborn, Michigan, June 1979.

References

Ayllon, T., & Azrin, N. H. *The token economy: A motivational system for therapy and rehabilitation.* New York: Appleton-Century-Crofts, 1968.

Ayllon, T., Layman, D., & Kandel, H. J. A behavioral and educational alternative to drug control of hyperactive children. *Journal of Applied Behavior Analysis,* 1975, *8,* 137–146.

Azrin, N. H., & Foxx, R. M. *Toilet training in less than a day.* New York: Simon & Schuster, 1974.

Baer, D., Wolf, M., & Risley, T. Some current dimensions of applied behavior analysis. *Journal of Applied Behavior Analysis,* 1968, *1,* 91–97.

Becker, W. C. *Parents are teachers: A child management program.* Champaign, Ill.: Research Press, 1971.

Becker, W. C. Behavior analysis and education. In G. Semb (Ed.), *Behavior analysis and education.* Lawrence: University of Kansas, Department of Human Development, 1972.

Becker, W. C., Engelmann, S., & Thomas, D. R. *Teaching: A course in applied psychology.* Chicago: Science Research Associates, 1971.

Begelman, D. A. Ethical and legal issues of behavior modification. In M. Hersen, R. M. Eisler, & P. M. Miller (Eds.), *Progress in behavior modification.* New York: Academic Press, 1975.

Bendix, S. Drug modification of behavior: A formal chemical violence against children? *Journal of Clinical Child Psychology,* 1973, *2*(3), 17–19.

Buehler, R. E., Patterson, G. R., & Furniss, J. M. The reinforcement of behavior in institutional settings. *Behavior Research and Therapy,* 1966, *4,* 157–167.

Clark-Hall, M. *Responsive parenting program*. Lawrence, Kansas: H & H Enterprises, 1977.

Cobb, J. A. Relationship of discrete classroom behaviors to fourth-grade academic achievement. *Journal of Educational Psychology*, 1972, *63*, 74–80.

Cowen, E. L. Nonprofessional human-service helping programs for young children. In V. L. Allen (Ed.), *Children as teachers*. New York: Academic Press, 1976, pp. 131–148.

Csapo, M. Peer models reverse the "one bad apple spoils the barrel" theory. *Teaching Exceptional Children*, 1972, *5*, 20–24.

Davis, M. Effects of having one remedial student tutor another remedial student. In G. Semb (Ed.), *Behavioral analysis and education*. Lawrence: University of Kansas, Department of Human Development, 1972.

Davison, G. C., & Stuart, R. B. Behavior therapy and civil liberties. *American Psychologist*, 1975, *30*, 755–763.

Dineen, J. P., Clark, H. B., & Risley, T. R. Peer tutoring among elementary students: Educational benefits to the tutor. *Journal of Applied Behavior Analysis*, 1977, *10*, 231–238.

Ethical principles in the conduct of research with human participants. Washington, D.C.: American Psychological Association, 1974.

Ethical standards of psychologists. Washington, D.C.: American Psychological Association, 1972.

Evans, G. W., and Oswalt, G. L. Acceleration of academic progress through the manipulation of peer influence. *Behavior Research and Therapy*, 1968, *6*, 189–195.

Fawcett, S. B., & Fletcher, R. K. Community applications of instructional technology: Teaching writers of instructional packages. *Journal of Applied Behavior Analysis*, 1977, *10*, 739.

Fixsen, D. L., Phillips, E. L., & Wolf, M. M. Achievement Place: The reliability of self-reporting and peer-reporting and their effects on behavior. *Journal of Applied Behavior Analysis*, 1972, *5*, 19–30.

Fixsen, D. L., Phillips, E. L., & Wolf, M. M. Achievement Place: Experiments in self-government with predelinquents. *Journal of Applied Behavior Analysis*, 1973, *6*, 31–47.

Goodall, K. Shapers at work. *Psychology Today*, 1972, *6*(6), 53–138.

Graubard, P. S., Rosenberg, H., & Miller M. B. Student applications of behavior modification to teachers and environments or ecological approaches to social deviance. In E. A. Ramp & B. L. Hopkins (Eds.), *A new direction for education: Behavior analysis—1971*. (Vol. 1) Lawrence: University of Kansas, 1971.

Gray, B. H. *Human subjects in medical experimentation: A sociological study of the conduct of clinical research*. New York: Wiley, 1975.

Greenwood, C. R., Sloane, H. M., Jr., & Baskin, A. Training elementary aged peer-behavior managers to control small group programmed mathematics. *Journal of Applied Behavior Analysis*, 1974, *7*, 103–114.

Greenwood, C. R., Hops, H., & Walker, H. M. The program for academic survival skills (PASS): Effects on student behavior and achievement. *Journal of School Psychology*, 1977, *15*, 25–35.

Greenwood, C. R., Hops, H., Walker, H. M., Guild, J. J., Young, K. R., Keleman, K. S., & Willardson, M. Standardized classroom management program: Social validation and replication studies in Utah and Oregon. *Journal of Applied Behavior Analysis*, 1979, *12*, 235–253.

Greenwood, C. R., Walker, H. M., Todd, N. M., & Hops, H. Selecting a cost-effective screening measure for the assessment of preschool social withdrawal. *Journal of Applied Behavior Analysis*, 1979, *12*, 639–652.

Guess, P. A functional analysis of receptive language and productive speech: Acquisition of the plural morpheme. *Journal of Applied Behavior Analysis*, 1969, *2*, 55–64.

Hamblin, R. L., Hathaway, C., & Wodarski, J. Group contingencies, peer tutoring, and accelerating academic achievement. In E.A. Ramp & B. L. Hopkins (Eds.), *A new direction for education: Behavior analysis–1971*. (Vol. 1). Lawrence: University of Kansas, 1971.

Hare-Mustin, R. T., Marecek, J., Kaplan, A. G., & Liss-Levinson, N. Rights of clients, responsibilities of therapists. *American Psychologist*, 1979, *34*(1), 3–16.

Harris, V. W., Sherman, J. A., Henderson, D. G., & Harris, M. A. Effects of peer tutoring on the spelling performance of elementary classroom students. In G. Semb (Ed.), *Behavior analysis and education*. Lawrence: University of Kansas, Department of Human Development, 1972.

Hentoff, N. The drugged classroom. *Evergreen Review*, December, 1970, 6–11.

Hilts, P. J. *Behavior Mod*. New York: Harper's Magazine Press, 1974.

Homme, L., Baca, P. E., Cottingham, L., & Homme A. What behavioral engineering is. In R. Ulrich, T. Stachnik, & J. Mabry (Eds.), *Control of human behavior: From cure to prevention* (Vol. 2). Glenview, Ill.: Scott, Foresman, 1970.

Hopkins, B. L. Behavioral competencies for evaluation of behavior modifiers: A response. In W. S. Wood (Ed.), *Issues in evaluating behavior modification: Proceedings of the first Drake conference on professional issues in behavior analysis*. Champaign, Ill.: Research Press, 1975.

Huxley, A. *Brave new world*. New York: Harper & Row, 1946.

Hyman, I., & Schreiber, K. Selected concepts and practices of child advocacy in school psychology. *Psychology in the schools*, 1975, *12*(1), 50–58.

Institutional guide to DHEW policy on protection of human subjects. Washington, D.C.: U.S. Department of Health, Education and Welfare, 1971.

Johnson, M., & Bailey, J. S. Cross-age tutoring: Fifth graders as arithmetic tutors for kindergarten children. *Journal of Applied Behavior Analysis*, 1974, *7*, 223–232.

Kale, R. J., Zlutnick, S., & Hopkins, B. L. *Patient contributions to a therapeutic environment*. Kalamazoo: Michigan Mental Health Research Bulletin, 1968.

Katz, J. *Experimentation with human beings: The authority of the investigator, subject, professions and state in the human experimentation process*. New York: Russell Sage Foundation, 1972.

Kazdin, A. E. Assessing the clinical or applied importance of behavior change through social validation. *Behavior Modification*, 1977, *1*, 427–452.

Keogh, B. K. Hyperactivity and training disorders: Review and speculations. *Exceptional Children*, 1971, *38*, 101–109.

Krasner, L. Behavior modification: Ethical issues and future trends. In H. Leitenberg (Ed.), *Handbook of behavior modification and behavior therapy*. Englewood Cliffs, N.J.: Prentice-Hall, 1976.

Krasner, L., & Ullmann, L. P. *Research in behavior modification: New developments and implications*. New York: Holt, Rinehart & Winston, 1965.

Krippner, S., Silverman, R., Cavallo, M., & Healy, M. Stimulant drugs and hyperkinesis: A question of diagnosis. *Academic Therapy*, 1973, *8*, 261–269.

Ladd, E. T. Pills for classroom peace? *Saturday Review*, November 21, 1970, 66–83.

Liberman, R. P., Teigen, J., Patterson, R., & Baker, V. Reducing delusional speech in chronic, paranoid schizophrenics. *Journal of Applied Behavior Analysis*, 1973, *6*, 57–64.

Lovaas, O. I. *The autistic child: Language development through behavior modification*. New York: Wiley, 1977.

Lovaas, O. I., Freitas, L., Nelson, K., & Whalen, C. The establishment of imitation and its use for the development of complex behavior in schizophrenic children. In O. I. Lovaas & B. D. Bucher (Eds.), *Perspectives in behavior modification with deviant children*. Englewood Cliffs, N.J.: Prentice-Hall, 1974.

Lovitt, P., Lovitt, T. C., Eaton, M., & Kirkwood, M. The deceleration of inappropriate comments by a natural consequence. *Journal of School Psychology*, 1973, *11*, 149–156.

Martin, R. *Legal challenges to behavior modification*. Champaign, Ill.: Research Press, 1975.

Mathews, R. M., & Fawcett, S. B. Community applications of instructional technology: Training low income proctors. *Journal of Applied Behavior Analysis*, 1977, *10*, 747.

May, J. G., Risley, T. R., Twardosz, S., Friedman, P., Bijou, S. W., & Wexler, D. Guidelines for the use of behavioral procedures in state programs for retarded persons. *M. R. Research*, 1975, 1.

McCarty, T. Griffin, S., Apolloni, T., & Shores, R. E. Increased peer-tutoring with group-oriented contingencies for arithmetic performance in behavior-disordered adolescents. *Journal of Applied Behavior Analysis*, 1977, 10, 313.

Michael, J. Panel discussion: Training behavior modifiers. In G. Semb (Ed.), *Behavior analysis and education*. Lawrence: University of Kansas, Department of Human Development, 1972.

Millenson, J. R. *Principles of behavior analysis*. New York: Macmillan, 1967.

Nelson, C. M., Worell, J., & Polsgrove, L. Behaviorally disordered peers as contingency managers. *Behavior Therapy*, 1973, 4, 270–276.

O'Leary, K. D. Behavior modification in the classroom: A rejoinder to Winett and Winkler. *Journal of Applied Behavior Analysis*, 1972, 5, 505–511.

O'Leary, K. D., & Borkovec, T. D. Conceptual, methodological, and ethical problems of placebo groups in psychotherapy research. *American Psychologist*, 1978, 33(9), 821–830.

Orwell, G. *1984*. New York: Harcourt, Brace, 1949.

Packard, R. G. The control of "classroom attention": A group contingency for complex behavior. *Journal of Applied Behavior Analysis*, 1970, 3, 13–28.

Patterson, G. R. *Families: Application of social learning to family life*. Champaign, Ill.: Research Press, 1971.

Patterson, G. R. The aggressive child: Victim and architect of a coercive system. In L. A. Hamerlynck, L. C. Handy, & E. J. Mash (Eds.), *Behavior modification and families*. I. *Theory and research*. II. *Applications and development*. New York: Brunner/Mazel, 1975.

Phillips, E. L., Phillips, E. A., Wolf, M. M., & Fixsen, D. L. Achievement Place: Development of the elected manager system. *Journal of Applied Behavior Analysis*, 1973, 6, 541–561.

Pierce, C. H., & Risley, T. R. Improving the job performance of Neighborhood Youth Corps aides in an urban recreation center. *Journal of Applied Behavior Analysis*, 1974, 7, 207–216.

Premack, D. Toward empirical behavior laws. I. Positive reinforcement. *Psychological Review*, 1959, 66, 219–233.

Renne, C. M., & Creer, T. L. Training children with asthma to use inhalation therapy equipment. *Journal of Applied Behavior Analysis*, 1976, 9, 1–12.

Robinson, D. N. Harm, offense and nuisance: Some first steps in the establishment of an ethics of treatment. *American Psychologist*, 1974, 29, 233–238.

Sajwaj, T. Issues and implications of establishing guidelines for the use of behavioral techniques. *Journal of Applied Behavior Analysis*, 1977, 10, 531–540.

Shore, M. F. Legislation, advocacy, and the rights of children and youth. *American Psychologist*, 1979, 34(10), 1017–1019.

Sidman, M. *Tactics of scientific research*. New York: Basic Books, 1960.

Skinner, B. F. *The behavior of organisms*. New York: Appleton-Century-Crofts, 1938.

Skinner, B. F. *Walden two*. New York: Macmillan, 1948.

Skinner, B. F. *Science and human behavior*. New York: Macmillan, 1953.

Skinner, B. F. The design of cultures. In R. Ulrich, T. Stachnik, & J. Mabry (Eds.), *Control of human behavior*. Glenview, Ill.: Scott, Foresman, 1966.(a)

Skinner, B. F. Freedom and the control of men. In R. Ulrich, T. Stachnik, & J. Mabry (Eds.), *Control of human behavior*. Glenview, Ill.: Scott, Foresman, 1966.(b)

Skinner, B. F. *Beyond freedom and dignity*. New York: Knopf, 1971.

Solomon, R. W., & Wahler, R. G. Peer reinforcement control of classroom problem behavior. *Journal of Applied Behavior Analysis*, 1973, 6, 49–56.

Starlin, C. Peers and precision. *Teaching Exceptional Children*, 1971, 3, 129–140.

Stolz, S. Why no guidelines for behavior modification. *Journal of Applied Behavior Analysis*, 1977, 10, 541–547.

Stolz, S. B., Wienckowski, L. A., & Brown, C. S. Behavior modification: A perspective on critical issues. *American Psychologist*, 1975, *29*, 1027–1048.

Stuart, R. B., & Davis, B. *Slim chance in a fat world: Behavioral control of obesity*. Champaign, Ill.: Research Press, 1972.

Sulzer-Azaroff, B., Thaw, J., & Thomas, C. Behavior competencies for the evaluation of behavior modifiers. In W. S. Wood (Ed.), *Issues in evaluating behavior modification: Proceedings of the first Drake conference on professional issues in behavior analysis*. Champaign, Ill.: Research Press, 1974.

Surratt, P. E., Ulrich, R. E., & Hawkins, R. P. An elementary student as behavioral engineer. *Journal of Applied Behavior Analysis*, 1969, *2*, 85–92.

Wahler, R. G. Child-child interactions in free field settings: Some experimental analyses. *Journal of Experimental Child Psychology*, 1967, *5*, 278–293.

Walker, S. Drugging the American child: We're too cavalier about hyperactivity. *Psychology Today*, 1974, *8*(7), 43–48.

Walker, H. M., & Hops, H. Increasing academic achievement by reinforcing direct academic performance and/or facilitative non-academic responses. *Journal of Educational Psychology*, 1976, *68*, 218–225.(a)

Walker, H. M., & Hops, H. A normative model for evaluating generalization and maintenance of treatment effects. *Journal of Applied Behavior Analysis*, 1976, *9*, 159–168.(b)

Walker, H. M., Hops, H., & Greenwood, C. R. Competency based training issues in the development of behavior management packages for specific classroom behavior disorders. *Behavior Disorders*, 1976, *1*, 112–122.

Warner, S. P., Miller, F. D., & Cohen, M. W. Relative effectiveness of teacher attention and the 'good behavior game' in modifying disruptive classroom behavior. *Journal of Applied Behavior Analysis*, 1977, *10*, 737.

Watson, R. I. *The great psychologists: From Aristotle to Freud*. New York: J. B. Lippincott, 1963.

Wiesen, A. E., Hartley, G., Richardson, C., & Roske, A. The retarded child as a reinforcing agent. *Journal of Experimental Child Psychology*, 1967, *5*, 109–113.

Wilson, J. A. B. *A clockwork orange*. London: Heinemann, 1962.

Winett, R. A., & Winkler, R. C. Current behavior modifications in the classroom: Be still, be quiet, be docile. *Journal of Applied Behavior Analysis*, 1972, *5*, 499–504.

Wolf, M. M. Social validity: The case for subjective measurement or how applied behavior analysis is finding its heart. *Journal of Applied Behavior Analysis*, 1978, *11*, 203–214.

Wood, W. S. *Issues in evaluating behavior modification: Proceedings of the first Drake conference on professional issues in behavior analysis*. Champaign, Ill.: Research Press, 1974.

Yohalem, D., & Dinsmore, J. 94-142 and 504: Numbers that add up to educational rights for handicapped children: A guide for parents and advocates. Washington, D.C.: Children's Defense Fund, 1978.

Zimmerman, E. H., Zimmerman, J., & Russell, C. D. Differential effects of token reinforcement on instruction following behavior in retarded students instructed as a group. *Journal of Applied Behavior Analysis*, 1969, *2*, 101–112.

Index